C000046495

Economic Diversification in Nigeria

Economic Diversification in Nigeria

The Politics of Building a Post-Oil Economy

Zainab Usman

ZED

LONDON • NEW YORK • OXFORD • NEW DELHI • SYDNEY

ZED BOOKS
Bloomsbury Publishing Plc
50 Bedford Square, London, WC1B 3DP, UK
1385 Broadway, New York, NY 10018, USA
29 Earlsfort Terrace, Dublin 2, Ireland

BLOOMSBURY, and Zed Books are trademarks of Bloomsbury Publishing Plc

First published in Great Britain 2022

Series design by Burgess & Beech
Cover image © Nuuman S. Ashaka

Bloomsbury Publishing Plc does not have any control over, or responsibility for,
any third-party websites referred to or in this book. All internet addresses
given in this book were correct at the time of going to press. The author
and publisher regret any inconvenience caused if addresses have changed or
sites have ceased to exist but can accept no responsibility for any such changes.

A catalogue record for this book is available from the British Library.

Library of Congress Cataloging-in-Publication Data
Names: Usman, Zainab, 1986- author.
Title: Economic diversification in Nigeria: the politics of building a post-oil
economy / Zainab Usman.
Other titles: Politics and development in contemporary Africa.
Description: New York: Zed, 2022. | Series: Politics and development in contemporary
Africa | Includes bibliographical references and index.
Identifiers: LCCN 2021052021 (print) | LCCN 2021052022 (ebook) |
ISBN 9781786993946 (hardback) | ISBN 9781786993977 (epub) |
ISBN 9781786993960 (pdf) | ISBN 9781350237674
Subjects: LCSH: Nigeria–Economic conditions–21st century. | Nigeria–Economic policy.
Classification: LCC HC1055.U867 2022 (print) | LCC HC1055 (ebook) |
DDC 338.9669–dc23/eng/20211021
LC record available at https://lccn.loc.gov/2021052021
LC ebook record available at https://lccn.loc.gov/2021052022

ISBN: HB: 978-1-7869-9394-6
          ePDF: 978-1-7869-9396-0
          eBook: 978-1-7869-9397-7

Series: Politics and Development in Contemporary Africa

Typeset by Integra Software Services Pvt. Ltd.

To find out more about our authors and books visit www.bloomsbury.com
and sign up for our newsletters.

Contents

List of Figures

Maps

List of Tables

Acknowledgements

Life is all about giving and taking chances. This ambitious book, to diagnose Nigeria's development challenges and proffer solutions, is a reality only because of the institutions and the individuals who facilitated the process of producing it. I owe the initial doctoral research which forms the foundation of the book to the University of Oxford, which also provided an excellent physical and intellectual space.

I am grateful to various academic and professional mentors throughout this nearly-decade-long journey. At Oxford, there was the late Abdul Raufu Mustapha Adeel Malik, Ricardo Soares de Oliveira, Emily Jones, and Monica Toft who were all reliable, encouraging and supportive. In the United States, special thanks go to Peter Lewis, Paul Lubeck, Ousmane Dione, Pierre Audinet, Albert Zeufack, and Tom Carothers.

I remain highly indebted to scores of individuals who made the actual data collection and analysis possible. Although I am constrained by space to list all these individuals and some would not like to be explicitly mentioned, I will single out a few. These include Lai Yahaya, Philip Osafo-Kwaako, Abdulmumin Jibrin, Yinka Oyinlola, Muhammed Sagagi, Obiageli Ezekwesili, Nasir el-Rufai, Suraj B. Yakubu, Aminu Umar Sadiq, Muntaqa Umar Sadiq, Bello Mandiya, and Fatima Aliyu among others. My immense gratitude goes to the former Statistician-General and the CEO of the Nigerian Bureau of Statistics (NBS) Yemi Kale for the timely response to numerous data requests over the years. Others include, Shamsuddeen Usman, Muhammed Hayattudeen, Aliko Dangote, Muhammad Sanusi (II), Ben Akabueze, the Lagos Chamber of Commerce and Industry, Ahmad Rabiu, the national branch of the Manufacturers Association of Nigeria (MAN) as well as the Kano branch, Malam Yusuf Dambatta, Engineer Rabiu Suleiman Bichi, Mr. Aigboje Aig-Imoukhuede, Tolu Ogunlesi, and others too numerous to mention. I can only hope that I do sufficient justice to these stories and insights they shared.

Special thanks to various individuals who read portions of the manuscript at various stages, including Lindsay Whitfield, Peace Medie, Alex Thurston, Ibrahim Gumel who drew the beautiful maps used in this document, Baba Olaleye, Ibrahim Waziri Jnr, and Fatima Rufai.

I cannot thank my family enough for their unconditional love and support, especially my mother, Justice Mairo L. Muhammed, for trusting my judgment, and my late father, Justice Usman Mohammed. My sister, Ummy, who passed away in the early stages of this process, my other siblings, Kaltume, Yaya Abba, and Yaya Ba'ana, Captain Shafi'i, and the rest of my large extended family.

Finally, to God almighty, who gave me this tremendous opportunity, to write exactly the book I set out to write, right from the summer of 2011 when I got the initial spark of an idea. I am eternally grateful.

Open access funding has been provided by The Carnegie Endowment for International Peace.

Acronyms and Abbreviations

ABC	Alpha-Beta Consulting
ABU	Ahmadu Bello University
AC	Action Congress
ACN	Action Congress of Nigeria
AD	Alliance for Democracy
AfDB	African Development Bank
AG	Action Group
ANPP	All Nigeria Peoples' Party
APC	All Progressives' Congress
APGA	All Progressives' Grand Alliance
APP	All Peoples' Party
ASUU	Academic Staff Union of Universities
BDP	Botswana Democratic Party
BPE	Bureau for Public Enterprises
BRT	Bus Rapid Transport
CAN	Christian Association of Nigeria
CBN	Central Bank of Nigeria
CDWA	Colonial Development and Welfare Act
CEO	Chief Executive Officer
CPC	Congress for Progressive Change
CTG	Cotton Textiles and Garment
ECA	Excess Crude Account
EFCC	Economic and Financial Crimes Commission
EITI	Extractive Industries Transparency Initiative
ERGP	Economic Recovery and Growth Plan
FDI	Foreign Direct Investment
FGN	Federal Government of Nigeria
GDP	Gross Domestic Product
GFC	Global Financial Crisis
GNI	Gross National Income

ICT	Information and Communications Technology
IFI	International Financial Institutions
IGR	Internally Generated Revenue
IMF	International Monetary Fund
IOCs	International Oil Companies
IPP	Independent Power Project
ISI	Import Substituting Industrialization
KACCIMA	Kano Chamber of Commerce, Industry, Mines, and Agriculture
LCCI	Lagos Chamber of Commerce and Industry
LGA	Local Government Area
LIRS	Lagos Inland Revenue Service
MAN	Manufacturers' Association of Nigeria
MDA	Ministries Departments and Agencies
MSMEs	Micro-, Small- and Medium-Scale Enterprises
NACCIMA	National Association of Chambers of Commerce, Industries, Mines, and Agriculture
NBS	Nigerian National Bureau of Statistics
NCNC	National Council for Nigerian Citizens
NEEDS	National Economic Empowerment and Development Strategy
NEITI	Nigeria Extractive Industries Transparency Initiative
NGF	Nigerian Governors' Forum
NIRP	National Industrial Revolution Plan
NITEL	Nigerian Telecommunications Limited
NLC	Nigerian Labour Congress
NNPC	Nigeria National Petroleum Corporation
NPC	National Planning Commission
NPC	Northern People's Congress
NPN	National Party of Nigeria
NSIP	National Social Investment Program
NV20:2020	Nigeria Vision 20:2020
NYSC	National Youth Service Corps
ODA	Official Development Assistance
OECD	Organization for Economic Cooperation and Development
OPEC	Organization of Petroleum Exporting Countries
PDP	Peoples' Democratic Party
PFM	Public Financial Management

R&D	Research and Development
SAP	Structural Adjustment Program
SDGs	Sustainable Development Goals
SEZ	Special Economic Zone
SOE	State-Owned Enterprise
SSA	Sub-Saharan Africa
STB	Standard Trust Bank
SWF	Sovereign Wealth Fund
TEF	Tony Elumelu Foundation
UBA	United Bank for Africa
WEF	World Economic Forum
YOUWIN	Youth Enterprise With Innovation in Nigeria

Glossary

Business Elite High-profile, wealthy, and influential entrepreneurs acting as individuals or as a group.

De facto Institutions that exist as a fact of life based on commonly understood norms and widespread acceptance in society.

De jure Formal institutions formally expressed in laws and regulations often in physical documents such as a constitution.

Economic Development A process of sustained economic growth, structural transformation from low to higher-productivity activities, and a deeper process of social change.

Economic Diversification An expansion of the sources of production, employment, trade, revenues, and expenditures in an economy.

Economic Growth The quantitative increase in economic output usually measured by increase in GDP.

Elite Bargain A consensus over the horizontal distribution of power among elites in society. Also known as "elite consensus" or "elite pact."

Elite Individuals, groups, or organizations who occupy the most powerful positions of authority in society. They could be political, business, bureaucratic, military, professional, or religious elite.

Growth Coalition A collaborative business–government relationship which drives growth in an industry or a sector.

Institutionalization The widespread acceptance and consistent enforcement of a mechanism or arrangement, such as the distribution of power and allocation of economic resources in society.

Institutions The rules that regulate human behavior and interaction in any social setting.

Political Elite Powerful individuals and groups with influence on, and access to, ruling elites without themselves necessarily possessing decision-making power.

Political Settlement The distribution of power in society among individual, group, and organizational actors.

Politics Activities around negotiating, acquiring and exercising power, and pursuing interests.

Power The ability to influence the behavior of others and to shape outcomes in one's interest.

Productivity Output per unit of production inputs.

Ruling Coalition An alliance between the ruling elite, other elite groups, and non-elite groups.

Ruling Elite Powerful individuals or groups who possess decision-making power in formal positions of authority.

Social Group Non-elite individuals with a common interest.

State A sovereign political entity that rules a population within defined geographical boundaries. In other words, a country. This is distinct from a subnational or provincial authority within a country, e.g., Kaduna State or the State of Virginia.

Structural Transformation The transition of a country's productive resources (natural resources, land, capital, labor, and know-how) from low-productivity activities such as primary agriculture to higher-productivity activities in the industrial and services sectors.

1

The Challenge of Achieving Economic Diversification

In February 2018, Francis Alimikhena made a forceful case on the floor of the Nigerian Senate. Standing up from the plush red seat of the "red chamber" as the vast Senate hall is popularly known, the Senator, from Edo state in southern Nigeria, lamented the crippling impact of the imports of palm oil from the south-east Asian countries of Indonesia and Malaysia. The previous year, Nigeria had officially imported 320,000 metric tonnes of palm oil. Added to the 400,000 metric tonnes smuggled into the country, these imports collectively accounted for over half of the country's consumption of the product.[1] In appealing to his colleagues in the Senate, Alimikhena noted with dismay that, on a visit to Nigeria in the 1960s, Malaysian officials had taken some palm seedlings back to their country. Through effective policies and committed leadership, the Malaysians used these imported seedlings to build a modern palm oil industry whose exports was now decimating Nigeria's. Therefore, Alimikhena proposed a motion to the upper house of the Nigerian parliament to "Halt the Importation of Palm Oil and its Allied Products to Protect Palm Oil Industry in Nigeria." The motion was adopted by all 109 Senators, across Nigeria's deep ethno-regional and partisan fault lines, for whom consensus is not easy to reach.

The Senator's consternation at the dismal fate of Nigeria's palm oil industry is one of the country's most enduring national myths. Growing up as a teenager in Nigeria in the early 2000s, I became socialized to this commonly held view on economic decline among the country's intellectuals. As with all national myths, it contains a grain of exaggerated truth. The reality is that West Africa used to be the world's main producer of palm oil. In the 1870s, British colonial administrators took the crop from eastern Nigeria to their other colonies in south-east Asia to meet growing demand from England's Industrial Revolution. By 1966, Indonesia and Malaysia surpassed Nigeria to become the world's largest palm oil producers.

Today, Malaysia is the world's largest exporter of the product, and has three of the world's five largest palm oil companies, IOI, Kuala Lumpur Kepong, and Sime Darby Bhd.[2] In addition to the large-scale palm oil cultivation, there are over 300,000 small-holder farmers. The industry is the fourth-largest contributor to Malaysia's economy, and directly employs more than 600,000 people, including both high-skilled and low-skilled labor. Malaysia not only exports palm oil; it has also developed the product's value chain, with investment in research and development, and has opened new downstream sectors including biofuels.

In contrast, Nigeria has been relegated to sixth place on the list of Africa's exporters of palm oil. It cannot meet its own domestic demand for the product and relies on small-scale producers for 80% of production. Nigeria has not produced any globally recognized company in the palm industry and is vulnerable to import competition and smuggling.

The fate of Nigeria's palm oil industry illustrates the decline of the country's other economic sectors. The cultivation of cocoa in the western part of Nigeria was vibrant until its decline accelerated in the 1970s. Throughout the first half of the twentieth century, Northern Nigeria was famous for its groundnut exports and a thriving cottons, textile, and garments (CTG) sector. Across the board, the story is similar. Nigeria's agriculture and manufacturing industries have been ravaged by global competition from more productive and better-organized firms. Except for the large oil sector, Nigeria, like many African countries, seems to be a passive participant in the global economy. Indonesia, Malaysia, and several other east Asian economies which had similar income levels to Nigeria in the 1960s have largely turned the forces of globalization to their advantage to build competitive industries accompanied by global conglomerates.

As Senator Alimikhena and his colleagues were busy legislating import bans to protect Nigeria's faltering agriculture sector, something else was happening in the financial industry. Several hundred kilometers away, in Nigeria's commercial capital Lagos, the conference center of the grand Federal Palace Hotel hosted an inaugural forum to kick off the fifth edition of Tony Elumelu Foundation (TEF) Entrepreneurship Program. The large WEF-style forum featured presidents Nana Akufo-Addo of Ghana and Uhuru Kenyatta of Kenya, prominent business leaders, and over 5,000 participants, mostly young entrepreneurs from African countries. Earlier in the year, TEF had hosted the French president, Emmanuel Macron, to a meetup with 2,000 young entrepreneurs. Founded in 2010 by Nigerian banker and investor Tony Onyemaechi Elumelu, TEF is a private-sector-led philanthropy supporting the entrepreneurship ecosystem across fifty-four African countries. The flagship TEF Entrepreneurship Program is a $100 million investment in empowering 10,000 African entrepreneurs over a ten-year period.[3] The program consists of a start-up enterprise toolkit, online mentoring, online resource library, meet-ups, the TEF Entrepreneurship Forum, seed capital, and alumni network. At the glitzy 2018 Forum, a continent-wide digital entrepreneurship hub was launched; it now has 800,000 users. The TEF has so far empowered 7,531 entrepreneurs.

Tony Elumelu's towering profile as an investor in African entrepreneurs was built on a career in Nigeria's banking sector. As the Chief Executive Officer (CEO) of one of Africa's leading banks, United Bank for Africa (UBA) until 2010, Elumelu was one of several bankers who drove the expansion and modernization of Nigeria's financial sector. In 1997, he led the takeover of a distressed medium-sized commercial bank, which became the Standard Trust Bank (STB). By 1998, the 34-year-old Elumelu was appointed CEO, the youngest of any commercial bank in Nigeria at the time. By 2005, STB had transitioned from obscurity to become one of the country's five largest commercial banks. That same year, Elumelu coordinated one of the largest mergers in the banking sector in sub-Saharan Africa, between STB and UBA. As chief executive, he helped spin UBA from a single-country commercial bank into a diversified multinational providing sophisticated financial services like asset management, investment advisory, stockbroking, and private equity.[4] Today, UBA operates in nineteen African countries, New York, London, and Paris. It ranks twenty-first among Africa's top 100 Banks, alongside other Nigerian banks such as Zenith, First Bank, and Access.[5] The emergence of these Nigerian banks is a testament to the grit of their investors, but also important policy reforms. Also, Elumelu's support for emerging African entrepreneurs aims to uncover Africa's untapped business potential.

From these two scenarios in agriculture and in finance, the Nigerian economy is not characterized by only stagnation or decline. As I will explain in this book, since Nigeria gained independence in 1960, its economic performance, especially in the twenty-first century, has been inconsistent over time and across different sectors. It has neither been uniformly good nor uniformly poor. Since the year 2000, sectors such as banking and finance, which have seen the emergence of tycoons like Elumelu, information and communications technology (ICT), and entertainment, as illustrated by Nigeria's homegrown *Nollywood* movies and the *Afrobeats* music industry, have expanded. However, others—like agriculture that policymakers like Senator Alimikhena seek to protect from global competition, manufacturing, and the oil industry—have seen slow growth and even decline. It is therefore necessary to have a comprehensive understanding of the challenges in the Nigerian economy and the opportunities that can be harnessed to improve its performance. This book identifies Nigeria's major economic development challenge as one of diversifying its economy. It also shows how this challenge has been shaped by the country's volatile political environment.

Neither the Resource Curse nor "African Culture" Explains Nigeria's Development Challenges

If the Nigerian economy is not characterized by inertia and decline, what then are the challenges to its sustained growth and development? In this book, I identify economic diversification as Nigeria's foremost economic development challenge. We can define "economic diversification" as sustained growth and the transition of an economy from dependence on primary activity such as oil and mineral extraction, and agriculture, to value addition in these activities. As I will explain in this book, this challenge of economic diversification is evident in aggregate national figures. Just one-tenth of Nigeria's GDP comes from the oil sector, but more than 90% of its exports and 50% of government revenue comes from it. This dependence on oil revenues is also acute at the subnational level. Nigeria's thirty-six states are mostly reliant on federal oil revenue transfers for their fiscal revenues even though these subnational economies are predominantly comprising non-oil activities in agriculture, trade, manufacturing, and services. As Africa's largest oil producer and exporter, a major economic policy goal is to sustain non-oil growth and employment in other industries. Thus, identifying economic diversification as Nigeria's main development challenge is not a profound statement. In fact, this is a problem widely acknowledged by many scholars, by policy makers, and by Nigerians themselves.

There is, however, much less understanding of the actual role of politics in this challenge of economic diversification in Nigeria. In this book, I argue that Nigeria's challenge of economic diversification is situated within a political setting of an unstable distribution of power among individual, group, and organizational actors. Within this volatile balance of power, Nigeria's ruling elites have lurched from one political crisis to another throughout the country's history, especially since the transition to democratic rule in 1999. In this perpetual state of crisis management, economic policy in Nigeria tends to be short term and episodic rather than the systematic, long-term orientation necessary to drive economic transformation. As I explain in the nine chapters of this book, the reason why Nigeria's economy is still dependent on oil exports and has not achieved sustained economic transformation lies in the interplay of volatile politics and economic policy making. Thus, the unstable distribution of political power shapes the policy choices that underpin the challenge of economic diversification. In this book, I present an alternative theoretical lens to conceptualize the challenge of economic diversification and provide building blocks for policy solutions.

Why the need for an alternative framework? Because the prevailing explanations of how politics shapes economic performance in resource-rich African countries like Nigeria are inadequate. These prevailing theories attribute Nigeria's failure to sustain growth and industrialize to some inherent characteristic in the country: the "oil curse" and a neopatrimonial culture.[6] These theories have persisted for decades even though their findings are increasingly being challenged, the flaws in their diagnoses evident, and the solutions they prescribe inadequate.

One of the most persistent explanations for Nigeria's economic development challenges is that the country is a victim of the "resource curse." As Africa's largest oil producer and the world's ninth-largest oil exporter, Nigeria is the poster child for the curse of natural resources. A large body of scholarship has, for decades, attributed the problems of slow growth, economic deterioration, and the decline of agriculture and manufacturing to the curse of resources and especially oil and gas, in some countries. According to this school of thought, the resource curse happens through at least two mechanisms—economic and socio-political.

The economic mechanism of the resource curse occurs through the "Dutch Disease."[7] Some economists argue that the large volumes of mineral export revenues during periods of high commodity prices, undermine the growth and competitiveness of other economic sectors. This happens for at least two reasons. First, the oil revenues are volatile since global commodity prices tend to swing precipitously. These rapid price swings also affect exchange rate stability in the exporting country because oil exports artificially inflate the value of the local currency and weaken the export price of non-oil goods like cash crops and manufactures of textiles and food processing. When international oil prices crash, the country finds itself in a dilemma—as the torrent of oil export revenue slows to a trickle, the country can neither afford its habitual imports of essential commodities nor produce these goods domestically because an overvalued exchange rate has already devastated domestic production. Indeed, the oil boom of the 1970s that led to an overvalued naira made it cheaper for Nigeria to import consumer goods—from soap and pencils to fruit juice—rather than produce them locally. Thereby the export of palm oil, cotton, other agriculture commodities, manufactures, and other industries whose output is internationally "tradeable,"[8] became more expensive, contributing to the economic stagnation and decline of the 1980s and 1990s. In those decades, the Nigerian economy fit the description of a "rentier economy,"[9] in which more than 60% of GDP came from oil-extraction, which thus crowded out other economic activities. Today, an important national aspiration often espoused by Nigerian policy makers is to restore domestic self-sufficiency in pencil manufacturing.

A second mechanism of the resource curse is socio-political. Some social scientists argue that oil and mineral wealth distort the institutions and incentive structures in resource-exporting societies away from more productive activities,[10] such as agriculture, manufacturing, and other tradable industries. Public policies pivot towards the allocation, distribution, and management of resource revenues and neglect the building of strong tax systems to generate non-resource revenues, enabling farmers, manufacturers, and other producers to thrive. Entrepreneurs' energies are diverted towards activities to service the oil and mineral industries. Therefore, many in business scramble to obtain oil-import licenses, run petrol stations, and secure government supply contracts rather than invest in building factories for manufacturing and agro-processing. Students in higher education are keen to study courses in oil and gas policy and to work in public and private oil companies. The whole of society: politicians, entrepreneurs, students, resource-producing communities become oriented towards profiting from easy oil wealth. The state therefore becomes a "rentier state" in which more than 40% of fiscal revenues are derived from oil rents.[11] Overall, the scramble to control these lucrative resources creates directly unproductive profit-seeking known as "rent-seeking" as well as corruption. Since individuals with access to lucrative import and oil licenses go to any lengths including manipulating elections and funding militias to maintain their economic privileges, political stability and democracy can be undermined by the resource curse, according to the theory's proponents.

Through these economic and socio-political mechanisms, the resource curse results in economic stagnation and institutional decay. Certainly, some aspects of the Dutch Disease and institutional malaise can be found in Nigeria. However, the resource curse thesis provides a limited and partial diagnosis of the causes, mechanisms, and outcomes of the economic challenges in resource-rich countries like Nigeria. Indeed, a growing number of scholars is pushing back on the resource curse thesis for at least three reasons.

The Dutch Disease can indeed erode the competitiveness of non-oil sectors and contribute to slow growth, but this is not inevitable, and economic growth is caused by a lot more than exchange rate stability. From the year 2003, Nigeria experienced strong economic growth averaging 5–7% until 2015. As we discuss in Chapters 5 and 6, although this growth happened at the time of an oil boom, it was driven by non-oil economic sectors, such as the banking sector, ICT, arts, and entertainment. Botswana, a diamond-rich country, experienced limited symptoms of the Dutch Disease because it successfully managed its resource revenues by adjusting exchange rates and building foreign reserves.[12] Ghana, a gold and oil-exporting country, was one of the world's fastest-growing economies between 2015 and 2019. Similarly, Malaysia and Chile have built strong economies and diversified their exports leveraging their natural resources including copper, petroleum, and palm oil. The economist, Jean-Philippe Stijns finds that natural resource abundance has not been a significant determinant of economic growth between 1970 and 1990.[13] He joins several economists who argue that resource-based development is possible, as the industrial success of advanced economies such as Australia, Canada, Finland, Sweden, and the USA resulted, in part, from drawing on their mineral resources while also investing heavily in knowledge accumulation in and around the sector.[14] Stijns concludes that what matters most is not the inherent character of the resources, but the nature of the learning process involved in extracting and developing these resources. Jonathan Di John also notes that oil abundance in many countries has coincided with both cases of long-run rapid growth and stagnation which "resource curse" theories cannot account for.

On the socio-political front, Nigerian society has long been infamously characterized by chaos around the management and distribution of oil wealth, especially during boom times. As we discuss in Chapter 6, during the fourth commodities super cycle from 2000–2015,[15] there were the familiar tales in Nigeria of large-scale theft of oil revenues by government officials, scams around inflated petroleum subsidies, sordid deals around the allocation of oil exploration and import licenses to private-sector cronies, etc., Yet, successive public policies in the 2000s deliberately enabled non-oil economic expansion through important reforms in the banking sector and public financial management (PFM). In addition, Nigerian entrepreneurs, like Tony Elumelu, have contributed to driving non-oil economic expansion. As Di John points out, these resource revenues do not generate uniform scales of corruption, rent-seeking, or terrible development outcomes across different countries—UAE versus Nigeria for instance—but also within one country over time, such as UAE's own varying experience over a thirty-year period. The path from natural resource abundance to economic deterioration and socio-political decay is neither linear nor inevitable.

As some resource-rich countries defy the predictions of economic stagnation by the resource curse, the theory's inadequacies are too evident to ignore. Key advocates of the resource curse such as Michael Ross have argued for years that oil producers are locked on a certain path of economic stagnation and institutional degeneration due to the "unusual qualities" of oil revenue.[16] As several countries in Africa and Asia broke out of slow growth in the 2000s, demonstrated improved governance, and achieved better human development outcomes, the deficiencies of resource curse claims became so evident, that even Michael Ross reconsidered some of his earlier assumptions. In his 2012 book, *The Oil Curse* for instance, Ross says that "real problem is not that resource-rich countries have experienced slow growth, but that their growth rates have been relatively normal rather than faster than normal given their enormous revenues."[17] He goes on to describe as "short-sighted" his own thinking a decade earlier that oil wealth causes weak economic growth and weakens institutions.[18] Despite this capitulation, Ross maintains that an oil "curse" independently causes problems for a country, although the precise nature of this curse varies.

The flawed diagnosis of the resource curse thesis around the economic challenges of countries like Nigeria is not abstract academic debate but has serious policy implications. The faulty characterization of a resource curse has long muddled our understanding of the actual and persistent problems faced by developing countries like Nigeria. Worryingly, its proponents have had enormous influence in prescribing insufficient policy solutions to problems they mischaracterized from the start. Take, for instance, the idea that countries should set up natural resource funds to park their oil rents both to manage revenue volatility from the Dutch Disease and to save the revenue for future generations. The countercyclical objectives of such resource funds are immensely helpful to countries in managing revenue volatility, along with the implementation of broader fiscal rules such as a medium-term expenditure framework. The savings part of these funds, such as Sovereign Wealth Funds (SWF) work especially well for Bahrain, Norway, Qatar, and other high-income countries with small populations, high living standards, and good infrastructure. A savings fund for future generations is certainly not the immediate priority for low-income African countries which need to invest in roads, schools, power-generation plants, hospitals, and other physical and human capital assets to increase future productivity.

Or take various international initiatives, especially the Extractive Industries Transparency Initiative (EITI) that emerged from the 2000s to address the corruption and governance challenges in the oil, gas, and mining industries.[19] The resource-rich countries that join such initiatives commit to and are applauded for disclosing resource revenues earned and contracts with multinational companies and for engaging civil society.[20] Indeed, it is due to the uptake of the EITI standard, that many countries make the laudable effort to publish resource revenue earnings. However, these transparency initiatives have failed to empower the public to hold the governments and companies to account.[21] More generally, these initiatives are unable to tackle the larger governance challenges in the management of natural resources including weak administrative capabilities for implementation, spending misallocation, lack of accountability, and weak oversight mechanisms that transcend the resource sector.

These policy solutions derived from employing a resource curse lens have neither addressed the problems they misdiagnosed, nor the actual challenges faced by resource-rich countries which they failed to conceptualize. Even erstwhile proponents of these initiatives, such as the famous Oxford economist Sir Professor Paul Collier, have publicly repudiated them. On a rainy summer day in 2015, at St. Catherine's college at the University of Oxford, Collier publicly excoriated these international transparency initiatives. It was a large conference featuring major international stakeholders on natural resources governance during which Collier said that:

> The lessons for the international community is we just did a misdiagnosis, we thought that the problem [of governance] was overwhelmingly transparency and accountability, it wasn't... is that a problem? Of course it is a problem. Is it *the* problem for natural resources? No it's just not. And so, the bulk of the international effort, things like EITI went into emphasis on transparency and accountability... EITI was the wrong focus... I did my best to promote EITI, but it's a subsidiary set of issues and if you just have that and nothing else, it just makes things worse... We need to focus on the entire economic decision-making chain, not [just] transparency and accountability...

Paul Collier's denunciation is worth watching on YouTube.[22] Yet, despite these landmark retractions by major advocates, the idea of a resource curse, its partial analysis and inadequate policy prescriptions have endured in the imaginations of many scholars and is uncritically accepted as gospel by policy makers and citizens of resource-producing countries.

Thankfully, a growing body of research is pointing to the actual problems that these countries face with more precision. These problems are not just of generating growth, but of sustaining it and diversifying its sources including and beyond natural resources; the problem of governance lies not just in a lack of "transparency" but, as Collier mentioned in the summer of 2015, in the "entire economic decision-making chain." Among this growing chorus of scholarly work pushing back against the flawed "resource-curse" thesis is Ha-Joon Chang and Amir Lebdioui's recent paper in which they identify "economic diversification not fiscal stabilization" as the best way to achieve macroeconomic stability in resource-rich countries in the long run. Specifically, they argue that, "the standard policy advice (which suggests that resource-rich developing countries should deal with the fiscal volatility associated with commodity prices through diligent fiscal rules to offset boom-and-bust cycles and by investing resource revenues in financial assets abroad) addresses only the short-term symptoms of commodity dependence (e.g., vulnerability to commodity price volatility) rather than its root causes (namely, the lack of diversified productive structures)." They emphasize that the case of an already advanced country such as Norway should not necessarily form the basis of lessons for policymaking in resource-rich developing countries because investment in financial assets is unlikely to lead to the productive transformation they need.[23]

In a similar fashion, this book aims to contribute to our understanding of the causes, mechanisms, and solutions to the economic development challenges of resource-exporting countries like Nigeria. As I will argue, this challenge of economic diversification is rooted in policy choices made within a country's political and institutional configuration.

Before we delve into how this book analyzes the challenge of achieving economic diversification, let us quickly examine, "neopatrimonialism" a second common explanation of Nigeria's failure to transform and industrialize its economy. The concept of neopatrimonialism has been used since the 1980s to explain how African countries south of the Sahara, are unable to develop modern states capable of supporting the process of economic transformation. A notoriously elusive concept to define, neopatrimonialism is often a shorthand for the political culture inherent in African societies. According to its advocates, the fusion of traditional and patrimonial authority structures with elements of a post-colonial modern state results in hybrid or neopatrimonial institutions.[24] These neopatrimonial institutions are the antithesis of Max Weber's conception of a modern state that is rational in its decision-making; has a strong bureaucracy to undertake its basic function of providing roads, schools and other public services; and is impersonal in representing all citizens and subjecting them to an impersonal rule of law irrespective of their socio-political identities. Rather, neopatrimonial authority structures undermine bureaucratic capabilities, rational decision-making, and the impersonal characteristics of a state.

Many comparative social scientists writing in the 1980s and 1990s invoked the concept to explain the economic and political crises in African countries, and why the region lagged behind parts of Asia and Latin America. They attributed these crises to the failure of "developmental states" to emerge in Africa due to neopatrimonial socio-political cultures which could only produce "predatory states." For instance, Peter Evans has developed an influential typology of state capacities in which he identifies the "developmental state" (presides over industrial transformation due to its corporate coherence, institutionalized ties to society and pursuit of collective goals), the "predatory state" (extracts at the expense of society because it lacks bureaucratic coherence, and therefore individual maximization and personalistic behavior by incumbents take precedence) and the "intermediate state" (presides over variable economic outcomes because it has some semblance of bureaucratic organization but not a high degree of coherence).[25] Evans, alongside several other scholars, describes Nigeria, and much of Africa, as "neopatrimonial" in contrast to Brazil, India, Indonesia, South Korea, and other Asian or Latin American middle-income countries.[26] While much of the scholarship on neopatrimonialism is Africa-focused to explain why the region is "different" from other parts of the world, the concept has also been applied to a limited extent to laggard countries such as Afghanistan and Uzbekistan in Asia and even Greece and Italy in Southern Europe.[27]

Among its various facets, the causal claims of how neopatrimonialism undermines economic transformation most directly relevant to this book merit closer examination. According to proponents, the mechanism by which these hybrid informal authority structures shape economic outcomes is a "neopatrimonial logic" and its driving force is "clientelistism." Clientelism is a form of political mobilization in which a "patron," say a politician running for office or a senior government minister, promises or provides benefits to their "client." In other words, the public official rewards those who voted or nominated them into office. These patron–client relations, which benefit narrow sectional constituencies, contrast with programmatic political mobilization around issues that affect the public (schools, hospitals, taxes, etc.). The patron–client relations also undermine prospects for an impersonal, rational, and bureaucratic state that works in the public interest. Through clientelism, public policies are thus oriented towards personalistic and sectarian ends which translate into corrupt practices and the predatory subversion of institutions by individuals in positions of power. Clientelism takes various forms: nepotism to family members, favoritism to ethnic or religious kin, cronyism to favored businessmen and women, etc. This "neopatrimonial logic" in African countries, thus operates through the application of public office to private ends resulting in suboptimal public policies such as expansionary monetary policy, and trade and industrial policies which encourage rent-seeking, yield low national savings, and obstruct the emergence of a productive business class.[28]

These descriptions of neopatrimonialism superficially fit a country like Nigeria. After all, various Nigerian public officials, from governors of its thirty-six states to legislators and heads of government agencies, exhibit predatory behavior: governors who may have vast private-sector experience in multinational companies often cultivate a larger-than-life image of the African "big man"[29] who subverts the public treasury to dispense cash gifts and other favors; legislators with advanced degrees from

Western universities often invoke ethnicity and religion to mobilize voters; technocratic cabinet ministers often bypass strict civil service rules on recruitment to favor family members, and ethnic and religious kin.

Beyond these partially accurate but cynical anecdotes, several scholars question the usefulness of the claim that African socio-political culture causes economic underperformance. Two of these questions are worth highlighting. First, does neopatrimonialism provide a reliable and measurable link between culture and economic performance i.e., growth, diversification, and transformation? This question arises because analyses of neopatrimonialism are densely descriptive of rich anecdotes of the flamboyant African big man and his contemptable rapacity, but light in analyzing the mechanisms through which these cultural factors produce economic outcomes. There is a problem of reverse causality that confuses cause and effect, because both a modern state with Weberian rational-formal authority and its distorted neopatrimonial variant result from, rather than precede, patterns of economic development, as Hazel Gray and Lindsay Whitfield point out.[30] It is the differences in economic structures, (such as an established private sector, the size of manufacturing industry, the clout of business associations, the size of the middle class, urbanization, etc.) that diminish the role of patron–client politics in advanced industrialized countries or sustain their prevalence in developing countries. As the Cambridge economist Ha-Joon Chang reminds us, until the early twentieth century, the Japanese were thought to be lazy and the Germans "too stupid, too individualistic and too emotional" to develop their economies; descriptions that contrast today's stereotypical image of these two nationalities as disciplined, innovative, and hardworking.[31] The Japanese and German cultures were transformed by economic development, as the demands of an organized industrial society made people behave in more disciplined, calculating, and cooperative ways. Therefore, culture is an outcome rather than a cause of economic development.

A second question that scholars are increasingly asking is: how does neopatrimonialism explain the differences in growth and economic performance among countries with similar levels of patron–client political cultures? This question became unavoidable after several African countries emerged out of the lost decade of the 1990s during the "Africa Rising" economic boom of the 2000s. Even though this decade-long growth crashed for countries like Nigeria and Angola, for others including Cote d'Ivoire, Ethiopia, Ghana, Senegal, and Tanzania, they sustained some of the world's fastest growth rates with noticeable declines in income poverty right up until the COVID-19 pandemic hit in early 2020.[32] If a "perverse" socio-political culture causes slow growth, resource dependence, and other poor economic outcomes, how are these neopatrimonial countries turning their economic fortunes around? Thus, neopatrimonialism is unable to explain variation in economic outcomes within one country over different periods of time—between Africa's "lost decade" of the 1990s and the "Africa Rising" decade of the 2000s. More precisely, it cannot account for the reality that economic growth in most countries occurs in episodes and spurts regardless of inherent characteristics, as emerging research shows.[33] This linear and cultural essentialist view cannot account for differences in outcomes even among industries or regions within one economy, say ICT and finance, versus agriculture, as we will see in this book.

Finally, cultures are not immutable because even a modern industrial economy can retain clientelistic characteristics or regress into neopatrimonialism for reasons related to economic underperformance. Indeed, strong aspects of clientelism are evident in Greece and southern Italy, as Francis Fukuyama highlights, in the patron–client dynamics that inform public sector recruitment.[34] In the United States, academics, journalists, and grassroots mobilizers bemoan what could be described as increasingly clientelistic forms of political mobilization. These include tactics employed by some state governors to increase the relative voting power of certain ethnic groups over others through "gerrymandering" or redrawing of electoral districts; or the provision of campaign contributions to Senators and Representatives from privileged business groups in exchange for legislation that favors them at the expense of consumers; or the use of presidential power to nominate individuals to federal courts on the basis of loyalties to the Democratic or Republican party in power; or more recently, former president Donald Trump's appointment of his daughter Ivanka and son-in-law Jared as senior advisors to the White House. These clientelistic aspects of political mobilization in America coexist with the innovation, dynamism, and profitability of Silicon Valley, Wall Street, and other axes of the American economy. However, these patron–client politics have become more noticeably debilitating to American politics since the turn of the century, with economists, such as Thomas Philippon, identifying them as symptoms of deeper economic underperformance in terms of lower labor productivity, stagnating wages, and weakening industrial competitiveness.[35] While this debate on inclusion, representation, and the relative power of privileged groups in American politics continues, it is clear that a neopatrimonial socio-political culture does not have an independent effect on economic development and it is not a uniquely African pathology.

If neither the curse of natural resources nor the effects of a neopatrimonial culture cause and explain Nigeria's economic challenges, then what does? This book aims to contribute to our understanding of the causes and mechanisms of the economic challenges that resource-exporting countries like Nigeria face towards more effective policy solutions. I will show that Nigeria's major development challenge is not an "oil curse," but one of achieving economic diversification beyond oil, subsistence agriculture, informal activities, and across its subnational entities. This challenge of economic diversification is rooted in the policy choices made within the country's unstable political configuration.

This Book: The Politics of Diversifying Nigeria's Economy

I began the research that informed this book by asking several key questions that a citizen of any resource-rich developing country is bound to ask at some point. No doubt, Nigeria's economy is underperforming despite its vast endowments. What is the reason for this underperformance? What role does Nigeria's resources, especially its oil wealth, play in this economic underperformance? How do power, politics, and decision-making affect this economic development challenge? If the resource curse, neopatrimonialism, and other prevailing explanations for Nigeria's development challenges are inadequate, how else can we better diagnose and tackle the problem? In addressing these questions, I identify Nigeria's main economic development challenge as characterized by the struggle to diversify its economy from the oil sector, subsistence agriculture, informal activities, and across its subnational entities. This challenge of economic diversification occurs within an institutional setting of an unstable distribution of political power among individuals, groups, and organizational actors. This unstable power configuration creates a volatile policy environment that generates intermittent growth that is insufficient to drive the economic diversification to which Nigeria aspires.

Using the lens of political settlements, I therefore argue that Nigeria is not forever beholden to neopatrimonial politics and doomed to perpetual economic stagnation. Neither is it a developmental state facilitating sustained economic growth and structural transformation. Rather, Nigeria is an intermediate state capable of episodic reform but, in its present configuration, incapable of driving economic transformation due to the unstable distribution of political power in which ruling elites are constrained to lean towards certain types of policy choices. Let us examine the constituent terms: challenges of economic diversification, unstable distribution of power, constraints, and economic policy choices.

Nigeria's challenge of economic diversification is characterized by irregular growth episodes, a dependence on the exports and fiscal revenues from the oil sector, and wide regional disparities among its thirty-six component states. The country's growth episode after the "lost decade" of the 1990s occurred in the 2000s, during the commodities super cycle. During this time, growth averaged 5–7% per annum until 2015. Even though there was a global hydrocarbons boom at the time, as we will discuss in Chapter 5, Nigeria's growth was not directly driven by the oil sector. In fact, the oil sector stagnated throughout this period, alongside agriculture and manufacturing, while services including ICT, banking and finance, trade, the arts, and entertainment expanded rapidly. Nigeria also rebased its GDP in 2014 to capture new economic sectors in national accounting statistics. Due to non-oil growth since around 2003 and, to an extent, GDP rebasing, the economy became more diversified; the oil sector now contributes just about 10% of GDP.

The problem though, is that the more diverse economic activities have neither translated into an export basket with a wider range of commodities nor a diversified fiscal base beyond the oil sector. A stagnating oil and gas sector still provides more than 90% of export earnings and more than 50% of government revenue. This dependence on oil revenues for government budgets is even more acute at the subnational level. Apart from two states, Lagos and Ogun, the other thirty-four states in Nigeria depend on federal oil revenue transfers for at least half of their government budgets. In short, Nigeria's economy has grown in terms of output, but this expansion has not occurred via industrialization and the associated improvement in productive capabilities.

What is the relationship between this inconsistent economic performance and Nigeria's unstable distribution of political power? The distribution of political power among individuals, groups, and organizations shape the choices and implementation of economic policies. Politics is central to economic policy processes and their development outcomes, and this truism is resurgent among scholars and policy analysts. Beyond the efficiency considerations and technocratic practices that are assumed to singularly dictate policy formulation and implementation, the policy process globally is highly political. Consider this: a governor of a province or a mayor of a city has a finite amount of government funds to spend among competing priorities within a budget cycle. In a low-income country, investing in transport infrastructure to improve the business climate is a crucial priority to enable growth. The province needs both a light rail system to improve urban transportation and feeder roads that connect remote villages to interstate highways. Economic analyses show that investment in rural roads could contribute up to 2.5 percentage points of GDP growth because farmers would have better access to regional produce markets for their harvests. An urban light rail system would contribute barely 1 percentage point even though it would reduce transportation costs for city workers, thereby increasing their disposable income and consumption. However, building the urban light rail system was an electoral promise by the governor in a province where 60% of registered voters are urban dwellers. It should not be surprising, therefore, that decision-makers prioritize investments in the light rail system because it helps them politically, even though it makes less economic sense, while postponing the work on rural roads. This sort of calculus is also not a uniquely Nigerian or African phenomenon.

The micro-level of the policy process which entails the allocation of scarce resources among competing priorities is highly political because it is influenced by the distribution of power in society. In any society, the ability to get things done, to exercise influence and shape outcomes lies in varying degrees among individuals, groups, and organizations having interests in different policy permutations and their outcomes, who will try to influence this policy process in their favor. Effective policies will yield results and thereby modify or create new incentive structures with rewards and sanctions, change behaviors thus creating winners and losers among these actors. The province we are using as an example now has a functional metro rail that reduces transport costs for many of the city's residents, but the inhabitants of surrounding villages feel neglected. An opposition politician could tap into these rural grievances by promising to build those feeder roads in their electoral campaign against the incumbent governor. This distribution of power among individuals, groups, and organizations shapes policymaking. The outcomes of the policies eventually chosen in terms of emerging and declining economic sectors will empower new actors, say wealthy businessmen, large conglomerates, trade associations, etc., with implications for the future distribution of power.

To explain how the distribution of power influences policy choices with implications for Nigeria's economic diversification, this book uses the lens of political settlements. A "political settlement," as conceptualized by the economist Mushtaq Khan, refers to the distribution of power among elites and the wider society. As a framework for analysis, the political settlement connects political power, policy, and economic outcomes. The concept, framework, and their application are discussed in Chapter 3. Through the lens of political settlements, we can better understand how power is distributed in society among actors such as political and business elites, trade unions, civil society leaders, grassroots activists, and social medial influencers; government entities like Central Banks, Ministries of Finance, and various regulators; and political institutions such as the executive, the legislature, and political parties. Using this political settlements lens, we can identify the mechanisms by which ruling elites or decision-makers are constrained to prioritize, choose, and implement specific economic policies at any point in time. This analysis also gives us an insight into how this distribution of power changes gradually over time or suddenly at a more critical juncture.

A key contribution this book makes therefore is to enhance our understanding of the mechanisms through which changes to the power configuration can affect economic policy choices. Therefore, various factors can cause a seemingly inert policy environment to become more dynamic and reform-oriented; or an erstwhile reform-oriented environment can become static. In this regard, the political settlement is an emerging framework for analyzing the politics of economic development.

In Nigeria, the economic policies prioritized and implemented within its unstable distribution of power or political settlement have resulted in bursts of economic growth insufficient to achieve exports and revenue diversification. In Nigeria's highly contentious power configuration, economic policy is oriented towards equitable distribution among competing actors rather than sustained growth. When decision-makers are constrained to act differently and the policy environment does become more reform-oriented, it results in a brief growth spurt that is not sustained. This was the dynamic that enabled Nigeria's decades-long growth episode between 2003 and 2014, as discussed in Chapters 5 and 6. However, this pro-growth reform-orientation was too brief to coordinate divergent interests towards the deeper policy reforms needed to sustain growth and translate Nigeria's diversifying GDP into an expansion of exports and its revenue base. These deeper policy reforms are those that can increase labor productivity, such as investment in transport and connectivity infrastructure, access to credit for businesses, tax harmonization, and intergovernmental policy coordination to support Nigeria's subnational economies. This is examined in Chapter 7 on Lagos and Chapter 8 on Kano.

This expanding economy, despite not diversifying the country's export and revenue base, is also changing the distribution of power with implications for future policy making and resulting economic outcomes. The actors and institutions that emerged and become empowered in this growing economy are now exerting their newfound political influence. The banking tycoon, Tony Elumelu, is one of several businessmen empowered by Nigeria's growing economy of the 2000s. Others include moguls like Aigboje Aig-Imoukhuede of Access Bank, Jim Ovia of Zenith Bank, Michael Adenuga of Globacom, Nigeria's homegrown telecoms multinational, and, of course, Aliko Dangote, the industrial magnate who became Africa's richest man during this time; all are members of various economic steering committees set up by the government and they play important roles in indirectly supporting the candidacy of individuals running for public office. We discuss these in greater detail in Chapters 5 and 6.

This book contributes to opening the black box of "political will" behind economic policymaking. It unravels the abstract notion of "political will" into its more tangible components of power, actors, and institutions, to better understand the drivers of decision-making in resource-exporting countries like Nigeria.

The book makes it clear that it is neither the presence of natural resources nor a peculiar neopatrimonial African political culture that singularly dictate the selection and implementation of suboptimal public policies, and the resulting outcomes of economic underperformance.

What this Book is Not About: Corruption, Democracy, and Prescriptions

Since this book examines the complex linkages in power relations, policy processes, and economic outcomes, it is crucial to delimit its scope. Through a process of elimination, I identify the three areas, all important on their own accord, but which are not this book's focus. They are corruption, democracy, and policy prescriptions.

Firstly, the book is not about corruption: grand corruption by high-level public officials, petty corruption by low-level civil servants or bribery by firms and businessmen. It does not identify or analyze corruption in its various manifestations as the central developmental challenge in Nigeria. To be clear, corruption is pervasive and problematic in Nigeria as various governance indices show. The theft of government budgets by state governors; the subversion of procurement processes for public services by politicians and their business cronies; the absence of medical supplies in hospitals from siphoned funds by administrators; and the demand for bribes by police and customs officers to undertake their responsibilities all hamper public policies and affect development outcomes.

However, there is confusion about what objectively constitutes corruption and how it differs from other distortionary practices that result in suboptimal outcomes but that are neither uniquely Nigerian nor obstructive to growth. Countries like Brazil, China, India, and Malaysia still have significant levels of corruption alongside their rapid economic transformation. We need better research to separate normatively undesirable practices from what is objectively corruption. For this reason, a lack of clear understanding of what constitutes corruption contributes to anti-corruption initiatives that so often fail. More importantly corrupt behavior is often a symptom of deeper challenges around insufficiently implemented rules, weak administrative capacity for implementation, misaligned incentives, low public trust, and weak accountability mechanisms.[36] It is these deeper drivers of corruption that I focus on in this book.

Secondly, the book is not an assessment of Nigeria's regime type: whether it is a true or pseudo democracy. It neither chronicles the evolution of democracy in Nigeria nor benchmarks the democratic credentials of successive governments against regional or global indicators. Rather the book analyzes and sheds light on the policymaking process that affects the country's economic performance in terms of growth, diversification, and transformation. The book does not test the quality of Nigeria's democracy in elections, political participation by interest groups or their representation in political institutions such as the legislature and the civil service. However, I do reference, and indeed examine, Nigeria's important political transitions from one government to another, through elections or military coups, to identify junctures—or crucial moments in time—during which powerful actors and their interests have changed and key economic policies have been introduced, sustained, or discontinued. The political transitions at these junctures shaped decision-making processes and, in turn, are shaped by the growth and economic outcomes of prior decisions, a phenomenon that social scientists call a "path-dependency."

Thirdly, this book is not a detailed review and prescription of individual economic policies in all of Nigeria's economic sectors. It does not engage in the normative undertaking of identifying, labeling, and prescribing policies as "good," "bad," "right," or "misguided." As I have already suggested, such normative endeavors, particularly with respect to addressing the so-called "resource curse," have proved distracting and even pernicious in some cases. What this book does is to provide a better understanding of how politics shape the decision-making processes around key policies in important sectors such as oil and gas, ICT, banking and finance, and manufacturing, and how those "good" or "bad" policies come to be.

How this Book is Organized

What does economic diversification mean for a resource-exporting African country like Nigeria? How do such countries achieve economic diversification? What are the roles for the state and the market in diversifying a country's economy? Chapter 2 addresses these questions and lays the groundwork for analyzing the interplay of political power and policymaking in Nigeria's challenge of economic diversification in the rest of the book. Chapter 3 on "Unpacking Politics: Power, Actors and Institutions" provides analytical tools to unpack the political foundations of the policies that address or exacerbate Nigeria's challenge of economic diversification. I present the political settlements framework for analyzing the distribution of power among political actors (individuals, groups, and organizations), how this balance of power sustains or changes institutions, and the implications for policy design and implementation.

This political settlement framework is then employed in the analyses in Chapters 4 to 6. In Chapter 4, I recast key moments of Nigeria's history to explain that, within an unstable power configuration, Nigerian leaders were constrained to make policy choices to stabilize the country but these decisions compounded the challenge of economic diversification. The chapter makes it clear that Nigeria's policy choices made during the oil boom of the 1970s and onwards were driven by factors independent of crude oil. However, oil windfall revenues were used in policy implementation, especially in efforts to blunt the fierce ethno-regional and religious competition that caused the 1967 civil war. In Chapter 5, I explain that during democratization in 1999, Nigeria's political settlement was characterized by a collective resolve to prevent a political collapse. Thus, an elite consensus on power-sharing stabilized political competition allowing for a policy reform-orientation focused on macroeconomic stabilization, rather than a structural transformation to diversify Nigeria's economy. Within this power configuration, Nigeria became Africa's largest economy in 2014 driven by an expansion in non-oil sectors, even as the challenge of economic diversification persisted. Chapter 6 examines in more detail how policy choices were made within this post-military political settlement to reform the telecoms and downstream oil sectors.

Specifically, I argue that external constraints of volatile oil prices and the resulting fiscal pressures pushed decision makers to successfully liberalize the telecoms sector. Yet, similar efforts to reform the downstream oil sector and clean up the wasteful fossil fuel subsidy regime stalled due to countervailing vertical constraints for redistribution.

The political settlement analytical framework is also employed in the two subnational cases in Chapters 7 and 8. Chapter 7 attributes, in large part, the status of Lagos as a major anchor of Nigeria's non-oil economy to the balance of power that has enabled relative policy effectiveness and continuity. I explain that, since 1999, successive Lagos ruling elites have built a political coalition to coordinate the state's advantageous factor endowments, skillfully leveraging the institutional provisions within Nigeria's federalism and have strengthened their administrative capacity for governance reforms. The chapter argues that Lagos ruling elites became reform-oriented not by accident, but in response to the existential threats to their survival from intra-party factionalization, population explosion, urban decay, violent crime, and fiscal insolvency. By contrast, as we examine in Chapter 8, Kano, another strategic anchor of Nigeria's non-oil economy, has been unable to overcome the global head winds of deindustrialization and realize its vast economic potential due to its underlying political settlement. I argue that Kano's ruling elites have not built a pro-growth coalition to address deindustrialization and its socio-economic impacts due to the political constraints they faced. To ensure their political survival, they succumbed to vociferous demands to extend Islamic Shariah law by an influential minority of activists in the Islamist revivalism of the early 2000s. Lacking a strong economic strategy, Kano's ruling elites have kept the large Kano business community at arm's length, even when some governance reforms were briefly implemented in 2011.

In the Conclusion, I outline five building blocks to better address the challenge of economic diversification in resource-rich countries like Nigeria. First, economic diversification must be seen for what it truly is: a political project of economic development. The aim of this political project would be to stabilize Nigeria's political economy and generate shared prosperity rather than just aiming to "build a strong economy" as the ultimate end. Second, this project would entail a political arrangement that stabilizes Nigeria's volatile distribution of power. How can this be achieved? I believe a systematic adoption and enforcement of the zoning power-sharing arrangement can help resolve collective action problems that so frequently destabilize the country. This power-sharing should go beyond an informal gentleman's agreement and should be incorporated in the federal constitution. A third building block for this political project would be to develop a shared vision for achieving structural economic transformation. This shared vision should entail an informed debate among Nigerians to settle the role of the state and the market in organizing the economy attuned to the realities of the twenty-first century, especially the fourth industrial revolution and climate change. It should also encapsulate the country's regional differentiations and their separate, but complementary, policy needs. Nigerians should also envision a strong mechanism for managing oil revenues in equitable and pragmatic ways to incentivize meaningful action.

A fourth building block to address Nigeria's challenge of economic diversification is to outline the urgent policy priorities for a post-oil future. These policy priorities should shift from stabilization to proactively creating markets and tackling market failures towards structural economic transformation. On the supply side, tackling these market failures would entail accelerating the pace of providing physical infrastructure and business finance, and closing the knowledge and technological gap to increase productivity. On the demand side, social protection instruments that help individuals and households to increase incomes and consumption, strengthen their resilience to shocks, and prevent destitution are crucial. For the Nigerian government to effectively tackle these market failures, it needs a competent and modern bureaucracy meaning that comprehensive civil service reforms cannot be avoided.

Finally, we as scholars must update our mental models on the challenges of economic development in Africa. To this end, an analytical framework focused on the dynamic interplay of power, policymaking, and economic outcomes gives us a vital insight into the political process of economic development. Using this political-economy lens confirms what we have always instinctively known—that no country is "cursed" by its natural resources or culturally averse to development. Our frameworks for analyses must be dynamic enough to account for ebbs and flows; and flexible enough to recognize new twenty-first century opportunities such as the digital revolution to address old challenges of economic development.

A Note on Methods, Data, and Sources

In writing this book, I drew on a wide range of sources. I consulted primary sources such as government reports, records, and other documents. I also collected my own data with over 120 interviews conducted between 2014 and 2015 mostly in Nigeria. These interviews covered politicians, senior bureaucrats in government agencies, industrialists, financiers and other business elites, oil company representatives, journalists, and civil society actors. This study also consulted data generated and maintained by the Nigerian government, multilateral agencies like the World Bank and the UN, and independent sources. I supplemented all these with news reports, memoirs, other studies, and other published material.

Economic Diversification: Concept, Application, and State–Market Relations

To most Nigerians, the one word that captures the essence of Eagle Square is "power." By virtue of its strategic location close to the presidential villa and the national legislature in Abuja, Nigeria's administrative capital, the crowds it draws, and the historic events it hosts, Eagle Square is powerful. So on 29th May 2015, Eagle Square hosted the inauguration of the newly elected president, Muhammadu Buhari, in historic circumstances. From where I sat with journalists, professionals, and others attending the swearing-in ceremony, I observed the arrival of various dignitaries to the VIP pavilion. Among those I spotted were billionaire tycoons Femi Otedola and Aliko Dangote, Zimbabwe's Robert Mugabe whose entry caused a brief commotion, and South Africa's Jacob Zuma. Overall, more than fifty heads of states from Africa, Asia, and other parts of the world were present. A few minutes after U.S. Secretary of State John Kerry's arrival, the presidential delegation entered the square with Buhari in an open-roof Mercedes SUV. Shortly after, Buhari took the oath of office as president, acknowledged the dignitaries attending, and thanked outgoing president Goodluck Jonathan. He then proceeded to lay out his vision to tackle corruption, provide electric power, fight insecurity, and address unemployment.

Eagle Square as a powerful site of historical firsts: it is where Nigerian presidents unveil their governing vision. Constructed in 1999 to host the democratic transition from military rule, the square is where all four of Nigeria's civilian presidents have ceremonially taken on presidential power in unique circumstances. Their inaugural address typically does several things simultaneously: it acknowledges the historic nature of their position, makes a commitment that defines their policy agenda and outlines their vision. When Olusegun Obasanjo was sworn into office on 29 May 1999 as the first civilian president of the Fourth Republic, he noted in his speech: "Twelve months ago, no one could have predicted the series of stunning events that made it possible for democratic elections to be held..." He then outlined his vision including a strident anti-corruption agenda and the restoration of Nigeria's external relations. In his inaugural speech in 2007, Umaru Yar'Adua admitted that the election that brought him to power "had some shortcomings" and committed "to examine the entire electoral process" and to "respect the rule of law." Yar'Adua then announced his Seven-Point Agenda, which included investing in power and transport infrastructure and addressing the security crisis in the oil-producing Niger Delta. Goodluck

Jonathan prefaced his vision for Nigeria's "Transformation" by acknowledging his status as the first president from the Niger Delta at his inauguration in 2011.

The vision statement announced by a president at Eagle Square is subsequently fleshed out in a policy document that guides budget and spending. The policy document is typically published about a year or two into the administration. Obasanjo's defining policy agenda, the National Economic Empowerment and Development Strategy (NEEDS), was published in 2003, in his second term in office. By then, signature initiatives such as anti-corruption, public procurement reforms, revenue transparency and privatization were well underway. Although Yar'Adua's Seven-Point Agenda comprising bullet points that took all of two pages, in 2009, his administration produced an elaborate long-term economic strategy called the Nigeria Vision 20:2020 which built on initiatives of the Obasanjo's administration and sketched out a vision for the next decade. The Transformation Agenda and the Economic Recovery and Growth Plan (ERGP) of the Jonathan and Buhari administrations respectively were only available nearly two years after their inauguration. Both policy agendas were presented as medium-term strategies under the umbrella NV20:2020.

There is a continuity in these policy documents which all aspire to build a strong and diversified Nigerian economy. Despite Nigeria's contentious presidential elections that produce these presidents, economic diversification is clearly articulated as the foremost policy objective. Starting with NEEDS in 2003, Nigeria partially returned to some version of economic planning after the SAP disruption of the 1980s and 1990s, with economic diversification as a major national aspiration. The Nigeria Vision 20:2020 then became the overarching framework for economic development for the eleven-year period between 2009 and 2020, through a series of medium-term strategies. The NV20:2020 retroactively incorporated Obasanjo's NEEDS (2004–2007) and Yar'Adua's Seven-Point Agenda (2007–2009) and was the basis on which Jonathan's "Transformation Agenda" (2011–2015) and Buhari's ERGP (2017–2020) were developed.[1] Specifically, the NV20:2020 identifies "… achieving significant progress in economic diversification" as one of its macroeconomic policy thrusts, and outlines the promotion of "… private sector-led non-oil growth to build the foundation for economic diversification" as one of the critical policy priorities.[2]

This post-military national aspiration for economic diversification is as old as Nigeria itself. Since independence in 1960, successive governments have sought to diversify the economy by catalyzing industrialization, notably since the first oil boom-and-bust cycle from 1973. Economic diversification is consequently a term whose meaning has evolved in parallel with Nigeria's revenue sources and development priorities. In the First and Second National Development Plans covering the 1962–1968 and 1970–1975 periods respectively, it meant "modernizing" agriculture and building a strong manufacturing and industrial sector to attain "self-sustaining growth" with less dependence on primary production and external sources of finance, capital, and capacity. In the wake of the oil boom of the 1970s, crude oil took an increasingly larger share of GDP, as oil and mining grew to 45% of GDP from 13%, while agriculture and manufacturing fell from 44% and 12% to 25% and 5% of GDP respectively by 1975.[3] Consequently, in the Third and Fourth National Development Plans covering the periods 1975–1980 and 1981–1985 respectively, a core goal was "... reduction in the dependence of the economy on a narrow range of activities" and specifically, "reducing dependence of the economy on oil as a source of public revenue and foreign exchange earnings..."[4]

This notion of "economic diversification" has since been firmly cemented in the lexicon of economic development in Nigeria. For as long as I can remember, it has been a staple feature in speeches by presidents and ministers and in policy announcements especially after a sharp collapse in oil prices. In the Nigerian conceptualization of economic diversification, it approximates to reducing the economy's debilitating dependence on its oil sector and, by implication, reducing its vulnerability to sharp oil price swings. In the minds of most Nigerians, a diversified economy is one that is more reliant on Nigeria's other endowments especially arable land, livestock, minerals and metals, and human resources as growth drivers, revenue earners, and employment providers. It also features strongly in public discourse in academic, civil society, and business circles.[5] One could even say that the term "economic diversification" now sounds like a cliché to many Nigerians because it is constantly invoked in unfulfilled policy promises.

Given this backdrop, the following questions come to mind: What does economic diversification mean for a resource-exporting African country like Nigeria? How do such countries achieve economic diversification? What are the roles for the state and the market in diversifying a country's economy? This chapter addresses these questions with respect to Nigeria, and thereby lays the groundwork for the analyses on the politics of building a post-oil Nigerian economy in the rest of the book.

Concept: What is "Economic Diversification" and Why Does it Matter?

At its most basic, economic diversification is an expansion of the sources of production, employment, trade, revenues, and expenditures in an economy. It is characterized by the transition from dependence on one or a few commodities such as crude oil, minerals, and agriculture produce. Achieving economic diversification is a policy challenge in many developing countries, especially in Africa, and is associated with the process of "structural transformation." And structural transformation is characterized by rising "productivity," sustained "growth," and results in "economic development." Let us look at each of these terminologies in turn.

Structural transformation is the transition of a country's productive resources (natural resources, land, capital, labor, and know-how) from low-productivity activities such as primary agriculture to higher-productivity activities in the industrial and services sectors.[6] It is characterized by a declining share of agriculture in GDP and employment, a shift of workers from low- to high-productivity sectors, increases in efficiency, urbanization as people move from rural areas to cities and the rise of a modern industrial and service economy. Economic growth is the quantitative increase in economic output usually measured by the increase in GDP. But growth can also be driven by rising factor intensity. For example, a farmer can increase the output on their 100-hectare tomato farm by hiring eight laborers to help cultivate the land using fertilizer, more hoes, and cow-driven plows. Output increases from 100 baskets per season to 150. Or growth can be driven by rising productivity. In this case, only the farmer and one hired help cultivate the land, but they use more fertilizer, higher-yield seeds, mechanized tractors, and modern refrigeration to produce and sell 300 baskets of tomatoes. Since "Productivity" is such an important concept to growth, structural transformation, and development, it merits closer examination.

At its most basic, productivity refers to output per unit of production inputs. Productivity growth is associated with higher efficiency in production, that is, an increase in output without necessarily a commensurate increase in inputs of labor, human, natural, and physical capital. Productivity improvement is essential to sustained economic growth. Our farmer thus increases their tomato yields by applying technology and new methods, rather than acquiring a larger farm or hiring more workers. The general consensus among economists is that total factor productivity accounts for the majority of income per worker differences across countries.[7] That is, with the same amount of inputs, i.e., workers, buildings, land, natural resources, raw materials, etc., some countries, sectors, and firms produce more than others.[8] Across sub-Saharan Africa (SSA) overall, labor productivity has lagged the global efficiency benchmark, using the United States as proxy.

One of the most important sources of firm-level productivity growth, i.e., for countries to push the production possibility frontier and catch up to the productivity leaders, is an increase in firm capabilities.[9] The economist Chad Syverson categorizes two determinants of firm capabilities: production practices (managerial capabilities, worker skills, technology adoption, process and product innovation, etc.) and the firms' external environments (R&D investments, physical capital such as infrastructure, human capital such as education, market efficiency, and the policy environment).[10] The average output per worker in sub-Saharan Africa, relative to the U.S., declined from 11.9% in 1960 to 7.7% in 2017, whereas for East Asian countries (Indonesia, Malaysia, Republic of Korea, Singapore, and Thailand), labor productivity increased from 8.5% in 1960 to 28.3% relative to the U.S. in 2014, according to a World Bank report.[11] Similarly, there has been a divergence in labor productivity between SSA and large emerging market economies like Brazil, China, and India which lagged behind Africa in 1960. In Nigeria, as we discuss in Chapter 5, labor productivity or output per worker has only now begun to increase after a three-decade decline.

Therefore, economic development is a process of sustained economic growth, structural transformation from low to higher-productivity activities and a deeper process of social change. Thus the process of economic development has at its core (1) sustained economic growth; (2) increased productivity; and (3) structural shifts towards a broad range of sectors, particularly manufacturing and services.

How do all these concepts relate to our focus—economic diversification? For a resource-exporting country like Nigeria, the process of economic development has, at its core, diversification and a transition from the oil sector, subsistence agriculture, and other forms of primary production towards value-added manufacturing, services, and other industry. To develop the Nigerian economy, its diversification is a prerequisite. In other words, economic diversification is the policy challenge to

Nigeria's development, and the characteristics of this development such as rising per capita incomes, reduced poverty, industrial transformation, and social change.

There are dimensions of economic diversification for any country, depending on its structural characteristics. The two most widely used conceptualizations of diversification are the sectoral contributions to employment and production, and international trade. In my paper with David Landry, we identified a third conceptualization, fiscal diversification, in terms of an expansion in the sources of government revenues and the targets of public expenditures.[12] Drawing from that paper, the three conceptualizations of economic diversification that apply to a large, resource-exporting African country like Nigeria, are discussed below.

The first conceptualization of economic diversification is the increase in the number of economic sectors that contribute to total employment and output, or GDP.[13] The diversification of GDP usually entails the transition from primary industries towards more technologically advanced sectors, a shift from informal towards formal sectors, or structural transformation as discussed above.[14] As this shift occurs, the growth in some economic sectors may provide intermediate inputs to the growth of others and thus diversify the sources of employment and output. For instance, underdeveloped financial markets create frictions that affect productivity and investment ratios. In developing countries, these financial frictions can have a severe impact on the manufacturing sector. According to Francisco Buera and colleagues, these frictions result in a 50% decline in productivity, higher relative prices of manufactures compared to services, and a 15% decline in investment ratios.[15] Hence, the informal sector such as petty trade or small-scale agriculture characterized by low wages, skills, and productivity, is prevalent in developing countries as the main source of output and employment. A more evenly distributed economic weight across industries, marked by a decline in agriculture's contribution in poor countries and in the oil and mining sectors for resource-rich countries, denotes a more diversified economy.

Across Africa, the informal sector makes up 86% of total employment and 72% when agriculture is excluded from the total (Figure 2.1). Though substantial variations persist between countries in North Africa (Algeria, Egypt, Morocco, Tunisia, etc.) and Sub-Saharan Africa, and within sub-Saharan Africa itself, African economies generally have high levels of informality. I examine the contribution of oil and gas relative to other sectors in terms of value added and employment in the Nigerian economy in Chapters 4–6, and to the subnational economies of Lagos and Kano in Chapters 7 and 8.

A second conceptualization of economic diversification—export diversification—focuses on a country's major trade sectors and partners.[16] Specifically, export diversification relates to an increase in the range of goods and services an economy exports to the rest of the world, or the markets to which they are exported. Export diversification generally entails a move from trading one or a few primary commodities to that of a wider set of goods and services. The IMF and the World Bank broadly define a resource-rich country as one in which minerals account for more than 25% of total exports.[17] Beyond expanding the export basket, export diversification can entail a growing number of destination countries for exports.[18] For instance, African countries are increasingly diversifying their trade partners away from former colonial powers in

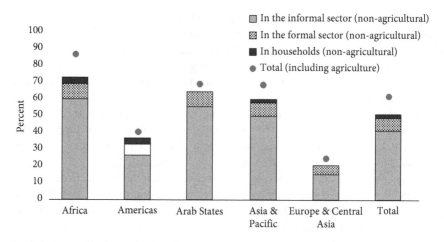

Figure 2.1 Africa has the World's Highest Levels of Informal Employment.

Source: International Labour Organization (2018, p. 67).

Europe. China and India recently surpassed the United States and the United Kingdom to become Africa's largest bilateral trade partners.

In this book, I focus only on the sectoral contribution to the export basket, in terms of export diversification. A more diversified export base is associated with structural change in the economy of the country in question. Regression analyses show a positive relationship between manufacturing value added as a percentage of GDP and exports diversification. In other words, as countries' manufacturing value added as a share of GDP grows, so does their export diversification. Similarly, for resource-rich countries, as their exports diversification increases, their dependence on natural resource rents decreases.

Across Africa, raw materials still make up the bulk of exports in many countries—52% of the total in 2017 (Figure 2.2). However, there is considerable variation on the continent, as Southern and East Africa have more diversified export baskets than West and Central Africa. At least twenty African countries are classified by the IMF as resource-rich, including Angola, Ghana, Nigeria, and Tanzania whose exports are comprising a large share of unprocessed oil, gas and minerals and agriculture commodities like cocoa. Resource-rich countries in other parts of the world like Chile, Malaysia, and Indonesia have a more diversified exports base comprising manufactures derived from petroleum, palm oil, and other value-added products. In Chapters 4 and 5, we discuss how crude oil has constituted more than 90% of Nigeria's export earnings since the 1970s.

A final conceptualization of economic diversification is an increase in the sectors that contribute to government revenues and that are targeted by governments expenditures. In my paper with Landry, we referred to this as "fiscal diversification." Governments usually tap various sources of finance including tax revenue, internal and external borrowing, currency issuance, and development assistance. Fiscal diversification therefore entails a move away from dependence on one or a few sources—especially

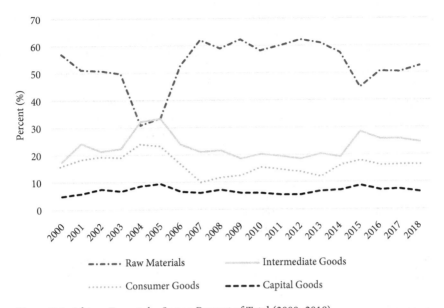

Figure 2.2 African Exports by Sector, Percent of Total (2000–2018).

Source: Zainab Usman and David Landry (Economic Diversification in Africa: How and Why it Matters, 2021, p. 9).

extractive industries in resource-exporting countries—toward more varied and sustainable domestic revenue mobilization.[19] It can also signify an expansion of the tax base and taxation instruments used, such as property or land taxes as taxes represent the most sustainable sources of revenue.[20] As economies grow, a gradual shift away from trade taxes to domestic sales taxes tends to happen. This diversification of tax sources occurs as governments move from collecting around 10% of national income as revenues towards roughly 40%, according to Timothy Besley and Torsten Persson.[21] The mechanisms for this shift include a shrinking informal sector which widens the tax net, the growth of larger firms which eases tax compliance, and the development of the financial sector which encourages transparent accounting procedures that enable tax collection.[22] Thus, the share of a government's budget collected from specific economic sectors can represent an important measure of economic diversification.

On the expenditure side, government spending can both catalyze and constrain the growth in employment and output of economic sectors. Through expenditures, governments can free up resources and reallocate them to sectors that provide higher economic and social returns.[23] Historically, governments around the world have used fiscal tools as part of industrial policies to catalyze structural transformation. Some governments—primarily North American, German and Italian late-industrializers, and the East Asian Tigers—succeeded in doing so. In other instances, however, the experience proved disastrous for economic development. For instance, the import-substitution industrialization polices adopted by many Latin American and African governments did not result in a sustained rise in manufacturing output. Africa's manufacturing value added remained largely stagnant between the early-1960s and mid-1990s. That said, a promising literature is rethinking the ideas surrounding industrial policy in Africa, as we will examine in the rest of this chapter.

Fiscal diversification is thus both an indicator of structural economic change (production, employment, and trade) and as the mechanism through which policymakers can catalyze this economic change. In this book, I focus on the revenue component of fiscal diversification at the national level and among subnational authorities in Nigeria's thirty-six states. Among resource-rich countries that rely on their mineral exports for more than 40% of their government revenues called "rentier states,"[24] fiscal diversification is even more urgent as the disruption in oil revenues can be catastrophic. These rentier states include African countries such as Angola, Equatorial Guinea, Gabon, Ghana, Nigeria, the Gulf Arab countries including Qatar and Saudi Arabia, as well as Russia. Interestingly, across African countries in the last two decades, domestic revenue generation has dramatically increased (Figure 2.3). As Mick Moore and others note, African governments are collecting taxes more effectively than governments in some low-income regions and are making consistent, gradual progress in improving their revenue systems.[25] In the same vein, net Official Development Assistance (ODA) or foreign aid as a share of national income (GNI) has declined from a peak of 5.1% in 2003 to 3% in 2017, though considerable cross-country variation exists. For instance, development assistance accounts for over 10% of GNI in Burundi, Liberia, and Malawi among others.[26] Furthermore, Africa remains

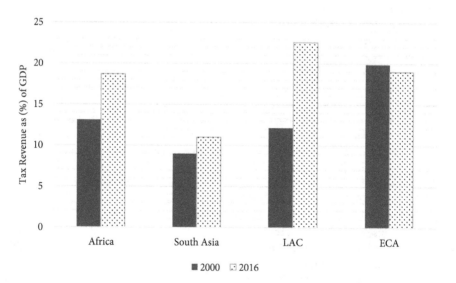

Figure 2.3 Tax Revenue Collection as a Share of GDP among Selected Regions (2000 and 2016).

Source: Zainab Usman and David Landry (2021, p. 13).

the region most dependent on ODA. In 2016, it received about 33% of total ODA from OECD donors, the most of any region.

The resource-exporting developing countries, especially in Africa, face urgent pressures to diversify their economies due to disruption to global supply and the demand for mineral resources. On the supply side, there are more oil and gas producers now than ever before. In Africa alone, by 2012 only five of the continent's fifty-four countries were not producing or looking for oil, and in 2013, six of the ten global discoveries in the oil and gas sector were made in Africa.[27] Furthermore, the US shale oil and gas revolution has partly contributed to a supply glut even as Organisation of Petroleum Exporting Countries (OPEC) struggle to control production and maintain high prices. To that effect, the US reduced its imports of Nigerian crude by 95% from a peak of 1 million barrels per day in 2007 to 58,000 in 2014.[28] On the demand side, the 2015 Paris agreement on climate change marked a decisive shift towards decarbonizing energy and transport systems. By some estimates, hydrocarbon-rich countries like Nigeria, Angola, and Gabon could experience a steep decline of up to 51% in oil and gas revenues by 2040.[29]

The writing on the wall for oil exporters is clear: they must take earnest steps to build post-oil economies. Realistically, the oil-guzzling technologies on which our daily lives depend such as the internal combustion engine and thermal power plants still have another decade or two of mileage. However, there is an accelerating global shift away from hydrocarbons, on which oil exporters like Nigeria have depended on since the 1970s. The combination of a supply glut, steadily declining demand, and the prospect of reserve depletion over the next two decades could throw oil-rich countries ino disarray unless they build more diversified economies.

Application: How do Resource-rich Countries Diversify their Economies?

How does a country achieve structural transformation towards a diversified economy? If an easy answer to this question existed, then a lot more countries than just sixteen out of 182 since the 1960s would have transitioned from low income to high income.[30] Scholars have documented the experience of the early industrializers in England and the USA, late industrializers in Germany, Italy, and Japan and the late "late" industrializers in East Asia in reaching high income. New technologies and changing geopolitics are shaping the tools, environments, and opportunities available for economic transformation. Based on this historical experience and changing conditions, we can identify roughly three pathways to achieving structural economic transformation in a way that diversifies and develops an economy. These are industrial transformation, leapfrogging industrialization through digital transformation and building "industries without smokestacks." Let us examine each of these in turn.

Manufacturing-based industrialization is the tried-and-tested pathway to achieving economic transformation. Industrialization is an integral part of this structural transformation process, in which technological innovation characterzes the production process and spreads across society. It is an integrated process of complementary agricultural productivity growth and non-agricultural activity and employment in manufacturing and services. The term "industry" generally consists of manufacturing, mining, services and construction, or any activity that involves widespread application of technology. Yet it is the manufacturing component of industry, (i.e., the physical or chemical transformation of agricultural and mineral materials, substances or components into new products) that have historically provided greater opportunities for sustained growth, innovation, employment creation, and poverty reduction.[31] This is due to the manufacturing sector's high productivity, diffusion of technological innovation to society, strong forward and backward linkages to other sectors and the fact that factory work can stimulate deep social change.[32] For instance, manufacturing creates demand for other sectors because factories are consumers of banking, transport, insurance, and communication services. Factory work can transform social relations in society by employing women in the "soft" activity of garment making, as has been the case in Bangladesh, Morocco, South Korea, and Vietnam, enabling them to join the labor force.[33]

All cases of rapid and sustained economic growth are associated with manufacturing-based industrialization. This was the case for the early-to-late industrializers who focused on developing the capabilities of their infant industries under protectionist trade policies such as Britain, Germany, and Japan. The late-late industrializers focused on export-led manufacturing under more liberal trading regimes such as Singapore. The manufacturing industrial sector is thus a key engine of growth in the economic development process.[34] Ha-Joon Chang underscores the significance of manufacturing-based industrialization because "... it is a fantasy to think that developing countries can skip industrialization and build prosperity on the basis of service industries."[35]

Sub-Saharan Africa, it is argued, has an opportunity to pursue the same labor-intensive export-led industrialization model. African countries can industrialize by adding value to their natural resources and exploiting their relatively low labor costs to provide specific skills or products to international production networks called global value chains (GVCs).[36] Many scholars note that the rise of wages in China as it transitions towards higher technology and skills-intensive production as with the rest of East Asia, will free up about 100 million labor-intensive manufacturing jobs for low-income regions like Africa to capture (see Box 2.1).[37] Some countries like Ethiopia seem prepared to capture manufacturing FDI from China, the USA, Spain, India and others, in places like the Hawassa Industrial Park.[38] For oil and mineral producers, opportunities exist to pursue resource-based industrialization through processing, linkage development, and technological upgrading of their natural resources sectors. In Malaysia and Chile, for instance, Amir Lebdioui and colleagues show that the leading engines of growth and exports have been resource-based sectors (petroleum, rubber, and palm oil) in the former and non-mining resource-based sectors (salmon, fruits, wine and wood-based) in the latter.[39]

Box 2.1. Will China Help or Hinder Africa's Economic Transformation?

China has become one of Africa's top economic partners now shaping the continent's development trajectory. Its rise as the world's second-largest economy, on course to take the top spot by 2030, occurred in parallel to its expanded global economic engagement. In Africa, China's engagement in manufacturing, infrastructure projects and as the continent's largest trade partner could help or hinder the region's economic development aspirations articulated in national strategies and the African Union's Agenda 2063. In terms of manufacturing, there are Chinese investments—accounting for the fourth-largest FDI stocks in Africa in 2019—in textiles in Lesotho, and flip flops, plastics, and tiles in Nigeria.[40] There are also Chinese investments in many of the 237 industrial parks and special economic zones (SEZs) across thirty-eight countries in the region.[41] Although the record for these China-Africa SEZs is mixed, studies show that industrial parks can help drive industrialization in specific sectors, as was the experience in China and now Vietnam, due to the potential for knowledge, skills, and technology spill overs.[42] China has now become Africa's leading financier for infrastructure projects outpacing other multilateral and bilateral development partners. Between 2010 and 2019, Chinese financiers committed $ 153 billion to the African public sector and at least 80% of these loans financed economic and social infrastructure projects.[43] China is providing both the financing and expertise for roads, ports, bridges, power plants, and telecoms infrastructure. New airport terminals in Abuja, Accra, Brazzaville, Dakar, and Lagos; the Addis light rail in Ethiopia; the Abuja-Kaduna and Lagos-Ibadan rail in Nigeria; the Mombasa rail in Kenya, etc., have all been built with Chinese financing and by its construction companies. Digital commerce platforms of the Ali Baba Business Group are enabling African SMEs, through the Electronic World Trade Platform (EWTP), to sell their products to new markets around the world, compared to the reticence of Western platforms like Amazon.[44] These digital and analog infrastructure investments are what African economies need to help increase their productivity. Finally, Africa–China trade has been growing by approximately 20% per year for the last two decades. In 2020, Africa–China trade amounted to $187 billion compared to $45 billion for the U.S. and $254 billion for the 27 EU countries combined.[45] It is the destination for Africa's exports, as well as the leading provider of consumer goods, from textiles to shoes to mobile phones. The mobile phone company Transsion leads Africa's phone market by units sold, displacing others like Finland's Nokia and South Korea's Samsung.[46] While the bulk of Africa's exports to China are crude oil, minerals, and timber, a few producers have started to add value to these commodities. Kenya has begun to export cut avocados; Rwanda and Uganda are working on selling processed coffee and Namibia and South Africa are shipping beef to China. Despite these opportunities and that China has none of what former Liberian minister Gyude Moore describes as the "historical baggage of colonial exploitation of Africa by European powers," there are risks.[47] The Africa–China relationship is asymmetrical, unless Africa presents a united front through the AfCFTA for example and skillfully balances its relationship with Western and Eastern powers. African countries are also taking on large volumes of loans from China to address their infrastructure deficits. This debt financing must be managed more transparently. Finally, African countries should strive to diversify their exports to China and indeed to the rest of the world beyond unprocessed mineral and agriculture commodities.

Some scholars have identified a second pathway to economic development in which a digital transformation allows the "leapfrogging" of the industrialization process. The idea that a digital transformation may provide an alternative to low-income countries, mostly in Africa but also in parts of Latin America and South Asia, stems from two shifts underway. The first shift is the so-called "fourth industrial revolution" in which an acceleration of technological change, especially digitalization, is transforming economic activities. Digital technologies such as autonomous vehicles, artificial intelligence, big data analytics, robotics, 3D printing, and the internet of things are disrupting business models, the production process, and even the nature of occupations in fundamental ways.[48] Automation in particular is disrupting the factory floor and integrated platforms such as Amazon, Facebook, and Airbnb are displacing their brick-and-mortar equivalents such as bookstores, newspapers, and hotels.

Another shift underway is the reorganization of value chains, due in part to the digital revolution as well as geopolitics. The process of globalization, in which capital flows of large Western and Japanese multinationals to lower-cost manufacturing jurisdictions in China, Malaysia, and other parts of East Asia helped drive Asia's industrial transformation, may be in reverse. This has been driven by the stagnation of wages and productivity in the aftermath of the global financial crisis (GFC) in industrialized Western countries. The COVID-19 pandemic also made it clear that many Western countries, perhaps with the exception of Germany, had lost domestic production capacity in essential industries including medical supplies, pharmaceuticals, aerospace, renewable energy components, and communications technology hardware. The combination of the GFC and the COVID-19 pandemic highlighted structural vulnerabilities in Western economies from the decades-long decimation of jobs from automation, off-shoring, and the transition to a service economy.[49] To that effect, French president Emmanuel Macron—a "champion" of globalization—declared in 2020 that supply chains will "need to become more French." Germany's Health Minister Jens Spahn similarly wants to minimize "one-sided dependencies in order to win back national sovereignty."[50] In January 2021, American president Joe Biden mandated federal agencies to purchases products made in the U.S.[51] These declarations point to the strong domestic political pressures in Europe and North America to reshore or bring back domestic manufacturing with increasingly protectionist trade policies in these countries.

Thus, the twin processes of digitization of manufacturing and globalization may result in "premature deindustrialization" for low-income countries. Dani Rodrik, one of the leading proponents of this school of thought, observed that poor countries are running out of industrialization opportunities sooner and at much lower levels of income compared to early and late industrializers in Europe, North America, and Asia.[52] In Africa and Latin America manufacturing is shrinking as a share of employment and value addition, the countries are transforming into low-productivity service economies without experiencing industrialization, and informality is expanding, unlike East Asia, where labor is moving from low- to high-productivity activities. Rodrik argues, thus, that the industrialization route to economic transformation may no longer be available to these countries. Besides, other low-income Asian countries like Bangladesh and Vietnam, which are more competitive than African countries due to better infrastructure and human capital, are already capturing this manufacturing FDI.[53] And according to a study on Ethiopia by Chris Blattman, Simon Franklin, and Stefan Dercon, the factory jobs that result from this low-cost manufacturing do not significantly increase incomes and well-being and, in the short term, created health risks.[54] For the low-income countries set to miss out on industrialization and stuck on a perpetual low-growth trajectory, their focus, according to this school of thought, should be on alleviating the suffering of the poorest, where possible using digital technologies, focusing on entrepreneurship, addressing informality, and providing social assistance. This claim that Africa may not be able to industrialize remains highly contested among scholars with a lot of push back.[55]

A third pathway to achieving economic transformation combines elements of the first two, in what is called "industries without smokestacks." In this pathway, Africa's economic transformation in the twenty-first century is unlikely to look like East Asia's experience in the twentieth. It will draw on a broader range of high-productivity economic activities including those that share characteristics of manufacturing called industries without smokestacks. These manufacturing-like industries include tourism, ICT, and other services as well as food processing and horticulture.[56] This school of thought argues that the twin processes of digitalization and globalization are creating new opportunities for African countries to focus on building and catering to integrated domestic consumer markets. Digitalization and the technology revolution are transforming non-manufacturing industries making them more tradable across time and space at lower costs. Therefore, these manufacturing-like sectors are outpacing the growth of manufacturing in many African countries, hold the potential for knowledge spillovers, have high value added per worker, and are tradable, thereby allowing for economies of scale and foreign exchange earnings.[57] A growing empirical literature from India, Pakistan, Sri-Lanka, and other parts of South Asia shows that services generate labor productivity, employment and reduce poverty at comparable or even higher levels than manufacturing.[58]

Overall, sustained growth for African countries may lie in the domestic production and regional export of services. In a climate of reshoring manufacturing investments and rising protectionism in Western countries, Africa can cater to its domestic and sub-regional markets.[59] The establishment of the Africa Continental Free Trade Area (AfCFTA) creates the world's largest single common market of 1.3 billion people with a combined GDP of $3.4 trillion across fifty-five countries. By improving trade facilitation and reducing barriers to intra-African trade, the single common market can contribute to Africa's economic transformation. A World Bank study finds that the AfCFTA can increase Africa's exports by $560 billion mostly in manufacturing. This is because intra-African trade has a higher composition of manufactures and intermediate goods than the region's exports to the rest of the world which is still comprising raw unprocessed commodities. For resource-rich countries, the AfCFTA can thus help with export diversification. Deeper regional integration allows countries that are small and landlocked, such as Lesotho, Rwanda, Zambia, and others to trade with their neighbors. Implementation of the AfCFTA can also help lift 30 million Africans out of extreme poverty and boost wages for both skilled and unskilled workers. There are studies on transport services, horticulture, and mobile payments in Kenya and healthcare in South Africa, among others.[60] These "industries without smokestacks," which focus on meeting domestic and regional demand, can also help address the continent's jobs crisis.

The State or the Market: Who Drives Economic Diversification?

Now that we have a sense of what economic diversification means and the three available pathways for African countries to achieve it, we need to understand who drives it. Is it the state, (a political entity that exercises legitimate authority over a sovereign territorial jurisdiction), the market (a place, institution, or network where buyers and sellers transact goods, services, and assets)[61] or both? What is the scope for the state and the market in driving economic transformation? In addressing these questions, we discuss the role of the state in facilitating economic transformation by creating, guiding, and regulating markets through any of the three pathways identified in the previous section. Then we delimit the scope of state participation in this process especially in coordinating a country's factor endowments and correcting market failures. We then identify elements of the institutional capacity and political character of an effective state in driving economic transformation.

The Role of the State in Guiding Markets to Drive Economic Transformation

The role of the state versus the market in economic transformation is the subject of recurring scholarly debate. Since the GFC of 2008 and more recently with the COVID-19 pandemic, this debate is resurging. Should economies operate on free market principles with minimal government intervention or should a state intervene in the public interest to create, guide, and correct markets, especially in the provision of public goods and in managing externalities? As we will discuss in this section, among economists and other social scientists this debate has come full circle. After the Second World War, in the 1950s, the focus was on government-led economic transformation. From the 1980s, there was a Washington Consensus on scaling back government involvement to allow unrestrained market forces to lead the economy. After the GFC from 2008 and with COVID-19 from 2020 there is a renewed emphasis on the role of the state to regulate markets, provide public goods, and address socio-distributional concerns.

My position having reviewed the large body of literature and the comparative historical evidence of the remarkable East Asian transformation in contrast to Africa's numerous failures, is unequivocal. African countries require strong and capable states to create, guide, and regulate markets towards economic transformation. Many African countries, unlike the Asian industrializers in the late twentieth century, and the European industrializers in the late nineteenth and early twentieth centuries have not struck a fine balance between the state and the market. In other words, I position myself in the school of thought which posits that Africa's failed industrial transition is a failure of effective government to "coordinate" the process of economic transformation. Therefore, Nigeria's challenge of economic diversification is a failure of effective government intervention to coordinate market forces towards this objective. This is the foundational assumption that underlies the rest of this book. Let me explain how I arrived at this assumption because it matters greatly in understanding why Nigeria and several other African countries have failed in this endeavor, and why many African policymakers remain confused and distracted about their roles in driving economic transformation.

This book's position on the state–market role in economic transformation touches on extensive scholarly debates on whether economies should conform to or defy their comparative advantage in organizing production and international trade. My position is derived from those taken by former World Bank Chief Economist Justin Yifu Lin and Cambridge University Professor of Economics, Ha-Joon Chang, Nobel Laureate Joseph Stiglitz, Professors of Economics Thandika Mkandawire and Mushtaq Khan, IMF researchers Reda Cherif and Fuad Hasanov and Ethiopian senior minister Arkebe Oqubay elaborated in several publications on industrial policy.[62] In summary, they argue that for a successful industrial transition to occur in Africa, economic activity should, at the onset, not deviate too far from a country's comparative advantage with an objective of eventually defying it, and that this process cannot happen purely through market forces but requires some kind of government intervention. Indeed, this government intervention is not just a prescription for Africa. It also reflects the experience of all prior industrializers in Europe, North America, and Asia, as Ha-Joon Chang carefully documents in his book *Kicking Away the Ladder: Development Strategy in Historical Perspective*.[63] Although there is considerable disagreement among these scholars on how closely a country should conform to its comparative advantage, they agree on the state's role in industrialization.

The question of whether countries' economic strategies should conform to their comparative advantage or defy it as an economic strategy has engaged economists for decades. This is whether countries should engage in production requiring inputs of the factor endowments they have in abundance,[64] i.e., labor, capital, technology, and natural resources—what they are good at—or whether they attempt to engage in heavy and technologically advanced industrial activity with scarce resources. Either of these strategies informs a country's international trade patterns as well as the substance and organization of economic activity because the optimal industrial structure is endogenous to the country's endowment structure.[65] In poor countries, this will mean at the onset focusing on labor or resource-intensive types of economic activities which they have in abundance to be competitive in domestic and international markets, rather than capital- or technology-intensive activities for which the factors are domestically scarce. In organizing production and exchange based on comparative advantage, since the 1980s, mainstream economic theorists favored a limited role for the state to unleash unregulated markets as the route to economic prosperity. Described as "Washington-Consensus" policies, they generally favored a reduction of public expenditures, financial and trade liberalization, among others.[66] In Africa, the seminal study by Robert Bates, for instance, argued that state intervention at the behest of bureaucratic, political, and urban elites distorted market forces in agriculture to the detriment of peasant farmers.[67]

In the twenty-first century, however, international consensus is inching towards a stronger interventionist role for the state to facilitate an industrial transition. Stemming from the rapid East Asian and Chinese economic transformation on one hand, and the devastating 2008 GFC in the West on the other, there were two interrelated realizations. First, the GFC forced mainstream economists, led by the IMF, to begin rethinking assumptions about the supremacy of market forces.[68] Frequent market failures, such as the vulnerability of consumers to predatory financial institutions in the USA which loaded low-income borrowers with high-risk mortgages that caused the financial crisis, indicated that market forces alone do not lead to Pareto-efficient outcomes and do not exist in a vacuum without policy. These market failures include information externalities on opportunities in the market and the problems of coordinating improvements in education, financial and legal institutions, and infrastructure.[69] In the USA, a policy response to the market failures of the 2008 GFC was the enactment of the Dodd–Frank Wall Street Reform and Consumer Protection Act law in 2010 which overhauled financial regulation. This included the creation of the Consumer Protection Bureau (CPB) to protect Americans from abuses related to credit cards, mortgages, and other financial products.

Second, the rapid East Asian economic ascent, including China's, has caused some introspection on the necessity of some state intervention to address market failures. The transformation of the economies of East Asian and China were driven by "activist" states compared to sub-Saharan Africa which experienced a decline in per capita income and deindustrialization.[70] In the 1950s and 1960s, classical economists such as Albert Hirschman and Alexander Gerschenkron, had elaborated on the active guidance of the state in "late development."[71] In addressing market failures, this government intervention could subsidize the costs of innovation for firms, close the knowledge and technological gap, provide infrastructure, and implement policies to facilitate a transition from their comparative advantage in, say, extractive industries and primary agriculture, to new industries like car assembly. In other words, move their human, capital, and financial resources from low to high-productivity sectors. In the United States for instance, the networking backbone that supports the modern global internet was first built by researchers funded by the Defense Advanced Research Projects Agency (DARPA), a unit of the Department of Defense. In fact, many of the technologies from Silicon Valley used widely today are rooted in DARPA-backed research: from the user interface that powers a Windows laptop to Siri, the voice of the Apple iPhone.[72]

This shifting global policy consensus underlies the seventeen Sustainable Development Goals (SDGs) which call on governments to design economic strategies to address the root causes of poverty. For instance, Goal 9 is "Build Resilient Infrastructure, Promote Sustainable Industrialization and Foster Innovation" and Goal 8 is "Promote Inclusive and Sustainable Economic Growth, Employment and Decent Work for All." This is a marked departure from the social development orientation of the predecessor MDGs, focused on humanitarian programs for poor countries while visibly lacking an economic development component. Thus, correcting market failures entails tackling supply-side constraints on the productivity, and demand-side constraints on people's incomes and their consumption capacity.

This state intervention is often framed as "industrial policy" which is increasingly being espoused today in wealthy countries. An industrial policy is any government policy which attempts to shape a country's economic structure through the sectoral allocation of human and physical resources and the selection of appropriate technology.[73] Governments in the USA, the United Kingdom, and the European Union have announced and implemented policies akin to state intervention in trade, manufacturing, and other economic sectors. Under Donald Trump's "America First" policy orientation, the United States imposed tariffs on imports of steel, aluminium and other manufactures from China, France, and Germany to help boost U.S. production in ways that contravened erstwhile "free market" principles. With the COVID-19 pandemic, the U.S. government initiated efforts to move medical supply chains away from China using tariffs and incentives such as tax breaks and subsidies, again policies that scandalized erstwhile "free market" advocates.[74] In one of the largest subsidy programs in the world, the EU spends $65 billion a year on agriculture impeding access to European markets for farmers in low-income countries. Similarly, massive government subsidies in the EU have helped scale up the region's investment in and adoption of renewable energy technology such as solar and wind.[75] This drive towards industrial upgrading, which involves risks and externalities, requires the government to play a "coordinating" role.[76] This ranges from making allocative decisions to creating an investor-friendly business environment and strategically allowing or blocking foreign competition.

The reality, however, is that state intervention to "coordinate" economic activity has had very mixed results in transforming poor countries. While there have been some successes in East Asia, industrial policies have been accompanied by economic crisis, the persistence of poverty and the "middle income trap" in sub-Saharan Africa and parts of Latin America and South Asia. Even in East Asia, the elaborate study by Joe Studwell shows a divergence in outcomes between the industrialized North East Asian countries of Japan, Taiwan, South Korea, and increasingly China, and those in the South East such as Indonesia and Thailand which are still middle-income countries.[77] Due to uncertain outcomes, mainstream economists have, for two decades, vociferously criticized industrial policies for simply picking winners, propping up failing firms, encouraging cronyism, and creating rent-seeking opportunities. However, the actual evidence from Asia points not to uniform success or failure, but to varied outcomes. Indeed, even among long-running critics of industrial policy such as the IMF, recent research has acknowledged the necessity of some state intervention.[78]

Beyond the recurring debate about the relevance of state intervention, a more important question for African countries is what distinguishes successful industrial policy from one prone to failure? There are at least three industrial policy principles based on which a government can effectively facilitate structural economic transformation.[79]

The first principle is to map economic strategies consistent with a country's changing or "dynamic" comparative advantage determined by its current or changing endowment structure. A typical agrarian and mineral-rich economy in Africa can have an industrial strategy that focuses on agro-processing of crops, a leather industry from livestock, mineral refining, and petrochemicals with the aim of transitioning to manufacturing more sophisticated products such as biofuels, luxury leather products, solar energy hardware, high-end jewelry, and cars. This would ensure that investment is not targeted at the wrong industries or the construction of unsustainable "white elephant projects" but at what a country is good at producing.[80] For example, it is odd that nearly all of Nigeria's thirty-six states have attempted to build their own "international airports" rather than pool resources around six to eight regional aviation hubs, while the remaining states build road networks to link far-flung villages to the large urban centers.

A second principle is to deliberately support technology and innovation in the pursuit of the so-defined economic strategy. In other words, governments guide the adoption of appropriate technologies which involves the capital–labor ratio that aligns with the country's factor endowments. This might mean making deliberate choices on R&D and capital investments in techniques to maximize employment (labor-intensive) rather than just efficiency of output (capital-intensive). With Africa's fertile land, livestock, and mineral resources, its governments would need to invest heavily in R&D around agriculture to increase productivity and modernize the sector and add value to mineral resources by applying technology and creating forward linkages to manufacturing industry and services (marketing, finance, etc.). Indeed, as Amir Lebdioui and colleagues show, Malaysia and Chile have sustained their export-led economic transformation and are on the verge of becoming high income from active industrial policy interventions to promote their leading resource-based sectors through government support for R&D, linkage development, competitiveness, and technological upgrading.[81] Government policy will thus enable the transfer of labor, capital, and knowledge from low- to high-productivity sectors, increase productivity through learning, remove barriers to the emergence of firms, and address externalities like pollution.[82]

The third industrial policy principle is an enforceable mechanism of accountability in the state–market relationship. Most scholars agree that what makes industrial policies effective is the government's ability to tie business support to performance targets. These targets weed out poorly performing firms by encouraging them to compete in domestic or international markets.[83] Although governments provide support to such domestic firms and use tariffs to protect them from foreign competition, what distinguishes successful protection, as was the case in East Asia, from unsuccessful ISI in many African and Latin American countries from the 1960s to the 1980s is the "export orientation." That is, state protection to domestic firms is temporary and tied to their achievement of performance targets for exports and competing in international markets. In East Asia, as summarized by IMF economists Cherif and Hasanov, firms receiving state support were subject to strict performance standards such as meeting export quotas in Korea or other conditions attached to preferred credit in Taiwan Province of China.[84] To compete in international markets, these firms invested in R&D, were innovative, and set up larger production capacities than they could have achieved had they been limited by the domestic market. Cherif and Hasanov further contrast unsuccessful ISI with successful export orientation illustrated by the different paths followed by Korea's Hyundai and Malaysia's Proton car companies. While Hyundai became a successful global brand, Proton remains a less-integrated car manufacturer relying on imported inputs such as Japan's Mitsubishi engine, with insignificant exports and a domestic market challenged by foreign automakers despite tariffs and subsidies.

Overall, as Arkebe Oqubay, a senior minister in Ethiopia and a leading thinker on industrialization in Africa, mentions "the state in Africa must play an activist and developmental role."[85] With Nigeria's endowments in oil, minerals, crop production, livestock, and a large population, the economic transformation strategy could both conform to comparative advantage in agriculture and minerals but also an industrial transition towards petrochemicals, agro-allied industry, mineral processing, and services. In a federation like Nigeria, this "coordinating" state formulates effective policies at both national and subnational government levels.

The Institutional Foundations for an Effective State to Facilitate Economic Transformation

The state's ability to effectively coordinate industrial transformation depends on its organization, cohesion, and authority, i.e., its institutional foundation and political character. By "institutional foundation," we are referring to the bureaucratic capacity and knowledge requirements necessary for promoting development and governing the markets.[86] Joe Midgal defines state capabilities to include capacities to penetrate society, regulate social relationships, and use resources in determined ways. This effective state is also referred to as a "developmental state." Based on studies on the rise of Japan, South Korea, Taiwan, Singapore, and Hong Kong, leading proponents[87] conceptualize a developmental state as one with a capable and coherent bureaucracy operating on rational-legal rules of meritocratic recruitment and internal cohesion. This bureaucracy or public service maintains close ties to the business community to be able to design business-compatible policies, but it can also evade policy capture by special interests. Such a developmental state can provide targeted industry-wide subsidies, such as tax holidays to support up-and-coming firms in a country's tech industry, but will not extend the same privileges to individuals or protect unproductive firms.

The effectiveness of a state's intervention in the market, whether facilitating and growth-oriented or distortionary and growth-retarding, lies in this institutional basis. Some scholars talk about less-stringent developmental states, which are nevertheless somewhat effective as "developmentalist states," such as Brazil, India,

Indonesia, Malaysia, and Thailand. In these countries, unlike those in North East Asia, only a few enclaves of the bureaucracy possess such cohesiveness, organization, and authority in a sea of general institutional dysfunction.[88] For African states to be developmental(-ist) in achieving sustained growth, increased productivity, and structural transformation, they would need to reorient their governance institutions. This entails sequencing a first order of economic objectives to build capabilities towards a second order of desirable "good governance" objectives of enforcing property rights, a rule of law, reducing corruption, and improving government accountability.

Unfortunately, the current Washington Consensus orientation of these states has reversed the sequence. Many African countries unhelpfully focus not on first order objectives such as strengthening governance capabilities to drive economic transformation but on second order objectives such as restraining governments from the necessary discretion to experiment with various policies until they figure out what works for them.[89] Mushtaq Khan explains further that, given the numerous governance challenges in African countries, this sequencing of what to prioritize at any point in time is crucial. The reality is that African countries cannot instantly become like Norway, Denmark, or any of the Scandinavian countries held up by mainstream development professionals as the ideal governance archetypes. African countries should rather prioritize building specific growth-enhancing governance capabilities, such as creating effective state–business relations to address market failures through experimentation and problem-solving rather than imposing ideal types of governance from elsewhere.[90] These "developmental" capabilities in federations like Nigeria, must exist at both the national and subnational levels of government.

A state's political character determines the institutional capacity to be "developmental" in sequencing its governance priorities for economic transformation (Figure 2.4). Relatedly, to understand policy decisions requires an understanding of the constraints and incentive structure for decision-makers, i.e., the political character of this "developmental state."[91] Thus, a developmental state cannot be imposed from outside. It must emerge from within the country's political economy. In the next chapter, we examine this notion of a political character and why in Nigeria and several African countries, it has not resulted in an institutional capacity to drive economic transformation.

*****

In summary, this book defines economic diversification in resource-rich countries as a core aspect of economic transformation. I identify at least three pathways to achieving economic transformation, through manufacturing and resource-based industrialization, leapfrogging, and industries without smokestacks. I take the position that to achieve economic transformation, economic activity in countries and their subnational regions should initially conform to their respective comparative advantage with a view to transitioning to higher-productivity industries over time. I also agree that governments have a critical role in guiding this economic transition by coordinating the country's factor endowments and correcting market failures.

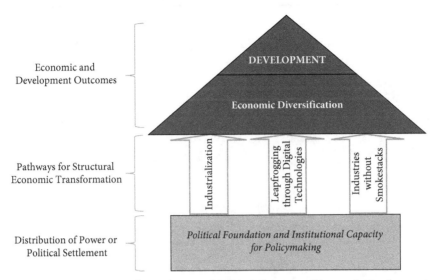

Figure 2.4 The Institutional Foundation and Political Character of Economic Development.
Source: Author's construction.

However, the effectiveness of state intervention in guiding this industrial transition depends on its institutional capacity determined by its political character. All Nigeria's civilian presidents since 1999 have proclaimed a political commitment to diversifying Nigeria's economy yet their actual achievements have fallen below expectations. Why has this political commitment not translated into a strong institutional capacity to guide economic transformation and thus diversify Nigeria's economy? What does the political character of a state mean? We address these questions in the next chapter.

Unpacking Politics: Power, Actors, and Institutions

On the cool evening of 15 November 2008, the vast halls of the edifice on the shores of the Mediterranean Sea hosted a grand ceremony. At the Bibliotheca Alexandrina in Egypt's second-largest city, Alexandria, the Ibrahim Prize for Achievement in African Leadership was given to Festus Moghae, the president of Botswana from 1998–2008. According to Kofi Annan, the Chair of the Prize Committee, and former Secretary-General of the United Nations, Moghae was given the award for his outstanding leadership for Botswana's continued stability and prosperity in the face of a HIV/AIDS pandemic which had threatened his country's future. President Moghae's stewardship of the Botswanan economy was recognized because it demonstrated how a country with natural resources can promote sustainable development. The previous year, Joaquim Chissano, the former president of Mozambique, had been the inaugural Ibrahim laureate for "achievements in bringing peace, reconciliation, stable democracy and economic progress to his country."

The award for Moghae's stellar leadership happened at an interesting juncture for global governance and economic management. In late 2008, much of North America and Europe were engulfed in the flames of the global financial crisis ignited by the excesses of the financial sector and weak regulation of the housing market in the United States. The financial meltdown had already brought down behemoths in investment banking such as the Lehman Brothers and Bear Sterns and was raging across the Atlantic Ocean through financial capitals in London and much of Europe, decimating businesses in its wake. Much of the African continent was barely affected by the global financial meltdown. However, many African leaders and intellectuals nursed a grievance from the year 2000, when the influential magazine, *The Economist*, had written off Africa as "the Hopeless Continent" whose "shortcomings owe less to acts of God than to acts of man" and whose societies are susceptible to "brutality, despotism and corruption... for reasons buried in their cultures."[1]

Thus, in 2006, this Ibrahim prize was set up by the Mo Ibrahim Foundation to counter the stereotypes around governance on the continent by celebrating excellence in African leadership. It is awarded to a former Executive Head of State or Government by an independent prize committee composed of eminent figures. The largest annually awarded prize in the world, the Ibrahim prize consists of: $5 million over ten years, $200,000 annually for life thereafter for the winner and a further $200,000 per year, for ten years, towards public interest activities championed by the winner. The significance of the prize lies not only with its winners but also with the annual buzz around leadership that it generates.

A closer look at Botswana's economic and socio-political achievements supports the rationale for the Ibrahim prize in 2008. The small southern African nation transitioned from a poor country, whose viability at independence was doubtful, to become one of Africa's most stable and prosperous middle-income countries today. At independence in 1966, Botswana was in a dire economic state: about 90% of the population was in absolute poverty with a per capita income of less than $80, an economy dependent on cattle exports, remittances from migrant labor in South Africa and foreign aid, and barely any infrastructure beyond 10 kilometers of tarred road. Its social development was similarly dismal: literacy was at 25% and life expectancy was just 48 years of age.[2] Diamond mining began in the 1970s and has generated between 30–50% of economic output since the early 1980s. By 2007, Botswana's per capita income grew to $5,600, after more than four decades of experiencing one of the world's fastest GDP per capita growth rates of 6.3%.[3] This economic growth was accompanied by dramatic improvements in social development indicators. Life expectancy increased to sixty-seven despite the HIV/AIDS epidemic, and literacy rates went up to 90% by the mid-2000s. Botswana is one of a few countries in Africa that has not experienced a military coup, war, or political violence.

Central to these laudable socio-economic outcomes is the leadership and policy choices around the management of Botswana's mineral wealth. Kofi Annan's description when presenting the Ibrahim Prize to Moghae in 2008 is fitting, that "Botswana demonstrates how a country with natural resources can promote sustainable development with good governance, in a continent where too often mineral wealth has become a curse."[4] Botswana has an effective and efficient mineral fiscal regime that appropriates diamond revenues while allowing mining investors sufficient returns to compensate for the cost of capital and risk. These mineral revenues have been prudently managed through strong macroeconomic policies that enabled the country to avoid the Dutch Disease; a public financial management framework that guided the investment of revenues in human, physical and social capital, and the accumulation of foreign reserves, including a well-managed SWF.[5]

Botswana's effective economic policies were formulated and implemented within an institutional context which allowed for vision, stability, and continuity in economic decision-making. Specifically, the broad political coalition that emerged after independence on the platform of the Botswana Democratic Party (BDP) incorporated various competing groups in society and thereby neutered rival power centers of economic elites, opposition parties, and traditional institutions. The BDP achieved this political dominance by appealing to powerful economic groups, especially the exporters of livestock and consumers of imports. To undercut opposition political parties, the BDP emphasized the tangible external threat from apartheid South Africa and invested mineral revenues for national development to defuse ethno-regional political competition. The party also incorporated traditional institutions, such as the *Kgotla* or village assembly of traditional chiefs, into the modern state to allow ordinary citizens to identify with government projects and policies.[6] The result was a national consensus around the BDP's vision for Botswana: for an active state in directing economic development, the centralization of natural resources as state assets and the strategic partnership with the multinational, DeBeers, around the mining and sale of diamonds in one of the world's best mining contracts. More practically, this broad-based political coalition cemented the BDP's recurrent electoral victory for over four decades. With this underlying political stability, there was economic policy continuity across successive governments.

Therefore, the 2008 Ibrahim Prize to Festus Moghae was a recognition of the stable foundation of visionary leadership right from presidents Seretse Khama and Quett Masire. This visionary leadership was enabled by Botswana's underlying political settlement anchored by the BDP. In recent times though, socio-economic changes from urbanization, the end of apartheid, and economic slowdown are starting to erode the political support of the BDP. Its high income and human development notwithstanding, Botswana is heavily dependent on diamonds for 80% of its export earnings and 60% of government tax revenues. Some scholars have noted that its strategy of investing diamond revenues in financial assets overseas has not contributed to economic diversification as its diamond reserves will be depleted by 2027.[7] The country also has remaining pockets of poverty and inequality outside the capital, Gaborone.

As Botswana reveled in the global recognition of effective leadership in 2008, Nigeria its large neighbor further up north, lurched from one political crisis to another. Nigerians had just secured a pyrrhic victory against attempts by former President Olusegun Obasanjo for a third presidential term between 2006 and 2007 beyond the constitutional two-term limit. The election of Obasanjo's successor, Umaru Yar'Adua, in 2007 was so flawed that even Yar'Adua acknowledged the irregularities that characterized the entire process.[8] It was an open secret that Obasanjo had positioned himself to receive an Ibrahim prize. Indeed, from 1999 when Nigeria transitioned to democracy—after almost two decades of military dictatorship, a short but chaotic civilian administration in the 1980s, a civil war in the 1970s and violent military coups in the 1960s—Obasanjo's administration had implemented substantial economic reforms that produced commendable results. As is discussed in Chapters 5 and 6, these included securing debt relief for Nigeria, establishing an anti-corruption agency, and liberalizing banking, telecoms, and other sectors of the economy. Coinciding with the oil boom of the early 2000s, the economy grew at an average of 7.6% per annum between 2000 and 2008 and the country earned billions of dollars from higher oil prices. Nigeria was also asserting its presence across Africa in ECOWAS through peacekeeping missions in Liberia and Sierra Leone, and in the African Union through the New Partnership for African Development (NEPAD). However, economic reforms and a growing geopolitical clout were not accompanied by improvements in income and human development for most Nigerians. Per capita income growth was an average of 5% between 2000 and 2008 while over 60% of the population lived below the national poverty line.[9] Thus, Obasanjo, the self-styled "father of modern Nigeria" was snubbed by the Ibrahim prize for African Leadership, alongside Ghana's John Kufuor and South Africa's Thabo Mbeki.[10]

What conditions allowed Festus Moghae to deliver governance results that positioned him for the Ibrahim prize? Why did Olusegun Obasanjo taint his respectable governance record with an attempt to extend his presidential term? Why has Botswana had stable leadership, policy continuity, and a consistent vision for natural resources management whereas Nigeria has struggled on all three counts? Why are Nigeria's political transitions from one administration to another crisis-ridden and chaotic? How does Nigeria's perennial political instability affect its longstanding aspiration of economic diversification? What do these divergent experiences tell us about the interplay of politics, institutions, and policies in African countries and their economic outcomes? The answer to these questions, as this book argues, lies in the political character of both countries.

Specifically, the distribution of power allows for a stable political coalition in Botswana across successive governments and policy continuity on natural resources management. In Nigeria, the distribution of power or the political settlement results in unstable coalitions that do not allow for smooth transitions across governments. In this unstable political configuration, economic policymaking is oriented towards stabilization and redistribution to pacify competitive political factions rather than a long-term focus on the herculean task of supporting structural economic transformation. This volatile power configuration is the political foundation of Nigeria's "intermediate" state which intermittently implements reforms, thereby driving bursts of economic growth rather than sustained policy reforms to diversify the economy. This chapter provides analytical tools to help unpack this political character and institutional capacity to implement economic policies.

Through a political settlements approach, we can better understand how the distribution of power in Nigeria creates unstable political coalitions whose policy orientation can only result in growth spurts at best and stagnation at worst. But this book does not just provide a static description of an institutional environment that is depressingly immune to change. On the contrary, a major part of this analysis describes and identifies the political factors that result in institutional change and policy reforms. However, even when changes in the distribution of power and institutions have led to pro-growth economic policymaking, these changes have neither been sufficient nor sustained in ways that drive industrial transformation in Nigeria as in the upper middle-income countries across Asia and Latin America. In this chapter, we present a framework for analyzing the distribution of power and institutional change. To apply this framework, we must identify the key actors (individuals, groups, and organizations) in this political settlement in terms of the power they wield and their influence in sustaining or changing institutions.

The Key Actors in a Political Settlement

To examine the distribution of power in Nigeria's political settlement we need to first identify the individual, group, and organizational actors who exercise this power. How do we identify them? What kinds of power do these actors possess and wield within this political settlement? Before proceeding with that task, it is essential to define the fundamental terms used here. To begin with, those who occupy the most powerful positions of authority in any society are the "elite." What distinguishes the elite from other privileged or wealthy social groups is their leading roles in authority in society.[11]

Understanding the processes of elite formation through relations of power sheds light on other non-elite "social groups." These social groups include trade unions, civil society, media, religious associations, and other interest clusters. The task of identifying the actors and mapping their interests and degree of influence is an exploration of their social class and status, in other words, their proximity to political power and economic resources in society. As this is no easy task, at least three filters can be used to identify the individual, groups, and organizational actors in a political settlement in terms of the economic resources they possess and the power they wield. These three filters are the history of state formation, the social makeup, and the economic structure of a society.

The first filter in identifying the elite and non-elite social groups in a political settlement is the history of state formation in a country. In the case of Nigeria, as with many African countries and indeed low- and middle-income economies in Asia, Latin America, and the Middle East, cobbled together by colonial rulers, the state is the central site for elite formation. Non-elite social groups also emerge from and operate in the state's orbit. The state, defined as the sovereign political entity that rules a population within defined geographical boundaries, is the ultimate embodiment of political power where various forms of authority or legitimate influence are expressed. These post-colonial states are both the main spheres of economic accumulation as described by Michael Watts, and the ultimate prize for domestic political contests as described by Ricardo Soares de Oliveira.[12] In Nigeria, the foundation for this dual economic and political function of the state was laid from the colonial period, even before the oil boom of the 1970s.

For the British colonial administrators, the Nigerian state—that they forged into being in 1914 from pre-existing precolonial empires, clans, and village republics— was an apparatus for the extraction of economic surplus from agricultural producers. However, colonial policy favored smallholder agriculture production by rural peasants rather than large-scale plantations by well-capitalized landlords as was the case in eastern and southern Africa. Specifically, the Northern Nigeria Lands Committee mandate in 1907, in collaboration with traditional rulers who controlled land, prevented foreign investments in large-scale land-lord agriculture plantations to superficially "protect the rights" of rural peasants, who never produced at a scale which allowed them to transform into large-scale producers.[13] These peasants ultimately were trapped in a cycle of subsistence agriculture and grinding poverty across generations. Therefore, there was no critical mass of a landed domestic or foreign oligarchic elite as in Latin America, the Philippines, or even southern Africa.

In colonial Nigeria, the economic elite emerged both independently from the trade in commodities and from the bureaucratic–administrative apparatus that appropriates these commodity revenues. In the Colony and Protectorate of Nigeria created in 1914, through the amalgamation of previously separate Northern Nigeria Protectorate and the Colony and Protectorate of Southern Nigeria, there emerged a distinct business and economic class despite the absence of a landed agrarian elite. There were successful traders some of whom were descendants of prominent merchant families in precolonial Nigeria; service providers in transport, banking and insurance, and after independence in 1960, emerging industrialists. Businessmen became wealthy due to the merchant trade in cocoa, groundnuts and other agriculture products that predated colonial rule. For instance, the wealthiest man in West Africa in the 1950s was Alhassan Dantata, a prominent trader in groundnuts and kolanuts, and who coincidentally is the great grandfather of Aliko Dangote, Africa's richest man today. The creation of marketing boards between 1947 and 1949 also provided a pathway for some administrators to transition to commerce, although many more industrialists emerged by transitioning from earlier involvement in trade.[14]

Besides, given the central role of the state in economic activity, this relatively autonomous business class operated in close proximity to the state. Many businessmen were in real-estate construction, and suppliers of goods and services to government. There was often a fluid movement between various political (public administrators, leading politicians, and traditional authorities) and business elites (wealthy businessmen), a "straddling" of both political office and economic accumulation and a "fusion of elites."[15] Unlike Francophone African countries or Kenya with their state-centric approach to private accumulation, upward mobility, and class formation, there have always been non-state avenues for capital accumulation in Nigeria.

This overlap of political and economic spheres was especially visible in northern Nigeria where the persistence of the traditional *emirate* system meant that dominant class formation involved the social and political coalescence of traditional rulers, administrative functionaries, and businessmen. This brings us to the second filter for identifying the individual and groups actors in a political settlement: the social makeup of society.

Regarding Nigeria's social makeup, one important factor is the regional differentiations in the patterns of class and elite formation between communities in southern and northern Nigeria. As noted by Richard Sklar,[16] in the south, class formation in the colonial period occurred within the context of modern social change—Western education, urbanization, and growth of commerce. By contrast in the north, class formation occurred within the context mainly of aristocratic birth and socio-political rank. More precisely, due to their proximity to the coast, parts of southern Nigeria had contact with Portuguese and other European slavers from the 1600s and later colonial administrators from 1861. Then, through the activities of Christian missionaries from the 1840s onwards, Western education as a vector of evangelism spread earlier in the southern colonies than in the protectorate of northern Nigeria. In northern Nigeria, the British employed indirect rule to govern the region, as in India and Uganda, relying on the organized precolonial administrative structures of the Islamic Sokoto Caliphate and Kanem-Bornu Empire. Therefore, the British opted for government-run schools in the north, which came late and were few and far between for the superficial reasons that the Muslim Emirs initially resisted the missionary-run schools. The reality, according to the historian Peter Kazenga Tibenderana, is that the British were also reluctant to invest in Western education in the north to discourage the emergence of anti-colonial-educated intellectuals as in Lagos, India, and other parts of the colonial empire.[17] Tibenderana documents cases in which the British refused repeated requests by northern emirs for funds to build a school dormitory for primary school pupils in Sokoto (in 1917) and to build separate girl's schools in Adamawa, Bornu, Ilorin, and Zaria among other places.

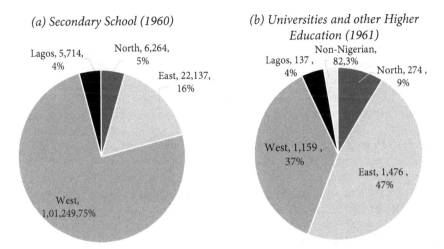

(a) Secondary School (1960)

Lagos, 5,714, 4%
North, 6,264, 5%
East, 22,137, 16%
West, 1,01,249, 75%

(b) Universities and other Higher Education (1961)

Non-Nigerian, 82,3%
Lagos, 137, 4%
North, 274, 9%
West, 1,159, 37%
East, 1,476, 47%

Figure 3.1 Student Enrolment in Secondary and Tertiary Education by Region of Origin, 1960/1961.

Source: Author's Calculations from the Federal Ministry of Education (1961) Annual Digest of Education Statistics 1961. Series No. 1, Vol. 1.

Consequently, the prior contact with Western education, the pattern of colonial rule and a relatively flexible class structure in southern Nigeria resulted in a higher concentration of the middle class at independence than in northern Nigeria. At independence, the north, despite having much higher population numbers, was severely underrepresented in educational attainment (see Figure 3.1). In 1960, there were only 6,000 students of northern origin enrolled in secondary schools, comprising 5% of the national total of 135,000, compared to 75% for the west and 16% for the east. Similarly, only 274 students of northern origin were enrolled in higher education institutions amounting to 9% of the national total compared to 47% in the east and 37% in the west.

Thus, trade unions, student groups, the press, and other markers of a middle class all had a more visible presence in southern Nigeria. These differentiations in class formation still persist, in terms of industrial and private-sector development, media ownership, incomes, and employment. These regional specificities also underpin disparities in the distribution of civil service appointments, composition of the army, the judiciary and other government institutions; and social inequalities in terms of access to education and health care between northern and southern states.[18] These regional differentiations in historical class formation, their persistence across generations, and their implications for economic policies and their outcomes are discussed from Chapter 4 onwards.

Finally, the economic structure of a society and the location of individuals and groups within is a third filter to identify the actors in a political settlement. By understanding the rights and ownership in economic activities in a society, also known as the means of production in classical economics, we can identify economic actors, the resources they wield, their status and thus the distribution of power in society.[19] Since economic activities vary in many countries, the participants of these activities as well as the resulting social relations are distinct. Thus, high-income advanced economies in Western Europe, North America, and parts of East Asia have strong manufacturing and services sectors; upper middle-income economies in Eastern Europe, parts of Asia, Latin America and the Middle East have growing manufacturing sectors as well as large agriculture and informal sectors; and mostly low-income and lower-middle-income economies across the African continent and parts of South Asia have small manufacturing sectors, a large agrarian sector comprising smallholder farmers, and a prevalence of informality—such as kiosk owners, petty traders, and cottage industries. The economies of oil- and mineral-exporting countries, including those in Africa, are structured around extractive industries and auxiliary services—oil production, petroleum marketing, state-owned enterprises, and a construction sector linked to the resource boom, retail, and hospitality industries—and less around the production process in manufacturing industry.

In resource-exporting countries like Nigeria, where exports and fiscal revenue are derived from the extraction of oil rather than trading and taxing goods and services from a production process on a factory floor, the structure of the economy has, for decades, been more extractive and less production oriented. Thus, the location of individuals and groups within economies structured around mineral extraction and supporting industries defines their access to and possession of political power. This is especially relevant because the state is heavily involved in the process of mineral and oil-extraction, the trading of these resources, and the appropriation and allocation of the resource revenues. Although Nigeria's manufacturing sector is one of the largest in West Africa, it is smaller than comparator middle-income countries (Figure 3.2). Therefore, many individuals and groups with high degrees of political power and economic resources, or the elite, not only emerge from production processes but

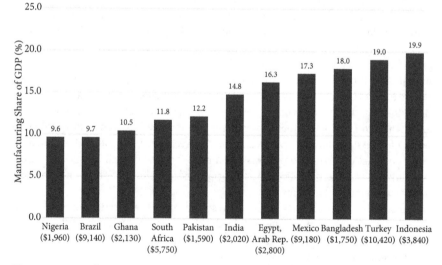

Figure 3.2 Manufacturing Share of GDP (%) in Select Middle-Income Countries, 2018.

Source: Author's calculations from World Development Indicators. Figures in brackets are the GNI per capita.

also from their proximity to the state.[20] Although powerful private-sector elites in finance and manufacturing are emerging from the expansion of non-oil sectors in the twenty-first century, the dynamic of elite formation from proximity to the state apparatus still applies.

Based on the application of the other two filters, we know that elite formation within the orbit of public administration predated the discovery of oil in Nigeria. However, the colonial patterns of elite formation and their regional differentiations were reinforced during the oil boom of the 1970s. The oil windfall led to a structural shift in the type and scale of earnings extracted, from agriculture cash crops to petroleum, from marketing boards to a national oil company (the Nigerian National Petroleum Corporation established in 1977). Consider this, government revenue increased over one hundredfold from N108 million in 1962 when agriculture commodities provided the bulk of Nigeria's exports to over N13 billion by 1979 at the peak of the first oil boom. The inflow of large volumes of oil revenues to state agencies made bureaucratic and political positions more lucrative, and commandeering the state became more urgent. From the 1970s onwards, the commodity traders, government suppliers, and other business elite, became more state oriented as economic activity revolved around a lucrative oil sector controlled by the state. Though economic reforms of the 1980s were partly meant to create more opportunities in other sectors by creating a market economy, the private sector still operated in close orbit of the state.

Through the application of these three filters of history of state formation, social makeup, and economic structure of society, we can better understand the process of elite formation in Nigeria. Non-elite social groups can then also be identified in relation to political elites who exercise control over the state's coercive instruments and can allocate economic resources. Among political elites, we can further distinguish between what Ricardo Soares de Oliveira[21] refers to as a "governing" segment (those with decision-making power) and a "non-governing" segment (those without decision-making power but with access to the governing segment and the ensuing privileges). Building on this conceptualization, I use the terms "ruling elite" and "state elite" to refer to those with decision-making power. "Political elite" encompasses influential actors without direct decision-making power. The ruling elite could also include a "bureaucratic elite" (senior officials in the civil service), the "traditional" and "religious" elites, the "military" elite, the "economic" or "business" elite (the top hierarchy of business and the private sector), and the "professional" elite (experts in certain professions and civil society). A "ruling coalition" refers to alliances between the ruling elite and other elite and non-elite groups.

Having identified the key actors in a political settlement by examining the process of elite formation, we will now analyze the distribution of power among them and how this configuration persists or changes. The analysis of the distribution of power and its persistence or change allows us better to understand the political foundations of a country. In the case of Nigeria, this would be the political foundations of its "intermediate" state which intermittently implements stabilization reforms, thereby driving episodic economic growth rather than structural economic transformation that diversifies the economy. As with Botswana and other mineral- and oil-exporting countries, a consensus over the allocation and use of resource rents is central to the distribution of power in Nigeria. Since the oil revenues on which Nigeria depends are derived externally, rapid swings in these revenue flows are politically disruptive by reinforcing the existing distribution of power or by reconfiguring the arrangement. The decisive actors at these moments, called critical junctures, are usually elites who preside over the allocation and distribution of these oil revenues.

The Distribution of Power among Actors in a Political Settlement

So, how does the distribution of power in Nigeria's political settlement result in unstable coalitions unlike Botswana? Why do these unstable ruling coalitions design and implement economic policies oriented towards short-term episodic growth rather than the structural transformation that diversifies the economy? To address these questions, we need to understand the distribution of power and how this political configuration can change or persist over time. The four dimensions of the distribution of power presented below are the first building block of this analysis. These are elite bargains, coalitions with non-elite societal groups, economic agenda, and formal institutions.

An elite bargain, or pact, is a consensus over the horizontal distribution of power among elites in society. It captures the event dimension of a political settlement, marking crucial milestones in ongoing political processes.[22] The elite bargain or pact is neither the sum total of political settlements nor is it synonymous with the peace agreements that are negotiated by warring sides at the end of a conflict, for example. It is, however, a commitment, often informal, among elites that they will not fight each other, and a consensus on the very foundation of how society is organized and its economic resources managed. Where economic resources flow largely from a central source, such as in oil-rich countries, the elite consensus constitutes the informal rules over their allocation in ways that result in productive or predatory outcomes. Formal institutions such as the civil service, the parliament, political parties, and intergovernmental transfers will either reinforce this informal consensus, or be distorted when there is no alignment with this underlying bargain. The durability of the elite bargain is based on the extent to which it includes powerful actors and is thereby fortified from contestation by excluded factions and whether it enforces actual agreements thereby preventing the exit of powerful members who can challenge it.

Broadly, some sort of elite bargain or consensus underpins the political and economic systems in all societies across the world. The organizational basis for fortifying this consensus could be a political party, the military, or the civil service.[23] In Botswana, since the 1960s, the BDP has served as the main platform for elite coordination. In Malaysia, the Barisan Nasional is a coalition of various ethnic political movements that rallied competing elites from the 1970s until 2018, when it was briefly displaced by an opposition movement. Whereas in countries such as Egypt, the armed forces, given their preeminent role in domestic politics and the economy, coordinate political and economic elites. Since the Free Officers overthrew the King in 1952, all of Egypt's presidents to date have had a military background. Finally, in the advanced democracies of the United States and the United Kingdom, the ruling coalition alternates between the two major political parties, i.e., the Democrats and the Republicans in the US; the

Conservative Party and the Labour Party in the UK. Most aspects of national politics and the economy in these advanced democracies revolve around the two liberal and conservative orientations—including newspapers, think tanks, and civil society.

These elite pacts are negotiated by a range of political, bureaucratic, economic, professional, and traditional elites, collectively referred to as a "ruling or governing coalition." However, these ruling coalitions also engage with other powerful actors beyond the capital city. These include subnational power brokers, such as grassroots organizers and international actors, such as the executives of influential multinational corporations and foreign aid donors.[24] In resource-exporting countries like Nigeria, the concept of elite bargains enables us to identify the role of powerful actors and marks discrete points in the political settlement, coinciding with mineral boom-and-bust cycles.

The second dimension of the distribution of power in a political settlement is vertical, within non-elite and societal groups. These groups could be youth movements, trade unions, traditional and religious associations, civil society, or even armed groups. The coalition could entail a vertical relationship between elites and a non-elite support base.[25] This vertical distribution of power refers to "the relative power of higher compared to lower factions within the ruling coalition." Within a political party for example, there is a distinction between top party officials, some of whom hold elective positions in executive and legislative branches of government and lower-level party officials, such as party delegates in local councils and provinces. Furthermore, societal groups could also wield autonomous power unrelated to elites. They can exert independent influence on elite pacts and challenge the power configuration. For example, grass roots organizers using social media ignited mass movements that toppled decades-old autocracies during the Arab Spring in Tunisia and Egypt in 2011, and also in Burkina Faso in 2014 and Sudan in 2019. Armed movements and insurgent groups can also pressure policy makers to take certain decisions. Thus, the relationship between elites and other societal groups could be top-down, such that elite negotiations affect citizens, or bottom-up, such that citizens exercise agency through collective mass revolt or the endorsement of legitimacy of elites.[26]

The third dimension of the distribution of power is the economic agenda. This is the economic policy regime which sustains a ruling coalition and determines resource production, accumulation, allocation, and exchange in society. It includes formal or informal mechanisms that define access, ownership, and the distribution of economic resources in society, also known as "rent management," or the allocation of resources.[27] In other words, this economic policy regime for rent management sets the balance in the relationship between the state and business in crucial areas such as property rights, investment, production, taxation, and trade.[28] Although these state – business relations can take different forms—the free market orientation of the United States, the state-led market orientation in China, Singapore, and Vietnam and other variations—it is the particular function they perform that matters. To put it differently, what is most crucial in an economic policy regime is not just its capitalist/socialist orientations or how state–market relations are structured, but whether this regime creates conditions that support or hinder sustained economic growth.

Therefore, we can envision at least two types of economic agendas based on the underlying nature of the business–state relations. One which enables basic economic activities which are at least reproducible, even if they are not growing the economy. Such basic production and exchange generate sufficient economic performance to sustain society and prevent economic collapse.[29] Consider, for instance, that despite the persistence of conflict in South Sudan, there are policies around the generation and management of its oil revenues. A second type of business–state relationships can be deeper and more complex. A cooperative business–government relationship which drives growth in an industry or a sector is a "growth-coalition."[30] This entails transferring economic privileges to capable business groups in a market or statist economy using strong performance targets such as export competitiveness as a precondition for such state support. The problem in developing countries, according to the economist Mushtaq Khan, is that the rents-transfer system privileges powerful groups who possess weak productive capabilities (say armed movements or political entrepreneurs) in order to maintain political stability and avert costly conflicts, while marginalizing the actual productive business groups who tend to be politically weak.[31] For instance, the leadership of an armed movement with mass support from residents in a restive region could receive lucrative government contracts due to the group's capacity to disrupt elections or incite social unrest. In contrast, a business association for food-processing companies employing thousands of people in productive jobs may receive no business support from policymakers because they lack disruptive political influence to incite violence. This economic agenda thus captures the ownership and distribution of economic resources and privileges in the political settlement.

The fourth and final dimension of the distribution of power in the political settlement is institutionalization. This refers to the widespread acceptance and consistent enforcement of the distribution of power and allocation of economic resources. The institutionalization can be informal when these arrangements become part of society's norms. Two examples suffice here. The United Kingdom famously has an unwritten constitution because many of its laws around the power and authority of the prime minister, the cabinet, parliament, etc., are rooted in norms and practices that have crystallized over centuries. In the United States, where there are loose regulations on minimum wage, a customer in a restaurant is expected to tip the underpaid waiter because in the trickle-down economics of the free market, the restaurant owner is expected, but not obliged, to share profits with these service workers. This institutionalization can also be formal, when enshrined in law and written in a physical document, say the constitutional separation of governmental powers in the American and Nigerian constitutions; intergovernmental fiscal transfers; on-budget food, higher education, and petroleum subsidies; or trade tariffs which favor certain business groups. More importantly, these rules must be enforceable or self-reinforcing to ensure that powerful actors adhere to them. To be self-enforcing, these rules must reflect the distribution of power in society, otherwise they will be undermined by powerful actors, as Adam Przeworski reminds us.[32] Once these rules become self-enforcing, an equilibrium is reached between the distribution of benefits attributed to particular institutions and the distribution of power across groups.[33]

So, the four dimensions of the distribution of power in a political settlement are: elite bargains, wider coalitions with non-elite societal groups, an economic agenda or policy regime, and institutionalization or enforcement. How is this political and institutional arrangement sustained or changed over time, especially in resource-exporting countries?

The Persistence and Change of Institutions over Time

The second building block of analyzing a society's political settlement is understanding how this power configuration persists or changes. There are conditions within which the political settlement emerges, evolves, or collapses, with implications for policymaking. I call these conditions "constraints." A society's power configuration can change suddenly under various constraints that compel powerful actors in specific ways or it can evolve through gradual incremental processes.

A window of change in seemingly fixed institutional settings opens at critical junctures, accounting for swift policy fluctuations. Critical junctures are periods when a constellation of economic, political, and social "contingent" conditions,[34] build up slowly or erupt suddenly, loosening the existing institutional order. As defined by the political scientists Giovanni Capoccia and Daniel Kelemen, critical junctures are characterized by the relaxation, for a short period, of the structural (that is, economic, cultural, ideological, organizational) influences on political action with two main consequences.[35] First, the range of choices for powerful political actors expands substantially and second, the consequences of their decisions for the outcome of interest are potentially more momentous. These conditions can be endogenous (social unrest, economic crises, and civil war) or exogenous (technological advancements, global economic shocks, and external aggression) to the political settlement. In resource-rich countries dependent on commodities exports, the boom-and-bust cycle is a major driver of these conditions. A sudden collapse can reduce resources distributed formally through, for instance, the government's budget for social spending on petroleum and electricity tariff subsidies, and informally through patronage to political supporters and business groups. The collapse in available resources to be redistributed can lead to riots and a fracture in political alliances in the ruling coalition, it can create a balance of payments crisis, foreign exchange shortages, and budget deficits. These conditions can "shock" and modify society's balance of power, leading to major changes in political and economic institutions.[36] Persistence or change is indicative of the durability or deficiencies respectively, of the power configuration in the face of internal and external conditions.

The response of powerful actors, especially ruling elites, to conditions at these historic junctures determines the maintenance of the institutional order (persistence),[37] or its collapse and replacement (change). As Capoccia and Kelemen note, re-equilibration or repurposing of an institution may be one of several outcomes of critical junctures.[38] As such, many institutions may remain unaffected with considerable continuity despite significant disruption at this critical juncture. For instance, some leaders may choose to deploy security forces to disperse mass protests in a country rather than implement policy reforms to modify revenue distribution to expand social welfare programs. To steer outcomes towards a new equilibrium of institutional persistence or change, the actions of influential actors, such as political leaders, bureaucrats, the military, and social activists, is crucial.[39] Similarly, James Mahoney argues that critical junctures are moments of relative structural indeterminism when willful actors have more leeway to shape outcomes than normal circumstances permit and the specific choices they make at this crucial moment can have reverberating and lasting impacts.[40] For example, deals struck by warring factions to end a civil war can have deep and lasting impacts on the quality of institutions in that country for years to come. Ultimately, these decisions at critical junctures close off alternative options and lead to the establishment of institutions that generate self-reinforcing processes, also known as "path-dependencies."[41]

However, the policy responses to ruling elites at these critical junctures are determined by the *nature of threats* these crises pose to them and the *capacity* to address them. The *nature* of specific threats these crises pose to the resource base and political survival of ruling elites shape the subsequent policy orientation, i.e., whether these threats are benign in the sense that they cause some discomfort, severe or existential in the sense that mass uprisings or electoral defeat can topple governments. The *capacity* of ruling elites is also crucial, in terms of their shared common vision for society and the availability of resources to draw on say, external financial reserves, technocratic knowledge, and productive business allies to invest in specific industries. Thus, capacity here can be organizational competence or the extent to which these rulers are cohesive or fragmentated. It could also be technical competence, i.e., the financial, managerial, and technological resources available and how these resources are deployed.[42] These two, the *nature of threats* and their organizational and technical *capacity to respond*, are collectively the "constraints" on a ruling coalition, illustrated in Figure 3.3.

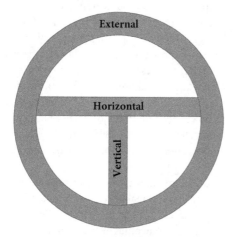

External Environment: foreign aggressors, donor partners, and global oil market

Horizontal-Ruling Coalition: balance of Power among political elite, and between political elite and business elite

Vertical-Wider Society: balance of Power between ruling coalition and ethnic, regional and religious groups, unions, militant groups, and other interests in society

Figure 3.3 Sources of Constraints in a Political Settlement.

Source: Adapted from Usman (2020) The Successes and Failures of Economic Reform in Nigeria's Post-Military Political Settlement, *African Affairs*, 119(474): 1–38.

These constraints operate at three levels, horizontal, vertical and external, and at each level, certain policy choices are more probable. These policy choices could be executed through formal institutions or informally. Richard Doner and colleagues reach a similar conclusion, that the interplay of three political constraints or "systemic vulnerability" inspires ruling elites to forego their otherwise individual interests in client-patron relations, in favor of a collective interest in improved economic performance.[43] For instance, political leaders may discontinue the side payments to the armed movements in a restive region in favor of supporting business groups whose increased productivity can allow the government to collect larger tax revenues. They argue that it is only the combination of these three constraints–pressures on the ruling coalition, the absence of natural resources and severe security threats from internal insurgencies or external military aggression—that can result in a developmental state capable of driving structural transformation from lower-value to higher-value economic activities. Whereas any of these three—coalitional, resource, or geopolitical—constraints individually may only lead to an intermediate state which drives inconsistent growth spurts.

Building on the work of Doner and colleagues, this book examines how these constraints individually elicit specific economic policy responses in Nigeria. Overall, the constraints on Nigeria's ruling elites elicit policy responses oriented towards economic stabilization to address the immediate crisis rather than proactive efforts to support structural economic transformation. Thus, Nigeria is an intermediate state; neither hopelessly predatory nor developmental. but can facilitate episodic reforms to generate economic growth to stabilize a crisis but not sustained improvements in productivity to support exports diversification and economic transformation. Let's take a closer look at each of these three levels of constraints.

First at the horizontal level within the ruling coalition, the constraints are characterized by the extent of the cohesion or fragmentation of the ruling coalition. With a fragmented elite, the constraint comes from the threat of a "palace coup" by a powerful rival faction. Reforms at times of such political crises are likely to focus on inclusion or pacification of excluded groups in the ruling coalition. A constitutional reform that incorporates inclusive arrangements by reducing the age of eligibility for public office or transfer of decision-making power and fiscal resources to restive regions is an example of conciliatory reforms induced by horizontal constraints. Reforms could also be economic that transfer privileges, rents, and subsidies to individuals, business groups, or even entire industries of interest. The outcomes of such economic reforms could be predatory or growth-enhancing depending on whether the recipients of these economic privileges are productive entrepreneurs or political operators with no business acumen. In David Kang's analysis on East Asia, he shows how the balance of power between economic and political elites is the decisive variable which spiraled into growth-retarding politics in the Philippines while reducing transaction costs and enabling sustained growth in South Korea.[44] The incumbent ruling elites could also seek external legitimacy by forming new coalitions with other actors including the masses, community organizers, trade associations, student groups, armed groups, and foreign entities to strengthen their support base. In the absence of the pacification of this excluded faction and an attempt to seek external legitimacy, the risk of political crisis and violent conflict is high as rival elites mobilize to upstage the incumbents.

A second level of constraints, vertically within wider society, is characterized by the extent to which non-elite groups accept or disapprove the distribution of economic resources. These groups can contest the status quo by withdrawing support for the ruling coalition during elections, through mass action or violence. These actions can undermine the survival of the ruling coalition. To stem this tide of discontent, the ruling coalition is likely to opt for redistributive policies. Mushtaq Khan describes such redistribution as politically organized transfers to sustain political stability rather than drive growth.[45] These transfers are provided across advanced and developing countries as a social compact with citizens, such as Europe's welfare state.[46] In Western Europe, a welfare state emerged in the early twentieth century to provide unemployment, housing, and other social insurance to citizens in response to mass political mobilizations and inroads made by communism. In the United States, redistribution schemes such as the Trade Adjustment Assistance supports workers who lose their jobs to import competition. In Japan and some other parts of East Asia, this social insurance is provided by large firms directly to their workers through lifetime employment, housing, and healthcare benefits. However, in many low and middle-income countries with weaker administrative capacities to manage elaborate income transfers, this social insurance takes the form of public works programs, on-budget electricity, fuel and food subsidies, employment in the public sector as well as off-budget payments to political brokers and armed groups.

At the final level of constraints in the external environment, ruling elites are pressured through the threat of military aggression, pressures from foreign donors or commodity price swings. A ruling coalition is likely to embark on extensive economic reforms to build economic resilience against geopolitical conflict, as conditions for international development assistance or to diversify volatile commodity exports. In resource-poor North-East Asia, ruling elites in Singapore, South Korea, and Taiwan faced regional insecurities from neighbors which impelled them to transform their economies for security reasons.[47] In oil-rich countries, where oil earnings make foreign aid relatively inconsequential and allow the state to acquire military capabilities, the impetus for economic restructuring has historically been global oil shocks. In Saudi Arabia, the collapse of oil prices between 2014 and 2017 led to an historic decision to aim for a public listing of Aramco, its national oil corporation, and to unveil an economic reform and diversification plan.[48] However, when commodity prices recover, an anti-reform impulse results from rising government spending and distributional demands on the state. This unsustainable consumption lays the foundation for vulnerability to future shocks and ensuing economic crises. Moreover, the sudden downward swing in oil prices, which reduces foreign exchange and government spending, can factionalize the ruling coalition and cause mass discontent. The interplay of constraints, policy responses, and economic outcomes is illustrated in Figure 3.3.

****

In conclusion, the analysis of the distribution of power in society, how it persists and how it could change gives us insights into the origin of policies that may support

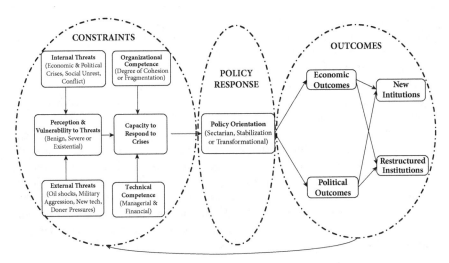

Figure 3.4 The Interplay of Constraints, Policy Responses, and Outcomes.

Source: Author's construction.

or undermine economic diversification. This chapter provided analytical tools to unpack the black box of politics into power, actors, and institutions, and how it relates to economic policy. Power in a society is distributed among individual, group, and organizational actors along the four dimensions of elite bargains, wider coalitions with non-elite societal groups, an economic agenda or policy regime, and institutionalization. This balance of power shapes the orientation of ruling elites and their economic policy priorities on short-term stabilization or long-term structural economic transformation through any of the available pathways identified in Chapter 2.

But this power configuration is not immune to change. It can change suddenly at critical junctures when powerful actors are constrained by crises and other contingencies to act in specific ways. The response of powerful actors, especially ruling elites, to conditions at these critical junctures determines the maintenance of the institutional order (persistence) or its collapse and replacement (change). Specifically, it is the nature of threats these crises pose to ruling elites and the capacity of these powerful actors that determines their policy responses at critical junctures. Thus, depending on the kinds of constraints on ruling elites, certain policy choices are more probable, say political reforms, industrial policies, redistribution social policies and public financial management reforms. Constraints can occur horizontally within the ruling coalition characterized by the extent of their cohesion or fragmentation. They can also be vertical within wider society in the extent to which non-elite groups accept or disapprove the distribution of economic resources. Finally, constraints from the external environment take the form of threats of external aggression, pressures from foreign donors, commodity price swings, or even disruptive technologies.

Based on the discussion so far, what does Nigeria's distribution of power look like? What constraints shape the policy priorities of ruling elites? How do these policy priorities shape Nigeria's longstanding goal of diversifying its economy? What kinds of policies are ruling elites constrained to pursue? We address these questions in the next chapter. For now, what we have learnt about the distribution of power is that it forms the political character and institutional foundation for an "intermediate" Nigerian state which intermittently implements reforms sufficient to enable growth spurts but not sustained policy reforms to diversify the economy. Like other major mineral exporters, rapid swings in externally derived oil revenue flows are politically disruptive in that they reinforce or reconfigure the institutional arrangement. Ruling elites are especially powerful in shaping systems and structures during oil boom-and-bust cycles because they preside over the allocation of large volumes of oil revenues and have significant leeway to implement policies that would ordinarily be difficult. In the next chapter, we examine how Nigeria's policy choices made within an unstable distribution of power contributed to oil dependence and institutional centralization for the purpose of maintaining political and economic stability after independence in 1960 through to the military period until 1999.

The Transition to Becoming Africa's Top Oil Producer

My mother came of age in the 1970s in the ancient town of Zaria in northern Nigeria during the first oil boom. Upon completing secondary school in 1972 at the age of 15, she enrolled in the School of Basic Studies at one of the country's five elite universities, the Ahmadu Bello University (ABU) in Zaria. She obtained the post-secondary diploma at age 16 in early 1974 and proceeded to university in 1978 after a four-year break. She spent three years at ABU studying for a law degree and graduated in 1981. Both the post-secondary diploma and law degree were sponsored by full government scholarships sufficient to cover the expenses for tuition, books, accommodation, and personal upkeep. At the time, most students in ABU and the other federal universities were on full government scholarships. The government also generously sponsored my mother's post-university transition. Immediately after graduation in 1981, she enrolled in law school in Lagos, Nigeria's commercial capital and at the time, its administrative capital. Not only was attending law school free, but my mother's cohort was paid a salary. Upon graduating from law school in 1982, she participated in the final step of post-university transition, the mandatory National Youth Service Corps (NYSC).

The NYSC is one of the flagship initiatives introduced to strengthen Nigeria's national unity after the devastating civil war of 1967–1970. Established in 1973, it requires all graduates of tertiary institutions to undergo a year of national service in a part of Nigeria outside their home region. This service year comprises two weeks of a paramilitary-style orientation at a "camp," then candidates undertake their primary assignment teaching at a school in an underserved area or an internship-style arrangement in any organization, and finally they graduate. This national service is such a vital aspect of post-university transition that, to date, no credible public or private organization will employ a graduate without an NYSC certificate. It also introduces many young Nigerians to their future employers.

During the one-year NYSC in Lagos, my mother was courted by various recruiters from government agencies and private enterprises. She received a job offer from one of Nigeria's top banks at the time, Union Bank, at their headquarters in Lagos. Some of the perks of the job included an apartment in the exclusive district of Ikoyi, and a subsidized car loan three months into the job, in addition to the generous salaries in the banking profession. However, my mother did not take up this offer. When she completed the NYSC in 1983, she moved back to Kaduna in the north to become a magistrate in the state's judiciary in 1984 and went on to have an illustrious career in the legal profession as a judge.

My mother's experience of higher education and the post-university transition was typical for a generation of Nigerians in the first three decades of independence. Through their eyes, my generation learnt of a Nigeria full of opportunities for upward social mobility enabled by a generous, confident, and competent government. In many ways, their experience at the time mirrored the pathways for upward social mobility in the industrial societies of North America and Western Europe, and the industrializing societies in parts of Asia and Latin America. This Nigeria is alien to my generation, raised in the 1990s and the 2000s, who attended decaying public schools, enrolled in underfunded universities and relied on dysfunctional government agencies. I started university in 2003, a year later than scheduled, because all public universities had gone on a characteristic nationwide strike to protest insufficient compensation and research funding. Strikes by the Academic Staff Union of Universities (ASUU) became common during military rule in the 1990s.

The oil windfall of the 1970s allowed for the increase in public investment that started in the 1960s after independence from British colonial rule. Airports, bridges, hospitals, and schools were built, roads connected remote villages to urban centers, and credible universities and research institutes were established. These were all financed by the Nigerian government, not by foreign aid, which at the time was an alien concept. In fact, between the 1970s and 1990s, it was Nigeria who provided foreign aid in development finance and investments to Chad, Guinea Conakry, Republic of Niger, and to the liberation movements in Angola, South Africa, and Zimbabwe; technical assistance to the government agencies in countries such as The Gambia; and championed the establishment of the Economic Community of West African States (ECOWAS).

The confidence Nigeria exuded during the oil boom was captured in an infamous remark in 1973 by the military head of state, General Yakubu Gowon, that "Nigeria's problem is not money, but how to spend it." There was, though, an underbelly to the large scale of government spending. The public sector expanded to the point of becoming bloated as the number of public enterprises increased from 250 in 1970 to more than 800 by the mid-1970s. Large prestige projects created a sense of national pride including the construction of a new capital city, Abuja, from scratch, but also left in their wake, a litany of uncompleted projects and the mismanagement of public funds. The infamous cement armada of the 1970s, in which 16 million metric tons of cement were shipped to the Lagos harbor beyond its handling capacity of four metric tons, illustrated the frenzy of the oil boom. Due to congestion at the port, some ships waited for almost a year to unload their cargo, incurring expensive demurrage fees in the process.

On the surface, the expansion of public spending during Nigeria's oil boom and the associated problems demonstrated the classic symptoms of the resource curse. As the political scientist Terry-Lynn Karl described, there was a "petrolisation of the policy environment."[1] The whole of society was drenched in the petrodollars of the windfall. Some Nigerians today have uncritically accepted that the "oil curse" is to blame for the country's economic underperformance and institutional dysfunction. It is common to hear some public commentators hope for global oil prices to crash to shock the country out of its oil-induced indolence. These prevailing explanations that focus on Nigeria's oil wealth are simplistic, incomplete, and misleading. In reality, both the pathologies of oil wealth and the sources of resilience of the Nigerian economy predate the oil boom. There were forces well underway before the first shipment of oil was exported in 1958 and these dynamics were only magnified by the oil boom. In this chapter I explain how the policy choices made during the oil boom onwards were driven by factors independent of crude oil but that used the oil windfall revenues in execution, especially efforts to blunt the fierce ethno-regional and religious competition that caused the 1967 civil war. Within an unstable power configuration, Nigerian leaders were constrained to make policy choices that aimed to stabilize the economy and polity but that compounded the challenge of economic diversification.

In this chapter therefore, I recast key moments of Nigeria's history using the lens of the political settlement to identify the policy responses by ruling elites to the constraints they faced. The first section of the chapter analyzes Nigeria's economic transition, from a production structure reliant on primary commodity exports to becoming Africa's largest oil exporter. In the second section, I discuss the political transition towards greater institutional centralization as a policy response that attempted to unite a country fragmented by ethnic, regional, and religious competition. The final section explains how institutions were sustained, adapted or changed by Nigeria's ruling elites in response to specific constraints including elite competition that erupted in a civil war, oil booms and busts that caused an economic crisis, and mass protests from declining living standards. The chapter covers three distinct time periods: the colonial period (1914 to 1960), the post-independence period (1960 to 1966) and the military period (1966 to 1999).

The Economic Transition from Commodities to Oil

Oil was discovered in Nigeria in 1956 at Oloibiri in the Niger Delta by Shell D'Arcy Petroleum, after about fifty years of exploration. Production began in 1958 when the first oil field came on stream to produce 5,100 barrels per day. In the same year, the first shipment was exported. From 1960, exploration rights were extended to other foreign companies, such as Mobil, Texaco Overseas, and Elf.[2] It was after 1970, with both the rise in oil prices and membership of OPEC, that Nigeria's status as Africa's largest oil producer and exporter was cemented. Before then, Nigeria was a major exporter of primary commodities such as coal, cocoa, groundnuts, palm oil, and rubber. How did the Nigerian economy transition from export-oriented agriculture and mining to crude oil? What were the major activities, growth drivers, and revenue sources in the economy? As this economic transition is already a well-covered subject, I will highlight key points in the contributions of economic sectors to national GDP, exports, and fiscal revenue.

Nigeria transitioned from an agrarian economy in the colonial period, to intermittent episodes of modernization in manufacturing industry in the post-independence period, to an oil economy in the military period. From the political unification of colonial Nigeria in 1914 until independence in 1960, the backbone of the economy was the production and export of primary agriculture commodities, including cocoa, cotton, groundnuts, palm oil, and rubber, and the extraction of minerals such as coal and tin ore. Production relied on small-scale cultivators on cocoa farms in the western region, in cotton and groundnut farms in the northern region and on palm produce in the eastern region. Laborers also worked the tin mines in Jos and coal in Enugu. These crops and minerals were purchased and sold abroad by the foreign trading monopolies, such as the United African Company (UAC).[3] By 1950, four major commodities accounted for more than 70% of total exports (Figure 4.1a). By independence in 1960, Nigeria was an agrarian society in which the bulk of economic production was oriented towards exports; emerging trade and transport services sectors supported this export orientation.

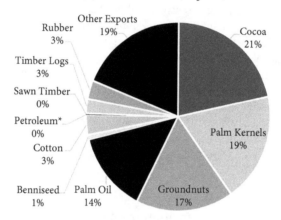

(a) Contribution to Exports, 1950

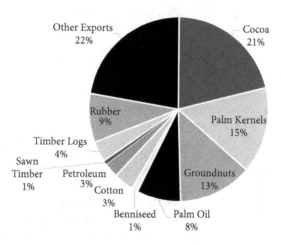

(b) Contribution to Exports, 1960

Figure 4.1 The Contribution of Major Commodities to Exports in 1950 and 1960.

Source: Author's calculations from data in the National Development Plan, 1962–1968, p.11.

In the first decade of independence, there were evident structural shifts towards oil and manufacturing industry even though the economy was still largely based on export-oriented agriculture. By 1960, petroleum accounted for 3% of exports (Figure 4.1b). Even in these early days, the government envisaged in the First National Development Plan that "by 1967, petroleum is likely to have displaced cocoa as the single most important source of foreign exchange."[4] While agriculture still constituted over half (56.7%) of GDP in 1960 and grew to 61% in 1962, it kept declining throughout the first post-independence decade, reaching 53% in 1969. The economy experienced some structural changes associated with the early stages of transformation. Growth was higher than the anticipated 4% per annum, and its sources were shifting to intensive industrial activities and expansion of food production.[5] Public policies also helped to drive growth, as rising government investments supported industrial expansion within the country's import substitution industrialization (ISI) strategy, discussed in more detail in the chapter. Growth was accompanied by considerable expansion in manufacturing, mining, and building and construction. Crude oil production, which began in the 1950s grew steadily, constituting 26% of total exports by 1962 and 42% by 1969.

Although growth slowed and crashed in the second half of the 1960s, it rebounded strongly by 1970 on the back of the oil boom. The quick succession of violent military coups in 1966 and the civil war in 1967–1970 compounded some of the structural deficiencies of the ISI and disrupted the pace of growth. Growth resumed at the end of the civil war in 1970. Real GDP in 1971, the first post-war fiscal year was about 30% above the average for 1963–1966 (Figure 4.2).[6] This post-war economic boom was

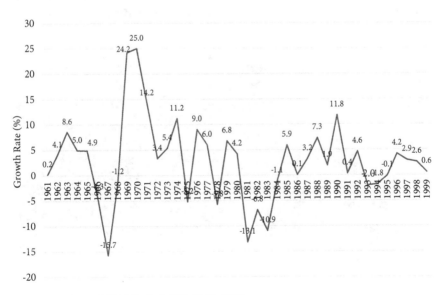

Figure 4.2 Annual GDP Growth (%), 1960–2019.

Source: Author's calculations from the World Bank's World Development Indicators.

characterized by a massive growth in oil production, which had commenced in the 1950s. There was a rise in global oil prices from less than $4 a barrel in early 1973 to $12 by year's end after the Arab embargo was lifted; this had increased to $14 by 1979, which resulted in an oil windfall. The windfall was also enabled by a nationalization of the oil industry, as other OPEC member states had done, which increased ownership of Nigeria's share of the oil companies from 35 to 55% and the revenues accruing to it. Therefore, the fortuitous oil boom drove a lot of the GDP growth—excluding oil, according to some estimates, GDP expansion was 7.5% (instead of 18.4%) in 1971, 0% (instead of 7.3%) in 1972, 6.2% (instead of 9.5%) in 1973 and 8.9% (instead of 9.7%) in 1974.[7] Oil export earnings nearly tripled, from N4.9 billion in 1975 to N11.2 billion in 1979 (Figure 4.3) and fiscal revenue also tripled from N5.5 billion in 1975 to N15.2 billion in 1980 (Figure 4.4).

The oil windfall provided resources to finance public investments in infrastructure and the purchase of inputs for other industries, especially the manufacturing sector. It enabled the country to strengthen its ISI begun in the 1960s, explained in more detail later in the chapter. As stated in Nigeria's Third National Development Plan, "the development strategy of the government [is] to utilise the resources from oil to develop the productive capacity of the economy and thus permanently improve the standard of living of the people... to create the economic and social infrastructure necessary for self-sustaining growth... a radical transformation of the economy."[8] Thus, the investment ratio increased from the projected 18.2% to 19.2% in 1972 and from 16.8% to 19.6% in 1973. Very importantly, these public investments became the major source of capital formation, indicating the strong government intervention in the economy. Between 1970 and 1974, the ratio of private to public investment was 58:42.[9] With the exception of agriculture, other key economic sectors including manufacturing, building and construction, trade and distribution grew. Starting from a small base,

Figure 4.3 Crude Oil Becomes Nigeria's Major Export Earner (%) from 1970 Onwards.

Source: Author's calculations from Central Bank of Nigeria (CBN) Data.

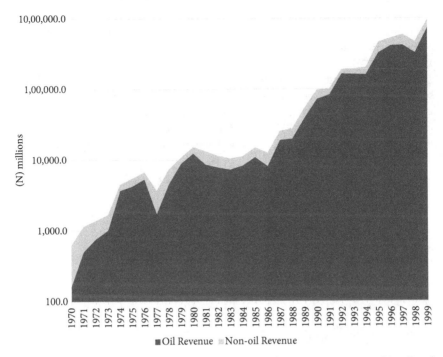

Figure 4.4 Oil Earnings Become Nigeria's Main Source of Government Revenue (N millions) from 1972.

Source: Author's calculations from Central Bank of Nigeria (CBN) Data.

manufacturing grew at an average 11% per annum since the 1960s, reaching 56.6% in 1975 (see Figure 4.5b) below. Although manufacturing grew in absolute terms during the oil boom, its growth was volatile and slower than the oil sector's—manufacturing grew from the extensive injection of petroleum-driven capital and was characterized by inefficiencies associated with the broader ISI strategy. Partly for this reason, its share of GDP did not exceed 10% (Figure 4.5c) and was lower than the 15–20% in other developing country peers and the 16% that the government had aimed for.[10]

Despite the large public investments in the tradables sectors, there was also an expansion of private-sector activity. The volume of oil earnings led to an appreciation of the naira, which made imports cheaper, and expanded the individual and industrial consumption of foreign goods. This, along with macroeconomic volatilities of the time, external debt, and public sector expansion, were symptoms of the "Dutch Disease." At the same time, there was growth in agriculture and manufacturing, although with considerable technical inefficiencies and weak backward and forward linkages. Tom Forrest goes beyond "Dutch Disease" to document the growth of the domestic private sector in import trading, distribution, construction, and in contracting; the oil boom increased profitability in commerce and the service economy, at the expense of small-scale industries in which many Nigerians were engaged.[11] The oil windfall also led to the expansion of government services, projects, and the public sector. For instance, the construction sector's share of GDP almost doubled in five years, from 5.8% in 1972 to 10.9% in 1977, while public administration and defense spending almost tripled, from 4.5% in 1972 to 12.1% in 1977.[12]

The technical inefficiencies of the agriculture, manufacturing and other tradables sectors and the ISI underpinning them were laid bare when global oil prices crashed in the 1980s. Nigeria's oil earnings fell dramatically from a peak of N13.6 billion in 1980 to N8.4 billion in 1982, triggering a major economic crisis. About 50% of manufacturing firms stopped production for some time,[13] and total exports almost

(a) Oil and Gas Growth Rate (%), 1963–1999

(b) Manufacturing growth rate (%), 1963–1993

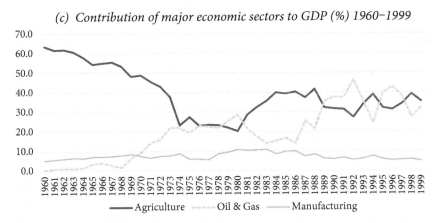

(c) Contribution of major economic sectors to GDP (%) 1960–1999

——— Agriculture ----- Oil & Gas ——— Manufacturing

Figure 4.5 The Manufacturing Sector Grew at an Average of around 10% but was Slower than the Oil Sector.

Source for Panel a and b: Author's calculations from FRN (1970) Second National Development Plan 1970–1974; FRN (1975) Third National Development Plan 1975–1980 and FRN (1981) Fourth National Development Plan 1981–1985 (p. 15) and the National Bureau of Statistics Data.
Source for Panel c: Author's calculations from the Nigeria National Bureau of Statistics Data, in current prices.

halved, from N14.1 billion in 1980 to N8.9 billion in 1986. To manage the crisis, a Washington Consensus-inspired Structural Adjustment Program (SAP) was designed and implemented from 1986. SAP comprising a sharp currency devaluation and deflationary fiscal measures that made capital- and import-intensive industries less competitive. Though structural adjustment addressed the debt crunch and fiscal crisis, it failed to stimulate sustained recovery of the productive sectors. This was within a broader context of low oil prices of $18 a barrel until the early 2000s. Within this period, the economy stagnated (see Figure 4.3), and the productive sectors contracted, until the early 2000s. Growth was at an average of just 0.7% a year for the better part of 1980 to 1999.

The Political Transition Towards Institutional Centralization

Nigeria transitioned to become Africa's top oil producer within a volatile political environment. Throughout the twentieth century, a precarious balance of power of fierce ethnic, regional, and religious competition and shocks from the global economy shaped policy design and implementation towards stabilization. Nigeria's military rulers favored the centralization of institutions to better capture the oil windfall and to stabilize an economy affected by oil price volatility and a polity torn apart by a civil war in the 1960s. Using the lens of political settlements presented in Chapter 3, we examine the changing distribution of power in Nigerian society and centralization of institutions to achieve stabilization along the four dimensions of elite consensus, coalitions with non-elite societal groups, national economic priorities, and institutionalization of political and economic structures.

Elite Bargains Strive to Unite Nigeria

Right from the colonial period, Nigeria's political elites have strived to negotiate commonly agreed pacts to blunt the sharp edges of ethnic, regional, and religious rivalries.

In the colonial period, an incremental negotiation of political autonomy from the British to Nigeria's regional political elites eventually led to independence. The differentiation in the patterns of elite formation between northern and southern Nigeria were hugely consequential in these negotiations. Colonial rule met a fully formed, hierarchical and administratively competent precolonial empire in northern Nigeria, in which entry into the ruling and bureaucratic class relied on class and lineage. In the (south)west, there were also hierarchical precolonial empires of Oyo and Benin, whereas the (south)east comprising small village clans. After the British military conquest of what became northern Nigeria in the early 1900s, the colonial system of indirect rule retained a façade of authority of the Muslim Amirs albeit in a diminished form, as with the Obas in the west. Indirect Rule reinforced the emirates' hierarchy—of Fulani aristocrats and Hausa nobility at the top, the free commoners or *Talakawas*, and an underclass that included ethnic minorities.[14] Indigenous merchants from aristocratic trading families were also closely tied to the emirate system, while craftsmen and peasants who never transformed into capitalist producers remained powerless as a socio-economic class. Even as access to Western education was expanding in the south, it was restricted in the north by the British in order to pre-empt the nationalist political agitation by educated intellectuals in the south, as discussed in Chapter 3. Eventually, nationalist movements comprising educated and economically empowered individuals from across Nigeria demanded greater inclusion in political institutions and the economy.

As the colonial state made incremental political and economic concessions to Nigerians, the vulnerabilities of each region became the driving force of political competition. The MacPherson Constitution of 1951 established three administrative regions which overlapped with ethnic identities. These were the Igbos in the eastern region, Hausas and Fulanis in the north, the Yorubas in the west and, and hundreds of minority groups in the north and east. Each region had a governing party—the National Congress for Nigerian Citizens (NCNC) in the east, the Northern Peoples' Congress (NPC) in the north and the Action Group (AG) in the west. However, there were deep fault lines resulting from disparities in educational advancement, geographic size, and population that regional federalism only magnified.

One major faultline was the north–south rivalry. The ruling elites in the predominantly Hausa and Fulani northern region feared domination by the educationally advanced southerners in public service and educational institutions. The southern regions on the other hand feared the north's political domination in parliament,[15] the federal cabinet and the army which it secured using its landmass and large population (Map 4.1). Very crucially, this north–south rivalry was inflamed by southern perceptions that persist to date, that colonial administrators favored the northerners. It did not help matters that the British often expressed "admiration" for the administratively advanced Muslim emirates in the north, which they regarded as more "cultured" and suited to leadership. For instance, Nigeria's first governor general

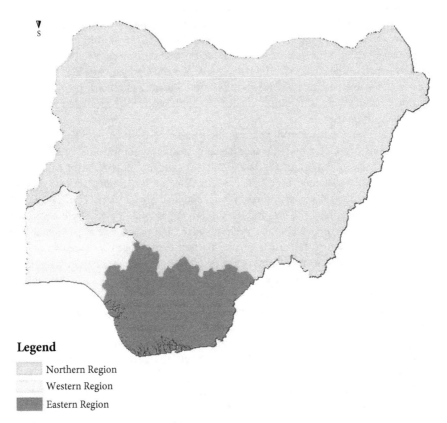

Legend

    Northern Region

    Western Region

    Eastern Region

Map 4.1 Map of Colonial Nigeria with the Three Regions.

Source: Author's construction.

Frederick Lugard said about northerners:[16] "Their traditions of rule, their monotheistic religion, and their intelligence enable them to appreciate more readily than the negro population the wider objects of British policy, while their close touch with the masses... mark them out as destined to play -an important part in... the development of the tropics." John Mackintosh, a historian and Labour MP similarly noted that "many features of Hausa culture give it dignity, status, and prestige: a comparatively rich historical tradition; a distinctive architecture; the pomp and splendour of its ruling class... ."[17] The reality was that the British easily related to the hierarchical northern emirates where class distinctions paralleled those in Victorian England rather than any genuine affection for northerners.

There were also other salient but understated fault lines. Within the south, there was and still is competition between Yorubas in the west and Igbos in the east, with the mega city Lagos as the battleground. From the 1940s, Yoruba elites who occupied the top bureaucratic, economic and political positions in Lagos due to their early head start in Western education felt threatened by those Igbos who were rapidly catching up and becoming assertive in business and politics.[18] This rivalry crystallized in the competition for electoral supremacy between Obafemi Awolowo-led A.G. and Nnamdi Azikiwe-led NCNC in the western regional elections of 1951. Within each region as well, the north and the east in particular, there were hundreds of minority ethnic groups—such as the Angas, Tiv, Ijaws, Itsekiris, and the Ogonis—who also wanted to be free of the overbearing influence of the Hausas, Fulanis, and Igbos. The foundation for inter-regional and inter-ethnic rivalry was built out of this social and economic imbalance of the regions.

Nigeria eventually secured political independence in 1960 as a federation of three regions negotiated by regional elites and colonial administrators at a series of constitutional conferences in the late 1950s. This fragile independence consensus, which was only sustained by a collective disdain for the colonial rulers, quickly unraveled after their departure. The pre-independence constitutional conferences did not address the regional rivalries and the underlying mutual fears of domination. For instance, the eastern NCNC found itself an increasingly "irrelevant" partner in the national ruling coalition because the major partner the northern NPC had a working majority in the parliament. Tensions reached boiling point with futile attempts by both the NCNC and the opposition western AG to contain the NPC's national political power which had tilted the distribution of federal spending in favor of the north. In a census in 1962, the NCNC's attempts to alter the representational ratio between the north and the south resulted in competitive population inflation by the regions. Allegations of plans by the AG to topple the NPC-led government to alter this regional balance of power undermined the 1964 general elections and led to a constitutional crisis.[19]

This simmering instability of Nigeria's First Republic violently erupted through a series of events, from a bloody military coup in 1966 to a civil war by 1967. On 15 January 1966, a group of mostly eastern-Igbo military officers assassinated Nigeria's prime minister, Sir Abubakar Tafawa Balewa and other high-ranking northern and Western political and military leaders, shattering the already fragile trust among regional elites. On 29 July 1966, a violent countercoup followed, when northern military officers overthrew the new military government and assassinated the eastern head of state General Johnson Aguiyi-Ironsi, who was perceived to be lenient to the first set of coup plotters.[20] Shortly after, were mass killings of Igbo military officers and civilians resident in the northern region after which the eastern region declared a secession from Nigeria. Finally, a civil war erupted in 1967 collapsing Nigeria's First Republic. A brittle elite consensus forged by naïve enthusiasm over independence, ushered self-rule amidst extreme regional rivalries and boiled over into a civil war by 1967.

Although the first coup in January 1966 opened the Pandora's Box of military rule, it was after the countercoup of July 1966 that an elite consensus emerged which lasted until democratization in 1999. The elimination of the highest echelons of the First Republic's civilian and military leaders by the January 1966 coup paved way for a new crop of political actors to negotiate a consensus around the distribution of power. Key participants in the July 1966 countercoup—such as 2nd Lt. Mohammed Sani Abacha, Lt. Ibrahim Babangida, Lt. Muhammadu Buhari, Major Theophilus Danjuma, Lt. Colonel Murtala Mohammed, Lt. Colonel Olusegun Obasanjo, etc.—would influence the political, military, and economic life of the country as heads of state, ministers, businessmen, and even run for elections decades afterwards

The emerging elite consensus was forged by a multi-ethnic northern military class alongside their western-Yoruba counterparts who organized the countercoup and fought a civil war to prevent the mostly Igbo-eastern "Biafra" region from seceding. Minority groups in the east such as the Ijaws, Urhobos, and Ogonis in the oil-producing Niger Delta did not overwhelmingly support the secessionist cause, as they felt their fate would be worse in an Igbo-dominated independent Biafra. The Niger Delta accounted for half of the east's total landmass, containing 95% of its oil reserves, seaports, and agricultural and fishing resources. Consequently, the Niger Delta's pioneering environmental activists such as Isaac Adaka Boro and Ken Saro-Wiwa fought or served the federal government against Biafra during the war.[21] Biafra was reintegrated into the federation by 1970 within a "no victor no vanquished" state policy that neither exacted retributions nor awarded victory. There was an amnesty for all "Biafran" fighters, some Igbo civilians who fled to Biafra were reinstated to the jobs they had held before the civil war, and Gowon also refused to award medals to Nigerian soldiers who fought in the war as "there could be no victory in a war between brothers."[22] Yet, there was a tacit understanding that Igboswould be excluded from strategic positions of military power and political authority due to lingering distrust after the violent January 1966 coup and the civil war. Alex Ekwueme, vice president in the brief democratic transition between 1979 and 1983, and of Igbo ethnicity, confirmed years later that:[23] "Definitely, my involvement in government... certainly gave some level of re-assurance to my people that they were now truly part of Nigeria and not a disgraced or conquered people."

The elite consensus forged in the wake of the countercoup in July 1966 was initially reinforced after the civil war and by the oil boom, but gradually destabilized until its collapse in 1998.

From 1973, there was an oil boom within this institutional setting of greater centralization, post-war reconstruction, and an unaccountable military government which transformed the whole of society. The psyche of many in the military was reoriented to aspire to lucrative government positions. This reorientation splintered the military vertically along class lines, and horizontally along ethno-regional and religious factions, with destabilizing consequences. Consequently, between 1966 and 1999, there were six military coups and three attempted/aborted coups. Nigeria's successive military regimes were highly unstable due to the risk of countercoups by excluded officers and their civilian backers such as businessmen, politicians, and media tycoons. As former military ruler, General Ibrahim Babangida explained: "we couldn't have done it without collaborators in the civil society... in the media... among people who have the means."[24] The underlying elite consensus transformed—from safeguarding the country's territorial integrity, fostering national unity and mediating a democratic transition—to one in which the military elite sought to retain power for itself, becoming increasingly distrustful of democracy in the process.

The factionalization of the military also mirrored the latent ethno-regional fears of domination which had persisted from the 1950s and further strained the delicate post-war consensus. The northerners in the ruling military elite were pitched against their southern counterparts; even among the northerners there were tensions between the mostly Muslim "core northerners" (Hausa, Fulani, Kanuri, and Nupe, etc.) and the mostly Christian "northern minorities," although these distinctions were not always clear-cut. For instance, General Ibrahim Babangida, accused towards the latter part of his regime (1985–1993) of favoring "core" and "Muslim" northerners is a northern ethnic minority of Gbagyi descent. Ironically, Babangida's regime had initially tried to make amends for the perceived pro-northern bias of his predecessor, General Muhammadu Buhari (1983–1985), by ensuring government agencies were ethnically balanced away from the Hausas and Fulanis.[25] However, the same suspicion trailed the second half of his regime after a cabinet reshuffle following a violent coup attempt in April 1990 by soldiers of northern-Christian and southern ethnic minority stock, thereby shifting the balance of power back towards the Muslim northerners. Religious tensions also flared up in 1986 when Nigeria became a member of the Organization of the Islamic Conference (OIC) to the consternation of many southerners and Christians.[26]

Beyond the military, various southern political, professional, and intellectual elites felt increasingly alienated from Nigeria's rulers, predominantly of northern extraction, and blamed them for squandering all the benefits of Nigeria's oil wealth. For the Yoruba in the west, the line was drawn when Babangida's military regime annulled the 1993 presidential elections, won by charismatic tycoon, Moshood Kashimawo Abiola, a Muslim of Yoruba ethnicity. Against the backdrop of a prevailing belief that the country would not have survived the civil war without their support, Yoruba intellectual and political leaders saw the annulment as an attempt by northerners to perpetually retain power. For instance, speaking on behalf of Yoruba traditional rulers, the traditional ruler Okunade Sijuwade, the Ooni of Ife, threatened that "if our son [Abiola] is not declared winner of the election, the Yorubas… are ready to pull out of Nigeria."[27] Concurrently, there were rumblings of dissidence by the oil-producing Niger Delta over the region's environmental devastation and underdevelopment. Through peaceful advocacies and armed rebellion, the Niger Delta demanded the right to a fair share of the oil wealth it produced and on which the Nigerian economy stood. The eastern-Igbo elite also quietly resented the humanitarian toll from the civil war and their exclusion from the highest echelons of military and political authority. These unaddressed grievances fractured the elite consensus which had held Nigeria together to overcome the tribulations of the violent coups and the civil war of the bloody 1960s.

The final straw that shattered the post-war elite consensus was the brutal repression by General Sani Abacha's regime. In November 1993, Abacha usurped an interim civilian government appointed on 26 August 1993 to organize fresh presidential elections. Abacha's regime was so repressive in crushing dissent by pro-democracy movements, the execution of Niger Delta environmental activists, and economic mismanagement, that the country teetered on the brink of total collapse. Tensions only eased from 8 June 1998 when Abacha died in mysterious circumstances, placing Nigeria back on a firm path toward democratization.

The path towards democratization in the transition government from June 1998 to May 1999 was underlined by a new post-military elite consensus to partially address the persistent regional fears of domination. At the core of this consensus was a power-sharing agreement to rotate presidential power periodically between the north and the south loosely based on a "zoning" power-sharing agreement formulated by the defunct National Party of Nigeria (NPN), the ruling party in 1979–1983.[28] This aimed to redress the Yoruba-western grievance over the annulment of the 1993 presidential election. As a founding member of the PDP explained to me,[29] Yoruba elites proposed this power rotation in the planned democratic dispensation with an understanding that power would shift to the north after one term of four years. Consequently, the major political parties presented presidential candidates from the region in the April 1999 presidential election. The candidates included Olusegun Obasanjo on the People's Democratic Party's (PDP) platform who became president and Olu Falae for the All People's Party (APP). This gentlemen's agreement on power rotation was negotiated by several military and civilian actors of the post-civil war consensus, on the platform of the PDP, and even inscribed in the party's constitution.

Thus, this "zoning" power-sharing agreement was the basis on which Nigeria's political elite agreed to end military rule on terms they negotiated to stabilize decades-old regional rivalries. This is not surprising because as the political scientist Barbara Geddes posits, military governments are more likely to step down before conditions reach crisis point and thus are likely to negotiate orderly transitions.[30]

The Political Exclusion of Non-elite Societal Groups

Nigeria's non-elite groups include productive groups, labor and trade unions, and other interest groups. From the colonial period through to the post-independence and military period, the redistribution concerns of these groups changed in line with their access to political institutions and economic resources.

In the colonial period, a gradual process of inclusion empowered various societal groups to challenge the domination of colonial rulers and traders. Discriminatory public policies had excluded most locals from the commodities' trade and obstructed the emergence of a strong landowning class.[31] The wage laborers, civil servants, artisans, petty traders, and an emerging merchant class, were unorganized and marginal to colonial power structures. With the expansion of education and health services from the 1920s, a generation of educated Nigerians benefited from the "Africanization" of the lower- to mid-tiers of hospitals, schools, and the public service. Concurrently, the lifting of discriminatory restrictions in the commodities' trade allowed for the greater participation of local merchants in the economy. Before the emergence of political parties in the 1940s, trade unions and other economic groups featured prominently on the political scene. For instance, the Lagos market women were the main mass base of Nigeria's oldest political organization, the Nigerian National Democratic Party (NNDP) established in 1923. From the 1940s, ethno-regional interest groups emerged from conditions enabled by colonial constitutional developments. Cultural associations such as the *Egbe Omo Oduduwa* in the west and the *Jam'iyar Mutanen Arewa* in the north, morphed into political parties, the AG and the NPC respectively. The MacPherson Constitution of 1951, which provided for the election and appointment of members into regional legislatures and executive councils, facilitated political party formation.[32] Thus, these grassroots cultural movements, the professional cadre of teachers, clerks, and students and trade unions constituted the pro-independence nationalist movements.

These economic and political groups which had fought colonial rule were further empowered after independence. The first generation of universities established between 1948 and 1965 produced a critical cohort of graduates who joined public service and the professions. These universities included the University of Nigeria Nsukka in the east, University of Ibadan in the west, and Ahmadu Bello University, Zaria, in the north.[33] Business men and women engaged in commerce, real estate, construction, industry, and government procurement and often associated with the governing political parties were further empowered through the allocation of patronage, i.e., loans, contracts, bank credits, and buying-agent licenses for commodity exports.[34]

The violent coups of 1966, the civil war and the oil boom transformed Nigeria's social structure by introducing individual military actors into politics and the economy. The size of the Nigerian army grew from 10,000 in 1966 to over 200,000 in 1970 due to enlistments to fight the war.[35] Military rule ingrained in the psyche of lower-ranking officers, the aspiration for political power seeing how their superiors got rapid promotions, appointments to cabinet and ambassadorial positions and opportunities for material enrichment. A nouveau riche class of serving and retired millionaire military officers emerged.

Within a changing social structure during the oil boom, concerns around economic redistribution and political representation became salient. From the 1970s, there was massive public investment financed by the proceeds of the oil windfall, which benefited my mother's generation. These included public sector wage increases, especially the famed Udoji Award, investment in transport and social infrastructure, business assistance, and indigenization policies in commanding heights of the economy. As economic inequalities widened during this time, class cleavages became a more explicit basis for political division in the Second Republic (1979–1983) while the political mobilization of ethnicity became more difficult.[36] However, redistribution issues were hardly at the forefront of public policy and there was no strong bottom-up pressure to deal with equity issues either in rural-urban or class terms. As Henry Bienen and Okwudiba Nnoli explain, peasant farmers and trade unions were not strong enough to advocate for income redistribution, while those in the urban informal sector did not constitute an effective force for radical change.[37] Although, upwardly mobile urban Nigerians were politically vocal, this voice did not translate into increased political participation.

The economic crises of the 1980s and the ensuing political transitions further marginalized Nigeria's professionals, trade unions, and civil society. In particular, General Muhammadu Buhari's military regime from 1983 alienated many with its harsh anti-corruption drive. State governors, ministers, and many prominent politicians were jailed on corruption charges; the Nigerian Medical Association and other professional associations were proscribed; the infamous Decree No. 4 "Public Officers" Protection Against False Accusation' criminalized critical journalism, and the regime's perceived ethnic and religious lop-sidedness in favor of northern Muslims, all gave it a draconian and regional flair. The regime's loss of its initial mass appeal created the momentum for a palace coup in August 1985 with wide support from media and civil society.

From 1985, General Ibrahim Babangida's far-reaching reforms to manage the economic crisis changed the relative balance of economic power among various groups. By taking a more consultative approach, Babangida's regime at the onset secured broad-based support from professional groups which lost incomes under Buhari, regional elites objected to Buhari's pro-northern bias, and the persecuted business and political elite. Therefore, in a national debate, Nigerians widely rejected an IMF loan in favor of a "homegrown" SAP. On the one hand, the SAP market reforms introduced new players into the non-oil economy. For instance, the relaxation of banking and foreign exchange controls in 1986 led to the tripling of banks, from forty to 120 over the next five years.[38] On the other hand, the failure of reforms to generate a supply-side response from the productive sector opened up rent-seeking opportunities around government contracting, import–export trade and speculation in commodities, real estate, currency, and financial markets.[39] Some of these bankers and business persons, such as Tony Elumelu, would constitute the private sector that would drive market-reforms in the Fourth Republic from 1999, discussed in Chapters 5 and 6. Specifically, southern, especially Yoruba-western economic interests, that benefited from the SAP market reforms, initially supported Babangida's regime.

Within this context of widespread rent-seeking that characterized Babangida's attempt to transition to a market economy, concurrent austerity measures profoundly antagonized societal groups. The currency devaluation, retrenchments in the public service, cuts in social spending and trade liberalization hit Nigeria's middle class hard. GDP per capita declined from \$840.5 in 1980 to \$571.7 in 1991, the percentage of the population subsisting below \$1.25 a day, rose from 54.1% in 1984 to 61.9% in 1992, and academics and professionals emigrated abroad en masse. Yet, a small group of banks, speculators, government officials, and importers prospered.[40] The squeezed middle class represented by a vibrant media and unions, aware of their deteriorating standard of living, took a militant position against economic austerity.

Empowered by a generation of university graduates espousing left-wing ideas of the Cold War, Nigeria's civil society radically opposed the very "homegrown" SAP they had once cheered. They were enraged further by the perceived inconsistency and opacity of the military regime in managing the economic crisis, favoritism to business cronies, co-option of journalists and repression of civil society groups such as the Civil Liberties Organization and the Constitutional Rights Project. The annulment of the 1993 presidential elections sparked widespread protests by the Campaign for Democracy (CD), the NLC, the National Association of Nigerian Students (NANS) and others, engulfing the country in its worst political crisis since the civil war.[41] The annulment radically alienated Babangida's regime from organized civil society and completely eroded its broad-based support.

The fallout of austerity and the aborted civilian transition resulted in antagonistic relations between a combative civil society, weakened productive groups, and autocratic military rulers until democratization in 1999. This military-society antagonism escalated under General Abacha's regime which discarded any pretentions of civility by harshly repressing dissent. For example, the regime sacked the executive council of the National Union of Petroleum and Natural Gas Workers (NUPENG), the Petroleum and Natural Gas Senior Staff Association (PENGASSAN), and the NLC and closed three newspapers: *The Punch, Concord group* and *The Guardian*.[42] It also intimidated and arrested civil society and political leaders such as Nobel laureate Professor Wole Soyinka, Brigadier Lawan Gwadabe, General Obasanjo (rtd), his former deputy, General Musa Yar'Adua, and others over an alleged coup plot in 1995. Finally, the regime executed Ken Saro-Wiwa and other Ogoni activists from the oil-producing Niger Delta in November 1995.

Very crucially, civil society was detached from the political processes of the democratic transition when key segments boycotted a national constitutional conference in 1994–1995. There was a deep grievance within a largely Yoruba elite and civil society over the persecution of Moshood Abiola, winner of the annulled presidential election. The umbrella body for civil society, the National Democratic Coalition (NADECO) formed on May 15, 1994 to press for the revalidation of the June 12, 1993 presidential election, was led by influential individuals from the Yoruba-west, a region with a heavy footprint in the professions, unions, and media due to historic educational and economic advantages. Even after General Abacha's mysterious death in June 1998, when a concrete path towards democratization had been carved, and an elite consensus had emerged for a Yoruba, Christian, southern president, much of civil society distrusted this transition process supervised by the military. As noted by a member of one of the political parties, an unintended consequence of civil society boycott of the democratization agenda of the military 1998 was to strengthen the elite's disproportionate influence in Nigeria's democratic process.[43]

By the time Nigeria democratized, the civil society groups which had been key to decolonization and in challenging military rule remained vocal, but were disempowered and excluded from the political process.

Economic Agenda Fails to Create Conditions for Industrializing Nigeria

Over the course of Nigeria's history, there have been at least three distinct types of economic policy priorities. During the colonial period, there was a laissez-faire and later, interventionist economic policy orientation. In the early post-independence years, there was state-led capitalism that was in global fashion after the Second World War. followed by a short-lived attempt to enable a market economy in the late 1980s.

Nigeria's colonial rulers adopted a laissez-faire approach to economic management with a brief pivot towards developmentalism in the twilight years of British rule. The economic agenda was initially defined by the "dual-mandate" philosophy of colonialism as articulated by Nigeria's first governor general, Lord Frederick Lugard as follows:[44]

> Let it be admitted at the outset that European brains, capital, and energy... never will be, expended in developing the resources of Africa from motives of pure philanthropy; that Europe is in Africa for the mutual benefit of her own industrial classes, and of the native races in their progress to a higher plane...

Britain's extractive economic interests were prioritized above the socio-economic development of the colony. Even the political unification of the north and south in 1914 was driven by the need to centralize administration for fiscal sustainability.[45]

Foreign enterprises dominated the commanding heights of the Nigerian economy. The leading sectors of cash crops and mineral exports, banking and shipping were held by European multinationals such as UAC John Holt and Company, Compagnie Française de l'Afrique Occidentale (CFAO) and Societe Commerciale de l'Ouest Africain (SCOA). Through colonial discriminatory policies in granting licenses, tax breaks, and the sole rights to import and distribute consumer goods, foreign capital was favored at the expense of indigenous enterprises.[46] While there were some large-scale merchants involved in West African trade, indigenous business generally occupied the lowest rung of the economic hierarchy as petty traders, low-wage earners, mine laborers, and small-scale producers.

A paradigm shift after the Second World War resulted in a more interventionist strategy of skeletal development planning. This shift was induced by mounting pressures from indigenous business for economic inclusion and the state's declining fiscal revenues. Under the framework of the Colonial Development and Welfare Act (CDWA) of 1945, the state was required to develop ten-year development plans to guide revenue allocation, such as the "Ten-Year Plan of Development and Welfare for Nigeria 1946."[47] They constituted a series of projects uncoordinated with any broader economic target for investment or industrial output, but aimed at the "bare minimum" improvements to social welfare, health services, and agricultural productivity to support the colonial export trade.[48] The Nigeria Colonial Government stated that: "it is not assumed… that Nigeria will become an industrial country as with its large population and area, a great deal of its future must rest in agricultural development… and the improvement of village industries."[49]

Even the limited efforts to establish light manufacturing industries from the 1930s was a strategic withdrawal by British firms to defend their imperial global market share from Japanese and other eastern competition.[50] This British withdrawal from certain industries paved the way for Levantine (Lebanese and Syrian) and Asian businesses to enter commerce, retail, and light manufacturing. It also allowed for the "Nigerianization" of business enterprises in 1956, requiring multinationals to increase Nigerian personnel, to use inputs sourced from within Nigeria in production, and to bar foreigners from certain aspects of distributive trade.[51] Although the indigenous business class was also able to make greater inroads into transport, distribution, and commerce, Nigerian private capital was generally fragmented and regional in outlook.[52] It was not until after independence that legislation and policies were pursued, such as the creation of Expatriate Quota Allocation Board in 1968.

On independence, a state-directed development strategy envisioned providing the springboard for an industrial economy and accelerate social development. This strategy was executed through a series of fixed-term development plans. In the First Development Plan from 1962 to 1968, the government aimed "to stimulate the establishment and growth of industries… " with a target of 4% growth per annum, annual public investment of 15% of GDP, economic modernization, macroeconomic stability, social development, and equitable income distribution.[53] Industrialization was to be attained through ISI, in which local manufacturing would satisfy local demand and replace imports. ISI entailed the use of agriculture and mineral exports earnings to import capital inputs for manufacturing industries and to invest in

Table 4.1 Distribution of Capital Expenditure on Areas of Major Emphasis (All Governments) 1955–1961 and 1962–1968

	1955–61 Plan		1962–68 Plan	
Item	Expenditure (£ Million)	Percentage of plan expenditure	Expenditure (£ million)	Percentage of plan expenditure
Primary production	8.7	3.7%	91.8	13.6%
Trade and Industry	6.9	2.9%	90.3	13.4%
Education	18.8	8%	69.8	10.3%

Source: Author's calculations from the (First) National Development Plan 1962–1968 (1962).

infrastructure and welfare. Therefore, industrial public investment was 13.4% in the 1962–1968 post-independence plan compared to the 2.9% in the 1955–1961 Ten-Year colonial plan (Table 4.1). The government explicitly promoted indigenous participation in industries "outside agriculture, wholesale and retail trade and road transport."[54] The objective was to break the monopolistic domination of the import trade by foreign multinationals. The Second Development Plan after the civil war in 1970, reflected the underlying elite consensus to foster national unity with a strong role for the state in post-war reconstruction and economic management. To drive growth, the government allocated the largest portion of development funds to agriculture, industry, transportation, manpower development, defense, and public utilities.[55]

The oil boom dramatically transformed the scope and priorities of the post-war economic agenda with two notable impacts on economic planning and the productive sectors.

First, rising oil export revenues expanded the scope of state interventionism to support the ISI. The policy instruments were the establishment of state-owned enterprises (SOEs) as well as the nationalization and indigenization of commanding heights of the economy.[56] To begin with, SOEs were established to compliment the indigenous private sector and compensate for the lack of indigenous financial, technical, and managerial expertise to drive modern economic development. For instance, attempts at developing large-scale agrarian plantations involved public enterprises such as the Nigerian Agricultural Bank, direct land acquisition, and the establishment of farms, poultry, and dairy ranches by government agencies.[57] And then nationalization and indigenization policies during the oil boom accelerated domestic enterprise expansion. The Nigerian Enterprises Promotion Decrees of 1972 and 1977 sought to radically increase Nigerian participation and ownership in the economy. These laws mandated a transfer of businesses within the competence of indigenous expertise (small-scale industry, services, and retail trade) and required a minimum Nigerian interest of 40% equity in enterprises which were technologically or organizationally more complex (large-scale light manufacturing, trade and services). The government also acquired at least 55% ownership stake in the oil companies, petrochemicals, and heavy industry.[58] There was also the Nigerianization of technical and managerial positions in heavy and capital-intensive industry.[59] Nationalization and indigenization provided investment opportunities for some of Nigeria's economic elite during the oil boom. Thus, state participation in the economy took the form of both the government's business assistance programs to local firms, as well as the establishment of SOEs. The state's role in the economy was ambiguous; from 1976, the government officially proclaimed a "mixed economy" of socialist leaning in some areas while permitting individual initiative and ownership in others.[60]

A second impact of the oil boom was a steep increase in public spending, especially around social policies and industrial sectors. Partly spurred by rising economic inequalities, there was a shift towards welfare objectives of building a "just, egalitarian society," "more even distribution of income," reduction of unemployment, and rural-urban income disparities in the Third Development Plan from 1975.[61] Public expenditure targeted education, health, housing, rural electrification, irrigation systems, and other public services, and a massive wage increase for civil servants under the Udoji Scheme of 1974–1975, all with a view to fast-tracking social development. However, rising public spending was accompanied by an expansion of the public sector—as the number of public enterprises increased from about 250 in 1970 to more than 800 within a decade.[62]

Although there were efforts to correct the serious dependence of the economy on oil revenue, these were futile until the global oil shock of the 1980s. For instance, in the Fourth Development Plan, monetary and fiscal policies were directed at "reducing the over-dependence on the oil sector as a source of public revenue."[63] Nevertheless, the Nigerian economy was badly hit when global crude prices collapsed in 1983. Total exports fell from N14.2 billion in 1980 to N7.5 billion in 1983, and of this, crude oil earnings which fell from N13.6 billion in 1980 to N7.2 billion (Figure 4.6). Total federal government revenue fell from N15.2 billion in 1980 to N10.5 billion in 1983, and of this, oil revenues which constituted 81.1% also lost close to half their value, from N12.35 billion in 1980 to N7.25 billion in 1983. Consequently, the economy contracted between 1981 and 1984 (Figure 4.2). It was impossible to immediately augment declining oil receipts with non-oil revenue. To make matters worse, Nigeria slid into a debt crisis from 1978, as public debt grew from N4.6 billion in 1979 to N22.2 billion in 1983. Inflation rose by 40% in 1984, external reserves fell by more than 50% in 1982, and by 1984, could not support up to two months of imports.[64]

From January 1986, General Ibrahim Babangida's military regime embarked on SAP to reform Nigeria's economy. As such, the regime implemented what Adebayo Olukoshi describes as the most "far reaching economic program to be implemented in… the post-colonial period.[65] The SAP sought to restructure the economy from state-led ISI to market-driven to address the oil and debt crisis in the immediate term and correct the structural deficiencies of import substitution in the longer-term. To stabilize the economy in the short term, there was currency devaluation from $1.50 to the naira in 1983 to about $0.5 in 1993, lifting of price controls, reduction of public spending, and a resizing of the public sector. In the long term, SAP sought to drive the transition to a market economy by moving to a floating exchange rate, liberalizing trade, eliminating import licenses and agriculture marketing boards, privatizing and commercializing SOEs and deregulating the banking system.[66] Under SAP, the

(a) Exports decline precipitously between 1980 and 1983

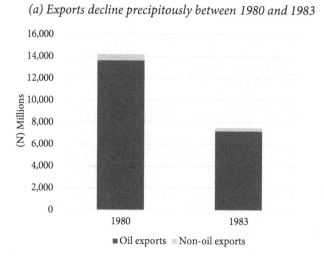

■ Oil exports   ■ Non-oil exports

*(b) Fiscal revenue declines precipitously between
1980 and 1983*

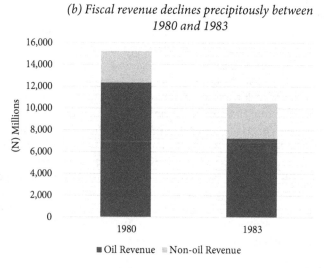

■ Oil Revenue   ■ Non-oil Revenue

Figure 4.6 Exports and Fiscal Revenues are Halved between 1980 and 1983 (N millions).

Source: Author's calculations from the Central Bank of Nigeria Database.

five-year fixed-term plans were replaced with a three-tier system consisting of a three-year rolling plan, an annual budget that draws from the plan, and a fifteen-year long-term plan.[67]

SAP mitigated some of the immediate effects of the economic crisis. Growth was restored from an average of -3.1% per annum between 1980 and 1986 to an average of 4.9% per annum between 1987 and 1992 reflecting primarily a recovery in agriculture and manufacturing.[68] Some of Nigeria's earlier anti-export bias in manufacturing disappeared under SAP as producers switched from imported to local inputs thereby strengthening some backward linkages in agro-processing and textiles manufacturing. By 1990, according to a Manufacturers Association of Nigeria (MAN) study, 78% of raw materials in the food and beverage sector were being locally sourced while, before SAP, Nigerian manufacturers imported over 75% of their raw materials. However, the assembly-based manufacturing sector, dependent on imported intermediate inputs and shielded from competition and market signals contracted. By 1993, the automobile industry which hitherto assembled over 100,000 vehicles was operating at only 10% capacity.[69] Growth was restored from -0.7% in 1986 to an average of 8.7% per annum between 1987 and 1992, followed by a contraction in 1992 and stagnation of around 2% until the early 2000s (Figure 4.3).

SAP did not, however, address Nigeria's structural economic problems and the dependence on the oil sector. On the supply side, it failed to provide the expected stimulus to the productive sectors. According to Peter Lewis, the Nigerian state was incapable of providing real inducements for productive activity, due to its weak institutional environment to elicit a significant supply response from the private sector; and a poor political environment to support productive capitalism.[70] Paul Lubeck and Michael Watts note that SAP's fiscal conservatism also depressed demand with social expenditure cuts, reduction of subsidies, wage freezes, and other austerity measures to plug budget deficits and reduce external debt.[71] According to the World Bank, the rebound in economic growth was insufficient to compensate for the drop in purchasing power from the collapse of oil prices as well as population growth of 3% per annum.[72] There are also external dimensions to the failure of SAP. The economists, Thandika Mkandawire and Charles Soludo, attribute SAP's failure to the global economic recession of the 1980s, its external imposition of policy prescriptions "unsuitable" to local conditions, and the limited agency of African governments in the entire process.[73]

Overall, weak institutions and rentier politics resulted in a weak supply-side response, austerity depressed demand, and external conditions undermined the reform program and resulted in a failed take-off of the market economy. The brief rise in oil prices in the early 1990s reinforced the sector's dominance. By 1995, crude oil accounted for 97% of exports and 70% of government revenue (Figure 4.4). Non-oil growth and productivity, which had improved slightly in the late 1980s, stagnated and, in certain sectors, declined. By 1995 manufacturing was around 5% of GDP while agriculture was over one-third. Although SAP's market reforms liberalized some opportunities for domestic accumulation, there were no productivity gains in the leading economic sectors.

Beyond SAP's failed economic outcomes, its social legitimacy was undermined by the differentiated impacts on ethno-regional groups, privileged elites, and wider society. SAP unintentionally exacerbated ethno-regional economic inequalities. The businessmen most positioned to take advantage of opportunities provided by liberalization and privatization were in the south-west. These disparities had already been widened by the indigenization policies of the 1970s as Tom Forrest documents.[74] The Yorubas, in their proximity to Lagos, Nigeria's commercial nerve center, with their head start in education and the professions were positioned to take advantage of the opportunity to join the boards of foreign companies and SOEs, and thus patronize the Lagos Stock Exchange.[75] This was in stark contrast to eastern-Igbo businessmen who, despite the early spread of Western education, had been significantly dispossessed by the civil war, or the northerners who had been educationally disadvantaged during colonial rule. Consequently, share transfers created a windfall for southern-Yoruba investors.[76] SAP reforms therefore deepened the regional economic inequalities from colonial rule that concentrated infrastructure, education, and administrative services in coastal cities like Lagos to facilitate the extraction of commodities.

A further dent in the social legitimacy of SAP was that business and the political elite appeared to gain from the government's distortionary interventions, whereas civil servants, students, professionals, and the wider society suffered hardship as a result of austerity policies. Across society, there was a perception that SAP was a repackaged version of the IMF's stabilization prescriptions, rather than a homegrown program "produced by Nigerians for Nigerians."[77] The perception of external imposition amidst socio-economic hardships alienated civil society and intelligentsia, and created an intense distrust of liberal economic policies, particularly those supported by the IMF and World Bank, which has persisted in the psyche of many Nigerians.

With the failure of SAP to rejuvenate the economy in a period of low oil prices in the 1990s, a new economic strategy was needed to address the persistent structural problems of industrialization. In November 1997, Abacha's regime unveiled an economic blueprint, the Nigeria Vision 2010. The major objectives were: to diversify the economy away from oil through industrialization, accelerate human and social development, implement institutional reform, and transition to becoming one of the world's top twenty economies by the year 2010.[78] Although Vision 2010 was the outcome of a consultative process and it outlined practical steps for Nigeria's economic transformation, its legitimacy was undermined by the authoritarianism of the Abacha regime and the resultant boycott of consultations by key sections of civil society, especially the Yoruba west.

The Vision 2010 economic blueprint was discarded in the transition to democracy as part of the elite bargain after Abacha's death in June 1998, to dissociate from any process produced by a "stolen mandate." When a new civilian administration was sworn in after 16 years of military rule on 29 May 1999, the development planning process had gone full cycle. As with the early colonial period, there was neither a clear economic agenda in place nor an explicit articulation of a national economic vision.

Institutions Inadvertently Entrench Sectarian Divisions

In the previous chapter, we defined institutions as the rules that set the parameters within which actors interact and operate in society. In the colonial period, institutions created and entrenched ethno-regional differentiations. In the military period, legal provisions were oriented toward centralization to blunt ethno-regional and religious cleavages in the polity and economy.

During colonial rule, the political institutions that emerged from successive constitutions unleashed regionalism as the basis for political mobilization and competition. Nigeria's first constitution unveiled by Sir Hugh Clifford introduced the elective principle in 1923, while its successor under Sir Arthur Richard in 1946 created regional councils as the basis for parliamentary representation at the center. This regional federalism from 1946 deepened the country's ethno-religious divisions in fundamental ways. As Abdul Raufu Mustapha highlights, colonial administrative regionalism consolidated the link between ethnic distinctiveness and administrative boundaries—Hausa and Fulani in the north, Igbo in the east, and the Yoruba in the west—while the ethnic minorities in each region were forced to accommodate themselves the best they could.[79] This regional differentiation was promoted by the British both as a "divide and rule" tactic to advance imperial interests, as they did in India between Hindus and Muslims,[80] but also for pragmatic administrative reasons of rallying the hundreds of ethnic groups into more compact identities.

Provisions of a new constitution in 1951 under the Governor John Stuart MacPherson allowed for the emergence of political parties and further entrenched ethno-regional political mobilization. As a result, cultural associations in each of the three regions transmuted into political parties, becoming the nucleus of political activity. The *Egbe Omo Oduduwa* in the western region and the *Jammiyar Mutanen Arewa* in the northern region became the ruling parties, AG and the NPC respectively, while the NCNC contained elements of the Igbo Union in the east. This tripodal-regional structure further undermined the development of a unified national consciousness by determining that access to power at the national level was to be derived from holding power at the regional level.[81]

Nigeria's constitutions in the early post-independence years held up the inherently unstable regional balance of power. As Richard Sklar rightly notes, the federal government of the First Republic (1960–1966) was erected upon a foundation of domineering regional power.[82] The 1960 independence constitution and the 1962 federal constitution embodied the underlying elite bargain from the constitutional conferences in Lagos and London, in which regional elites agreed to independence on the basis of relative autonomy. Some important provisions skewed the balance of political power and economic resources in favor of the north. These included a regional quota system in the army and the civil service, a form of affirmative action to ensure fair representation of educationally "backward" regions, especially the north. In addition, the region's large landmass and population gave it more representatives in the federal legislature: 174 members more than the east (73), west (62), and Lagos (3) combined.[83] These highly contested provisions were accepted, partly in acknowledgement of the need for equity, but mainly because the north negotiated hard using its numerical strength and its initial refusal, with British cooperation, to accept the motion for independence proposed by southern parliamentarians during the constitutional conferences. The eagerness to attain independence foreclosed a sobering assessment of the implications after. As Billy J. Dudley describes, "so overwhelming was the imagery of 'the platter of gold' that principles were freely conceded before the seemingly pragmatic consideration that independence was worth any price."[84]

The friction among the three regions over the asymmetry of power in the federal constitution spiraled into political crisis. The contested areas included resource allocation and population numbers especially after a shambolic census in 1963 failed to alter the regional balance of power.[85] In elections in 1964, a coalition between the eastern NCNC and the western AG, the United Progressive Grand Alliance (UPGA), lost the election to the Nigerian National Alliance (NNA) a coalition of the northern NPC and a breakaway faction of the AG. Having failed to achieve a rebalancing of population numbers through the 1963 census, the president, Nnamdi Azikiwe and leader of the NCNC, refused to accede to the request of Prime Minister Sir Abubakar Tafawa Balewa of the NNA to be reappointed as the head of government. This created a brief but severe constitutional crisis, which revealed the deep cracks in the body politic of the First Republic. The violent coup of January 1966 indicated a total collapse of the independence political settlement with the suspension of the constitution and the descent into civil war by 1967.

The aftermath of the 1966 coups and the civil war undermined the role of the constitution as the final arbiter of political power in favor of more informal elite bargains. Military rulers were not beholden to the constitution since they ruled by decrees and edicts. A military government's power is typically de facto, derived from their appropriation of political authority structures and instruments of violence, rather than formal or *de jure* constitutional rules. Therefore at any time, they could suspend the constitution, eliminate checks and balances from the legislature, and generally remain unaccountable. In Nigeria, the Supreme Military Council (SMC) and later the Armed Forces Ruling Council (AFRC) from 1986, comprising military officers and some civilian politicians and bureaucrats, was the final decision-making authority. This symbiosis of the military rulers with civilian technocrats in the policy process further helped to remove checks and balances and reinforced the centralization of administrative power that began with Ironsi's Unification Decree in 1966. Decisions with far-reaching implications were made by the SMC/AFRC without any institutional oversight since the constitution was no longer the main reference point.

Within this constitutional vacuum, the military's approach to managing Nigeria's deep ethno-regional divisions was to centralize government institutions. This centralization began with a Unification Decree 34 passed by General Aguiyi-Ironsi in May 24 1966 in an attempt, albeit disastrous, to abolish regional federalism as the institutional backbone of the contending ethnic forces obstructing national identity, according to political scientist Abdul Raufu Mustapha.[86] Although in August 1966, Yakubu Gowon repealed the Unification Decree, specific aspects of the post-war reconstruction initiatives outlined in a Nine-Point Transition Program in 1970 to blunt regional rivalries strengthened the central government. These include the creation of twelve states out of the four regions, implementation of a national economic plan for the war damaged economy, and revisions of the revenue allocation formula that weakened the fiscal power of the regions. The major revenue allocation revisions include, Decree No. 13 (1970) which allocated the bulk of revenue to the federal government, Decree No. 9 (1971) which allocated all offshore rents and royalties to the federal government, Decree No. 6 (1975) requiring all revenues to be shared by the states through a distributable pool account, with the exception of 20% onshore mining rents as derivation for mineral producing states,[87] and the Land Use Decree of 1978 transferred control of land and mineral rights away from local communities to the federal government. This centralization set the federal government on a future collision course with the oil-producing Niger Delta.

To their credit, military rulers tried to mitigate Nigeria's visceral ethno-regional competition that degenerated to a civil war the best they could, but within a constitutional vacuum they also became factionalized and corrupted. Gowon's Nine-Point Program to reconcile, reconstruct, and rehabilitate after the civil war remade the country in fundamental ways. A Federal Character principle expanded the previous "quota" system to ensure that the civil service, the armed forces, and other public institutions reflect Nigeria's linguistic, ethnic, religious, and geographic diversity.[88] The multiparty system sought to encourage consensus and political parties with a national as opposed to ethnic or regional character. A new constitution in 1979 provided for an American presidential system with a three-tiered federal structure to eliminate the regional animosities of the parliamentary-style First Republic. Within the framework of this new constitution, Nigeria transitioned to a short-lived Second democratic Republic headed by the civilian president Shehu Shagari. By 1983, a deterioration of governance and an economic crisis was the final push that the military, too used to plotting coups, needed to overthrow Shagari's government.[89] In fact, the idea of a permanent "diarchy," a joint civilian and military government, was floated at some point as a way of disincentivizing coups.[90]

Another serious attempt at constitutional reform was made a decade later. The Babangida regime supervised public consultations to provide the institutional framework for a botched democratic transition to a Third Republic in 1993. Abacha's regime organized the 1994–1995 national constitutional conference towards a transition in 1998. Insights from one of the participants, the former vice president Alex Ekwueme are instructive:

> Before Abacha's death, 'The Constitution of the Federal Republic of Nigeria 1995' had been finalised [at the 1994-1995 National Constitutional Conference] and was to... come into effect on October 1, 1998. This constitution introduced some fundamental changes to Nigeria's previous presidential constitutions (1979 and 1989) based on experience garnered over almost four decades of Nigeria's independence, all calculated to conduce to a stable Nigerian polity within which all Nigerians could truly feel a sense of belonging...

These fundamental changes in the draft 1995 constitution aimed to squarely address the perennial regional rivalries and fears of domination that undermined Nigeria's national cohesion. The provisions aimed to diffuse federal executive power, rotate principal executive offices across the country, reduce "winner takes all" through proportional representation in the federal and state cabinets, and eliminate the abuse of incumbency in the electoral process with a single one-year term.[91] For instance, to diffuse federal executive power, six principal offices were proposed: the office of the president, vice president, prime minister, deputy prime minister, President of the Senate, and Speaker of the House of Representatives. On power rotation, the constitution grouped the thirty-six states within six geopolitical zones and proposed three senatorial districts in each state, with provisions that office of President and

Governor would rotate among the six geopolitical regions and the three senatorial districts in each state respectively. This principle of rotation would be implemented over a 30-year period during which it was expected that at the national level each of the six geopolitical zones would have filled the six principal offices for a term of five years each. Ekwueme adds that "Thereafter, the cry of 'marginalization' would have been a thing of the past. The 30-year period would have been used to... promote state level and national integration at all levels, following which all positions could then be filled on... merit and competence in the true democratic spirit."

Proportional representation in cabinet positions was meant to dilute the potency of the "winner takes all" in political competition. Therefore, the provision in the draft constitution was for an all-party government with ministers drawn from all political parties with at least 10% of the seats or the total votes cast at the national legislative election. The recurring controversy as to which geopolitical region should present the next president would have been narrowed down to manageable proportions, according to Ekwueme.

Unfortunately, the constitutional framework that Nigeria's political elites finally settled for in the democratic transition in 1999 was an amended version of the 1979 constitution rather than the one proposed under the Abacha administration. As Ekwueme opines:

> [With] Abacha's untimely death in June 1998, 'the Constitution of the Federal Republic of Nigeria 1995' was never promulgated... Nigeria therefore lost the benefit of some of its well-thought out provisions which were intended to promote justice, equity, and national unity in the process of transforming... from a country of many ethnic nationalities into a modern nation-state within a 'transition period' of 30 years.

Thus, the military elite consensus on democratization settled for a modified version of the 1979 constitution while jettisoning the draft 1995 constitution which had explicit provisions to address the ethno-regional and religious forces that have obstructed cohesion.

Institutional Centralization to Stabilize Politics and the Economy

Over the course of a century Nigeria's economy transitioned to dependence on oil exports. Its institutional arrangements became more centralized to stabilize a country riven by ethno-regional and religious competition. Both oil dependence and institutional centralization were shaped by policy choices of ruling elites within this unstable balance of power. In turn, the economic underperformance and institutional centralization further destabilized the balance of power by aggravating elite competition and sectarian divisions. Some aspects of the institutional configuration survived the recurrent turbulence with some modifications, for example maintaining active state participation in the economy despite the attempt to transition to a market economy in the 1980s. In other cases, these institutions collapsed and were replaced, for example replacing the British-style parliamentary system with an American-style federalism in 1970 after the civil war. What were the conditions that catalyzed institutional persistence and change? What kinds of constraints did these conditions impose on decision makers? What were the policy responses of decision makers to these constraints? Using the framework outlined in Chapter 3, let us identify the critical junctures at which certain conditions constrained decision makers to adopt specific policy reforms. These constraints occurred at horizontal, vertical, and external levels:

- The struggle for survival in the immediate post-independence period: 1960.
- Post-war reconstruction of Yakubu Gowon's military regime: 1970.
- The failed reforms of Ibrahim Babangida's military regime: 1986.
- Abdulsalam Abubakar's transition regime: 1998.

The Struggle for Post-Independence Survival: 1960

At independence in 1960, Nigeria was at a critical juncture where external and horizontal constraints resulted in major political and economic policy responses. Externally, a collective disdain for colonial rule and the necessity of economic self-sufficiency propelled Nigeria's ruling elites to ensure the new nation-state survived despite their conspicuous ethnic, religious, and regional differences. Horizontally, the three regions now acutely aware of their relative weaknesses were spurred to economic buoyancy to survive the intense political competition that ensued.

These existential threats to the country's survival, and to the individual regions constrained ruling elites towards inclusive and pro-growth policy responses. To consolidate national unity, the NPC/NCNC coalition government established a quota system to ensure the most educationally disadvantaged region was not marginalized in the public service and the armed forces. To attain economic self-sufficiency, the First National Development Plan articulated the country's economic aspirations, ISI orientation and focused on using public investments to reduce foreign dependence, build an industrial economy and improve human development. Concurrently, regional development plans outlined each region's aspirations and economic and social development strategies in relation to their resource endowments. Politically, the 1962 constitution balanced power between the national and regional governments.

These policy responses to the existential impulse of post-colonial survival were insufficient to blunt the fierce sectarian rivalries. Therefore, invidious competition among the regions for national power in parliamentary representation, public service employment and, for the advantages of population numbers, strained the nation-building process. The post-independence political settlement increasingly became incapable of managing competing horizontal–elite interests. These tensions generated severe crises which erupted in the succession of violent coups of 1966, the collapse of the First Republic and eventually the civil war from 1967 to 1970.

The Post-war Reconstruction: 1970

General Yakubu Gowon's regime was constrained by regional elite competition which prompted extraordinary efforts at nation-building for the country's survival. The regime presided over a divided country on the brink of collapse, and a citizenry traumatized by the violent coups of 1966 and the 1967–1970 civil war. Consequently, in October 1970, the regime unveiled the elaborate Nine-Point transition program for restoring national unity under the banner of "Rehabilitation, Reconstruction and Reconciliation." This process of promoting national cohesion was engineered by a military regime under which the constitution, the legislature, political parties and other *dejure* formal political institutions were proscribed while defacto informal institutions prevailed. On the economic front, military rulers restored national planning to place the country back on a track of economic self-sufficiency through industrialization. The Second and Third National Development Plans between 1970 and 1979 provided the framework for public investments and social spending. From 1973 onwards, an oil boom aided this post-war reconstruction, giving the regime the resources to implement its ambitious development plans.

The key decisions taken in this period would strongly influence long-term institution-building in at least three ways. First, the process of state creation became a convenient mechanism for addressing economic redistribution demands by ethnic, regional, and religious groups. All subsequent military regimes, except Buhari's, created new states to placate recurrent advocacies for political inclusion. Second, the centralization of allocative and decision-making power in the federal government strengthened it politically and economically at the expense of the subnational units. Economic institutions also reflected this centralization as the state became a major player in the economy and took new responsibilities for economic management through import substitution, nationalization, and the establishment of SOEs in major industries. Third, the oil boom had what Terry-Lynn Karl describes as a structuring effect on emerging institutions by "petrolizing" the policy environment.[92] Karl argues that when oil booms coincide with the initial stages of state building, public spending becomes the primary mechanism of "stateness" as money is substituted for authority. Such choices persist over time and make building administrative authority more difficult.[93] At this critical juncture of post-war institution-building to blunt ethno-regional divisions, oil revenues which financed the expansion of the public sector, and the concentration of power in the federal government only exacerbated the situation.

A Failure of Market Reforms: 1986

General Ibrahim Babangida's regime came to power in December 1985 amidst a spiraling economic crisis caused by the external collapse of global oil prices which revealed the structural defects of the ISI. The regime also met horizontal–elite and vertical–societal tensions incubated in the predecessor Buhari regime's delay in outlining a democratic transition timetable, its draconian war on corruption, and its crackdown on the political elite and civil society. The policy response by the Babangida regime to this economic crisis was the SAP market reforms. SAP, as described by Paul Lubeck and Michael

Watts, was an alliance of international, state, and private capital to institutionalize conditions to enable Nigeria "grow" its way out of economic crisis.[94] The regime's policy response to the political crisis was an elaborate democratic transition program with a new constitution, a two-party system, and further creation of eleven states.

Although SAP failed to generate a supply-side response from the productive sector, it left a lasting mark on Nigeria's economy. Privatization, economic liberalization, and other market reforms brought new players into the economy in shipping, oil services, financial, and other service sectors, which laid the groundwork for private-sector activity in the post-military period from 1999. For instance, Tom Forrest notes that a strong advance in the banking sector, unparalleled in other sub-Saharan African countries was evident from the 1980s, encouraged by high profits, more relaxed conditions for entry, and the prospect of access to foreign exchange.[95] However, the labor-intensive sectors of agriculture, agro-processing, and manufacturing on which most of the northern states relied, all stagnated. Therefore, economic liberalization further eroded the economic power of the northern states in Nigeria.

Transitioning to Electoral Democracy: 1998

General Abdulsalam Abubakar became head of state in a caretaker military regime at a critical juncture immediately after General Abacha's mysterious death in June 1998. Abubakar's regime was constrained by horizontal–elite and vertical–societal pressures from the fallout of the annulment of the 1993 elections and Abacha's violent repression of political opposition in his quest to become a civilian president, all of which risked erupting into social unrest. Abacha's economic mismanagement, corruption, and odious debts within a climate of consistently low global oil prices stymied growth and left the country economically vulnerable. Extensive human rights violations, such as the hasty trial and execution in 1994 of the environmental activist, Ken Saro-Wiwa, left the regime internationally isolated.

Abacha's death thus was an opportunity to chart a new course towards democratization. At least four key elements defined the post-military political settlement from 1999. First, the regime outlined the transition timetable accompanied by a constitution for the new democratic order but without a coherent economic strategy. The Vision 2010 economic blueprint drafted by the Abacha regime was not carried along. Second, because Abubakar's caretaker role was a consensus within the largely military political elite, a distrustful civil society largely boycotted the transition process. This boycott further consolidated the unchecked political dominance of politicians of both military and civilian backgrounds after democratization. Third, the transition constitution was a revised version of the 1979 constitution rather than the draft produced under the 1994–1995 constitutional conference which was more equipped to address Nigeria's ethno-regional and religious competition. Fourth, the democratization elite consensus enabled the emergence of a Christian president from the Yoruba-west to heal the wounds of the annulled 1993 presidential elections. This shift of presidential power to the south was on the understanding that power would shift to the north after four years. It was based on this emergent political settlement that Nigeria democratized in 1999.

The Transition to Becoming Africa's Largest Economy

The month of May in Nigeria is typically one of the hottest. For participants of the World Economic Forum (WEF) on Africa between May, 7 and 9 2014, they barely felt the stuffy heat in Abuja, Nigeria's administrative capital, as they navigated the air-conditioned conference halls in the prestigious Transcorp Hilton and Sheraton hotels. The mood among these participants—which included presidents, investment bankers, finance ministers, and journalists in global media corporations—was upbeat. It was, after all, the zenith of the "Africa Rising" zeitgeist in global circles. And Nigeria was basking in this newfound global optimism towards African economies. Just a month prior, in April 2014, revised national accounts had recalculated the size of the Nigerian economy, as Africa's and the world's 26th largest following a decade of strong growth. Hosting the WEF Africa summit in Abuja was no small feat. The gathering for the world's most exclusive policy discussion was a stamp of recognition of Nigeria's economic clout and renewed global status. WEF Africa summits are usually hosted in Cape Town South Africa, although Tanzania, Ethiopia, and Rwanda had taken a shot at it.

The opening question during one of the highlights of WEF Africa, the "Africa Rising" panel, departed from the upbeat tone. Adrian Finnigan, an anchor of Aljazeera News who was moderating the panel, posed the question to Ngozi Okonjo-Iweala the then Nigerian Minister of Finance and Coordinating Minister of the Economy on what the government was doing about the violent insurgents, Boko Haram. Just three weeks prior in Chibok in the north-east, the group had kidnapped 276 schoolgirls. Following that question was an extensive discussion on how these security challenges and other political risks could scare away investors and put the brakes on Nigeria' decade-long economic growth.

Okonjo-Iweala's irritation at the question was barely concealed. More than anyone, her deep global connections as a former managing director in the number two position at the World Bank was instrumental in bringing the WEF Africa to Nigeria. From her perspective, therefore, the line of questioning on the insurgency fit a broader trend in which international media sensationalized problems in Africa and deliberately understated the continent's achievements. And Africa's good economic performance was the result of deliberate policies implemented by decision makers who got little credit globally. At some point, the Minister remarked that given the globalization of terrorist violence beyond Nigeria from Boston to London and Nairobi, "investors are looking at more fundamental issues than we might think." She was keen to steer the conversation back to the opportunities, the potential, and indeed the challenges, of Africa Rising.

Like a shadow, the violent Boko Haram insurgency raging in Nigeria's northeast loomed over the entire WEF Africa, tempering the air of optimism. In a sense, the violent insurgency is a microcosm of the socio-political factors that trail Africa's growth episode of the twenty-first century. Described as "jobless growth," this strong economic performance has not been accompanied by the rising productivity and non-farm jobs that characterized East Asia's growth episodes of the 1980s and 1990s. What economists refer to as "structural transformation" during periods of rapid growth in which labor moves from small-scale and rural agriculture to factory jobs in urban centers is happening differently in Ghana, Kenya, Nigeria, and many other parts of Africa. People are moving from rural areas to cities not to factory jobs but to petty trade and other informal activities. The peaceful resolution of conflicts of the 1990s in Angola, Cote d'Ivoire, Liberia, Sierra Leone, Sudan, the Congos, etc., enabled this economic performance. School enrollments have increased, infant and maternal mortality have declined, and life expectancy is also on an upward trend.

By late 2014, however, the socio-political dimensions of this jobless growth including youth unemployment, persistence of poverty, and more evident inequalities, could no longer be ignored. Multinational beverage companies such as Diaego and Nestlé that invested in Africa from 2010 to tap into the growing market for consumer goods scaled back their operations when they struggled to make profit. Apparently the purchasing power of Africa's rising middle class, as the African Development Bank projected in 2011, was vastly overestimated and the commodity price collapse in 2015 pushed some of this demographic teetering on the brink of precarity back into economic vulnerability.[1]

Nigerian citizens were using various platforms to express their frustrations around distributional concerns, economic exclusion, and political marginalization. Even before the WEF Africa, local newspapers devoted column inches to questioning whether Nigeria was indeed Africa's largest economy given the rising incidence of poverty and unemployment. Many ordinary Nigerians questioned why they were not feeling this "growth" in their pockets.[2] Two years earlier, the government's decision to remove petroleum subsidies had been hastily overturned because tens of thousands of Nigerians had poured out on the streets to protest the decision. While the economic logic for removing the inefficient subsidies was sound, the social implications were felt by the millions of Nigerians who had come to rely on these subsidies as the only "benefit" they got from the state in the absence of elaborate social protection systems. Then there were those who employed more violent means to register their discontent with economic exclusion as in the armed groups of the oil-rich Niger Delta, fought their neighbors in competition for scarce natural resources as in the herdsmen–farmer conflicts in Nigeria's north central states and were disillusioned with democratic governance as in the foot soldiers recruited by Boko Haram.

The events surrounding WEF Africa captured the strengths and underlying socio-political challenges of Nigeria's economic performance. The strong decade-long economic growth, albeit without industrial transformation, defied the predictions of slow growth by scholars who held up Nigeria as the poster child of the "resource curse." The decision making that enabled this strong economic performance also showed that the policy environment was more dynamic than the sweeping expectations of persistent dysfunction in a so-called neopatrimonial state. However, the Bring Back Our Girls protests of the government's tepid response to the violent Boko Haram insurgency were part of a wider current of growing disaffection to the policy environment. As Okonjo-Iweala also admitted on the WEF panel, "the growth that we have... the quality of the growth is not good enough because we are rising with inequality... and without creating jobs... and we're rising without a basic social protection system for our poor people... " In turn, protests, both peaceful and violent, ethno-regional alliances, party politics, the new democratic institutions, and external shocks, all shaped the calculus of Nigeria's decision-makers and the kinds of policies they formulated and implemented.

In this chapter therefore, we examine the economic and political foundations of Nigeria's transition since the turn of the century to becoming Africa's largest economy. Within this time, the challenge of economic diversification of exports and fiscal revenue persisted, even as the economy's composition changed beyond the oil sector. I argue that policy choices made at democratization from 1999 within Nigeria's power configuration in which a collective resolve was made to prevent a political collapse shaped the economy's performance. In this power configuration, an elite consensus on power-sharing stabilized political competition allowing for a reform-orientation in policymaking focused on macroeconomic stabilization, rather than facilitating structural transformation to diversify Nigeria's economy. This elite consensus unraveled as new individual, group, and organizational actors emerged from the democratic process and a growing economy. The first section of the chapter examines Nigeria's recent economic transition in the twenty-first century to become Africa's largest economy. The second section discusses Nigeria's balance of power in this period, characterized by an elite power-sharing agreement and the emergence of new political actors from political liberalization.

Nigeria's Economic Transition beyond Oil and without Industrialization

In the twenty-first century, Nigeria broke the cycle of economic stagnation until growth crashed in 2016. Between 2000 and 2010, growth averaged 7.7% per annum and 5% between 2011 and 2015 (Figure 5.1). This economic growth offset years of economic stagnation averaging 0.7% between 1980 and 1999 below annual population growth of 2.5%. In April 2014, Nigeria became Africa's largest economy, and the twenty-sixth largest in the world with a GDP of N81 trillion or $521.8 billion (at 2014 market exchange rates) after a "rebasing" exercise. Basically, Nigeria upgraded the base year of its national account series used to calculate the GDP, from 1990 to a more recent price structure of 2010. However, the economy contracted in 2016, and has since struggled to crawl out of recession. In 2020, Nigeria's GDP was $432 billion much less than its 2014 volume, but still ranked as the twenty-fifth-largest economy in the world according to the World Bank.[3] The economy has taken a further hit from the shock of the COVID-19 pandemic.

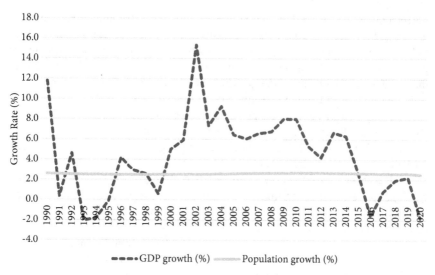

Figure 5.1 GDP Growth Finally Overtakes Population Growth in the 2000s (annual %).

Source: Author's calculations from the World Bank's World Development Indicators.

There are two features of this economic performance that are crucial to the challenge of economic diversification in Nigeria that is this book's concern. The first feature is that non-oil sectors have been the growth drivers in the twenty-first century. Secondly, the oil sector is no longer the major contributor to GDP in terms of value addition and employment, although it is the main source of exports and fiscal revenues.

The Non-oil Drivers of Economic Growth

Nigeria's economic growth in the twenty-first century has been driven by non-oil sectors. In the ten-year period from 1999 to 2009, the fastest growing sectors of at least 10% were non-oil. These include services (12%), especially telecommunications whose average was 122%, trade (11%) and agriculture (10%), as Figure 5.2a shows. Within this period, the oil and gas sector's average growth rate was 1%. Non-oil sectors were also the largest contributors to growth, while the oil sector, which alternated between sharp growth and contraction, was the fourth-largest contributor to growth (8%), as Figure 5.2b shows. From 2000 to 2009, agriculture accounted for an average of 40% of GDP growth, followed by services (22%), trade (22%) and the oil sector (8%).

These changes in the growth drivers became more evident in 2014 after Nigeria upgraded the base year for its GDP in national accounting, from 1990 to 2010. Between 2011 and 2019, the sectors with the highest growth rates were manufacturing (7%), solid minerals (7%) and construction (6%), as Figure 5.2a shows. However, oil contracted by an average of 3%, despite high global oil prices of around $100 per barrel. However, the non-oil economy is still vulnerable to oil price swings. For instance, the collapse of global oil prices (from a peak of $111.63 in 2012 to $43.64

(a) Average growth rates (%) by sector, 1999–2019

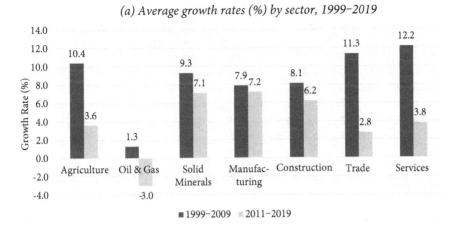

■ 1999–2009   ▪ 2011–2019

(b) Contribution to aggregate economic growth (%) by sector, 1999–2019

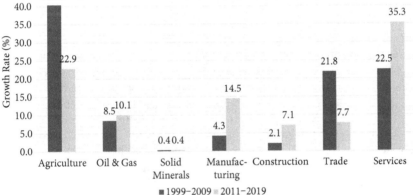

■ 1999–2009   ▪ 2011–2019

Figure 5.2 Non-oil Sectors Drive Nigeria's GDP Growth between 1999 and 2019, Adjusted in 1990 and 2010 Prices.

Source: Author's calculations from the Central Bank of Nigeria database.
Note: Data from the pre-revision figures is used for 1999 to 2009, while the revised figures cover 2010 to 2019. Rebasing makes direct comparisons with pre-rebasing figures difficult since they measure economic data differently (NBS, 2014a).

in 2016) and reduction in Nigeria's oil output (from a peak of 2.44 million bbl/d in 2005 to 1.46 million bbl/d in 2016) slowed economic growth, reduced international reserves, and disrupted private-sector activity.[4] Although growth rebounded in 2018 (1.9%) and 2019 (2.3%), the economy contracted in 2020 (-1.8%) from the sharp fall in international oil prices, reduced demand for Nigeria's oil and disruptions to non-oil activity from the COVID-19 pandemic. The shifts in the drivers of economic growth are even more evident when the contributions of individual sectors are assessed. As Figure 5.2b below shows, the largest contributors to growth on average post-rebasing, between 2011 and 2019, were services (35%), manufacturing (14%), and agriculture (23%). Oil as a share of growth was 10%.

From this data, there is an evident shift from the traditional centers of growth, from agriculture and oil to a range of services, although manufacturing witnessed a recent surge of growth, especially in the food and beverage sub-sector rather than intermediate or heavy industries.[5] This is not a shift towards industrial growth, but towards services. Specifically, the oil sector's growth rate and share of GDP have precipitously declined despite high oil prices between 2003 and 2014. The oil sector contracted by 4.6% between 2011 and 2017 compared with growth of 6.8% for the non-oil economy. This changing growth drivers has important implications for policy and the broader processes of economic transformation, as we discuss in the next section.

The Changing Composition of the Nigerian Economy beyond Oil

In the last two decades, there have been structural shifts in the composition of the Nigerian economy beyond oil but without industrialization. Oil is not the major contributor to GDP in terms of value addition and employment, although the sector is the main source of foreign exchange and government revenues. A more diversified economic activity on the one hand does not translate into more diversified exports and revenue sources on the other due to low levels of productivity growth since the 1980s. Let us examine each of these: the sectors' value addition and employment share of GDP, composition of exports and government revenues, and productivity.

The composition of GDP is diversified beyond oil in terms of value addition and employment. Given that Nigeria rebased its national accounting statistics in 2014, a useful way to read the data is to divide it into three phases: the immediate post-military economic data in 2000, the pre-rebasing data in 2009 and post-rebasing data from 2010. In 2000, three activity sectors, oil, agriculture, and trade accounted for over 85% of GDP (Figure 5.3a), at 49, 27, and 9% respectively. By 2009, there were evident changes. The share of the oil sector declined to 30%, agriculture (37%), trade (16%) and services (12%) had all increased, while manufacturing (2%), construction (1%), and solid minerals (0.2%) had stagnated. Although oil, agriculture, and trade still accounted for over 80% of economic activity in 2009, their share of GDP was changing.

The rebased GDP figures covering 2010 onwards captured more of this changing economic structure. Between the first post-rebasing year in 2010 and 2019 (Figure 5.3b), the oil sector's contribution to the economy declined from 15 to 9%, and agriculture, from 24 to 22%. The sectors that expanded by 2019 include manufacturing (12%(, building and construction (6%), trade (16%) and services (35%). The number of economic activities accounting for over 70% of GDP increased to six, including agriculture (22%), oil (9%), trade (16%), information and Telecoms (8%), manufacturing (12%), and real estate (6%). Overall by 2019, the oil and gas sector declined to 9% of GDP from 49% in 2000. Services, including trade, accounted for 51% of GDP.

With regard to national employment, most Nigerians are engaged in small-scale economic activities in the informal economy. According to a government survey, 59.6 million Nigerians—76% of the labor force—are employed in micro-, small- and medium-scale enterprises (MSMEs) (Figure 5.4a). These are enterprises with a capital

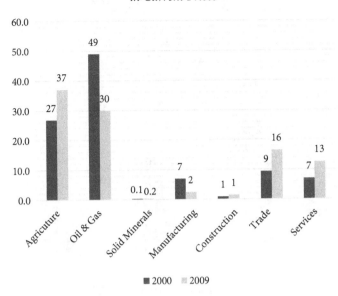

(a) Sectoral Contribution (%) to 2000 and 2009 GDP in Current Prices

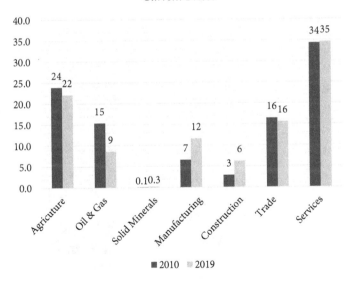

(b) Sectoral Contribution (%) to 2010 and 2019 GDP in Current Prices

Figure 5.3 The Composition of Nigeria's GDP is Diversified beyond the Oil Sector.

Source: Author's calculations from NBS data.

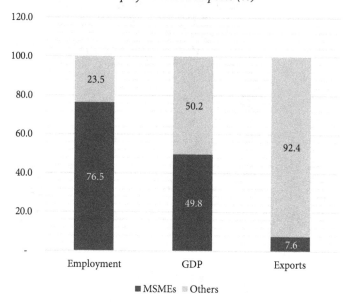

(a) Contribution of MSMEs to National Output, Employment and Exports (%)

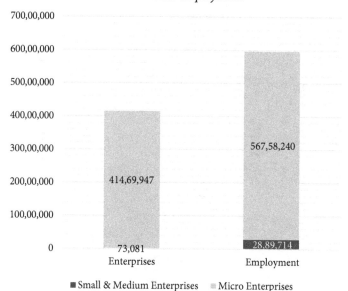

(b) Microenterprises are more in number and generate the most employment

Figure 5.4 MSMEs Contribution to Output, Exports, and Employment in 2017.

Source: Author's calculations from SMEDAN & NBS (2017).

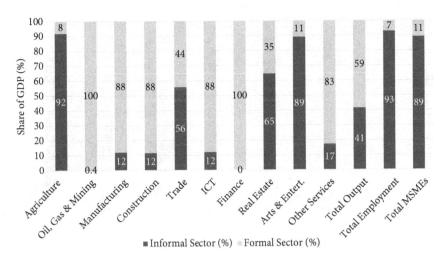

Figure 5.5 The Formal and Informal Sectors (%) in Nigeria's GDP (Output and Employment).

Source: Author's calculations from NBS (2016), SMEDAN & NBS (2017) and ILO (2018) data.

base of less than N10 million ($27,778 at 2017 exchange rates) in the case of micro enterprises, less than N100 million ($277,778) for small enterprises and N1 billion ($2.8 million) for medium-scale enterprises which collectively employ fewer than 200 people. More than 60% of these MSMEs are in trade (42%) and agriculture (21%). Millions of Nigerians are also engaged in other services (13%), manufacturing (9%) and accommodation & food services (6%). Crucially, nearly eight in ten of these MSMEs operate in the informal economy (Figure 5.5). Informal activities constitute nearly half or 41% of Nigeria's GDP (Figure 5.5) and employ 93% of the labor force according to the International Labor Organization (ILO). This informality is more pronounced in agriculture (91.8%), arts & entertainment (89.1%), real estate (64.7%), and trade (55.7%). Thus, micro enterprises in which fewer than ten people are employed, with a capital base of $27,778, account for 73% of total employment in Nigeria (5.4b). This includes enterprises such as kiosks, food sellers, petty traders, and others.

Overall, there is some evident economic diversification, partly attributable to Nigeria's revisions of the GDP base year, which now capture forty-six economic sectors rather than thirty-three in the old series.[6] However, the decline of Nigeria's oil sector is indicative of a growing non-oil economy markedly different from other large African oil producers. Even though Nigeria is Africa's largest oil producer (Figure 5.6), it is the only major oil exporter whose hydrocarbons industry contributes less than 10% of GDP.

Nigeria's exports earnings and revenue composition, however, are still heavily concentrated around its oil industry. In 2019, the oil sector constituted 84% of export earnings, barely declining from 99% in 2000 (Figure 5.7a). Concurrently, government

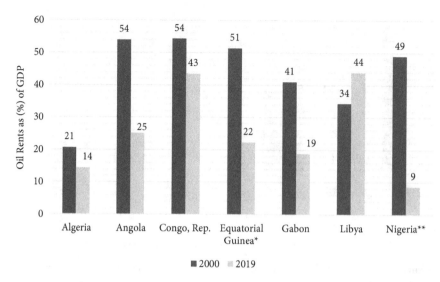

Figure 5.6 Oil Rents as a Percentage of GDP in Africa's Top Producers, 2000 and 2019.

Source: Author's calculations from the WDI database and NBS (2020) data. Note: This figure includes only veteran oil-rich countries which were exporting oil by the year 2000. It excludes Cameroon (due to the small scale of production) and DRC (due to the abundance of other minerals and metals).
* Equatorial Guinea's 2000 figures are from the year 1999.
** Nigeria's figures are from NBS data for consistency. Calculations using the NBS data result in figures close to the WDI ± a few percentage points explained by differences in exchange rates, nominal or constant values, and base year used (e.g., 1990 or 2010).

revenue composition is changing slowly. This indicates a weak translation of the increasingly diversified economic activities driving GDP growth into international trade. The share of non-oil revenue increased from less than 20% in 2000 to 46% in 2019. Several factors account for this decline in oil receipts including the disruption of oil production in the Niger Delta as well as low global oil prices, and more recently, OPEC production cuts. Non-oil revenues also grew in absolute terms due to improvements in tax collection indicating some diversification towards non-oil sources of fiscal revenue. Although a closer assessment reveals that tax revenues are just 6% of GDP in 2017, much lower than the Africa average of 19%, and according to the IMF, one of the lowest in the world.[7]

The dependence of government revenue on oil earnings is more acute at the subnational tier of government. For Nigeria's thirty-six states, the monthly disbursal of oil revenue—in which the federal government is allocated 52.7% and the state governments' share 47.3% with local governments—is the primary source of fiscal finance. The diversification of state government revenue measured by the extent to which the states generate their revenue from domestic sources or Internally Generated Revenue (IGR), has been similarly dismal (Figure 5.8). Except for Lagos, and more recently Ogun, every state has depended on federal revenue transfers for more than 50% of its annual budget since the late 1970s. Even regional economic hubs

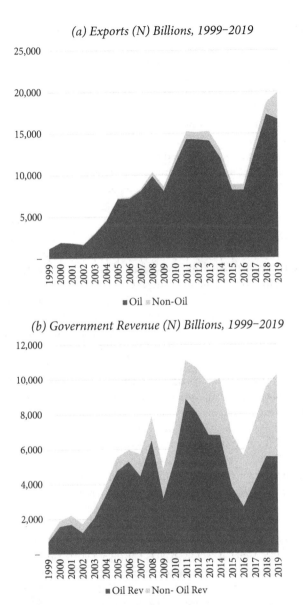

Figure 5.7 Nigeria's Exports and Government Revenues are Heavily Dependent on the Oil Sector.

Source: Author's calculations from CBN statistics database.

like Anambra, Kano and Rivers generate less than 50% of their budgetary revenues from non-oil sources. There is also significant variation in the states' dependence on these federal disbursements, especially between regional economic hubs and the smaller states. While Lagos State generated 76% of its revenue from internal sources in 2018, states like Bayelsa, Borno, and Niger generated the equivalent of 8, 9 and 15% respectively (Figure 5.8).

With oil accounting for up to 50–90% of government revenues at both national and subnational levels, Nigeria remains a rentier state. A rentier state is defined by Hazem Beblawi as one in which more than 40% of fiscal revenue is derived from external rents, and in which the government is the main recipient.[8] However, it does not have a rentier economy in which oil earnings constitute 60–80% of GDP because, in Nigeria's case, oil is just 9% of GDP. While the economic structure is increasingly diversifying towards a service-oriented economy which depends to a large extent on what the IMF describes as "the recycling of petrodollars,"[9] exports and government finances are dominated by oil rents. This discrepancy may have to do with low levels of productivity in Nigeria.

In Nigeria, labor productivity, or output per worker, has only now begun to recover from a three-decade decline. From a peak of 0.271 in 1978 relative to the U.S., and much higher than the East Asian Tigers as well as the sub-Saharan Africa average, labor productivity plummeted by more than 76% to 0.065 in 1986. Productivity steadily declined throughout the 1990s during which the Asian countries and several other African countries (including Angola, Botswana, Mauritania, Mauritius, and Sudan) surpassed Nigeria, reaching 0.015 in 1998, the nadir of its post-independence economic history (Figure 5.9a). It began to pick up in the 2000s, and at a faster rate from 2005 at 0.105, reaching 0.155 in 2014, now higher than the African average. Yet, output per worker is still below the 1970s levels. Very importantly in this six-decade period, output per worker was largely explained by factor accumulation, rather than total factor productivity at least until the 2000s (Figure 5.9b). In other words, when a small farm increased its output, this came about not by improved farming techniques or the adoption of new technologies such as tractors, but by either increasing the size of the cultivated land or employing more workers, especially family members. As former Central Bank Governor Lamido Sanusi explained to me, the recent expansion of the agriculture sector is driven by factor accumulation, i.e., more workers tilling the land, rather than the use of new technologies, improved skills, and managerial practices.[10]

With this persistence of low productivity, it is no wonder that micro enterprises that employ less than 10 people account for 73% of total employment, and 99% of them operate in the informal sector. In an economy in which output and employment come from small-scale and informal enterprises, their low productive capabilities undermine their export competitiveness. Strikingly, these MSMEs, despite accounting for nearly half of Nigeria's GDP, only account for 8% of exports. Similarly, these 37 million or 89% of MSMEs do not substantially contribute to tax revenues, even though they fall prey to informal taxes at the municipal level.

Overall, the conundrum in which Nigeria's diversified economic output and employment do not translate into diversified exports and government revenues beyond the oil sector is explained by persistent, economy-wide, low productivity.

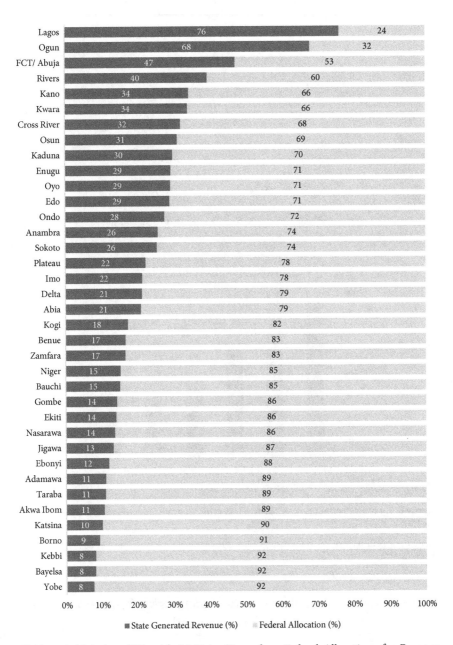

Figure 5.8 Majority of Nigeria's 36 States Depend on Federal Allocations for Revenue (2018 figures).

Source: Author's calculations from Nigeria Bureau of Statistics data.

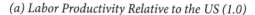

(a) Labor Productivity Relative to the US (1.0)

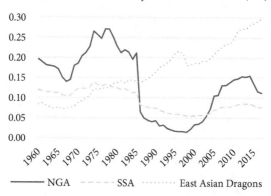

(b) Share of Labor Productivity Explained by Factor Accumulation and TFP (%)

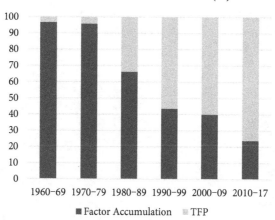

Figure 5.9 Labor Productivity in Nigeria Has Only Begun to Recover from a Two-Decade Decline.

Source: Cesar Calderon (Boosting Productivity in Sub-Saharan Africa: Policies and Institutions to Promote Efficiency, 2021, page 146).

The Post-Military Political Transition towards Institutional and Societal Fragmentation

Nigeria transitioned to become Africa's largest economy within a democratizing political environment after military rule ended in 1999. Democratic rule and a growing economy empowered various individual, group, and organizational actors. An elite consensus on "zoning" or the regional rotation of presidential power provided some political stability that enabled a policy reform-orientation. Against the backdrop of the turbulence of the twentieth century, policymaking was again geared towards macroeconomic and political stabilization, rather than sustained economic transformation to diversify Nigeria's economy. What is the distribution of power in Nigeria's post-military political settlement? How did a changing balance of power engender a policy orientation of stabilization rather than transformation?

Elite Bargain on Zoning Strives to Stabilize Nigeria's Politics

An elite consensus on power-sharing between the north and south, called "zoning" was the foundation on which Nigeria exited decades of military rule in 1999. As we saw in Chapter 4, democratization was a last-ditch effort to manage horizontal–elite competitive regionalism that threatened to tear the country apart. In the wake of General Sani Abacha's death in June 1998, Nigeria's isolation by the international community, odious debt, and a stagnant economy, democratization was the most expedient course of action. This specific elite consensus aimed to stabilize political competition by rotating presidential power and other principal elective positions between the north and the south, Christians and Muslims and among Nigeria's ethnic groups, until its reset with the electoral defeat of the PDP in April 2015. While this elite consensus stabilized Nigeria's politics for a while, the emergence and empowerment of new actors strained its enforcement.

What were the pillars of this consensus? How did it unravel by 2015? The first pillar was an informal power-sharing agreement for presidential power to alternate between the north and the south and within its six geopolitical zones, or "zoning" as a founding member of the PDP explained to me.[11] The initial terms in 1998 was to alternate power between the north and the south for a single term of four years for thirty years. The origin of this arrangement lies in the power-sharing arrangement of the National Party of Nigeria (NPN), the ruling party of the Second Republic (1979–1983). As former vice president of Nigeria (1979–1983) and Board Member of the PDP, Chief Alex Ekwueme, noted: "The NPN was the party that introduced zoning into the political lexicon of this country and the idea was that every part of this country should have a sense of belonging."[12] However, after president Obasanjo completed his first term in 2003, he was allowed by the PDP to run for another term on the understanding that power would shift to the north after eight years. Although the Nigerian Constitution did not recognise "zoning," it was both in the PDP's constitution and was adopted by other political parties.

The second pillar of the elite consensus was a tacit agreement to appease the Yoruba south-west for the annulment of the 1993 presidential election won by the charismatic tycoon of Yoruba ethnicity, Kashimawo Moshood Abiola. Therefore, in 1998, all the major political parties presented Yoruba candidates for the presidential elections. Olusegun Obasanjo, a former military head of state (1976–1979), emerged as the first president under this arrangement on the PDP's platform. The third pillar was that the new 1999 constitution was an amended version of the 1979 constitution, while the constitutions drafted in the 1990s by the derided regimes of Generals Babangida and Abacha who had usurped the 1993 elections, were discarded. As a founding PDP member explained to me[13] "... by the time he [Abacha] died, the General had become something of a pariah leading those who succeeded him to treat his legacy with open contempt."

The fourth pillar of the bargain was an inclusion of the old guard elite in the new democratic political institutions. This comprising mostly the military elite from the previous regimes, but it also included politicians from the first and second republics, businessmen, and traditional leaders. Thus, prominent military officers converted *de facto* power into *de jure* power by becoming politicians and businessmen. Many officers who held positions in previous military regimes ran for elective positions or were appointed into Obasanjo's cabinet. These include General Theophilus Y. Danjuma (Defense Minister), Vice Admiral Murtala Nyako (State Governor), Colonel David Mark (Senate President), Major General Muhammad Magoro (Senator), Air Commodore Jonah Jang (State Governor), Admiral Augustus Aikhomu, Anthony Anenih (Works and Housing Minister), former Chief of Army Staff Chris Alli (interim administrator of Plateau State) among many others. Other military generals retained back channels of influence as members of political parties, especially the PDP, or indirectly through their children and protégés appointed as cabinet ministers or presidential aides. The PDP was thus the reincarnation of the ruling NPN in the Second Republic, and was a vehicle for democratization on terms that protected the military's interests.

These were the four pillars on which Nigeria transitioned from military rule to the Fourth Republic of civilian rule, with the PDP as the organizational basis for sharing power and for elite coordination.

However, economic growth, political liberalization and the entrenchment of democratic institutions altered elite formation in ways that strained this zoning arrangement until its reset in 2015. Previously, as described by social scientist Inge Amundsen, the process of elite formation was characterized by a "fusion of elites": political elites in executive, military, and legislative positions; bureaucratic elites in ministries, departments, and agencies and then traditional and religious leaders.[14] Amundsen explains that this process begins with possession or proximity to state power by military or bureaucratic elites, they then convert this political power to economic power, and then they use economic extraction, particularly of oil wealth, to reinforce their political power. Amundsen's thesis is, to a certain extent, correct; it explains elite formation at a point in time in Nigeria, particularly during military rule. However, political liberalization, the entrenchment of democratic institutions and economic growth are all producing new individual, group, and institutional actors not party to the 1998 zoning bargain in ways that are changing the very nature of horizontal–elite competition in Nigeria. What are these changes to elite formation in Nigeria?

Political liberalization created new power centers that are incrementally displacing the military old guard. This commenced with massive purges of senior and mostly northern military officers in the armed forces by Olusegun Obasanjo in his first four-year term. On June 10, 1999, less than a month after his inauguration as president, Obasanjo compulsorily retired all generals in all three military branches who had held political office in previous military administrations. This included fifty-three officers from the army, twenty from the navy, sixteen from the air force, and four from the police. In August 2000, 459 army officers were redeployed and in September 2000, thirty-seven military officers were compulsorily retired for "over ambition."[15] The official line for this decision was "to provide a clean break with the past… to ensure the survival of democracy in Nigeria… and the permanent subordination of the Nigerian military to civilian rule."[16] This purge neutralized the influence of powerful generals from previous regimes who were veterans in plotting and executing coups.

Simultaneously, the crystallization of formal democratic structures produced powerful new actors to displace the military and the old guard. In particular, an electoral mandate in a constitutional democracy formally subordinated the military and traditional rulers to elected officials. There is the President as the Commander in Chief of the Armed Forces with the power to appoint hundreds of individuals and oversee segments of the economy including the oil industry. There is also the presidency as a consortium of principal officers including the chief of staff, the Secretary to the Government of the Federation, the scores of senior advisors, etc. The National Assembly or the legislature is constitutionally empowered to check the national executive and to make laws. There are also the thirty-six state governors who are the chief executives of their respective states, with annual budgets of millions of dollars, vast electoral power as the subnational leaders of their political parties and influence over their state legislature. Finally, there are political parties, the formal platforms for political participation and coalition building. Older power centers, such as traditional rulers, retain significant but declining influence. Although technocrats and bureaucrats, such as finance ministers, central bank governors, etc., have access to financial resources, intellectual capital, and international networks, they remain beholden to the president, and are mostly without a political base of their own.[17]

The emergence of state governors as dynamic political actors cannot be discounted in eroding the power base of the old guard that negotiated the 1998 bargain, especially the military. Nigeria's thirty-six state governors, by virtue of their financial resources and electoral mandate, have become influential actors. During the peak of the oil boom in 2013 for instance, states like Lagos, Rivers, Akwa Ibom, Delta, and Bayelsa had budgets that rivaled those of other mid-sized African countries (Figure 5.10). Individually, a state governor is the leader of the local chapter of their political party, is instrumental in selecting and financing state party executives, and can shape the outcome of state presidential elections. Collectively, governors often organize and mobilize on the platform of the Nigerian Governors' Forum (NGF). This is a cross-party association of all thirty-six state governors for consensus building, sharing best practices on governance, and setting policy agendas.[18] This individual and collective power of governors has raised their political profiles since 1999. It is not a coincidence that the two successive presidents who came after Olusegun Obasanjo, were governors. In 2007, Umaru Musa Yar'Adua, a former governor of Katsina state, was elected as president with Goodluck Jonathan, a former governor of Bayelsa, as the vice president, and later as president in 2010. This is indicative of the political power of governors and as the anchors of the zoning power rotation.

Relatedly, old guard northern and southern (east and west) power structures have been disrupted by emerging elites from the oil-rich Niger Delta. Specifically, some governors of oil-producing states have an elevated status due to the financial resources

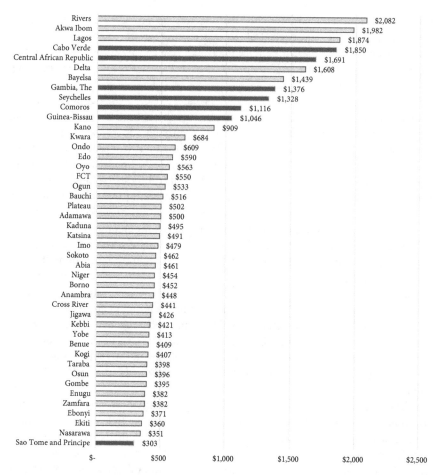

Figure 5.10 The Revenues of Some Nigerian States are Larger than the GDPs of Some African Countries, $ Millions (2013 market exchange rates).

Source: Author's calculations from Central Bank of Nigeria and WDI data.
Note: African countries in dark-shaded bars.

at their disposal. In 2004, under political pressure, a legislative amendment approved the extension of the 13% derivation for oil-producing states to include offshore oil production which dramatically increased their monthly federal oil revenue allocations. Therefore, at the peak of the oil boom in 2013, the annual federal oil receipts for major oil-producing states including Rivers ($2.08 bn), Akwa Ibom ($1.98 bn), Delta ($1.61 bn) and Bayelsa ($1.44 bn) individually dwarfed the total receipts of four other states combined. Since then, governors from the region have come to occupy a prominent role in Nigerian society. Diepreye Alamieyeseigha of Bayelsa state shot to national infamy for dressing up as woman in 2005 to skip bail out of the United Kingdom for charges of laundering $3.2 million.[19] James Ibori of Delta state was one of the first governors to be convicted of grand corruption by the anti-corruption agency, the

EFCC in 2012. Goodluck Jonathan, another former governor of Bayelsa state, became president in 2011. Rotimi Amaechi, the former governor of Rivers was instrumental to the construction of the APC coalition in 2013 which achieved the first electoral defeat of an incumbent political party in Nigeria's history in 2015. In a way, the Niger Delta is belatedly occupying its rightful spot in national prominence as a region that generates more than 90% of Nigeria's exports and over 50% of its fiscal revenues, but for decades suffered unconscionable economic exclusion, political marginalization, and environmental degradation.

Finally, economic growth has been accompanied by the emergence of private-sector elites especially in liberalized industries such as banking, telecommunications, manufacturing, and trade. These business elites' proximity to the ruling party allows them to influence economic policy, which they reciprocate with donations to political parties under banners such as "Organized Private Sector" or "Corporate Nigeria." Corporate Nigeria, loosely modeled after Corporate America in the US, became a prominent donor to the PDP from 2003. Pioneered by the then Director-General of the Nigerian Stock Exchange, Ndidi Okereke-Onyiuke, it was comprising industrialists like Aliko Dangote, bank CEOs such as Pascal Dozie of Diamond Bank, Jim Ovia of Zenith Bank, and other prominent private-sector operators. In the run-up to the 2015 elections, they contributed 65% of the N21 billion ($106 million) of the PDP's publicly declared donations.[20] An important initiative of members of Corporate Nigeria was the establishment of a state-backed conglomerate, the Transnational Corporation (Transcorp) in 2004. It was initially modeled along the South Korean Chaebols to facilitate Obasanjo's privatization program from 2003 and to facilitate investments by Nigerian firms across Africa as Nasir el-Rufai, former minister under Obasanjo and now governor of Kaduna state, explained to me.[21] Transcorp controversially acquired concessions in the oil sector, the Nigerian Telecommunications Limited (NITEL) and other public enterprises below their market value.

Partly due to the growing influence of these new actors, such as governors, there were strains on the post-military elite consensus on zoning. Olusegun Obasanjo unsuccessfully attempted a third presidential term in 2006. His successor Umaru Yar'Adua, a northerner, died in his third year in office in 2010. The northern wing of the ruling party, the PDP, felt that his death in 2010 before completing an expected two-terms until 2015 had "cheated" the north of its eight-year turn at the presidency.[22] Goodluck Jonathan, a southerner from the Niger Delta and Yar'Adua's deputy, ascended to the presidency in 2010 and defied the power rotation to the north by running for office in 2011. Northerners in the PDP opposed Jonathan's candidacy, as a breach of the existing gentleman's agreement struck in 1999. A letter by the northern wing of the PDP addressed to the party leadership in September 2010 stated that:[23]

> If we follow our party's practice and constitution... the party must nominate a northerner as our presidential candidate and a southerner as our vice-presidential candidate because the existing Yar'adua/Goodluck ticket is zoned to the north not the south. To do otherwise would amount to injustice and the violation of our party's *grundnorm*.

As one of the authors of the letter and founding member of the PDP explained to me:[24]

> The breaching of *zoning* was a big moral burden for the PDP and for Jonathan in particular. People are quick to say 'why should Nigerians care [about power rotation]?' That would be in an ideal situation whereby Nigerians really don't care about where their presidents come from. But people should remember that this whole idea about power shift... emanated from a certain section of the country [south-west]. Zoning was instituted during the NPN days... After buying into the argument for power shift, then all of a sudden... everyone abandons the idea of power shift, [claiming] it is only merit that counts. If we had accepted that there is absolutely no difference in Nigeria, no ethnic and religious differences... if we had grown walking on that platform, it makes sense to abandon sharing power that way. But the truth of the matter is that... the state level, every state is sharing power according to that [zoning] arrangement, if you go to local government [it is the same thing]...

Therefore, the emergence of Goodluck Jonathan as presidential candidate of the ruling PDP in the 2011 elections unraveled the 1998 consensus on "zoning" the position of president. Zoning was, however, still applied to other elective positions such as the Senate President and Speaker of the House of Representatives. In 2015, the PDP was defeated in the presidential elections by Muhammadu Buhari, a northerner of the APC.[25] For his re-election in 2019, Buhari's challenger was another northern candidate, Atiku Abubakar of the PDP, showing that zoning was very much in place, after its reset in 2015. There is an expectation that from 2023, presidential power will shift to the south, the failure of which, going by past precedents, would further destabilize Nigeria.

The Exclusion of Non-elite Societal Groups

There is a variety of non-elite societal groups that embody the political views and socio-economic interests of Nigerians. Due to structural shifts from the economic transition and political liberalization of the last two decades, the average Nigerian is now young and underemployed in a low-wage and low-skilled job. Traditional groups such as trade unions, media outlets, and interest groups which are comprising middle-aged professionals and senior activists are increasingly detached from Nigeria's demographic realities. Structural shifts creating a mass of Nigerians on the margins who are finding representation in new spaces and platforms.

The ethno-regional associations, trade unions, and media that were crucial to advocacies against decolonization and the excesses of military rule are no longer fully representative of most Nigerians. Ethno-regional interest groups which were influential in the mid-late twentieth century are now reincarnated in associations like Afenifere (Yoruba-west), Ohanaeze Ndigbo (Igbo-east), Arewa Consultative Forum and the Northern Elders' Forum (north), Movement for the Survival of the Ogoni People, Ijaw Youth Council (Niger Delta), Middle Belt Forum (some Christian minority groups in the northern states), among various others. They articulate the political positions of the people they claim to represent by advocating for representation in the public service and regional balance in public spending. Contrastingly, they exercise limited influence in advocating for programmatic socio-economic issues such as community development, in shaping economic policies and in actual voter mobilization during elections. The prominent trade unions and professional associations represent formal sector workers. These unions include the Nigerian Bar Association (NBA), Nigerian Medical Association (NMA), National Association of Nigerian Students (NANS) the Academic Staff Union of Universities (ASUU), and the umbrella unions Trade Union Congress (TUC) and the Nigeria Labour Congress (NLC). As we saw earlier in this chapter, about 93% of Nigeria's labor force is employed in the informal sector, and these workers may not necessarily be represented by traditional trade unions.

Finally, the Nigerian print and broadcast media is one of the most vibrant in Africa today. With over 100 independent newspapers, the country enjoys media pluralism. Although they do a comparatively better job at reporting on the socio-economic conditions of Nigerians than the interest groups, the media are often reactionary to politicians and ethno-regional considerations. These include corruption scandals, ethno-regional balance of political appointments and government spending, rifts between high-profile personalities and other such headline-grabbing news. As the managing editor of one of Nigeria's most prominent national newspapers explained to me[26] "instead of covering, we cover up some institutions, we cover up some individuals...." Journalists are often denied access to information by government officials, police and sometimes the public, and are frequently intimidated by powerful governors. Therefore, Nigeria ranked 115 out of 180 countries on the 2020 World Press Freedom Index.

These traditional and mainstream societal groups are no longer encompassing of a vast majority of Nigerians due to economic and demographic shifts that have occurred in the twenty-first century. The decade-plus strong economic growth did not create jobs or increase incomes for most Nigerians. Instead, most found themselves in low-skilled, low-wage, informal jobs in MSMEs. Within this period also, economic policy, as we will examine more closely in this chapter, was reform oriented towards macroeconomic stabilization, but was neither productivity enhancing nor pro-poor. There were limited efforts to create jobs, increase incomes, and establish formal safety nets for the vast majority of Nigerians. In the first decade of the 2000s, poverty across Nigeria, especially in the northern regions, increased (Figure 5.11). The political transition to democracy was a hurried process engineered by the military, to pull the country back from the precipice of instability. There was limited, if any, participation of civil society in this process.

Rapid demographic shifts are also rendering traditional platforms for organizing, especially unions, unrepresentative of most Nigerians. The country's current demographic structure, according to the United Nations is such that the median age is about 18, compared to Bangladesh (25), Brazil (30), India (26), Indonesia (27), South Africa (25), and Turkey (29). The average Nigerian is therefore young and underemployed in a low-wage, low-skilled job. Trade unions, as well as mainstream media and interest groups, are comprising middle-aged professionals and even

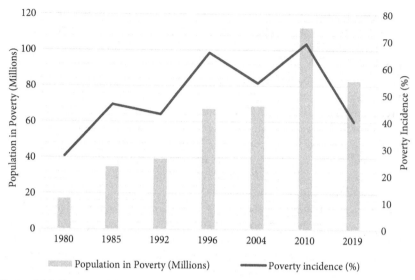

Figure 5.11 Poverty in Nigeria, 1980–2019.

Source: Author's calculations from Nigerian Bureau of Statistics data (2012; 2020).

geriatric activists. And new platforms—such as religious movements, armed groups, and social media—are emerging to organize and mobilize younger Nigerians on various political causes.

Religion is an important platform for Nigerians to address socio-economic concerns and advocate for contentious political positions. According to the Pew Research Center's Forum on Religion and Public Life, the 200 million-strong population is almost evenly split among 51.1% Muslim and 46.9% Christian, projected to be 53.7 and 44.2% respectively by 2030.[27] While the majority of Christians are in the southern states and most Muslims are concentrated in the north, there are large religious minorities in both—and this is why most Nigerians bristle at the description of a "Muslim-north and Christian-south" in international media. The transition to democracy in 1999 coincided with the twin global forces of the ICT revolution and religious revivalism. As Monica Toft and colleagues noted, globalization and democratization facilitated the rise of Islamists and Pentecostals, the swift transmission of fringe and radical ideas, and a capacity to undermine the authority of orthodox religious values.[28] Within this global climate of concurrent Islamist revivalism and Christian Pentecostalism, religious resurgence in Africa's most populous country took a dramatic turn, resulting in confrontational discourse.

A major catalyst to increased confrontational discourse between Christians and Muslims is the introduction of full Islamic shari'ah law in some northern states. Pioneered by Ahmad Sani Yarima in 1999, the governor of the north-west state of Zamfara at the time, the advocacy for full implementation of shari'ah extended Islamic law to the criminal justice system, previously restricted to civil matters such as divorce, inheritance, and domestic disputes.[29] Northern Nigeria was caught in the tide of

Islamist revivalism that swept across Egypt, Indonesia, Pakistan, Tunisia, Turkey and other parts of the Muslim world where campaigns to extend shari'ah-inspired public policies feature in electoral politics.[30]

The shari'ah movement was a turning point in the politicization of Islam as a formal policy platform. There were fears that governors in multi-ethnic northern states would exclude Christians and other religious minorities in the distribution of public resources especially when shari'ah-compliant states like Borno, Kano, and Zamfara appointed Muslim clerics in government positions. These anxieties tapped into long-standing grievances around exclusion of non-Muslim minority communities in the northern states since the 1980s from practices such as state government sponsorships of Islamic pilgrimages to Saudi Arabia and the restriction of water, sanitation, and other municipal services to Christian districts, according to the Christian Association of Nigeria (CAN).[31] A fierce resistance to the implementation of shari'ah ensued in 2000 by a mostly southern media, civil society, religious minorities in the affected states, and some Muslims who defended the secular constitution.[32]

Since 2007, there has been a dramatic decline in the deployment of political-Islam rhetoric by northern political actors. The glaring governance failures of Ahmad Sani Yarima and other populist shari'ah advocates eroded grassroots support. Zamfara, the origin of the movement, remains one of the poorest states in Nigeria, with over 82% of the population in multidimensional poverty in 2019.[33] A survey by Human Rights Watch shows that, by 2004, many Muslims had become disillusioned with the way shari'ah was implemented; while in reality many governors reluctantly introduced it under pressure from popular clerics.[34] According to the sociologist Fatima Adamu, with the exception of Kano, few states made any headway in building institutions, such as Hisbah Board, for implementing shari'ah.[35]

As political Islam was growing, Christian advocacy groups also became vocal on the national stage. CAN emerged in the 1980s as an umbrella group of various Christian denominations to promote the interests of adherents in national discourse and public institutions. The motivation of CAN is encapsulated in a speech by its former president Ayo Oritsejafor in April 2014 parts of which go thus: "it is time to raise the political awareness and consciousness of every Christian in the country... Christians must be more active in governance and must vote candidates who will protect the interests of the Church. This is not to say that we are against any religion, but to ensure that there is a level playing field for everyone."[36]

The context of CAN's vocal public advocacy to defend Christian interests occurred at a time of growing financial clout of Pentecostal movements in Nigeria. The Pentecostal church with its evangelism, pragmatic response to everyday concerns of members, and lively sermons, quickly attracted millions from the poor and urban middle class in Nigeria and other African countries—Ghana, Kenya, South Africa, Uganda, Zimbabwe, etc. Pentecostal churches also have economic assets worth millions of dollars invested in housing estates, elite schools and universities, processing plants, publishing houses, and other enterprises. Pastors such as Enoch Adebayo of the Redeemed Christian Church of God (RCCG), David Oyedepo (Living Faith Church World), Chris Oyakhilome (Believers' Loveworld Ministries), and the late Temitope. Joshua (Synagogue Church of All Nations) are among the richest clergymen in the world,[37] with transnational churches and congregations of millions. The Nigerian brand of the Pentecostal church is one of the country's exports across Africa and Europe.

With economic power, national visibility, and followers in the tens of millions for Pentecostal religious movements, comes political influence. For instance, one of the closest advisors of President Goodluck Jonathan (2010–2015) was the president of CAN, Ayo Oritsejafor. Oritsejafor frequently intervened in national politics and participated in presidential delegations. In September 2014, Oritsejafor's private jet was used to convey $9.3 million to informally procure weapons from private arms contractors in South Africa for Nigeria's war against the Boko Haram insurgency, causing a diplomatic standoff between the two countries.[38] Furthermore, Vice President Yemi Osinbajo to President Muhammadu Buhari (2015–present), a lawyer by profession, is also a high-ranking pastor of a Lagos branch of the RCCG.

The mutual fear of domination that has characterized Nigerian society since its colonial creation has resurfaced in the post-military period on starkly religious terms in the competition for political power. Between Islam and Christianity is a zero-sum contest to join ruling coalitions, influence the distribution of state resources, and stave off political exclusion. Even in the ethnically homogenous Yoruba south-west, the sociologist, Ebenezer Obadare explains how a more Charismatic Islam emerged from the mid-2000s in direct response to a perceived Christianization of the region's public sphere by Pentecostalism,[39] although the more established religious authorities—such as the Catholic Church in Nigeria and the Nigerian Supreme Council for Islamic Affairs—are less inclined to engage in partisan politics and can be voices of moderation. Overall, as Said Adejumobi observes, in the context of a deepening social crisis and shrinking material provision by the state, identity politics assumes a major means of accessing public resources.[40]

A second emerging platform for younger Nigerians on the margins of society is often violent in nature. Political liberalization in the last twenty years has provided an opening for militant and millenarian movements, to champion the causes of Nigerians on the fringes. Two important such groups are worth highlighting. In the north-east, the Jama'atul Ahlus Sunna Liddawati wal Jihad (JAS), also known as "Boko Haram," exploded onto the national consciousness in 2009 from a history of radical Islamist movements since the 1980s in the north. In its quest to violently carve out an "Islamic state" in the north-east, free of the corruption of the Nigerian state, the group recruited and coerced thousands to its cause, provided social assistance to its members, attacked Christians and Muslims who did not conform to their world view and had caused the death of 37,500 Nigerians by 2020 according to the Council on Foreign Relations' Global Conflict Tracker.[41]

Armed movements in the oil-producing Niger Delta are also violently challenging the region's economic marginalization and environmental degradation from hydrocarbons extraction. These groups include the Movement for the Emancipation of the Niger Delta (MEND), the Niger Delta People's Volunteer Force (NDPVF) and the Niger Delta Avengers (NDA), some of which emerged in the 1990s. From the 2000s, they adopted more violent tactics to address these historic advocacies destroying oil facilities, abducting workers from international oil companies and engaging in oil theft.[42] The armed advocacies in the Niger Delta became so disruptive to oil production—a precipitous decline from 2.5 million barrels per day down to just 500,000 in 2008—that the government was forced to negotiate an unconditional amnesty in exchange for the cessation of hostilities. This amnesty was an historic attempt to address the grievances of the Niger Delta which had exploded into a violent insurgency against the state. The ebb and flow of continuing armed rebellion in the region costs Nigeria up to 10% of daily production, according to senior officials at the NNPC.[43] These armed groups are distinct from criminal gangs in that they espouse clear political objectives, contest the state's authority, and use violent means to address real socio-economic grievances.

The third and final platform to mention here is social media, which non-elite Nigerians are increasingly using to participate in the public sphere. Through Facebook, Instagram, Twitter, and WhatsApp, among other social networking platforms, people organize on various public causes such as gender equality, religious discrimination, unfavorable government policies, and elections mobilization. Entrepreneurs also use social media for e-commerce. These entrepreneurs operate in event management, entertainment, fashion design, and food catering industries which serve a large domestic market for weddings and parties. Bloggers are often the source of breaking news which is then taken on by the traditional print and broadcast media. Linda Ikeji, for instance, is a popular blogger who is a major news source on entertainment, gossip, and national issues for her 6.5 million followers on Instagram and Twitter. Ikeji is now worth an estimated $40 million and is also diversifying into TV production.

The rise of social media platforms is a global phenomenon propelled by the ubiquity of mobile phones, internet access, and online platforms towards new forms of political mobilization. Unsurprisingly, this global trend has taken a life of its own in Africa's most populous country. With 139 million internet subscriptions as of July 2021, Nigeria has the largest number of internet users in Africa.[44] Thus, the most prominent mass protests in Nigeria since 2010 began on social media and spilled onto the streets. In 2012, the Occupy Nigeria movement, sparked by influencers on Facebook and Twitter, rallied thousands against the removal of petroleum subsidies and government corruption.[45] Similarly, the #EndSARS protests on police brutality in October 2020 rallied thousands. In both cases, young people started these conversations online, mobilized one another to protest offline in Nigeria's major cities of Lagos, Port Harcourt, Kaduna, and at Nigerian embassies abroad. In the same vein, these platforms are vectors of fake news that allow individuals and groups to exploit residual anxieties around Nigeria's fault lines of ethnicity, region, religion, and occasional bouts of anti-foreigner sentiment. The separatist group, the Indigenous People of Biafra, in Nigeria's south-east successfully uses social media to incite violence against government officials. A recent report finds that WhatsApp is the tool of choice in spreading "fake news" around elections but is also used to counter disinformation.[46]

Therefore in twenty-first century Nigeria, there is a waning influence around established civil society organizations such as ethnic associations, trade unions, and the media in the public sphere and an ascendance of religious movements, "extremist" armed groups, and social media influencers.

Economic Agenda is Reform-oriented but not Transformational

The political settlement which ushered electoral rule in 1999 initially had no coherent economic strategy. The priority at democratization was to bring Nigeria back from the brink of political implosion, restore relations with the international community, and avert a relapse into military rule while retaining the influence of the old guard. However, significant reforms began from 2001 in the Obasanjo administration. The successive governments of Yar'Adua, Jonathan, and Buhari also designed their respective four-year economic strategies with significant continuities among them: macroeconomic stabilization, enabling growth, and selective public sector reforms. Despite modest achievements, the policy agenda was not devoted to tackling market failures and increasing productivity for economic diversification.

In the first decade of the twenty-first century, macroeconomic stabilization was pursued due to external constraints on Nigeria's economy. Volatile swings of global oil prices battered the economy and created a recurring balance of payments crisis stretching back to the 1980s. An acute dependence on oil exports and macroeconomic mismanagement during military rule created currency instabilities. Inflation had decimated people's assets and savings. A heavy debt burden alongside corruption eroded fiscal revenues. In his first term in office in 1999–2003, Olusegun Obasanjo's priority was to stave off the specter of military rule and restore Nigeria's external relations. His frequent foreign trips to mend Nigeria's diplomatic relations were derisively described by local media as "frequent junkets abroad." However, from 2003, in his second term, he embarked on a different path. Obasanjo appointed a competent team of technocrats to develop a coherent reform strategy, the NEEDS. According to the members of his cabinet, Obasanjo had a personal desire to leave a legacy by laying the foundation for Nigeria's economic rejuvenation, in the mold of his friend and role model, Singapore's former strongman, Lee Kuan Yew.[47] More practically, Obasanjo's administration faced severe fiscal pressures. The global price of oil, on which Nigeria depended for over 90% of exports and 80% of government revenues was low (Figure 5.12); nearly half of available revenue was committed to debt servicing.

Therefore, a series of macroeconomic reforms were implemented to address these severe fiscal pressures. First, efforts were made to secure debt relief to free up government revenues. The low global oil prices, at $18 per barrel in 1999 (Figure 5.12), reduced the resources available to service Nigeria's debt of $3 billion per annum by 2004 or 41% of the annual budget.[48] Negotiations began from around 2003 to secure debt relief from the Paris Club, multilateral and commercial creditors,[49] and the return of stolen public assets from the UK on the condition that Nigeria would develop a comprehensive economic reform program. Nigeria was to have 67% of its debt stock written off in March 2006 subject to a satisfactory review by the IMF. A homegrown reform blueprint, the NEEDS, was developed to pre-empt the ideological opposition to the IMF Poverty Reduction Strategy Paper (PRSP) by Nigerian civil society, stemming from the bitter experience with SAP in the 1980s, as we saw in Chapter 4. The program was approved by the IMF Board in September 2005, paving the way for the implementation of the debt-relief agreements.[50] Finally, in 2006, external creditors

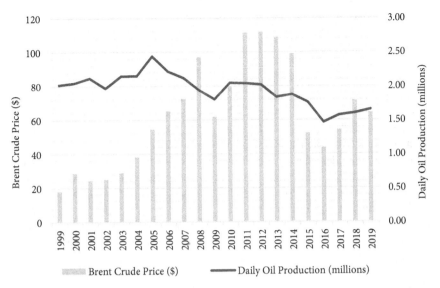

Figure 5.12 Regardless of Oil Prices, Nigeria's Oil Production is on a Declining Trend.

Source: Author's calculations from Energy Information Administration (EIA) data.

wrote-off $18 billion of Nigeria's debt after net payments of $12 billion and upon satisfactory implementation of NEEDS.[51]

A second set of stabilization policies were countercyclical in nature, introduced to manage the volatility of oil prices, stabilize revenue flows, and contain the impact on the rest of the economy.[52] In 2004, Nigeria introduced an oil-price-based fiscal rule to detach government expenditure from the vagaries of global oil prices. The rule set an oil price benchmark, typically lower than the global price, as well as a cap on the non-oil-deficit based on which government budgets were prepared. The Fiscal Responsibility Bill, signed by President Umaru Yar'Adua in November 2007, enshrined the oil-price-based fiscal rule into law. These countercyclical policies were part of broader public financial management (PFM) reforms around the stability and transparency of government revenues. The PFM reforms also included the monthly publication of all revenues at all tiers of governments, and the adoption of the Extractive Industries Transparency Initiative (EITI). Finally, efforts were made to save excess oil revenues for a rainy day. As oil prices rose steadily from 2003, the earnings in excess of the benchmark set in the oil-price-based fiscal rule were saved in an Excess Crude Account (ECA) established in 2004. Beyond the foreign reserves that every country maintains, the ECA strengthened the fiscal buffer that Nigeria could draw on during an oil price crash as was the case in 2015. By 2008, the ECA had accumulated a staggering $17 billion, boosting foreign exchange reserves to US$60 billion as Nigeria entered the global financial crisis.[53] Legislation in 2011, under Goodluck Jonathan, approved the establishment of the Nigeria Sovereign Investment Authority (NSIA), a sovereign wealth fund to replace the ECA. However, both currently exist. Nigerians now take for granted the oil-price-based fiscal rule on which government budgets are designed, the ECA, and the monthly publication of oil revenue disbursements, but they were not always the norm.

Successor administrations sustained these macroeconomic reforms introduced under Obasanjo but also came up with additional policy solutions to address persistent fiscal pressures. Under Yar'Adua and later Jonathan's administrations, the macroeconomic fundamentals were stable. Inflation was a steady 11% between 2007 and 2012. However, oil exports and, by implication, government revenues were precipitously declining. Despite high global oil prices (Figure 5.14), Nigeria lost revenue due to disruptions in oil output from a violent insurgency in the oil-rich Niger Delta. Decades of neglect under military rule and the heavy-handed tactics of the Obasanjo administration in quelling unrest in the region further radicalized advocates of resource-control. The groups took up arms, kidnapped expatriate staff of oil companies, vandalized pipelines, and other oil-sector equipment and created a general climate of insecurity in the Niger Delta. There was an urgency to restore oil production, the lifeblood of the economy, which by 2008, had declined to 1.9 million barrels per day from a peak of 2.5 million in 2005 (Figure 5.12).

In June 2009, the Yar'adua administration negotiated a peace settlement with the Niger Delta's armed movements. The government came up with an amnesty program, a homegrown disarmament, demobilization, and reintegration (DDR) initiative to address armed conflicts in the region.[54] Under the program, the government offered MEND and other groups blanket amnesty from prosecution in exchange for their renouncement of violence. There were also monthly payments, training, scholarship opportunities, and other empowerment initiatives to re-integrate repentant militants into society. The expectation was that sustainable peace would restore oil production, address the region's socio-economic grievances, and lay the foundation for the Niger Delta's economic development. Yar'Adua died in May 2010, less than a year after launching the amnesty program, leaving his successor Goodluck Jonathan, who was also the first head of state from the Niger Delta, to flesh out the details of the initiative. The Buhari administration encountered renewed rebellion in the region and had to continue the payments of the amnesty program to restore oil output. Various scholars have criticised the program for being heavy on "amnesty" from prosecution and failing to tackle the region's structural problems.[55]

The second thread of commonality in economic strategies pursued in the last two decades is the pro-growth initiatives. Starting with Obasanjo, successive governments implemented a policy agenda that created conditions for generating economic growth. Throughout the late 1980s and 1990s, as we saw in the previous chapter, Nigeria was in a low-growth trap and average population growth of 2.5% exceeded economic growth of 0.7% per annum (Figure 5.1). Nigeria had to meet donor conditions for securing debt relief. As one member of Obasanjo's reform team explained to me, the government consciously adopted a growth orientation[56] "to demonstrate to the world... that Nigeria had changed its past ways of profligacy... that Nigeria would make judicious use of revenues... to ensure debt relief would not just be squandered."

Policy documents, including NEEDS, identified an objective of achieving economic diversification through the generation of growth in non-oil sectors. Therefore, the government pursued economic liberalization to attract (foreign) private investments in key non-oil sectors, especially telecommunications, banking and financial services, and trade. There were also unsuccessful attempts at deregulation through the reform of subsidies and tariffs in sectors such as agriculture, oil, power, and trade, as we discuss in the next chapter. Box 5.1 provides a closer look at the continuities in the successful banking sector reforms.

Box 5.1. A Modern History of Nigeria's Banking Sector Reforms

Nigeria's banking industry has experienced significant restructuring in the twenty-first century. Until the late 1980s, the sector was rooted in its colonial origins with an oligopolistic structure dominated by three big commercial banks: First Bank, United Bank for Africa, and Union Bank.[57] From 1986, during SAP, economic liberalization attracted private investments into the industry. Nigerian investors seized this opportunity to acquire or establish banks, insurance firms, and other financial institutions. Throughout the 1990s, along with Nigeria's general economic malaise, the banking sector was in crisis. Bank failures were frequent in which thousands of customers routinely lost their savings while senior executives stripped the assets of the collapsing entities. Deregulation tripled the number of banks and resulted in an explosion of nonbank financial institutions. There were also few regulatory mechanisms for risk management, due diligence and effective deposit insurance. By 2003, many of Nigeria's eight-nine banks had severe structural and operational weaknesses, including low capital base, insolvency, weak corporate governance, and an ethno-regional customer base. During the 2000s, the financial sector was completely overhauled under the stewardship of Central Bank Governor, Professor Chukwuma Charles Soludo in reforms popularly known as the "Banking Sector Consolidation."[58] Among various measures taken, commercial banks were recapitalized to a minimum of N25 billion ($190 million at 2004 exchange rate) shareholders' funds. This resulted in mergers and acquisitions of previously small and weak banks into today's behemoths, like Access Bank, First Bank, UBA, and Zenith. Twenty-five large banks emerged with an aggregate capital base of $5.9 billion, some with a transnational presence beyond Nigeria. The emergence of these banks also heralded the visibility of their CEOs as financial titans including Tony Elumelu of UBA, Jim Ovia of Zenith Bank, Pascal Dozie of Diamond Bank, and Aigboje Aig-Imoukhuede of Access Bank. There was also strong enforcement of anti-money laundering measures. This allowed for new investment flows of about $3 billion in just the first year. There was also more regulatory oversight of the sector, including the Central Bank, the Nigerian Deposit Insurance Corporation (NDIC), Nigerian Stock Exchange (NSE), and the Securities and Exchange Commission (SEC). However, other aspects of the reforms lagged, especially supervision, risk management, corporate governance, and lending to MSMEs and the real sector. Thus sudden capital inflows resulted in financial instability, and several banks engaged in unethical practices of hiding their true financial position.[59] In 2008, the banks' weaknesses were further exposed when the global financial crisis and the subsequent collapse of oil prices crashed the capital markets where they had engaged in share buybacks. To prevent the sector's collapse, which like its Western counterparts, had become "too big to fail," drastic steps had to be taken. From 2009, the new Central Bank Governor Sanusi Lamido Sanusi, embarked on another round of financial sector reforms to restore corporate governance and to address the sector's volatile financialization which threatened to engulf the rest of the economy. To restore stability and market confidence, the CBN published a list of major debtors[60]—a rollcall of business and political elite including director of the Nigerian Stock Exchange, shareholders of Transcorp, and CEOs in the oil, airline, and construction industries. It also injected N620 billion ($4.1 billion in 2009 exchange rates) of liquidity, replaced the leadership at eight banks, and introduced capital controls to mitigate the volatility of rapid financialization.[61] In addition to stabilizing the sector, a major objective of the banking reforms was to shift lending from politically connected individuals, government entities, and big business, towards agriculture, the power sector, transportation[62] and especially MSMEs; financial inclusion, and diversification of banking services. Consequently, the banking sector financed the oil and gas sector local content initiatives from 2010 and the privatization of power sector assets in 2013. When global oil prices crashed in 2015, Nigerian banks became saddled with contingent liabilities from the power and oil and gas sectors, among others. Access to credit remains a major constraint to the productivity of MSMEs. Nigeria's financial sector lags in the adoption of mobile money services, at less than 100 accounts per 1,000 adults compared to more than 1,000 accounts in Ghana and across East Africa.[63]

The third thread of commonality in economic strategies pursued by successive Nigerian governments since 1999 is in the public sector. With varying results, several initiatives aimed at improving transparency and efficiency, reducing waste and corruption, and enhancing coordination. During Obasanjo's administration, there were at least two reasons why they prioritized public sector forms. The first was to rebuild the capacity of public agencies to allow the government carry out its day-to-day activities because Nigeria transitioned to electoral democracy with a hollowed-out civil service from decades of military rule. The second reason was to demonstrate to international donors and creditors that Nigeria would judiciously utilise the resources to be freed-up from debt relief through a rejuvenated public sector. The country ranked at the bottom of global indices on corruption and governance.

Therefore, Obasanjo's administration opted for four main approaches to public sector reform. There were efforts at instituting transparency, competition, and fair costing in public procurement, known as "Due Process." Due Process saved Nigeria N200 billion ($1.3 billion in 2009 exchange rates) between 2001 and 2009 from inflated contract prices.[64] There was also a privatization program, undertaken by a newly established Bureau for Public Enterprises (BPE), in which 127 state-owned enterprises were privatized, including public utilities like the Nigeria Telecommunications Limited (NITEL). An anti-corruption drive saw the establishment of the Independent Corrupt Practices and Other Related Offences Commission (ICPC) and the EFCC to reverse global perceptions about Nigeria as a hotbed for corruption and fraud. The EFCC received global acclaim for the high-profile prosecutions of financial crimes, including state governors like James Ibori of Delta, Saminu Turaki of Jigawa, and Joshua Dariye of Plateau State; the former Inspector General of Police Tafa Balogun; bank executives such as Cecilia Ibru and Erastus Akingbola and perpetrators of internet and financial fraud. Finally, new agencies that operated on technocratic principles were insulated from the sea of civil service decay. These agencies include the BPE, EFCC, the Federal Inland Revenue Service (FIRS), the National Agency for Food and Drug Administration and Control (NAFDAC). As documented by Joe Abah, these technocratic islands of effectiveness succeeded due to a convergence of a strong mandate for their services, effective managerial leadership, and political backing from the president.[65]

While these public sector agencies and reform initiatives exist with varying degrees of effectiveness today, there has been no comprehensive overhaul of Nigeria's civil service. The federal civil service is inefficient with thousands of ghost workers, lumbering with redundant agencies, and aging as over 60% of the workforce is over forty with sub-clerical skills.[66] The situation is even worse at subnational level, as Nigeria's thirty-six states and 774 local governments devote about 50% of their budgets towards payments of salaries and allowances of underperforming civil servants.

The inertia to modernize Nigeria's civil service is confounding because successive governments since 1999 did make attempts. Obasanjo's government established the Bureau of Public Service Reforms (BPSR) in September 2003 and a Public Service Reform Team headed by Nasir el-Rufai to reform some ministries, departments, and agencies (MDAs) stopped short of comprehensive civil service overhaul. Yar'Adua's government in 2007 set up another civil service review committee. Goodluck Jonathan's government appointed a presidential committee headed by Steve Oronsaye, a former head of the civil service, in August 2011. In April 2012, the committee submitted its 800-page report in which it made sweeping recommendations, including the abolition and merger of 102 of Nigeria's 541 MDAs to cut the cost of governance.[67] Buhari's 2015 administration promised to reform the civil service. Its commitment in September 2019 to implement recommendations of the Oronsaye report is yet to fully materialize, although it has implemented PFM reforms to reduce waste and increase transparency. These PFM reforms include the Treasury Single Account (TSA), which manages all government payments and revenues the Central Bank, and the Integrated Payroll and Personnel Information System (IPPIS) which centralizes the payroll of the civil service. Yet, in the absence of an overhaul of the civil service, the capacity of the Nigerian state remains handicapped, even with lauded PFM reforms and islands of technocratic excellence.

The failure to reform the civil service was closely linked to the absence of a proactive agenda to tackle the market failures of economic transformation. These market failures are supply-side constraints on the productivity of firms and workers, and demand-side constraints on people's incomes and their capacity to consume goods and services. Thus, addressing these market failures means increasing productivity on the supply side and implementing pro-poor initiatives on the demand side. Productivity growth, has only just begun to recover from more than two decades of contraction

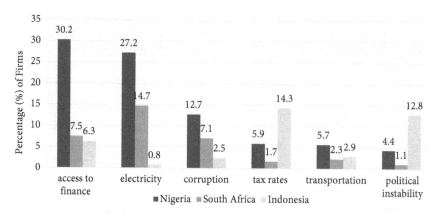

Figure 5.13 The Biggest Obstacles to Firms in Nigeria, 2014.

Source: Author's calculations from World Bank Group Enterprise Surveys database.

(Figure 5.10a) as discussed earlier in this chapter. Since the 1990s, enterprise surveys reveal that productivity growth has been hampered by constraints, most of which are yet to be addressed. Access to affordable, reliable electricity, for example, remains one of the most critical obstacles to firm productivity (Figure 5.13). Remember, over 90% of firms in Nigeria are micro enterprises, employing fewer than 10 people, with a capital base of $27,778; they are unable to scale up due to these supply-side constraints. On aggregate, MSMEs operate in sectors, such as agriculture, trade, manufacturing, and hospitality and absorb 76% of the labor force. Therefore, the objectives of economic diversification are linked to increasing the productivity of Nigeria's MSMEs in ways that modernize agriculture, increase its value addition, create meaningful employment, and increase incomes.

Unfortunately, these economic strategies since the 2000s have not addressed these supply-side constraints on productivity. Efforts to reform Nigeria's electricity sector and to increase access have recurrently stumbled. Investments in infrastructure—including roads and rail lines—have been insufficient, the projects bedeviled by corruption, partisan bickering, and weak coordination. Belatedly, Nigerian policymakers are waking up to the realization that they need sustained infrastructure investment. Since 2015, the Buhari government has completed large infrastructure projects started by his predecessors and has initiated several of his own, mostly with Chinese and also some European financing. These include airport terminals in Abuja, Lagos, and Port Harcourt; interstate federal highways and the completion of three major rail projects: Abuja Metro Rail, the Abuja-Kaduna Rail, the 327-kilometer-Itakpe–Ajaokuta–Warri Rail started in 1987 and completed in 2020, and the Lagos-Ibadan Rail started in 2017.[68]

The second policy blind spot of post-military Nigerian governments is the absence of sustained pro-poor initiatives. These pro-poor initiatives help to address demand-side constraints that affect people's incomes and their consumption capacity. Until around 2012, there was no systematic strategy to address destitution by providing opportunities for the poor to earn an income, increase consumption, build economic assets, and be resilient to shocks. In other words, there was no comprehensive social safety net system for the poor in Nigeria, especially those in the informal sector. These social safety nets are a subset of social protection instruments that help individuals and households to increase incomes and consumption, access education and healthcare, and increase resilience to disruptions to livelihoods, thereby preventing destitution.[69] Most countries that have transitioned from low to middle- or high income have extensive social protection policies and instruments.

Until recently, poverty reduction was marginal to the economic policy agenda of Nigeria's post-military governments. Olusegun Obasanjo's administration set up a National Poverty Eradication Program (NAPEP) to coordinate various pro-poor initiatives which failed and faded into oblivion. Although the freed-up resources from debt relief were channeled towards investments in primary health and basic education, only 5% of the funds were devoted to social protection.[70] Goodluck Jonathan's administration piloted social protection initiatives using savings from the partial removal of petroleum subsidies. These include conditional cash transfers (CCTs) under the Subsidy Reinvestment Program (SURE-P) and the YOUWIN financing for young entrepreneurs. Under Buhari, more social protection initiatives were scaled up in the National Social Investment Program (NSIP) including CCTs, school feeding programs, labor market programs for the youth, and business support initiatives for MSMEs. The NSIP's social safety net program now has 12 million direct beneficiaries or roughly 6% of Nigeria's population of 200 million, the largest in the country's history.[71] Overall, comprehensive social protection in Nigeria is bedeviled by low spending at just 2.6% of GDP, limited coverage of the poor, lack of effective coordination, and accurate demographic data.[72] Nigeria, therefore, lags behind its comparators in Africa and globally on comprehensive social protection.

Therefore, the economic policy agenda since the 2000s has been oriented towards stabilization rather than supporting structural transformation. There were macroeconomic policies to address the fiscal pressures resulting from oil price volatility; economic liberalization to generate growth, and selective public sector reforms to improve transparency, fight corruption, and enhance government coordination. But this policy agenda did not proactively tackle market failures that affected prospects for diversifying Nigeria's economy. Thus, there have been no consistent efforts to address both the supply-side and demand-side constraints on productivity.

Institutions Strengthen New Centers of Power

As discussed, democratization in 1999 was a last-ditch attempt to pull the country back from the brink of political implosion. An elite consensus spelled out terms for the rotation of presidential power between the north and the south through the PDP's "zoning" principle while retaining the military's influence. The key actors in this bargain settled for a modified version of the 1979 constitution as the 1999 constitution. Despite its imperfections—and Nigerian intellectuals constantly despair at the undemocratic process through which it was imposed by the military—the 1999 Constitution of the Federal Republic of Nigeria has empowered and entrenched new centers of power beyond the military. These include the national legislature, political parties, and state governors.

There is, of course, the office of the president, which is powerful in the grand scheme of things. The individual and the coalition of actors around him, is known as the presidency. The president is the most powerful individual in the country with immense powers granted by the constitution over the armed forces, veto power over legislative bills, appointment of ministers and other key public officials, economic policy design, management of 48% of the country's revenues, to mention but a few. In particular, the vast power over the oil sector, coercive apparatuses, and leadership of the ruling party are all instrumental to dispensing patronage, rallying political support, and coordinating elite cohesion or fragmentation. However, at least three other centers of power institutionalized by the constitution constrain, in significant ways, the executive power of the president.

Nigeria's legislature, at least at the national level, is a vibrant center of power and an important check on the executive. In this American-style presidential system, the legislature, called the National Assembly, is bicameral comprising an upper chamber, the Senate, and a lower chamber, the House of Representatives. Formally empowered by the constitution, the bicameral National Assembly is also a center for formal and informal elite negotiations. The legislature is a crucial check on the use and abuse of presidential power. The National Assembly effectively constrained some of Olusegun Obasanjo's overreaching tendencies, nearly impeaching him in 2002 on seventeen charges of constitutional breaches.[73] Crucially, the National Assembly thwarted a covert attempt at tenure extension in 2006 by rejecting Obasanjo's proposals for a constitutional amendment which would have allowed him run for a third presidential term.[74] Finally, it was a resolution by the National Assembly on February 9, 2010 that defused the political crisis over the prolonged absence and incapacitation of President Umaru Yar'adua. Yar'Adua, who had been ill for months, and had not been seen in public, but his inner circle was reluctant to allow a smooth political transition. The National Assembly stepped in to pass a resolution that designated Vice President Goodluck Jonathan as acting president.

Regrettably, the legislature is neither as vibrant nor as effective at the subnational level. Just like the American federal system, each of Nigeria's thirty-six states has its own State House of Assembly. Like their national counterparts, the parliamentarians of these state legislatures are also elected. However, because the state governors exercise disproportionate influence at the state-level of party politics and have unrivaled financial resources, they can dictate the course of legislative elections and the composition of the House of Assembly. Once this House of Assembly is constituted, it does little by way of being an effective check on the state governor, earning the popular moniker "rubber stamp legislature" among Nigerians. Many governors frequently drown their states in debt from domestic lenders because their House of Assemblies seldom perform effective oversight functions. Sometimes the legislators plausibly justify the free pass they give to the governors in order not to unnecessarily block development initiatives. As several state legislators admit, the House of Assemblies are not independent because their funding comes directly through approvals from the office of the governor.[75]

Nigeria's political parties constitute a third center of power empowered by the constitution. Despite constitutional provisions for multiparty democracy, for over a decade the PDP was the main institutional basis for elite coordination, including not only civilian politicians, but also the military and the business class. Other major parties such as the All Nigeria People's Party (ANPP), the Action for Democracy (AD), the All Progressives Grand Alliance (APGA) and the Congress for Progressive Change (CPC) have not had the PDP's staying power. These opposition parties have undergone significant changes in name, structure, and membership since 1999; some have splintered or disappeared entirely. In 2015, the electoral defeat of the PDP by a coalition of opposition parties of the APC points to a gradual, if chaotic, institutionalization of the party system. This is a departure from descriptions of African political parties by leading political scientists such as Nicolas Van de Walle and Kimberly Butler as having weak organization, low levels of institutionalization and weak links to society.[76]

Finally, Nigeria's state governments are formally empowered by the constitution as component units in a federalism with fiscal and political autonomy. Governors have national oil receipts, an electoral mandate, and influence on their state political parties and legislatures in ways that can shape the fortunes of their states, as discussed in Chapters 7 on Lagos and 8 on Kano. Furthermore the 13% derivation and other revenues accruing to the oil-producing Niger Delta states have raised the profile of the region's governors, especially Rivers and Akwa Ibom, with the highest oil receipts. Finally, through the institution of the NGF, the governors often collectively check the president, sometimes more effectively than the National Assembly. According to development partners, the NGF secretariat,[77] became an avenue through which development partners channeled interventions to the states, bypassing the red tape of Nigeria's hollowed-out civil service. The governors collectively remain influential in deciding who becomes president. It is instructive that since 1999, two of the four presidents and three of four vice presidents have all previously been governors.

*****

By 1999, democratization was a last-ditch attempt to pull Nigeria back from the precipice of implosion from decades of military rule and crises. The basis on which Nigeria exited military rule was a "zoning" power-sharing agreement that rotated presidential power and other principal elective positions between the north and the south, Christians and Muslims. This elite consensus stabilized political competition for a while. However, structural shifts from political liberalization and the economic transition empowered new actors not party to the zoning agreement, which strained enforcement until it was reset by the 2015 presidential election. Some of the new elites that eroded the power base of the old guard include state governors, especially wealthy states in the oil-producing Niger Delta, and large regional hubs like Lagos and Kano. Other actors in ascendance are religious movements, armed groups, and social media influencers who are supplanting trade unions and other established civil society organizations in representing the average Nigerian who is young and underemployed in a low-wage, low-skilled job. The 1999 constitution is also entrenching new centers of power beyond the military including the national legislature, political parties, and state governors.

Within this evolving balance of power, Nigeria transitioned to become Africa's largest economy. Although the priority in 1999 was the prevention of political collapse, an economic agenda of stabilization eventually crystallized. In the early

2000s, external constraints of low global oil prices on which Nigeria depended for over 90% of exports and 50% of government revenues caused a severe fiscal crisis for the Obasanjo administration. Debt relief and a series of economic reforms were simultaneously pursued to relieve the fiscal pressures, enable growth, improve transparency, fight corruption, and enhance coordination. These stabilization reforms were continued, with varying degrees, by Yar'Adua, Jonathan, and Buhari, but fell short of the structural transformation needed to achieve economic diversification. To that effect, the overall policy agenda was neither oriented to increasing productivity through systematic civil service reforms and sustained infrastructure investments nor on pro-poor initiatives. Nevertheless, these limited stabilization reforms enabled Nigeria to break the cycle of economic stagnation until growth crashed in 2016. Growth averaged 7% per annum between 2000 and 2010, and 5% between 2011 and 2015. Today, oil is no longer the major contributor to Nigeria's GDP but, due to low levels of productivity growth since the 1980s, it remains the county's main export sector and source of fiscal revenues.

6

The Successful and Failed Policy Choices of Becoming Africa's Largest Economy

"Nothing is impossible" is inscribed on a plaque on the large desk in the expansive office. As we approach the desk, Aliko Dangote seated behind it, motions to me to sit. He is on the phone talking numbers and scribbling on a notepad. Another curious item on the desk is an ordinary calculator, the type commonly used by vendors in market stalls. Dangote punches on the calculator buttons, speaks some more, scribbles on his notepad and works the calculator again. Dangote concludes his phone call less than five minutes later. We exchange pleasantries, and thus begins my nearly two-hour long discussion with Africa's and the world's richest black man, Aliko Dangote, on his experience of building a Nigerian industrial conglomerate, on government policy and the business environment, and on his vision for the future.

Dangote's journey to becoming an industrial magnate closely mirrors the transition of Nigeria's non-oil economy to what it is today and what it could be in the future. It is no secret that Dangote comes from an affluent and aristocratic family in Kano in northern Nigeria. As we saw in Chapter 3, he is the great-grandson of the wealthy commodity trader Alhassan Dantata who, during his time in the early 1900s, was West Africa's richest man. With a N500,000 loan from an uncle, Dangote set up a bulk commodity trading group in 1978 to take advantage of the liberalization of commodity imports. Through his family wealth, social networks, and government connections, the Dangote Group secured import licenses like several other business-minded Nigerians, to trade and process food including pasta, flour, sugar, and beverages throughout the 1980s up to the mid-1990s.

From the late 1990s, however, Dangote began a decisive paradigm shift, from trading to manufacturing for import substitution and backward integration. On a business trip to Brazil, as he explained to me, he visited a factory which employed about 4,600 people. He was fascinated by "... the number of people walking into the factory to work, and walking out after work, and how all those people depended on the owners of the factory, and their families, and how they organised themselves."[1] He realized how manufacturing adds value to society in a more holistic manner than trading—various products are made from a raw material, buildings are erected, workers are employed, local demand is met, there is backward integration with the rest of the economy and the whole of society benefits. At the time, he continues, Brazil was experiencing "hyper-inflation... the currency was devaluing almost every minute... worse issues than us in Nigeria." So Dangote wondered why Nigeria "... couldn't progress with industrialization" despite not having Brazil's severe macroeconomic challenges. It was this epiphany in Brazil that motivated Aliko Dangote to venture into manufacturing the same products he had for decades been importing to sell in Nigeria. Unstated, perhaps, is the realization of the profits to be made from manufacturing consumer goods.

Dangote's business reorientation also coincided with a stabilizing policy environment that departed from the haphazardness of military rule in the 1980s and 1990s. The Nigerian government under Obasanjo was keen to liberalize the economy, attract private investment, and encourage domestic entrepreneurs. In banking and finance, as well as ICT, as we shall examine in this chapter, economic reforms attracted domestic investors who acquired licenses to set up telecoms companies, banks, pension administrators, and other financial firms in ways that fundamentally transformed and modernized these industries. In sub-sectors of agriculture and manufacturing, the policy direction was less consistent, taking the form of substituting imports with domestic produce and manufactures to build national self-sufficiency. For instance, in 2002, Obasanjo's government hiked tariffs and banned imports of African print fabrics, biscuits, fruit juice, pasta, certain pharmaceuticals, sugar, and frozen poultry among others that had domestic substitutes.[2] The objective was clear: to help develop domestic production capacity and protect Nigerians from substandard imports. Yet, the beneficiaries of these import bans also happened to be highly connected business elites, including Obasanjo himself who owned Ota Farms, a livestock farm producing at scale, which benefited directly from a ban on frozen meat imports. Another major beneficiary of this import substitution was the Dangote Group which was already processing flour, pasta, rice, salt, sugar, and other food staples.

Although Aliko Dangote was a household name in Nigeria by the late 1990s, it was really his foray into cement manufacturing that made his empire the transnational colossus it is today. During the privatization program of the early 2000s, he acquired state-owned cement companies, Benue Cement Company in 2000 and Obajana Cement Plc in 2002, as well as other government enterprises such as Savannah Sugar. In the background, the government also had restricted cement imports. In 2007, the Dangote Group commissioned the Obajana Cement plant with two production lines and capacity of 5 million tonnes per annum, making it the largest plant in sub-Saharan Africa. As Dangote explained to me, it cost over $1 billion of which $472 million was borrowed from various lenders including thirteen of Nigeria's recently recapitalized banks and the International Finance Corporation (IFC). When a list of high-profile debtors was released by the Central Bank of Nigeria in 2009, as part of efforts to clean up nonperforming loans, Dangote's companies featured as some of Nigeria's top borrowers.[3]

Obajana began operations in 2006. From then onwards, Dangote's rise was meteoric. In 2008, he was Nigeria's richest man according to *Forbes* magazine. The company also began to expand operations abroad to Ghana, South Africa, and Zambia by 2012. Nigeria is now able to meet its domestic demand for cement due, in large part, to Dangote Cement, which supplies 12Mt of cement, representing a 65% share of the Nigerian market. Other important players in the cement industry include local firm Bua and the French company Lafarge. In June 2020, Dangote began to export bulk cement across West Africa from an export terminal he had built, thereby earning foreign exchange for Nigeria.

Today, the Dangote Group has a presence in seventeen African countries and is a market leader in cement on the continent. The conglomerate is a diversified portfolio of cement manufacturing, sugar milling, sugar refining, port operations, packaging material production, and salt refining, with an annual turnover of $4 billion. The Group is currently constructing Africa's largest petroleum refinery, petrochemical plant, and fertilizer complex.[4] In September 2021, Aliko Dangote's net worth was $12.4 billion as estimated by *Forbes*, crashing from a peak of $25 billion in March 2014 due in part to the collapse of the Nigerian naira.[5] He still retains the title of Africa's richest man, and the world's richest black man, which he earned in 2011 when he edged out Ethiopian-Saudi billionaire Mohammed al-Amoudi and America's Oprah Winfrey.

While Aliko Dangote is largely celebrated in Nigeria and beyond, there are those who see him as representing an economy rigged in favor of the highly connected. Various government policies including tax waivers and import restrictions disproportionately benefit Dangote and other large-scale entrepreneurs to the detriment of foreign competitors and smaller enterprises. His deep social networks allow him extensive influence on policy individually, and as an important member of industry groups such as "Corporate Nigeria" and MAN, that some describe as policy capture. Thus, a combination of favorable policies, political influence, and Aliko Dangote's own evident business acumen[6] as first mover in some industries has yielded impressive returns for his conglomerate. In some industries, Dangote is seen to have leveraged his scale of operations into monopoly power to choke foreign competitors and smaller-scale domestic entrepreneurs, according to a leaked U.S. government memo.[7]

In response to these criticisms, Dangote implies that as a first mover in the industries he operates within Nigeria's tough business environment, he personally provides public services which then become public goods. As he explained to me, "in all Dangote factories we generate our own power and we're not relying on the national grid at all, we're not even connected to them." They also build their own road networks and housing estates for workers; more recently building export terminals at Nigeria's seaports in Lagos and Port Harcourt. In building the Obajana Cement Plant in Kogi in north-central Nigeria, he said:

> we ended up building a gas pipeline – 92km – to supply gas for the generators... for electricity. The place was a no man's land – no housing to rent, the closest place was Lokoja, 38km. So we had to build about 472 houses. The water table was terrible... so all the boreholes we built collapsed... we had to build a dam; you can see the dam over there [he points to blow up photo on his wall].

With all these unforeseen expenses, "the Obajana factory cost us about $1 billion, up from the initial $490 million."

The private provision of these services generates positive externalities becoming public goods used by host communities. As he explained

> … wherever we land to do a business, the government will just run away, and they leave us with the community. We are the ones to make sure that they go to school… right now we have a place in Ogun state (Igbesu), we have issued road projects worth over N6 billion – we are doing the roads. Even now after doing the roads, the community [we are] repairing their schools, we have given them N250 million to do projects that they badly need.

Other benefits to society including being the largest employer of labor beside the government, adding value in manufacturing, generating foreign exchange through exports in exchange for the tax waivers and other policies that allow the Dangote Group to break even, turn a profit, and open up that industry to other players. Interestingly, similar arguments are put forward by Nigeria's international oil companies which provide some public services—including roads, schools, and hospitals in their host communities in the Niger Delta—although their impact on jobs creation and value addition is negligible.

The activities of Dangote and other large-scale entrepreneurs contributed to the growth of non-oil sectors of the Nigerian economy since the turn of the century. The expansion of food and beverage production, cement manufacturing, banking and finance, and ICT resulted from a combination of privileged political access and favorable policies for powerful entrepreneurs with demonstrable business acumen. Indeed, the future transformation of Nigeria's other non-oil industries especially agriculture, manufacturing, and tech, may very well follow a similar trajectory of cement, telecoms, and finance. Therefore, a good understanding of what it would take to diversify Nigeria's economy towards a post-oil future in the twenty-first century may lie in taking stock of recent experience. In this stocktaking, we unpack the combination of deliberate government policies, privileged political access, and entrepreneurial acumen.

This chapter, therefore, examines how deliberate policy choices were made for crucial sector reforms within Nigeria's post-military political settlement. We discuss how external constraints of volatile oil prices and the resulting fiscal pressures pushed Nigeria's policymakers to liberalize the telecoms sector quickly and successfully. Yet, at this critical juncture, efforts to reform the downstream oil sector by boosting domestic fuel refining, removing subsidies, and investing in public services stalled. The fiscal pressures from global oil prices were insufficient to embolden successive governments to deregulate a downstream sector characterized by fuel imports to meet domestic demand and an expensive fossil fuel subsidy regime that consumes more government revenues than social expenditure that is popular among ordinary Nigerians. Instead, wider redistribution concerns for cheap fuel used in private generators due to insufficient grid electricity and in passenger vehicles due to sufficient mass transit disincentivized downstream oil sector reforms.

The Liberalization of the Telecoms Sector is driven by Domestic Capital

One sector where liberalization was successfully pursued is telecommunications, a major growth driver in the first decade of Nigeria's democratization. The reforms succeeded due to a combination of external fiscal pressures on Nigeria's ruling elites, the privileged allocation of rents in the form of mobile licenses to connected business elites and their entrepreneurial savvy in the productive use of these mobile licenses to build a telecoms industry that was founded on domestic investments and foreign technology. Let us take a closer look, then, at the sector's underlying problems, the constraints and catalysts for reform, the actual policies undertaken, the key actors involved, and the outcomes.

By 1999, when Nigeria transitioned to democratic rule, the telecommunications sector was in dire straits. The sector was largely state-run with the public enterprise, the Nigeria Telecommunications Limited (NITEL) at its core. The notorious inefficiency of NITEL prompted the government to pencil the utility alongside 140 other SOEs for privatization during structural adjustment between 1988 and 1993.[8] The Nigerian Communications Commission (NCC) was set up as a regulator in 1992, while General Abdulsalam Abubakar's military government promulgated the Public Enterprises Act of April 1999. Unlike, say, banking and finance, the government was not able to attract sufficient private investments in telecoms during structural adjustment. By the mid-1990s, any hope of attracting foreign investments vanished as Nigeria became an international pariah during General Abacha's rule and multinationals outside the oil sector were wary of getting involved with the country. Towards the late 1990s, Nigeria still pressed on with efforts to attract private investments, especially in the new technology around cellular networks, and therefore efforts were made to auction mobile licenses. Overall, the efforts to extend telephone lines across Nigeria failed spectacularly within a broader context of insufficient investments, bureaucratic dysfunction, and the country's persistent political crisis. Between 1985 and 2000, more than $5 billion was spent on digitalizing the telephone network that ended up with just 400,000 connected users for a population of 122 million people at the time.[9]

So, within this context, what was the catalyst for a change in mindset towards substantive reforms in the telecoms sector? Using the political settlements framework outlined in Chapters 1 and 3, I argue that external constraints on ruling elites enabled a pro-reform mindset to liberalize the sector. The business elites within the ruling coalition that stood to gain from liberalization also made the government more committed to the reforms, with Nigerian rather than international capital as central players. And this is how it all played out.

Despite professing a nominal commitment to liberalizing the telecoms sector, President Obasanjo only became committed upon realizing the potential for generating non-oil resources. His administration initially revoked the twenty-seven mobile operation licenses provided to investors by the previous military regime of General Abacha, which had placed Obasanjo on death row.[10] Therefore, the first attempt at

GSM licensing in 2000 failed due to the power tussle among Obasanjo, former military ruler General Ibrahim Babangida, and other military elite. It was only when Obasanjo's government realized the wealth-generation potential that a second bid round was conducted in the UK in 2001.[11] This is within a context in which, as we discussed extensively in Chapter 5, Nigeria had limited fiscal resources due to low global oil prices and a heavy external debt burden, the servicing of which consumed nearly half of the annual budget. Specifically, Obasanjo's government was encouraged by the high bids for the three licenses, each auctioned at $285 million, by Communication Investments, Econet Wireless Nigeria, and MTN. This amount far outstripped the $100m quoted for each license—the most expensive issued in Africa at the time according to the Econet CEO Strive Masiyiwa.[12] Thereafter, the administration became more committed to pursuing liberalization.

These external constraints also came from development partners and regional competition pressured the Obasanjo administration to liberalize the sector. Conditional assistance by the Bretton Woods institutions, OECD countries and the World Trade Organisation (WTO) facilitated liberalization. As a precondition for debt relief during low oil prices, Nigeria had to develop a reform strategy approved by the IMF. Consequently, in July 2000, the government pledged to minimize spending on restructuring NITEL as a precondition for a $1 billion standby agreement.[13] There was also neighborhood rivalry within West Africa. The realization that earlier failures had left Nigeria's telecoms network several years behind those of Ghana, Ivory Coast, and other regional rivals may have expedited the GSM auctions in 2001.[14]

Given these external pressures, business elites in the ruling coalition shaped the direction of liberalization to be driven largely by domestic rather than international capital. Officials and business partners of previous military regimes owned shares in these first wave telecoms firms. For instance, Colonel Sani Bello (rtd.), a former military governor and ambassador and an oil tycoon, owned a minority stake in MTN Nigeria, one of the three beneficiaries of the 2001 auction.[15] Econet Wireless Nigeria (now Airtel Nigeria), the first telecoms firm to operate in Nigeria, had a consortium of twenty-two all-Nigerian financiers including Diamond Bank, the Lagos and Delta state governments, military generals who were founding members of the PDP, and industrialists such as Oba Otudeko, who had made fortunes during military rule in the 1980s.[16] Many multinational telecoms firms at that time were wary of investing in Nigeria given the widespread perception of fraud about the country. It wasn't all rosy though, as there was bribery and underhand dealing in the license auctions. For instance, Econet Wireless Nigeria was asked to pay $9 million in bribes to senior politicians who mobilized financial investments for the license. According to the firm's CEO Strive Masiyiwa, his refusal to authorize the illegal payments led to the cancellation of Econet's management contract by Nigerian shareholders.[17] Another international operator was invited to replace Masiyiwa's Econet as technical partner, the name was changed from Econet to V-Mobile, then to Vodacom, Zain, Celtel, and finally to Airtel today.

The liberalization in August 2001, marked by the introduction of cellular networks, the Global System for Mobile (GSM), engendered the telecoms sector's expansion. From 400,000 phone lines in 2000, there were 328 million connected mobile and fixed

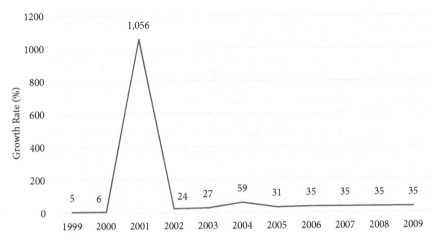

Figure 6.1 Growth Rate (%) of the Telecommunications Sector, 1999–2009.

Source: Author's calculations from NBS data.

lines and 139 million internet subscriptions by July 2021,[18] the largest mobile market in Africa. The telecommunications sector expanded from just 0.1% of GDP in 2001 to 8.2% in 2019, growing at an average of 122% from 1999 to 2009 (Figure 6.1). Nigeria is the biggest market for the South African mobile firm Mobile Telecommunications Network (MTN), in terms of subscriber base, constituting about 27% of its 273 million subscribers across twenty-one countries.[19] Nigerian-owned Globacom, is a major player across Africa.

This involvement of domestic private sector was a watershed for market reforms in Nigeria as the business men allied to ruling elites championed the telecoms liberalization. They demonstrated their capacity to generate new resources or economic rents and to ease budgetary restraints, which although one-off, allowed key elites to position themselves in emergent economic sectors and created a model for replication in other sectors. In particular, the Dangote Conglomerate among others, as we discussed at the beginning of this chapter, benefited from the allocation of monopoly rents in the cement and fruit juice industries through the "Backward Integration Policy" which allowed Nigeria became a net exporter of cement by 2013.[20] The counterfactual is that, even without the involvement of local financiers, GSM would eventually have spread to Nigeria, but would have been wholly led by multinational firms.

Therefore, through the political settlements lens, we identify how external constraints enabled the emergence of a growth coalition in Nigeria's telecoms sector. At the turn of the century, a ruling coalition was able to drive market reforms in the telecommunications sector, despite oil wealth, ethnic pluralism, or the "neopatrimonial logic" which would otherwise obstruct growth. The story is, however, remarkably different in most parts of the oil and gas sector, particularly the downstream of petroleum refining, transportation, and distribution.

Distributional Pressures Prevent the Deregulation of Petroleum Prices and Effective Subsidy Reform

In Nigeria's oil industry, reforms have been comparatively less effective. The sector overall has trended towards steady stagnation and decline. For instance, the oil sector grew at an average of 1.3% between 1999 and 2009, and -3% between 2010 and 2019 despite high overall economic growth until 2015. On the one hand, the oil sector's decline as a share of GDP from a peak of 49% in 2000 to 9% in 2019 indicates diversification of output. However, the sector's absolute decline points to a deeper malaise. Since 2013, production averaged 1.9 million bbl/d below peak capacity of 2.4 million bbl/d, and the target of 4 million bbl/d.[21] Nigeria's proven reserves have not grown from 37.2 billion barrels despite targeting 40 billion barrels.[22] Oil earnings routinely disappear through leakages across the industry value chain. Nigeria lost $217.7 billion from 1970 to 2008, and $20 billion between 2010 and 2012.[23] The Petroleum Industry Bill meant to harmonize the disparate legislations governing Nigeria's oil industry stalled for two decades before its passage in August 2021. A paper by political scientist Alex Gboyega, finds that "every institution along the extractive industries value chain that potentially could prevent fraud is weak. Although these weaknesses allow for manipulation,... the necessary underlying conditions for... best practice in petroleum governance are not in place. The responsibility is political."[24]

Specifically, the dysfunctions in the downstream sector of petroleum refining, transportation and distribution of Nigeria's oil industry affect public finances and service delivery. These dysfunctions are at least threefold. First, Nigeria spends billions of dollars annually to secure fuel supplies to power economic activities. These fuels include premium motor spirit (PMS) or gasoline, automated gas oil (AGO) or diesel, household kerosene (HHK), aviation turbine kerosene (ATK) or jet fuel, and low-pour fuel oil (LPFO) among others. Therefore, it spends billions of dollars importing fuel, usually among the top three largest import items including capital goods and industrial supplies (Figure 6.2a) and also spends heavily on subsidizing the final consumer prices below market rates. In 2019, Nigeria spent N2.5 trillion importing processed fuels equivalent to 15% of total imports (Figure 6.2a). Although the 2019 figures mark a decline from the nearly 30% (N3.8 trillion) in 2018 and 27% (N2.6 trillion) in 2017, it is still very high. For fuel subsidies' expenditure, the figures are hard to come by as they frequently spill into extra-budgetary spending. In 2011, for instance, Nigeria spent N2.1 trillion on PMS subsidies although it had budgeted only N245 billion for both PMS and HHK.

A second aspect of this dysfunction is that the billions spent on importing and subsidizing fuel come at the expense of public services, especially electricity and transportation infrastructure and social protection. These subsidies alone in 2011 were more than double the N878 billion spent on education, health and social services combined; and the N697 billion on agriculture, transport and other economic services (Figure 6.2b). Although the subsidy regime has been significantly cleaned up with a less-rigid pricing regime, closure of extra-budgetary leakages, and lower global oil prices, Nigeria still spent more than N1.5 trillion on this expenditure item in 2019.

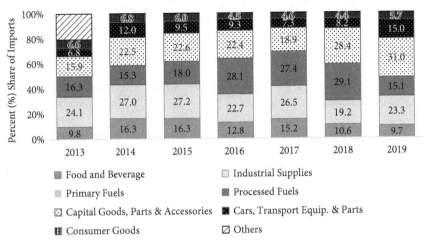

(a) Processed fuels is one of Nigeria's largest import items but its share in the total is declining

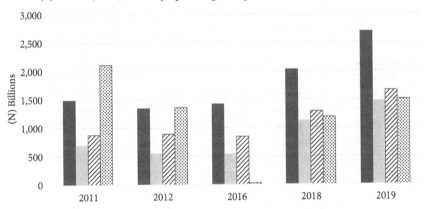

(b) Petrol (PMS) Subsidy Spending Compares to Social Spending in Nigeria

Figure 6.2 Nigeria Spends Billions of Dollars on Importing and Subsidizing Processed Fuels.

Source for Panel a: Author's calculations from NBS data.
Source for Panel b: Author's calculations from data from Central Bank of Nigeria, BudgIT (2019, p. 2) and Daily Trust (2017).

Finally, any effort to drastically reduce spending on fuel subsidies is fiercely resisted by many Nigerians. As discussed in Chapter 5, Nigeria's national trade unions, NLC and TUC, and those in the oil and gas sector PENGASSAN and NUPENG[25] often coordinate mass resistance to the removal of petroleum subsidies. While this advocacy is driven by concerns about rising costs of living associated with fuel price hikes, it often translates into hostility to broader reforms that introduce market forces in the downstream petroleum sector. Major increases in petroleum prices are accompanied by paralyzing strikes. Most notably, the partial removal of fuel subsidies in January 2012 which raised gasoline prices from N65/liter to more than N141/liter, led to unprecedented mass protests. Thousands of people poured out onto the streets in Nigeria's major cities of Abuja, Benin, Kaduna, Kano, Lagos, Port Harcourt, and at Nigerian embassies abroad in the UK and the USA.[26] The protests tagged "Occupy Nigeria" pressured the government to partially restore the subsidies several days later. In light of this resistance, governments settle for incremental adjustments to the pump price of gasoline when convenient.

These dysfunctions in Nigeria's downstream oil sector are rooted in certain structural characteristics of the economy which create redistribution pressures on policy makers to continue these suboptimal policies. These structural characteristics include a large demand for fossil fuels as a major energy source in the economy, a supply gap resulting from weak domestic refining capacity, and an unhealthy dependence on fuel imports to balance supply and demand.

Before we examine these structural characteristics, it is important to situate and contrast this discussion within the prevailing global discourse on fossil fuel subsidies. This reality of how fuel subsides are deeply intertwined with the structural characteristics of the Nigerian economy eludes many reform advocates who misdiagnose the reason why these subsidies persist. It is assumed that Nigerian decision-makers are irrationally pursuing a bad policy of maintaining the fuel subsidies that are: economically inefficient because they subsidize consumption, fiscally wasteful because they are prone to corruption, socially regressive because they benefit the urban middle class at the expense of the rural poor, and environmentally harmful because they encourage more consumption and higher emission of greenhouse gases.[27] Since 2010 or so, the policy literature and donor interventions have evolved to incorporate political-economy approaches to better understand how powerful actors can support or obstruct subsidy reforms.[28] I was part of several such initiatives during my time at the World Bank at a global level, and in Morocco, Nigeria, and Zambia.[29] Despite these analytical advances, these political-economy approaches to studying and reforming subsidies remain limited in their focus on the role of powerful stakeholders. These studies are not sufficiently in-depth in understanding how structural factors shape the behavior of these powerful actors.

My position goes thus: it is not just that decision-makers are irrational, ignorant of "good policies," are bad communicators, susceptible to unethical tendencies or forever beholden to corrupt cronies, although all of these are partially true. The reality is that the mechanics of the way fuel imports and subsidies are intertwined with the quotidian activities in the Nigerian economy compel even the most well-intentioned decision-makers to retain them. Within this economy, policy makers are expected by Nigerians to keep fuel prices artificially low as a form of redistribution to cushion their inflationary impacts on the cost of living. Let us now examine the structural characteristics of the downstream petroleum sector that compel the retention of fuel subsidies.

Despite being Africa's largest oil producer, Nigeria is unable to meet its domestic demand for refined oil products, especially petroleum, diesel, and kerosene. On average, the country consumes 56 million liters of gasoline (PMS) daily for residential, productive, and transport uses (Figure 6.3a).

Nigeria's 200-million-strong population translates into many fossil fuel consumers. Furthermore, fossil fuels are a main energy source for electricity generation for residential and productive uses, with gas and oil accounting for more than nearly 90%, according to the International Energy Agency.[30] Absent reliable grid power, private electricity generators powered by gasoline (PMS) and diesel (AGO) contribute to 32% of electricity generation in Nigeria. These fuels are also major energy sources for transportation, which itself accounts for 80% (17.8 million tons of oil equivalent Mtoe) of total fossil fuel final energy consumption (22.2 Mtoe).[31] With insufficient mass transit systems, Nigerians rely on their individual solutions to intracity and interstate transportation such as passenger vehicles and light trucks, the second highest in sub-Saharan Africa in 2015.[32] Although there has been a recent push to complete inter-

(a) Average Daily Refined Petroleum Imports and Consumption

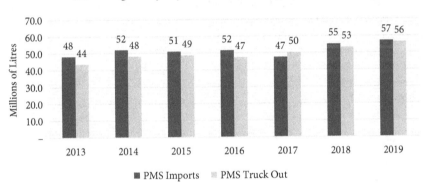

(b) Average Daily Refined Diesel (AGO) and Kerosene (HHK) Imports and Consumption

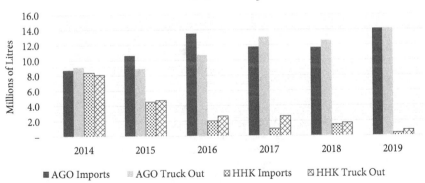

Figure 6.3 Average Daily Refined Fuel Imports and Consumption in Liters (millions), 2014–2019.

Source: Author's calculations from NBS data.
Note: Truck Out is a proxy for consumption. It refers to the amount of fuel transported and distributed in trucks.

city rail networks, such as the Abuja-Kaduna Rail; the Itakpe–Ajaokuta–Warri Rail, and the Lagos-Ibadan Rail Project, Nigeria lags on effective and reliable mass transit systems, including urban transit, for its size and income. Finally, Nigeria also consumes large volumes of HHK as cooking fuel for lower-income households (Figure 6.3b). It is used in stoves and complements the coal, firewood, and other biomass that collectively account for more than 73% of cooking fuels, in the absence of cleaner energy options.[33] Therefore, there is a large demand for refined oil products for residential, productive, and transportation uses due to structural attributes of a large population, a deficit of electricity and mass transit systems, and lack of affordable clean cooking fuels.

A second structural attribute of the downstream petroleum sector is that this large demand for fossil fuels in Nigeria is not met by domestic refining capacity. In other words, there is a supply gap for petroleum and kerosene, and until recently, diesel. Taking petroleum in particular, Nigeria consumed an average of 56 million liters daily in 2019, of which it imported 57 million liters (Figure 6.3a). The discrepancy between the imports and final consumption is not a glitch—Nigeria tends to import more fuels than it consumes due to the byzantine nature of the downstream sector. As several policy makers explained to me, imported and subsidized fuels are illicitly re-exported at higher prices to neighboring West African countries through the Republic of Benin.[34] West Africa consumes 22 billion liters of PMS annually of which imports account for over 90%.[35] In theory, Nigeria should be able to supply its own domestic needs from its refineries. It has five operational refineries of which four are NNPC-state-owned, with a combined installed capacity of 446,000 bpd per day. These are spread across the country's vast landscape in Kaduna in the north, three in Port Harcourt and Warri in the south, and a fifth, private 1,000 bpd complex (Table 6.1). At present, Nigeria has Africa's fifth-largest refining name-plate capacity after Egypt, Algeria, Libya, and South Africa, although actual output is very low.

Table 6.1 Status of Nigeria's Public and Private Refineries

Refineries	Number	Description	Capacity	Status
NNPC Refineries	4	Conventional plant capable of producing transportation fuels PMS, HHK, AGO; heating oils' LPFO, and petrochemicals.	445,000	Operational
Niger Delta Petroleum Resources	1	Modular plant capable of producing naphtha, dual purpose kerosene (DPK), AGO, marine diesel, Liquefied Petroleum Gas (LPG).	1,000	Operational
Dangote Oil Refinery Company	1	Conventional plant capable of producing transportation fuels PMS, HHK, AGO; heating oils' LPFO, and petrochemicals.	650,000	Advanced construction stage, nearing completion
Other Conventional Refineries with Active Licenses	5	Conventional plant capable of producing transportation fuels PMS, HHK, AGO; heating oils' LPFO, and petrochemicals.	700,000	At various stages of construction

Refineries	Number	Description	Capacity	Status
Modular Refineries with Active Licenses	20	Modular plants capable of producing naptha, PMS, HHK, AGO, LPFO, and LPG.	295,000	At various stages of construction
Refineries with Expired Licenses (All Modular)	17	Modular plants capable of producing naptha, PMS, HHK, AGO, LPFO, and LPG.	655,000	Mostly sourcing funds with some at early stages of construction
Grand Total	**48**		**2,746,000**	
Total excl. NNPC	*44*		*2,301,000*	
Total Modular Refineries	*38*		*951,000*	
Total Conventional Refineries Excl. NNPC	*10*		*1,350,000*	

Source: Author's Analysis Based on Information from Nigeria's Department of Petroleum Resources, Dangote Refinery Company, and the Niger Delta Petroleum Resources.

Since the late 1990s, these NNPC refineries have operated at way below capacity with deteriorating performance although recent private investments could soon ramp up output. In 2019, the combined capacity utilization of the four state-owned refineries was less than 10% (Figure 6.4). Various efforts at rehabilitating the government refineries, through Turn Around Maintenance (TAM) over the last two decades have been costly and unsuccessful. In 1997, Abacha's regime awarded a $215 million contract for the Kaduna refinery. In 1998, the Abdulsalam regime awarded a $92 million contract for the four refineries. Under Obasanjo $254 million was spent on them. Nearly

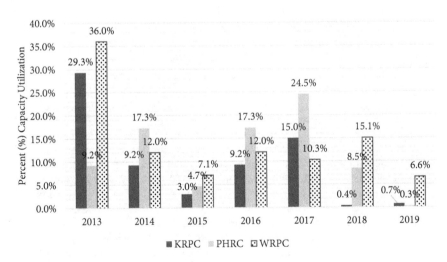

Figure 6.4 NNPC Refining Capacity Utilization (%), 2013–2019.

Source: Author's calculations from NNPC (2019) Annual Statistics Bulletin 2019, p. 28.
Note: KRPC—Kaduna Refinery and Petrochemical Company; PHRC—Port Harcourt Refinery Company; WRPC—Warri Refinery and Petroleum Company.

$1 billion in 2011 and $1.6 billion in 2013 were spent under Goodluck Jonathan.[36] An attempt at privatization in the twilight of the Obasanjo administration in May 2007 was immediately reversed by the successor Yar'Adua government for various reasons including an ideological aversion to a full market orientation in commanding heights of the economy and fears that Obasanjo was conducting a fire sale of national assets to cronies.

Since 2004, forty-four (six conventional and thirty-eight modular refinery) licenses with a combined capacity of 2.3 million bpd have been issued to domestic and private investors (Table 6.1).[37] Of the thirty-eight low-cost modular refinery licenses, only the Ogbele Refinery by the Niger Delta Petroleum Resources with a 1,000-bpd capacity is operational; a few others are nearing completion. Among the six conventional refineries, only the Dangote Petroleum Refinery Company is at an advanced stage of construction (see Box 6.1). If completed, the Dangote Refinery alone could address Nigeria's supply gap for refined oil products and help realign incentives around downstream oil sector reforms. The modular refineries, which have smaller capital outlays and are more labor intensive, can help support private-sector development, job creation, and address illegal oil refining and its associated environmental degradation in the Niger Delta. Overall, if these refineries were to be completed and become operational at even 50% combined capacity of 1.35 million bpd, they could address the supply gap for refined fuels in the whole West Africa sub-region.[38] Nigeria could become one of Africa's top three largest producers and exporters of refined fuels and petrochemicals with spill over effects for jobs and industry. Until then, nearly all of Nigeria's demand for refined fuels is met by imports rather than local refining.

Box 6.1 Can the Dangote Petroleum Refinery Help Address the Dysfunctions in the Downstream of Nigeria's Oil Industry?

The Dangote Oil Refinery could be one of the solutions to addressing the supply gap for refined fuels in Nigeria. It is a 650,000 bbl/day integrated refinery project under construction in the Lekki Free Zone near Lagos in Nigeria. The project is set to be Africa's largest oil refinery and the world's biggest single-train facility. A license was approved after an unsuccessful attempt to acquire the Kaduna and Port Harcourt refineries in May 2007 through a consortium, called Bluestar, for $750 million in the twilight of the Obasanjo administration.[39] In 2013, Dangote signed a financing deal with a consortium of local and international banks to begin construction for his new refinery. Total costs are estimated to reach $19 billion. Despite various challenges, including the sharp currency devaluation that accompanied the collapse of global oil prices from 2015 and extended timelines, the complex is scheduled for completion in late 2022. The refinery holds the promise of addressing some of the debilitating dysfunctions in the downstream of Nigeria's oil industry and of alleviating the burden on government revenues. With a capacity to process 650,000 barrels of oil daily, the refinery can bridge the supply gap for petroleum, kerosene, and other fuels that power quotidian economic activities. It can also export the surplus across the West Africa sub-region, as the cement industry, thereby easing pressures on Nigeria's foreign reserves. Crucially, boosting domestic refining could eliminate other costs around imports, transportation and distribution that may finally make fuel subsidies redundant. The implication thus is of an impending removal of fuel price controls to allow market forces prevail for the refinery to turn a profit. Finally, the refinery will create jobs in the domestic economy, as Aliko Dangote explained to me. This is estimated at 4,000 direct and 145,000 indirect jobs around production, transportation, and distribution of the fuel products as well as auxiliary services like real estate and hospitality. These benefits notwithstanding, there are risks to the success of the refinery and to Nigeria's oil industry overall. Nigeria's challenging business environment could derail the project's successful completion, take-off, and profitability. For instance, congested ports at Lagos delayed by more than three years the project's initial completion date and infrastructure constraints resulted in the relocation of the refinery site. Dangote is pulling all the stops to mitigate these challenges. The refinery is funded by a combination of equity ($3 billion), debt financing ($6 billion) from local and international banks and a $2.7 billion equity investment by the NNPC, including a $1 million grant to develop human resources from the United States Trade and Development Agency. It will feature its own infrastructure such as a pipeline system, access roads, tank storage facilities, and crude and product-handling facilities; a marine terminal, and a fertilizer plant.[40] Given Dangote's antecedents in import substitution in the cement industry, this refinery could transform the regulated downstream oil sector into a monopoly. With its sheer scale, the refinery will easily have the dominant market share for fuels and petrochemicals in most of West Africa potentially restricting competition. If the refinery does succeed as intended in helping eliminate fuel imports and the associated subsidies, new risks could arise from the stakeholders who lose out of this new equation. In other words, powerful actors such as fuel traders who are suddenly cut off from their lucrative enterprise could organize politically to resist this new economy that excludes them. These potential grievances combined with full deregulation that results in higher fuel prices, could be leveraged by politicians to undermine the social legitimacy of the Dangote Refinery, and the conglomerate more broadly. Finally, there are risks to the environment from the refinery's carbon emissions and industrial waste. The global transition underway towards cleaner energy could render a refinery of this scale redundant and its assets stranded in a future powered by clean energy. Overall, the Nigerian government has an important regulatory role to play in anti-trust initiatives, consumer rights, environmental protection, and public service provision.

A final underlying characteristic of Nigeria's downstream oil sector is that the large gap in supplies for refined fossil fuels for domestic consumption is bridged through imports. Nigeria imports nearly all the 56 million liters of PMS, 14.1 million liters of AGO and 740,000 liters of HHK it consumes daily (Figure 6.3a/b). These imports are undertaken in institutionally opaque and fiscally wasteful circumstances. Through the NNPC, the government barters 210,000 barrels of crude oil per day that are neither exported nor provided to domestic refineries, in exchange for refined PMS, HHK, and other derivatives. This barter arrangement became widespread from 2010 when the performance of the four state-owned refineries severely deteriorated. Thus, large volumes of fuel were imported to meet daily demand and prevent a return to the dreaded long queues at petrol stations that were ubiquitous in the 1990s. Initially, this barter took the form of short-term "oil-for-product swap" or "offshore processing agreements" between various arms of the NNPC and commodity traders. These traders include Aiteo Energy Resources, Duke Oil, Nigermed, Sahara Energy, Societe Ivorienne de Raffinage (SIR), and Trafigura.[41]

The terms of some of these secretive crude swap agreements have been very unfavorable to Nigeria. The American NGO, NRGI, estimates losses of up to $381 million in one year (or $16 per barrel of oil) from just three provisions in one of the seven crude swap contracts Nigeria entered into between 2010 and 2015.[42] Some of the contracts also contained troubling clauses, such as those that permit "destruction of documents after one year."[43] After the scandal around subsidies exploded in 2012, the crude swaps were replaced in 2016 with a more transparent and cost-effective Direct-Sale-Direct-Purchase (DSDP) arrangement in which the NNPC directly sells crude oil to refiners and purchases refined oil products from them.[44] Yet, the DSDP still involves some of the same commodity traders that exploited Nigeria in the past, and will continue until at least 2023 when it is expected that domestic refining capacity would have improved.

Until 2016, private-sector actors were also involved in importing refined fuels. Since at least the 1970s, the government provides import licenses to businessmen to buy refined petroleum from abroad and distribute to the domestic market. For a long time, the import license regime was riddled with cronyism, opacity, inefficiencies, and severe revenue leakages. An investigation by the lower chamber of the federal legislature in 2012 found that the number of private importers of refined fuels increased exponentially from 6 in 2006 to 19 in 2008 and 140 in 2011; and marketers who distribute these fuels increased from 45 in 2009 to 128 in 2011.[45] In one egregious instance, one hundred and twenty-eight payments of equal installments of N999 million each were made within twenty-four hours in January 2009, to unknown beneficiaries involved in the import trade that did not supply a drop of oil.[46] Fuel import and marketing licenses became a way of dispensing patronage during a period of high oil prices from 2010 and a tense political environment after President Yar'Adua's death and right before the 2011 elections when the PDP's northern caucus opposed to Jonathan's presidential bid. Unsurprisingly, the list of twenty-three oil marketers investigated at the time included the sons of two former PDP chairmen, Senator Ahmadu Ali and Bamanga Tukur.[47] Although the regime of private-sector fuel importers has been cleaned up since 2016, the transportation and distribution system to get the product to vendors and the final consumer is still maddeningly inefficient and byzantine.

Let us now tie up this intricate information together. Due to these structural characteristics of Nigeria's downstream petroleum sector, decision-makers are constrained to continue spending billions of dollars to subsidize fuel imports to meet domestic demand. The exact expenditure on fuel subsidies is unknown because it is a complicated expense item that spills beyond the actual annual budget. For instance, the NNPC documents that N780 billion was spent on subsidizing PMS imports in 2019, but the Senior Special Assistant to the president announced a figure closer to N1.5 trillion.[48] The amount spent on subsidies closely tracks global oil prices, with higher expenditures during high oil prices, such as between 2011 and 2013 when oil was over $100 per barrel and vice versa during low oil prices, bearing in mind the leakages and inefficiencies (Figure 6.2b). So, it is not that policy makers are unaware of the waste and inefficiencies in the fuel subsidy regime as some economists and donors tend to assume. Without addressing the underlying structural characteristics of the downstream oil sector around the infrastructure deficiencies driving demand, the fuel supply gap resulting from weak domestic refining capacity and thus the reliance on a deeply flawed import regime, it is nearly impossible for any government administration to effectively reform fuel subsidies.

Even severe external fiscal pressures on policymakers from the sudden collapse of oil prices, are insufficient to drive sustained reform of the subsidy regime which is a core element of Nigeria's social contract. Each government during the last twenty years, regardless of political affiliation or ideological orientation has announced the removal of these subsidies but with little to no actual reforms taking place. The Buhari administration announced in June 2020 that it had effectively ended all fuel subsidies.[49] In principle, subsidy payments decline significantly with low global oil prices. This should be the opportunity to painlessly remove price controls and then allow market forces to prevail with an effective communications campaign to convey to the public, the movement of global prices. Yet, no government can withstand the intense pressures to restore these subsidies from Nigerians experiencing the inflationary impacts of rising electricity and transportation costs from higher fuel prices. As some recent studies have shown, given these severe structural constraints, subsidy removal has inflationary impacts that are detrimental to the poor, to households, and, most importantly, to the productivity of firms.[50] According to a World Bank assessment, successive Nigerian governments have aimed to provide benefits to the population in the form of lower fuel prices, which can directly affect welfare through savings on fuel expenditure, as well as bring indirect benefits through lower costs of transportation.[51] Even well-designed communications campaigns, as are often suggested by donor interventions, are insufficient to compensate for the absence of electricity, transportation, and social protection for the poor.

Overall, the downstream oil sector consumes Nigeria's fiscal revenues, undermines service delivery, and undercuts the sector's efficiency. From this discussion, the problem in Nigeria's downstream sector is not, as is often framed by much academic and policy-oriented scholarship, of an unhealthy dependence on wasteful and inefficient fuel subsidies. It is not the fuel subsidies that cause the dysfunctions around refining, distribution, and large-scale consumption of fossil fuels. It is rather the structural attributes of the Nigerian economy. The dependence on fuel subsidies is not an immutable characteristic of a country afflicted by a "resource curse" since an oil-rich country like Iran was, from 2010, able to establish an effective cash transfer program for poor households to compensate for the removal of petroleum subsidies.[52] The direction of causality is the reverse.

The unhealthy dependence on these inefficient subsidies is caused by a structural dysfunction in the downstream sector resulting from insufficient infrastructure and public services. Nigerian policymakers could have used the billions of dollars wasted in the maintenance of the obsolete refineries. They could have adopted a phased approach to reallocating subsidy expenditure towards policy solutions to address these structural problems. For instance, investing in electricity provision, mass transit, petroleum refining and expanding social protection coverage to renew the social contract with society beyond an unhealthy dependence on wasteful subsidies. Thus, policymakers are frequently in a conundrum, they understand that petroleum subsidies are wasteful expenditures on consumption. When constrained by fiscal pressures, their immediate policy response is to remove subsidies without addressing the structural factors. This knee-jerk reform receives a swift backlash from Nigerians bearing the brunt of inflationary impacts until the subsidies are restored. Hence the vicious cycle and blame-game continues.

****

To conclude this chapter, the diversification of Nigeria's economy towards a post-oil future lies in its recent successes and failures in reforming specific sectors. The varied experience of successfully liberalizing the telecoms sector while struggling to reposition the oil industry provides insights into the mechanics of economic reforms in Nigeria. Whether certain reforms are successfully implemented owe to the political constraints on policymakers that incentivize them to pursue a specific course of action to empower capable entrepreneurs such as the telecoms investors. External constraints of global oil prices that created a severe revenue crisis motivated the ruling elite to overcome internal squabbles and quickly liberalize the telecoms sector with domestic capital and foreign technology in the front seat. Declining revenues at the critical juncture of democratization in 1999–2000 and also from 2015 have not constituted sufficient pressures for a radical overhaul of the oil industry, especially the downstream sector of petroleum refining, transportation, and distribution. The vertical–societal pressures for cheap fuel to compensate for the absence of electricity access, mass transit systems, and social protection services prevailed in disincentivizing sustained reforms. However incremental policy changes including the provision of refinery licenses and the completion of some refineries in the next few years may gradually allow Nigeria to address its domestic fuel supply gap, and thereby reorient incentives of ruling elites around substantial oil sector reforms.

Lagos: The Political Foundations of Economic Diversification in Nigeria's Commercial Capital

Bangkok, the capital city of Thailand is notorious for its chronic traffic congestion. In September 2019, I found myself stuck in such traffic gridlock in the city. I had arrived the day before, to present a paper at a United Nations conference. After the conference concluded, I went sightseeing since I had several hours of free time before my flight back to the United States. Within five hours, I had covered some of the biggest Buddhist temples including the Temple of the Reclining Buddha; the Chinese district; the monarch's palace; and finally ended at a mall downtown. At the mall, I decided to take a taxi back to my hotel which was about 4 to 5 kilometers away. The taxi headed towards an intersection that connected to a bigger road that led to a busy highway. We never made it to the intersection. The car was stuck in traffic about fifty meters away from the intersection. It took nearly fifteen minutes before the car crawled another ten meters, and then stopped again. We were barely moving. After more than thirty minutes of crawling through the mass of vehicles, I got out of the car and approached some motorbikes parked beside the road. One of the motorbike taxi drivers gave me a helmet to wear, motioned that I hop on behind him, and we sped off. The motorbike taxi quickly snaked through the mass of cars onto the highway. Minutes later, I was back in my hotel. For me, Bangkok was a déjà vu of a similar experience in Lagos, Nigeria, five years earlier.

In July 2014, I found myself stuck in traffic gridlock in Lagos. It was a few days after my arrival in the city for what was to be weeks of interviews, meetings, and symposia for research. On this particular day, I had taken a taxi at around 9am from where I resided in FESTAC Town with the intention of arriving early to my 11am meeting at Ikeja, another district. We drove easily through the expansive roads of FESTAC Town until we were about 200 meters away from the estate's exit gates. The taxi crawled to a stop behind other vehicles. It moved no more than 100 meters in the next hour-and-a-half and we were firmly stuck in traffic. I got out of the vehicle and found a motorcycle taxi or "okada" in local parlance, to take me to the nearest bus stop. Despite being of Nigerian origin, I had never resided in Lagos for an extended period. Thus, I was unfamiliar with how chronic the traffic congestion could get in some districts. Apparently, the nearest bus stop was at the Mile 12 junction, where extensive highway and light rail construction works were underway. The motorcycle ride to the bus stop was rough. I worried I would fall off into a puddle or hit my head on unpaved portions of the wide roads we used to bypass the congested traffic of polished sedans, trucks, and the signature yellow public buses. Unlike the experience in Bangkok five years later, neither the driver nor I wore helmets, even though regulations mandating their use existed on paper. I was eventually dropped off at Mile 12 from where I boarded a bus to Ikeja. Two days later, I moved to another neighborhood in Lekki which had less traffic than FESTAC.

This chronic traffic gridlock in Bangkok and Lagos is a common feature of mega cities globally. Across Africa, Asia, Europe, and Latin America, the very elements of dynamism in such mega cities also hobble their efficient functioning. As we will discuss in the rest of this chapter, Lagos is a rapidly growing megalopolis of 15–20 million people, very much in the mold of Cairo, Dhaka, and Mumbai. While Bangkok has a smaller population of around 10.5 million, it is the administrative, commercial, and cultural capital of Thailand. Being at least two centuries old, Bangkok is a fusion of a rich history of Buddhist temples, ancient districts, and traditional markets with gleaming skyscrapers, upscale malls, and modern amenities. Bangkok thus pulls in migrants from other parts of Thailand, tourists from all around the world and the regional hubs of multinationals. While Lagos is no longer Nigeria's administrative capital since Abuja was commissioned in 1991, it is the country's commercial center and embodies much of Nigeria's urban transformation, dynamism, and challenges. In both Bangkok and Lagos, deficiencies in urban planning and transport infrastructure exist alongside rapid urban growth. Both cities have invested in bus rapid transit (BRT) systems and city rail lines to ease chronic traffic congestion.

Urban chaos, infrastructure decay, violent crime, and fiscal insolvency are some of the severe policy challenges in Lagos that its decision-makers have attempted to address since Nigeria's electoral transition. The city has cleaned up dramatically since the dark days of the 1990s when parts of Lagos were uninhabitable, buried under mountains of rubbish, being devoured by the rising tides of the Atlantic Ocean, conquered by violent criminal gangs and arenas of social unrest. In the second decade of the twenty-first century when its governance reforms started to yield visible results, Lagos received glowing academic and media acclaim. In a 2012 article, the *Financial Times* wrote that "The reinvention of Nigeria's commercial capital is offering a model for how African megacities can cope with soaring populations."[1] Lagos is now ranked alongside its peer megalopolises in other middle-income countries such as Brazil, Egypt, India, and South Africa. Between 2000 and 2016, Lagos attracted the second highest amount of FDI inflows in Africa at $658 million after Johannesburg's $944 million, according to UN Habitat.[2] International franchises in retail, luxury hospitality, fast-food, and services have set up across Lagos, as the gateway to the Nigerian economy. Most of the country's fast-growing tech start-up are located in the city. The quality of subnational governance is also a model, in some ways, for Nigeria's thrity-five other states. Dynamism and dysfunction exist side-by-side in Lagos in ways that are not much different from other mega cities in middle-income economies around the world.

Overall, the Lagos economy outperforms the national average. Its economy is larger and more diversified than the other states and its fiscal revenue base is more diversified beyond oil revenues. Lagos is rather important for Nigeria's post-oil economy. In this chapter, we explain that the status of Lagos as a major anchor of

Nigeria's non-oil economy is due to the balance of power that has enabled relative policy effectiveness and continuity. Although the combination of its structural attributes, in terms of its geography, resources, and human capital also help, they are not the decisive determinants. In other words, since 1999, successive Lagos State governments have built a political coalition to coordinate their advantageous factor endowments, skillfully maximize the institutional provisions within Nigeria's federal system and strengthen their administrative capacity for tax and other reforms. This political coalition has attempted to directly address the constraints of fiscal pressures, urban dysfunction, and intra-elite factionalization.

Specifically, I argue in this chapter that successive Lagos ruling elites became reform-oriented in response to threats to their political and physical survival. These constraints on Lagos rulers are horizontal pressures of intra-party factionalization, vertical–societal pressures from population explosion, urban decay, and violent crime and external pressures of fiscal insolvency. I argue that the relative effectiveness of successive Lagos governments was neither coincidental nor driven by taxation reforms and an "emerging social contract" as some have argued.[3] The causality is the reverse. Rather, in response to the existential threats they faced, Lagos' ruling elites built a political coalition to pursue tax and other reforms resulting in a somewhat more responsive social contract.

The chapter is structured as follows. I present the diversifying economic structure of Lagos as Nigeria's largest subnational economy, increasingly comprising services and with a growing non-oil revenue base that outperforms the national average. Then I outline its factor endowments (i.e., natural resources and geography, human capital, infrastructure and finance capital, and entrepreneurial talent) and explain how these structural attributes position Lagos as Nigeria's largest subnational economy, oriented towards services and with a large non-oil fiscal base. The chapter then goes into more detail to examine how the distribution of power in Lagos has created the conditions for a reform-orientation among policy makers. Overall, the existential threats to the survival of Lagos ruling elites constrained them to build a political coalition that envisioned the transformation of Lagos into a global megacity and is strengthening the bureaucratic capacity to implement policy reforms. The result is fiscal diversification, urban renewal, and an emerging, if fragile, social compact across successive Lagos State governments.

The Diversifying Economy of Lagos

In examining the structure and composition of the Lagos economy, three characteristics are important. First, the Lagos economy is Nigeria's largest subnational economy. Second, it is oriented towards services and trade rather than agriculture. Third, it has an increasingly diversified revenue base reliant on tax income rather than federal oil revenue transfers. These three characteristics illustrate how Lagos serves both as an anchor of the Nigerian non-oil economy and of the country's services-oriented economic expansion in the post-military period.

On the first characteristic, Lagos is Nigeria's largest subnational economy. With a GDP of around N20 trillion ($107 billion) in 2014, it contributes 22% to the national economy (Figure 7.1a) even though it contributes roughly 6% of Nigeria's population (Figure 7.1b). If Lagos were a separate country, it would rank as Africa's seventh-largest economy as its GDP in 2014 was larger than Kenya, Ethiopia, Ghana, and Tanzania (Figure 7.1c). Second, the Lagos economy is oriented towards services and trade rather than agriculture. A decomposition of the GDP figures yields some important findings.[4] Three activity sectors account for over 75% of GDP—these

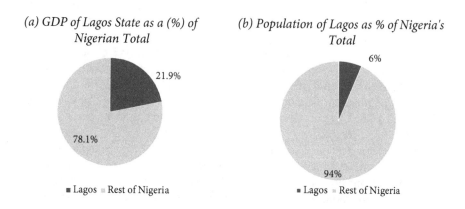

(a) GDP of Lagos State as a (%) of Nigerian Total

(b) Population of Lagos as % of Nigeria's Total

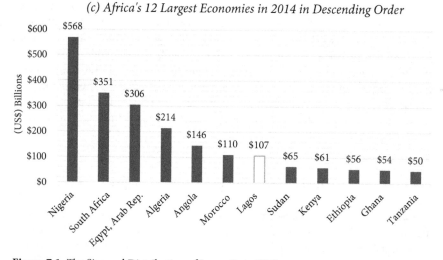

(c) Africa's 12 Largest Economies in 2014 in Descending Order

Figure 7.1 The Size and Distribution of Lagos State GDP.

Source: Author's calculations from NBS data for the year 2014 in Panel a; NPC 2006 Census data for Panel b; World Bank and NBS data for Panel c.

Note: 2014 figures are used because no updates are available for Lagos State GDP.

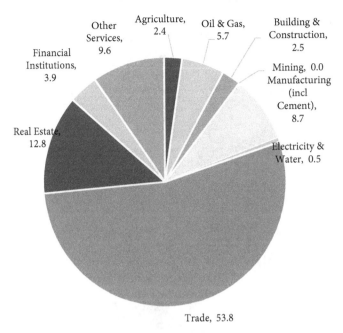

Figure 7.2 The Sectoral Distribution of Lagos State GDP (%) 2011.

Source: Author's calculations from NBS data for the year 2011.
Note: The year 2011 was the last year for which the national bureau of statistics calculated Lagos State GDP. Although more recent data for the GDP of other states exist, the Lagos State Government voluntarily opted out of NBS state-level GDP calculation and reconciliation exercises.

are trade, real estate, and manufacturing (Figure 7.2). In 2011, the latest year for which data are available, Trade was the largest sector at 53.8%. The four other large activity sectors for the same year are real estate (12.9%), manufacturing (8.7%), oil and gas (5.7%) and financial institutions (3.9%) (Figure 7.2). This indicates a relatively diversified economy, although services and trade collectively account for 80.1%. Crucially, these figures indicate a trading economy despite significant manufacturing activity relative to the national average and oil deposits. In 2016, Lagos officially became an oil-producing state, with a production capacity of 40,000 barrels per day.[5]

Looking more closely at the Trade sector reveals that it is largely comprising both informal and small-scale enterprises. As we saw in Chapter 5, 42% of the country's 41.5 million microenterprises are engaged in Wholesale and Retail Trade. These microenterprises have a capital base of less than $10,000, they employ fewer than ten people and are largely informal. In Lagos, there are 3.3 million MSMEs, the largest number of all Nigeria's states, and 8,395 SMEs (Figure 7.3).

The fact that the real-estate sector is the second-largest indicates an active private sector, the flow of investments and of urban expansion. Various policy and media reports captured the property boom in Lagos during the growth cycle of the last two decades: luxury apartments, office complexes, residential buildings, hotels and

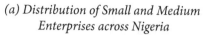

(a) Distribution of Small and Medium Enterprises across Nigeria

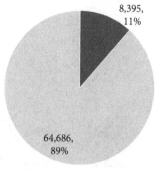

■ Lagos   ▪ Rest of Nigeria

(b) Distribution of Micro Enterprises across Nigeria

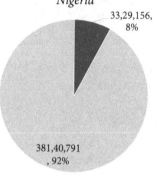

■ Lagos   ▪ Rest of Nigeria

Figure 7.3 Lagos Has the Largest Number of MSMEs among Nigeria's Thirty-Six States.
Source: Author's calculations from SMEDAN & NBS (2017).

shopping centers. In 2019, Lagos was ranked as the fourth costliest city in Africa according to Mercer's annual Cost of Living Survey, driven up by expatriate demand, the oil boom, and Nigerians returning from the diaspora.[6] The Lekki Free Zone, a multi-purpose commercial, industrial, and residential are is an example of a large real-estate investment project initiated in 2006 by a consortium of Chinese, public, and private investors. The size of the manufacturing sector, as the third largest is also indicative of the status of Lagos as one of Nigeria's major industrial hubs—alongside Ogun, Kano, Onitsha, and Kaduna. Lagos accounts for about 60% of industrial investments and manufacturing output in Nigeria.[7] In 2011, the manufacturing sector accounted for 8.7% of GDP, compared to the national figure of 7.3% for that year. There is significant oil and gas activity which comprises 5.7% of GDP. While there is no oil refining activity showing up in the data, several refining projects are on course for completion in the next few years.

The third characteristic of the Lagos economy is the diversification of its fiscal revenue base beyond federal oil revenue transfers. Across a two-decade period, from 1999 to 2019, there was an evident increase in non-oil revenue generation, higher than any other state in Nigeria.

Lagos relies more on its own internal revenue sources than federal oil receipts. In 2000, Lagos State relied on monthly oil revenue statutory allocations from the federal government for 52% of its total revenue while Internally Generated Revenue (IGR), mostly from non-oil sources, constituted 42.9% (Figure 7.4a). IGR includes taxes, fines and fees, licenses, rent on government property and other miscellaneous funds. Lagos State IGR gradually increased as a percentage of total revenues, reaching 74% a decade later in 2010, and a peak of 84% in 2017. A closer look at the composition of IGR reveals that taxes are the largest component (Figure 7.4b). Since the year 2000, taxes have comprising an average of 80% of total IGR excluding loans and bonds, reaching 86% in 2017 (Figure 7.4b). This increase points to the government's success at generating internal non-oil revenue through tax reforms and improved PFM, although the state's debt stock as a share of total revenues had increased sharply to 26% by 2017 (Figure 7.4a). We examine these PFM reforms in more detail further in the chapter.

This snapshot of the Lagos economy shows Nigeria's largest subnational economy as relatively diversified, largely comprising trade and services and an increasingly diversified revenue base reliant on non-oil sources of income.

(a) Distribution of Lagos State Revenue, 1999–2017

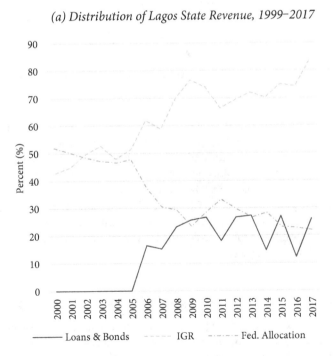

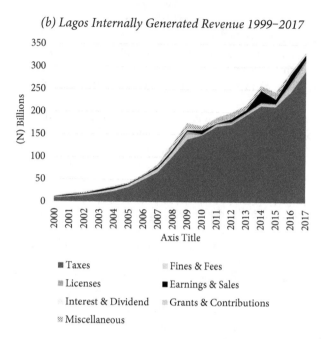

(b) Lagos Internally Generated Revenue 1999–2017

■ Taxes   Fines & Fees

■ Licenses   ■ Earnings & Sales

Interest & Dividend   Grants & Contributions

※ Miscellaneous

Figure 7.4 Composition of Lagos Fiscal Revenue 1999–2017.

Source: Author's calculations from: World Bank (Nigeria—Lagos State: States Finances Review and Agenda for Action, 2007) for 1999–2003 figures and Lagos State Government (Digest of Statistics: 2013, 2013; Digest of Statistics: 2015, 2015; Digest of Statistics: 2018, 2018) for 2004–2017 figures.

Note: IGR figures in panel (a) include loans which are classified by the Lagos Bureau of Statistics under capital receipts. Federal Allocation includes VAT.

The Endowment Structure of Lagos Supports Economic Diversification

The increasing economic diversification of Lagos in terms of output and fiscal revenue is underpinned by the structural attributes that orient the state towards a services and trading economy. These structural attributes are called factor endowments, which refer to the stock of factors of production.[8] These endowments include natural resources and land, labor and human capital, physical and finance capital, and the character of entrepreneurship. As explained in Chapter 2, the direction of a country's economic growth and transformation is shaped by the ways in which public policies coordinate endowments towards economic objectives. How do these structural attributes shape the orientation of the Lagos economy?

Natural Resources and the Advantages and Limitations of Geography

The first factor endowment is geography and natural resources. We take an expansive definition here to include both resources with a finite stock such as agriculture, land, and minerals,[9] and climatic, topographic, and geographic resources.

As a coastal city with the country's major shipping and trading port, the geography of Lagos positioned it towards a service and trading economy even before colonial rule. From around the 1700s, Lagos easily became a West African port trading in slaves and commodities with Portuguese and later British merchants. The port was an important interface between the hinterland of the most populated of the African British colonies.[10] From 1914, the city naturally became the capital of colonial Nigeria. It generated most of colonial Nigeria's revenue until after the Second World War and was the administrative capital until the move to Abuja in December 1991. The presence of Nigeria's two largest seaports, the Lagos Port Complex in Apapa and Tin Can Island Port with a third being built at the Lekki Free Trade Zone, has maintained Lagos's status as Nigeria's premier trading hub.[11]

An important way in which the coastal location of Lagos affects its economic performance, is that the trade sector, which is the largest contributor to Lagos GDP, is enabled by the proximity to the ports. Since many goods traded by both MSME and large-scale commercial enterprises are imported, there are far lower transportation costs than for those in hinterland regions such as Kano as we will discuss in Chapter 8. Due, in part, to the absence of an efficient rail freight infrastructure, there is a wide gap between the cost price and profit margins for imported goods between Lagos in the coast and Nigeria's hinterland regions. That may soon turn around for the better as rail infrastructure projects to connect Nigeria's hinterlands to the coast, such as the 327-kilometer-Itakpe–Ajaokuta–Warri Rail are coming to life.

The region's climate and topography can also negatively affect economic activity. As a low-lying coastal zone, Lagos is prone to periodic floods that displace households, commodities markets, and disrupt livelihoods. The landmass is less than 15 meters above sea level, of which 22% consists of water in lagoons and creeks. Lagos also has a long coastline of 180 kilometers comprising 22% of the nation's total coastline and is therefore vulnerable to increased storm surges and coastal erosion.[12] In addition to the city's low elevation and rainfall intensity, the problem of flooding is compounded by human developments. These include land reclamation, the uncontrolled expansion of the built-up area, the lack of good infrastructure, and a failure to maintain and expand storm water drainage. These near-annual floods affect Lekki, Ikeja, Oshodi-Apapa Expressway and other commercial nerve centers, leading to annual losses of millions of naira for individuals, households, and firms.[13]

Lagos has some mineral deposits but faces acute land scarcity that constrains agriculture. It has significant deposits of oil and gas, silica sand and clay, but these resources are underdeveloped. In May 2016, Lagos officially became an oil-producing state following the discovery of offshore oil and gas reserves by the Yinka Folawiyo Oil Company. For renewable natural resources, the scarcity of arable land applies a major brake to agricultural productivity, because 40% of all land area is swampy.[14] Consequently, agriculture accounts for only 2.4% of Lagos GDP, of which livestock and fishing constitute 60.8%. At 0.7 million hectares, Lagos has the smallest land mass of Nigeria's states—although this keeps expanding through unplanned settlements.[15] Due to this land scarcity, there is very little agriculture activity, especially crop production compared to Nigeria's vast hinterland regions.

Within this small landmass, Lagos faces acute demographic pressures on public resources. As Nigeria and West Africa's commercial hub, Lagos attracts economic migrants. This phenomenon of rapid population growth in the region has accelerated in recent years. The population of Lagos has increased from 3.5 million in 1985 to 7.3 million in 2000, to over 10 million in 2010 and is projected to reach 15.8 million in 2020 according to UN Habitat estimates.[16] Lagos is now Africa's largest city, with a high rate of immigration, growing at over 2.91% per annum.[17] This rapid population growth is inevitably stretching scarce resources, and straining harmonious community relations. Specifically, underlying tensions between indigenous Yoruba communities and Igbo migrants are further aggravated by a competition for scarce resources alongside partisan politics as we will examine further along this chapter.

Labor and Human Capital

The second factor of production in economics is labor and human capital. Here, we focus on the educational attainment and skills composition of a given population, especially the productive segment or the labor force.[18] The size and quality of the human capital stock in Lagos predispose it to a service economy. A concentration of skilled labor in Lagos relative to the national average across Nigeria underpins the growth of trade, real estate, financial services, ICT, and other services sectors in the state. Across three indicators for educational attainment and skills composition, Lagos outperforms the national average.

On youth educational attainment, Lagos outperforms the national average. According to a recent government survey, 94% of the Lagos youth population from age 15 to 35 is literate, with at least a primary school education (Figure 7.5a). This is the highest in the country, compared to the national average of 74%. Nearly 60% of young people in Lagos have secondary school education, higher than the national average of 47%, and 31% of Lagos youth have post-secondary education compared to a national average of just 14.4%. Also crucial is the capacity of young people to adapt in a modern service economy. Across the third indicator, computer skills, Lagos outperforms the national average yet again: 53% of young people have computer skills compared to a national average of 21% (Figure 7.5c). There is a better gender balance

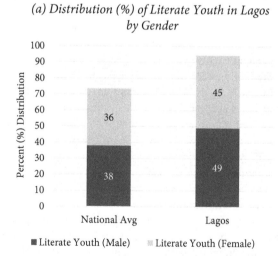

(a) Distribution (%) of Literate Youth in Lagos by Gender

(b) Distribution (%) of Lagos Youth by Educational Attainment

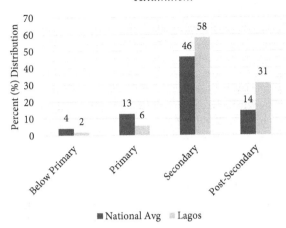

(c) Distribution (%) of Lagos Youth with Computer Literacy

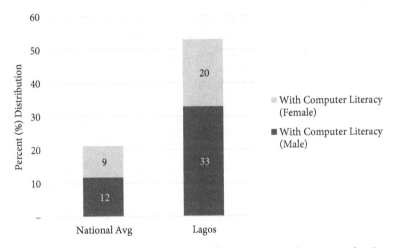

Figure 7.5 Educational Attainment among the Youth Population (15–35 years) in Lagos is Above the National Average (2012 figures).

*Literate youth is defined here as those with a minimum of primary education
Source: Author's calculations from *NBS* (National Baseline Youth Survey, 2012, pp. 72–73; 106).

in Lagos as well. Of the female Lagos youth surveyed, 45% are literate compared to a national average of 36%; 20% are females with computer skills compared to a national average of 9%. This educational attainment and skills composition make Lagos more conducive to a service economy. Indeed, most headquarters and branches of banks, financial institutions, real estate, and IT firms as well as NGOs and multinationals are located in Lagos although there is a push to decentralize to other regional poles in the country.

There are at least two reasons for the above average human capital stock in Lagos.

First, Lagos has historically attracted migrants from within Nigeria and West Africa in search of economic opportunity. Fom the 1800s, well before the British annexation of the territory, merchants and migrants were drawn to the city. These included European merchants, freed slaves from Brazil and Cuba, Sierra Leoneans, and Hausas and Nupes from the northern interior.[19] As Lagos became the capital of colonial and post-colonial Nigeria, migrants, merchants, and traders contributed to its growth.[20] From the 1970s, the development of a major wage labor market, combined with the oil boom and the demographic transition of the Nigerian population, attracted more people to Lagos such that it became sub-Saharan Africa's largest city. Since the 1970s, Lagos became more appealing to other African migrants including Beninois, Cameroonians, Congolese, Ghanaians, and Togolese.[21]

A second reason for the relatively high stock of human capital in Lagos is that residents prioritize educational attainment and skills acquisition. As we discussed in Chapter 3, the region's early contact with education from proselytizing Christian missionaries and British colonial rulers in the 1800s gave it a headstart on Western education. Then, in the latter days of colonial rule and the early years of independence, there was massive public investment in universal, free, and compulsory primary education (UPE) by the western regional government (comprising Abeokuta, Benin, Colony, i.e., including Lagos) from 1955 under the stewardship of the regional premier, Sir Obafemi Awolowo. This push for UPE laid a strong human development foundation for Lagos because it linked educational attainment to economic prosperity and political power. As Nicholas Nwagwu notes, the western region's ruling elites as well as their counterparts in the East, saw the production of popular education policies as one of the surest ways of staying in power, because of the scramble to fill vacant posts left by departing British officers in federal public service at independence.[22] Consequently, the high achievement-orientation of Lagos residents may also explain the higher-than-average concentration of human capital. Like many commercial capital cities around the world, the fast-paced nature of life amidst a rapidly growing population creates a competitive environment in which people are pressured to constantly upgrade their skills.

Despite the large human capital stock in Lagos, many employers lament the skills deficit within the workforce. Both large corporates and formal MSMEs frequently express concerns about the steep costs of (re)training new hires, even those with tertiary education. As we discussed in Chapter 5, Nigeria has an extremely low labor productivity to output ratio, lower than counterparts in Brazil, India, and other middle-income countries. This is despite the fact that among Nigeria's states, Lagos has one of the highest value-added per worker, at $6,740.[23] The dearth of skilled labor is a major constraint on productivity for most firms.

Physical, Finance, and Social Capital

The third factor endowment in economics is capital. Capital, here, refers to assets that yield income and other outputs over time.[24] These include machinery and economic infrastructure, as well as soft infrastructure such as finance and social networks. The physical, finance, and social capital stock in Lagos position it to be Nigeria's largest and most diversified subnational economy.

Some of Nigeria's most developed hard infrastructure can be found in Lagos. This includes a network of roads, bridges, flyovers, ports and other transport infrastructure; arts centers and national institutes; housing estates; schools, hospitals, and other public facilities which make the state more amenable to a wide range of economic activity. Most of this infrastructure was the legacy of the city's status as Nigeria's administrative capital until the mid-1990s, and especially, the result of major investment during the oil boom from the 1970s to the 1990s. For instance, the 11.8 kilometers long Third Mainland Bridge links the Lagos "mainland" to the commercial nerve center and highbrow areas of Ikoyi, and Victoria Island. At the time of its opening by the Ibrahim Babangida's military regime in 1990, the bridge was the longest in Africa and remained so until 1996 when Cairo's 6th October Bridge was completed. Other construction projects include the 1004 estate, FESTAC Town, and the National Theatre. Since the early 2000s, the Lagos State Government has made significant strides in urban renewal and infrastructure rehabilitation, as discussed later in this chapter. One notable initiative is Eko Atlantic, a multibillion dollar modern residential and business development modeled on Manhattan in New York City, being built on 10 million square meters of land reclaimed from the Atlantic Ocean.[25]

However, inadequate urban planning and years of neglect have created a serious infrastructure crisis in Lagos. Even the investments in infrastructure made by military rulers were far below the recommended threshold by urban planners. As Matthew Gandy and Laurent Fourchard note, the military governments focused only on prestige buildings and road projects to the detriment of housing, sewerage, and other important recommendations by the UN.[26] The decades-long recurrent congestion on the road arteries leading to and from Nigeria's major port complex in Apapa is a case in point. Successive governments have failed to expand this artery to accommodate the growth of commercial and vehicular traffic. To ease traffic especially after the infamous "cement armada" of the 1970s, the Fourth National Development Plan of 1981 committed resources to establishing additional ports, the Tin Can Island Port in Lagos, and the Calabar Port in Cross River state. However, progress on these alternate port complexes has been slow. Furthermore, the relocation of the federal capital to Abuja in 1991 has left many buildings in a state of decline; some of which were taken over by Lagos State, such as the now-privatized Federal Secretariat.[27] Overall, the national malaise of the 1990s precipitated by prolonged military rule also affected Lagos as existing infrastructure fell into acute disrepair. Therefore, hours-long traffic jams such as the one I experienced in FESTAC Town in 2014 are a common sight on neglected federal roads, incurring heavy losses for traders and commuters.

As a center of commerce, Lagos has a soft infrastructure of networks, finance and social capital that enable an emerging service economy. Historically, Lagos was a trading city. Its business quarter dates back to the trade in slaves and commodities of the eighteenth century. The trading imperative developed into huge retail operations such as the Alaba international market, a pillar of the large informal sector in Lagos. In the latter part of the colonial period, industrial estates in Apapa and Ikeja played a role in the food and drink industries anchored by multinationals such as Cadbury,

Nestlé, Guinness, and Nigerian Breweries.[28] Since 1999, more foreign, especially South African, capital has flowed to retail, hospitality, and entertainment such as the drinks multinational SAB Miller and the entertainment chain DSTV to cater to a growing middle class.[29] Presently, Lagos has ten large industrial estates accommodating several hundred enterprises as well as many smaller industrial zones for MSMEs.[30] It also has the most sophisticated built-up consumer markets and distribution channels in West Africa.[31] Lagos houses the headquarters of ninety-five diplomatic missions and consulates, multinationals, international media, large domestic firms, and international NGOs. For example, the Chinese telecoms giant, Huawei, has located one of its eight global innovation centers in Lagos and has invested $6 million in the city.[32] The American social media company, Facebook, has also established a tech hub for start-up in Lagos, which is also the heartbeat of Nigeria's rapidly growing music, movie, and entertainment industry. All these provide access to regional and global networks, lower information asymmetry, and increase economic opportunities for individuals, households, and firms resident in Lagos compared to the rest of Nigeria.

Finally, Lagos borrowers receive the largest share of bank loans compared to other economic hubs in Nigeria. An examination of data on credit and deposit of commercial banks shows that lending to entities in Lagos is disproportionately higher than the city's contributions to deposits (Figure 7.6a). In other words, Lagos entities are financed by savings from other parts of the country acquired by financial institutions headquartered in Lagos but with a national spread. In 2015, Lagos received a disproportionate 78.5% of Nigeria's total commercial loans while providing only 50.7% of bank deposits (Figure 7.6a). Let us contrast these figures from other economic hubs across Nigeria. Rivers state provided 5.8% of total savings but received 5.1% of credit; the administrative capital, Abuja, provided 13.4% of deposits but received only 3.1% of credit while Kano accounted for 1.6% of total savings, but received slightly less, 1.4% of all credit. Therefore, there is some imbalance between savings and lending in Lagos, that outpaces other economic hubs around the country.

On the surface, this distribution of bank finance suggests that individual and enterprise borrowers in Lagos have better access to finance capital. This proposition may seem even more plausible when one considers that the city is home to the largest number of banks and financial institutions—by the number of branches and headquarters located there. Of the country's twenty-two commercial banks, all except one have their head offices in Lagos.[33] The reality, though, is that large firms, conglomerates, and high net worth individuals are the main beneficiaries of these bank loans rather than MSMEs. Indeed, only 36.1% of sole proprietorships in Lagos are able to access bank finance, compared to a national average of 49.5% (Figure 7.6b). According to a World Bank study, "there is very little difference between firms based in Lagos and those elsewhere. Being close to the center of the nation's banking sector does not appear to confer any advantage on Nigerian businesses."[34] This was confirmed by the founder and then CEO of Access Bank, Aigboje Aig-Imoukhuede, to my question on whether MSME location affects their access to finance:[35]

No. Money… transcends religion, tribe etc. If you are a good entrepreneur, if I know you are the next Steve Jobs, Bill Gates and so on, my money will be in your pocket very quickly. It is an economic decision, always.

*(a) Distribution of Bank Credit and Deposit in
Economic Centres, 2015*

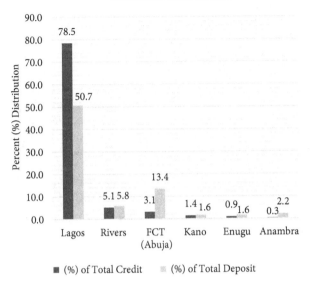

■ (%) of Total Credit   ▧ (%) of Total Deposit

*(b) Access to Bank Finance by State (Sole
Proprietorship) % Distribution*

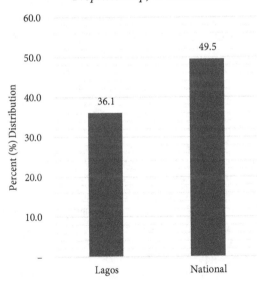

Figure 7.6 Lagos Receives a Disproportionate Share of Bank Credit that Does Not Benefit Small Enterprises.

Source: Panel a—NBS (Banks Credit and Deposit by States in Nigeria: 2010–2015, 2016)Panel b—NBS and SMEDAN (National survey of micro-, small-and medium-scale enterprises (MSMEs) 2017, 2017).

In fact, a major break on productivity and growth identified by MSMEs in Lagos is the limited access to finance in ways that mirror the rest of Nigeria as we discussed in Chapter 5. This was also confirmed to me by a representative of the Lagos Chamber of Commerce and Industry (LCCI).[36] As we discussed in Chapter 5, Nigeria's banking sector is not fully integrated into the real economy, i.e., agriculture, manufacturing, and industry overall, a situation Central Bank reforms have sought to address. Although consolidation reforms from 2004 made the Nigerian banking sector more liquid, reduced nonperforming loans (NPLs) and increased asset quality, credit to the private sector remains constrained. Lending mostly goes to the government, oil importers and large corporations which are often Lagos-based, to the exclusion of MSMEs in agriculture, manufacturing, and other real sectors, as the banking tycoon Imoukhuede elaborated.[37] MSMEs are, in turn, discouraged by high interest rates and steep collateral. Many economists are of the view that a financial system will work better if governments have moderate borrowing needs and rely on markets, rather than pressure banks, to obtain their funds.[38] Although there have been recent efforts by the Central Bank to boost lending to MSMEs, the problem surrounding cost and access to finance to MSMEs persists in Lagos and across the country.

Entrepreneurial and Managerial Ability

The fourth and final group of factor endowments in economics is entrepreneurial and managerial ability. A concentration of entrepreneurial talent in Lagos is another element of its endowment structure which orients the economy towards services. I work with the definition of an entrepreneur as someone who manages and assumes the risks of an enterprise, and entrepreneurship as the process of discovering new ways of combining resources.[39] To that effect, I use the terms entrepreneur and businessmen/women, interchangeably, and therefore refer to "business class" and "economic elite" as the collective of entrepreneurs especially the large-scale and influential ones.

There is a concentration of entrepreneurial talent in Lagos. It has Nigeria's largest number of MSMEs, at 3.3 million. Besides, most of Nigeria's billionaire tycoons listed by *Forbes* such as Aliko Dangote, Femi Otedola, Mike Adenuga, and Folorunsho Alakija,[40] and most commercial banks, are headquartered in Lagos. Although many of these firms—from manufacturing to financial services—have their headquarters in Lagos while the actual operations are dispersed around Nigeria. There are strong historical continuities in the city's attraction to local entrepreneurs and foreign investors. As the anthropologist Kaye Whiteman notes, the trade in Lagos, was never totally dominated by foreigners (unlike in Francophone, Eastern and Southern Africa) despite the favors given to European firms by the colonial government.[41]

In addition to historical precedents, the concentration of entrepreneurs in Lagos is complemented by other factor endowments. These include access to seaports, a rapidly growing population, a relatively skilled labor force, better infrastructure, and stronger economic networks compared to the rest of Nigeria. As Aliko Dangote, the industrial magnate, who is headquartered in Lagos explained to me:[42]

I come from Kano, and no matter how much I want to help my people in Kano, whatever I am going to do must be sustainable, then I am better off putting my plant where it can be sustainable... Then I can dedicate the profit to be sharing it among the people there... Even the raw materials, since we don't have a port [in Kano], the raw materials will still come, and you have to transport it... So with my flour mills, it is cheaper for me to produce the flour here [in Lagos] and take it down there [Kano] and sell... than to open a factory and produce... there.

Entrepreneurs are attracted to Lagos because the business environment allows for economies of scale. With a dynamic technology start-up ecosystem, Lagos is ranked as the top innovative city in Africa by GSMA.[43] According to the World Bank, the Lagos ecosystem has scale due to the availability of skilled manpower via the various technology institutes in the country, bandwidth, infrastructure, and venture capital as well as sectors and markets that can sustain innovation.[44] It is the entry point from where Nigeria connects to seven submarine internet cables that have huge available capacity. In 2013, the MainOne company, in partnership with the Lagos State Government, deployed a fiber-optic pilot for broadband internet in the Yaba district where several tech hubs and start-up are located. With the large number of tech creatives, over sixty primary and secondary schools, three higher institution campuses, and home to over thirty established tech companies, the Yaba district is frequently compared with Silicon Valley, with names such as Yabacon Valley and Silicon Lagoon.[45] Lagos is thus a mature and active ecosystem with dynamic incubators, venture capital companies, and digital start-ups (See Box 7.1). This tech community, mainly in Yaba and in other parts of Lagos, positions Nigeria alongside South Africa, as having the most advanced tech ecosystem in Africa.

Box 7.1 Will the Lagos Tech Scene Drive Nigeria's Digital Transformation?

The Co-Creation Hub (CcHUB) in Lagos is the leading technology (tech) hub incubating digital entrepreneurship in Nigeria today. The CcHUB is an open living lab and multi-purpose incubation space which nurtures creative tech ventures designed to address social problems. Through various incubation and acceleration programs, the CcHUB supports tech start-ups admitted into the program to take off, grow, and achieve economies of scale. This support includes the provision of free workspace with high-speed internet, a cash investment of $5,000–$25,000, mentorship from industry experts and hands-on support on product development.[46] Since its inception in 2010, the CcHUB has supported over ninety tech ventures, some of which have become fully-fledged standalone firms with a footprint in their respective industries.[47] These include BudgIT, a civic tech organization focused on transparency, citizen engagement, and accountability in public finance; Life Bank, which delivers medical supplies to hospitals using technology solutions and WeCyclers, which provides convenient recycling services. The CcHUB has gone from strength to strength: it acquired one of Nairobi's most prominent tech hubs in September 2019 and is collaborating with the Bill & Melinda Gates Foundation, Facebook, Google, and the MacArthur

Foundation, among others. Tech hubs like CcHUB, Andela, Wennovation, and dozens of others have helped position Lagos as the top innovative city in Africa, with over forty tech hubs.[48] While Lagos contains more than half of Nigeria's eight-five tech hubs, there are other emerging ecosystems in cities like Abuja and Port Harcourt, with the potential to expand to Enugu, Jos, Kaduna, and Kano. With Nigeria's 41 million MSMEs, it has a long and established culture of entrepreneurship which is now spilling into the digital economy. To realize the promise of Nigeria's digital transformation through the growth of digital firms, challenges such as a difficult business environment, lack of early-stage financing, limited market opportunities outside of Lagos and Abuja, and investments in digital skills must be addressed.[49] This would help ensure that digital revolution in the Lagos tech scene becomes a truly Nigeria-wide phenomenon.

This analysis of the factor endowments in Lagos illustrates how the region is positioned to be Nigeria's largest subnational economy, based on services and with a large fiscal base. The advantages conferred by these structural attributes are not assured, however, without deliberate public policy around infrastructure, investments, trade, and social development to leverage them. And it is politics that determines the orientation and effectiveness of these public policies. In post-military Nigeria, public policy reforms have contributed to positioning Lagos as Nigeria's largest and most diversified subnational economy built on services, trade, and non-oil activity. How did these policy reforms emerge? Who drove them? Why have they achieved a modicum of success? Are they sustainable? We address these questions in the next section.

Subnational Policy Reforms Enable Fiscal Diversification in Lagos

The economic performance of Lagos is not just a function of luck, history, or geography although they certainly contribute. Beyond its factor endowments, public policies in Lagos have increased non-oil revenue generation, rejuvenated the city, and enabled its fiscal diversification. State government initiatives in urban renewal, PFM reforms, and social development, have drawn popular attention in global policy and media circles. Lagos under the leadership of Bola Ahmed Tinubu (1999–2007) and Babatunde Fashola (2007–2015) was a pilgrimage destination for other Nigerian state governors keen to copy the "Lagos Model" in urban renewal and non-oil revenue generation. *The Economist*, the *Financial Times* and other leading publications have applauded the state's urban regeneration initiatives.[50] A large stream of academic publications assess Lagos governance and tax reforms.[51]

I attribute Lagos' policy effectiveness to the nature of politics in the state. Lagos ruling elites built a political coalition to coordinate their resource endowments and harness institutional arrangements to address severe socio-economic pressures. Using the lens of political settlements outlined in Chapters 1 and 3, we identify these pressures as external constraints of fiscal insolvency and tense relations with the federal government, horizontal constraints of political factionalization and vertical–societal constraints of rapid population growth, urban decay, and violent crime. In responding to these pressures, decision-makers in Lagos built a political coalition that was managerially competent, administratively capable of designing and implementing policy reforms, that espoused a grand vision for the city's transformation like other global cities in Asia and Latin America and that leveraged existing institutions within Nigeria's federalism. The result is fiscal diversification, urban renewal, and an emerging if fragile social contract.

The Lagos Ruling Elite is Constrained towards a Reform-orientation to Diversify the Revenue Base

When Nigeria transitioned to electoral rule, Lagos, as much of the country, was at a critical juncture of existential threats that required responsive leadership. The city was the poster child for urban decay and chaos in international media and policy circles. For instance, in February 1994, Robert Kaplan writing in *The Atlantic* magazine described Lagos as a city " ... whose crime, pollution, and overcrowding make it the cliche par excellence of Third World urban dysfunction... "[52] Horizontal–elite factionalization within the ruling political party, vertical–societal constraints of urban decay and violent crime amidst exploding population growth, and the external constraint of declining federal revenue all threatened to collapse on the city. A political coalition emerged from attempts by Lagos ruling elites to address the severe threats that these partisan, urban, fiscal, and social crises posed to them. How did these constraints push ruling elites to build a reform-oriented political coalition?

The first major constraint, at the horizontal–elite level, is the factionalization within the ruling party that spurred a reform-orientation in Lagos State. Specifically, continuous intra-party power struggles put successive state governors under constant pressure to seek external legitimacy beyond the confines of their adversarial political party. They secured this legitimacy through both service delivery and by granting political favors to influential social groups such as street gangs known as "area boys," market women, transport unions, and other informal networks. For instance, the first post-military governor of Lagos State, Bola Tinubu, drew the anger of influential party elders of the then Alliance for Democracy (AD) over his appointment of political outsiders to cabinet positions. In addition, when Tinubu selected Babatunde Fashola as his successor in the 2007 election, it was considered an imposition by many influential party members. Fashola's selection led to mass defections of prominent AD party leaders such as Senator Afikuyomi, Jimi Agbaje, Senator Musiliu Obanikoro, and Remi Adikuwu Bakare. Tinubu eventually gained the upper hand in the party by building relationships with key social constituencies, traditional leaders and utlizing grassroots networks.[53]

For Fashola, his relationship with his benefactor Tinubu eventually deteriorated in his second term from 2011. He therefore sought legitimacy beyond the party from Lagos residents based on his record of service delivery.[54] Fashola's successor, Akinwunmi Ambode, did not survive this internal power struggle and failed in his attempt to run for a second term as governor when he fell out of favor with the grand patron of the APC in Lagos, Bola Tinubu (see Figure 7.7).[55] Therefore, partisan factionalizations

Figure 7.7 Timeline of Lagos State Governors and their Political Parties since 1999.

Source: Author's construction.

impelled governors Tinubu and Fashola to build an external and popular support base beyond the political party through both service delivery and the allocation of rents to informal networks.

The second major constraint, at the vertical–societal level, is the urban disorder that spurred governance reforms and urban renewal. The city was consumed by infrastructure decay and pervasive violent crime. Matthew Gandy vividly illustrates the chaos that characterized Lagos in the 1990s and early 2000s:[56]

> The recent history of Lagos has been marked by a stark deterioration in quality of life… the city has lost much of its street lighting, its dilapidated road system has become extremely congested, there are no longer regular refuse collections, violent crime has become a determining feature of everyday life and many symbols of civic culture such as libraries and cinemas have largely disappeared. The city's sewerage network is practically non-existent and at least two-thirds of childhood disease is attributable to inadequate access to safe drinking water. In heavy rains, over half of the city's dwellings suffer from routine flooding…

As discussed earlier, Lagos faced demographic pressures from a rapidly growing population which severely strained its existing infrastructure. On average, 1.6 million people migrate to the city each year, placing severe pressure on housing, transport infrastructure and social services that were inadequate to begin with and already decaying from unplanned urban growth, industrial decline, and federal government neglect. In essence, infrastructure that was in place when Lagos had 5 million residents now served a population of over 15 million people, as the Commissioner for Economic Planning and Budget explained to me.[57] In 1991, Lagos was named the world's dirtiest city by the UN.[58] By the turn of the century, Lagos had become a hotbed of armed robbery, ritual murders, and other violent crime which severely undermined security and deterred investors. The police force covered a few wealthy neighborhoods while others relied on private security or vigilantes.[59] There was a pervasive atmosphere of entrenched disorder. The "area boys" extorted residents, while the ethnic militia Oodua People's Congress (OPC), which provided vigilante security, frequently clashed with non-Yoruba residents, especially Hausa-speaking "northerners." As one analyst explained to me "Lagos faced the threat of imminent infrastructural collapse."[60]

All strata of society, including the middle class and the elite, were affected by this prospect of infrastructural collapse and urban anarchy. Former chief of staff to Bola Tinubu and now Federal Minister of Information, Lai Mohammed, explained to me[61] that due to intense traffic gridlocks and the "… heaps of refuse, some roads were impassable… " Civic advocacy also helped to pressure decision-makers to respond to urban disorder. Due to the favorable initial conditions described earlier in this chapter, Lagos has a substantial middle class and is the fulcrum of national civil society. Lagosians were therefore better positioned than other Nigerians to make programmatic demands of their elected leaders for improved public services, according to Diane de Gramont.[62] To that effect, government officials in Tinubu's first administration felt strong pressure from both its citizens and the media to start addressing the city's problems as soon as they took office. Since state government performance was and still is compared to accomplishments of revered past leaders such as Chief Obafemi Awolowo and Lateef Jakande,[63] public demands increased over time. As the ruling elite realized, they were not immune to the crisis posed by urban decay and insecurity, and middle-class advocacy further intensified this pressure on decision-makers.

The third major constraint, at the external level, was a fiscal crisis that forced Lagos decision-makers to implement PFM reforms. By 1999, the Lagos State Government simply did not have sufficient revenue to address the collapsing infrastructure, rising insecurity, and to fund the day-to-day business of public administration. In 2002, the state government's personnel costs alone exceeded its statutory allocation from the federal government, which was already depressed from low oil prices. Based on Nigeria's complex revenue distribution formula, which considers several criteria including landmass, population, internal revenue generation, and fiscal efficiency, among others, Lagos is one of the states that receive the largest share of statutory allocations. In 2018, Lagos received N119 billion of federal revenues, the fifth fastest growing largest of Nigeria's thirty-six states (Figure 7.8). However, demographic pressures and the public services needs render these federal funds grossly inadequate. In the same year, Lagos

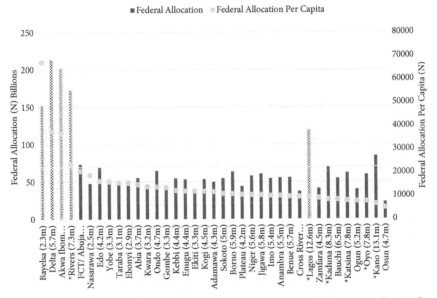

Figure 7.8 Federal Allocation to Nigeria's Thirty-Six States Ranked in Descending Order in (N) Billions, 2018.

Source: Author's calculations from NBS and estimates the annual abstract of statistics 2017.

Notes: Bars shaded in dots represent the top five federal allocation recipients. States with an asterisk (*) represent Nigeria's five most populous states.

received only N9,484 per capita even though it is one of Nigeria's two most populous states. In comparison, a state like Bayelsa with an estimated 2.3 million residents, less than a quarter of Lagos, received N153 billion of federal revenues which amounts to N67,211 per capita, more than sixfold the amount received by Lagos.

There were also roadblocks to securing other external sources of finance. For instance, Lagos could not take out loans on capital markets indefinitely without proving it could repay them by having a steady revenue stream.[64] A difficult situation became worse when the federal government, during Obasanjo's presidency, withheld Lagos State statutory allocation for its local governments when, in 2004, Tinubu's government created thirty-seven additional local councils that were not recognized by the constitution.[65] Consequently, government authorities were under pressure to creatively diversify their revenue base to cater to their fiscal and developmental needs.

Thus, elite factionalization within the ruling party, urban degeneration, and insufficient public finances constrained Lagos' decision to adopt a reform-orientation.

A Reform-oriented Ruling Elite in Lagos Harnesses Federal Institutions to Achieve Fiscal Diversification

In responding to these severe pressures, the ruling elites in Lagos built a reform-oriented political coalition. This was managerially and administratively capable of identifying the city's problems and articulating a vision for transforming Lagos into a world-class mega city. They also harnessed the institutional arrangements of Nigeria's federalism to strengthen their administrative capacity towards their grand vision for Lagos. This administrative capacity allowed them to upgrade urban infrastructure, adopt a pro-business orientation, and implement tax reforms for non-oil revenue generation. Let us examine the elements of the ruling elite's reform-orientation: managerial competence and skillful negotiation of federal institutional arrangement.

To begin with, the post-military ruling elites of Lagos State demonstrated managerial competence to pursue a reform-orientation. Since 1999, the succession of state governors in Lagos have been well-educated, capable managers, with a deep understanding of the city's problems. The first post-military governor, Bola Ahmed Tinubu, had been an accountant with the multinational Mobil and was a prominent member of Nigeria's pro-democracy movement, NADECO, against the military. As Tinubu's former chief of staff, Lai Mohammed explained to me,[66] "Asiwaju (Tinubu) had definite ideas about governance," and shortly after his inauguration, he requested development assistance from the United States and his former private-sector colleagues. Tinubu handpicked his successor, Babatunde Fashola, his chief of staff, an accomplished lawyer and a Senior Advocate of Nigeria (SAN), the highest achievement for lawyers in Nigeria. Mohammed explained further[67] "the crowning factor was the ability to choose a successor who understood what governance was about."

Furthermore, the state governors articulated a clear vision to transform Lagos into a world-class city to be achieved by upgrading urban infrastructure and adopting a pro-business orientation. In the Lagos State Development Plan (2013), the city aspires, by 2025, to become "Africa's model mega-city and a global economic and financial hub, one which is safe, secure, functional and productive." As the Commissioner for

Economic Planning and Budget at the time explained to me:[68] "infrastructure has been at the heart of the reform agenda… We adopted a development policy thrust: sustainable economic growth and poverty eradication through infrastructure renewal and development…." There is also a pro-business orientation. In his inaugural address in May 2007, former governor Babatunde Fashola stated that: "we are also determined to create more job opportunities for residents of Lagos State. During my term of office, Lagos will remain a pro-business city State…."[69] With a GDP that ranks as Africa's seventh largest if Lagos were a separate country, the ruling elite exhibit a sense of exceptionalism (Figure 7.1c). They see the state as detached from the rest of Nigeria.[70] Consequently, in their drive to become a functioning and prosperous city-state, the Lagos State Government benchmarks itself against Dubai, Johannesburg, and other global cities. Fashola, as his personal aides informed me, made several trips as governor to Singapore to meet Lee Kuan Yew and consult the city's planners for ideas. It is to actualize this vision of building a world-class mega city that successive governments focused on self-sufficiency through non-oil revenue generation and urban renewal.

To implement this vision of a functioning world-class megacity, the Lagos ruling elite had to strengthen the state's weak bureaucratic capacities. Like the rest of Nigeria, military rule had corroded the administrative structures of Lagos State by the time of the democracy transition in 1999. The government lacked a basic capacity to collect or monitor tax revenues, there was virtually no urban transport system and Lagos was literally disappearing under mountains of rubbish. Taxes were routinely paid in cash to revenue officials who gave out handwritten receipts creating multiple opportunities for corruption and the poorly-equipped revenue administration staff found it difficult to effectively track payments.[71] Faced with these bureaucratic deficiencies across the board, there was need for "process re-engineering," as the Commissioner for Economic Planning and Budget explained to me.[72]

To strengthen their bureaucratic capacity, the Lagos ruling elite harnessed the institutional provisions of Nigeria's federalism which provides for fiscal and political autonomy of state governments. As a federation, the American-style Nigerian Constitution distributes power between the federal government and subnational authorities, that is the states and local governments. The jurisdiction of these tiers is classified as Exclusive, Concurrent, and Supplementary, in which the Federal, the State, and both authorities can legislate on respectively.[73] Therefore, state governments have significant fiscal autonomy in the Nigerian Constitution to envision an economic agenda within their respective jurisdictions, formulate policies, generate revenue, establish MDAs and appoint their heads,[74] and allocate resources to actualizing this agenda. The constitution also empowers state executives with vast political autonomy. As elected chief executives, state governors possess a political mandate, they are the leaders of the state chapters of their political parties and are influential in their state legislatures. Thus, Lagos has attained atypical fiscal diversification among Nigeria's thirty-six states because it has harnessed this fiscal and political authority provided by the constitution to achieve specific policy objectives.

In harnessing the institutional arrangements of Nigeria's federalism, Lagos State governance reforms were initially ad hoc focused on relieving immediate fiscal pressures. This ad hoc approach to governance reforms was most evident in tax collection in which creative measures that maximized its constitutional fiscal authority were used to source non-oil revenues. Since the early 2000s, the strategy consisted of stronger enforcement of subnational tax authority outlined in the Concurrent List of the constitution such as personal income, property, and land taxes. Personal income tax, which has driven most of the increases in IGR, constitutes 80%.[75] As the Lagos Commissioner for Economic Planning and Budget explained to me,[76] they started with high-income earners in large corporations and the public service, and then used public campaigns to link tax collection to visible infrastructure projects. Private consultants such as the Alpha-Beta Consulting (ABC) did the heavy lifting in collecting taxes to supplement weak administrative capacity at the Lagos Inland Revenue Service (LIRS). By 2014, tax payment compliance among large corporations reached 80%, up from 30–40% in 2005. Consequently, tax revenues expanded exponentially from an average N900 million per month in 2000, to N6 billion in 2007, N18 billion in 2014 and over N26 billion in 2017 (Figure 7.9). Efforts are now focused on expanding tax coverage to include the informal sector which constitutes more than 70% of economic activity.

The Lagos State reformers also invested in deeper subnational institutional building, especially around urban renewal and infrastructure upgrading. In Tinubu's second term from 2003, the policy reforms became less ad hoc in at least two ways. Firstly, new agencies were built from scratch such as the Lagos Metropolitan Transport Authority (LAMATA) to manage urban transportation and the Lagos State Traffic Management Authority (LASTMA) to enforce traffic laws. These enforcement agencies were crucial to the infrastructure push in rehabilitating roads, establishing a Bus Rapid Transport (BRT) system and building an intracity metro system. A second long-term approach

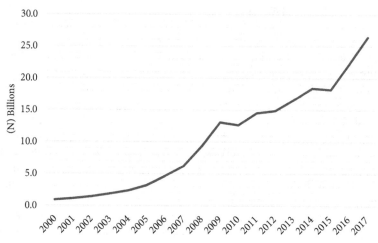

Figure 7.9 Average Monthly Taxes, Fines and Fees, and Licenses Earnings for the Lagos State Government, 2000–2017.

Source: Author's calculations from: World Bank (Nigeria–Lagos State: States' Finances Review and Agenda for Action, 2007) for 1999–2003 figures and Lagos State Government (Digest of Statistics: 2013, 2013; Digest of Statistics: 2015, 2015; Digest of Statistics: 2018, 2018) for 2004–2017 figures.

was to draw on a diverse range of public, private, foreign, and multilateral sources to finance infrastructure and major capital projects. In 2007, Lagos State came up with a ten-year infrastructural development plan, costed at $50 billion.[77] They have since explored various options to finance this plan, as explained by the Commissioner for Economic Planning and Budget. For example, major highway overhauls were made possible by public–private partnerships, such as the Lekki-Epe Expressway and Toll Concession arrangement with the Lekki Concession Company. The world-class Eko Atlantic project, or West Africa's "Dubai," was financed by a consortium of domestic and foreign investors.

The successes in implementing reforms to actualize the vision of megacity, have emboldened Lagos ruling elites to negotiate for an expansion of their fiscal authority in the constitution. Specifically, they want more authority to set statutory rates for income, consumption, corporate, and other taxes.[78] They also want more control on transportation, power, and security infrastructure currently in the Exclusive List. Infrastructure is thus a sphere of political contestation with transport management often weaponized by both federal and Lagos politicians. As the Lagos Commissioner for Economic Planning and Budget explained to me,[79] their plans to pursue Independent Power Projects (IPP) and an intracity railway project were delayed for years by the federal government's lethargy: in approving their requests to use the rail corridor, float bonds, and obtain external development assistance. There were accusations that a former Federal Minister of Transport, out to settle partisan scores in Lagos, frustrated attempts by the state government to secure a $77 million World Bank facility for the state transport agency LAMATA.

The Lagos ruling elite also weaponized urban spaces, especially motor parks, and markets to check the federal government, to the detriment of the city's urban planning. According to Fourchard, since the 1980s, major sources of revenue such as motor parks levies have been outsourced to transport union leaders who are allowed to levy discretionary taxes in exchange for electoral support.[80] Lagos ruling elites ironically expect the federal government to both pull its weight but also regard it as a hindrance. As the Commissioner for Economic Planning and Budget explained to me:[81] "Without doubt, we would be further ahead without hindrances by the [federal] government... to borrow funds, we have to go all the way to the minister of finance...." With these perceived and real restrictions, Lagos has been at the forefront of advocating for "fiscal federalism" or greater decentralization of political and fiscal power to subnational governments.

Fiscal Diversification and Urban Renewal Result in a Fragile Social Contract in Lagos

The results of these initial policy reforms provided the building blocks for a fragile social contract in Lagos State. Tangible progress towards fiscal diversification in terms of rising IGR and urban renewal in terms of transport infrastructure rehabilitation strengthened the legitimacy of Lagos ruling elites among at least three key constituencies: business groups, middle-class professionals, and grassroots networks. This legitimacy is helping to construct a fragile state–society compact crucial to sustaining policy initiatives in the long term. Yet, political factionalization within the ruling party and rising disenchantment with the looming influence of Bola Tinubu in public finance could unravel this nascent social contract. Let us examine in more detail the nature of the social compact with each of these key constituencies and the risks therein.

The reform-orientation of Lagos decision-makers is strengthening state–business relations between the government and business groups. Various policy coordination platforms exist to engage the private sector in economic policy. According to the Lagos Chamber of Commerce and Industry (LCCI),[82] the private sector participates in policy formulation and in tracking progress. Since 2000, a bi-annual investment forum, called "Ehingbeti," has provided a "platform to enhance policy formulation and implementation dialogue" for the Lagos State Government, investors, and other stakeholders.[83] Due to its success and visibility, other Nigerian states adapted the idea of a state–business forum, notably the northern state of Kaduna which now organizes very glitzy annual investment summits with multinationals and global policy leaders in attendance.

Stronger state–business relations are helping to advance the policy objectives of improved security and tax reforms. The Lagos State-Security Trust Fund is another instance of state–business collaboration. Established in 2007, this fund accepts contributions from the private sector and other stakeholders to support the police and federal security forces stationed in Lagos.[84] Since 2008, these funds have been used to support the 1,600 officers of the state's Rapid Response Squad to combat violent crime:[85] with a monthly allowance in addition to their federal salaries; supply of uniform and equipment including bulletproof vests, ammunition, and patrol vehicles; life insurance and housing. A Security Command and Control Center has been set up with CCTV cameras, a toll-free emergency number, and other communications infrastructure. Stronger state–business ties are also enhancing tax collection. On this front, the LIRS works closely with organized private sector, such as the LCCI, to encourage compliance among private firms, reign in illegal practices by tax collectors, and mediate disputes.[86] These are some instances where stronger state–business ties are helping to advance government policy objectives.

A second constituency with which a social compact is emerging with the Lagos State Government around service delivery is tax-paying middle-class professionals. The government is using the evidence of service delivery to persuade more professionals in private practice such as lawyers, doctors, and chartered accountants to pay tax.[87] As the Lagos State Commissioner for Budget and Planning explained to me,[88] many people did not previously pay taxes because they saw no "connection between their … taxes and … any goods and services of government." However, the extension of physical infrastructure upgrading from the highbrow Victoria Island to middle-class dwellings in the Lagos Mainland have convinced more salaried professionals to pay tax, according to finance ministry officials.[89] Billboards at government construction sites link the ongoing project with "tax payers' money at work." A 2009 survey showed 83.9% of Lagosians were satisfied with the government's work on roads, and a 2010 survey found that receipt of public goods was correlated with a willingness to pay tax.[90] It also helps that Lagos has a large tax base. As the country's commercial capital with a large stock of literate residents, it has a critical mass of salaried staff who can pay income tax.[91] Consequently, voluntary tax compliance is rising alongside an emerging social contract with a taxable population.

The third constituency with which a social compact exists is grassroots actors who provide political support in exchange for government employment and patronage. Certain government agencies are effective because they perform dual functions of public service provision as well as patronage employment to key social groups. The Lagos State Traffic Management Authority (LASTMA), which employs about 3,000 people has in its ranks many "area boys" who assisted in political campaigns.[92] Similarly, the Lagos State Waste Management Authority (LAWMA) employs over 24,000 street sweepers from key electoral constituencies. The roots of this compact lie in Tinubu's involvement in street politics with the powerful Lagos State Market Women's Association and the National Union of Road Transport Workers—NURTW.[93] The market women's association has been an influential electoral constituency since the franchise was extended to women in 1950s because they constituted the majority of female voters in southern cities. As the son of the leader of the Lagos market women association, Tinubu also found it easy to associate with this powerful group. Successive Lagos ruling elites have since the 1980s also relied on the NURTW to supply thugs and votes during governorship elections. According to Laurent Fourchard, ruling elites often diverted resources meant for upgrading urban infrastructure, such as motor parks, to greasing these clientelist ties with NURTW leaders.[94]

In addition to gaining an electoral advantage, this compact with grassroots associations has contributed to advancing the policy objective of tax collection. Lagos State officials have complemented formal enforcement with informal ties to these associations to extend the tax net to the informal sector.[95] According to tax officials at the LIRS, without the cooperation of these market associations, it would be difficult to collect taxes from smaller associations of traders operating out of informal markets. Market leaders have, in turn, taken on much of the state's monitoring and compliance role, providing LIRS with lists of traders in their domain and helping with outreach. The government is adapting this street-smart strategy to extend the tax net to artisans.[96]

While there is an evident state-society compact emerging, it could be unravelled in its infancy by the very elements that forged it. Specifically, the looming influence of the grand patron of the APC ruling party in Lagos, Bola Tinubu, could undermine the nascent state–society compact he single-handedly built. His political hegemony is a double-edged sword. On one side, the political structure he has built since 1999 has fostered continuity by insulating decision-making from the factionalization of party politics. This political structure was inherited from the Action Group built by Obafemi Awolowo, the Yoruba Premier of the western region who ran Lagos from the 1950s and has never been disbanded.[97] The AG became the UPN in the Second Republic (1979–1983), formed part of the SDP in the aborted Third Republic (1990–1993), became the AD and then ACN between 1999 and 2013 in the current Fourth Republic, and is a key building block of the now national ruling party, the APC. This party, under various names, has won every governorship election in the state and dominates the legislature. It successfully re-captured south-west politics since 2011, from controlling just Lagos State in 2007 to an additional three states: Ogun, Osun, and Oyo by 2015. Tinubu's political dominance of the ruling APC has provided a strong policy coherence in Lagos and much of the south-west that is rare in the turbulence of Nigerian politics.

The other side of this sword is that a growing and critical mass of political adversaries could consolidate forces to upstage Tinubu in the long run and unravel the two-decade policy coherence he has engineered. By sheer political heft, Tinubu has prevailed over intra-party divisions. In his first term, he battled influential AD party elders over appointments. At the end of his second term in 2007, he overcame the strong pushback from party elders to his nomination of Babatunde Fashola as successor which prompted major defections. The crowning of Akinwunmi Ambode as Fashola's successor in 2015 also led to mass defections from the APC. And when Ambode fell out of with the grand patron, he suffered a humiliating defeat in the party primary to Babajide Sanwo Olu who eventually became governor. Despite these intra-party schisms, there is always an effort to present a united front, suggesting commitment to a broader vision of building a functioning megacity.

The perception of a narrowing political tent in the APC for an increasingly diverse Lagos society could strengthen the otherwise disorganized opposition and unravel the prevailing political consensus. The opposition party, the PDP, lacking a Tinubu-like charismatic and influential father-figure, is structurally weak and highly fragmented with several formidable factional leaders[98] some of whom have defected from the APC. Yet, the APC's margin of victory has fluctuated with each election cycle as the PDP sometimes puts up a strong challenge. It garnered an unprecedented 44% of the vote compared to the APC's 54% in 2015 for instance (Figure 7.10).

APC's fluctuating electoral margins can be linked to rising tensions between Yoruba indigenes and the large Igbo minority in Lagos which surfaced during the 2015 governorship election. During the electoral campaigns, the APC candidate Akinwunmi Ambode implicitly represented Yoruba interests, while the PDP candidate Jimi Agbaje positioned himself as the protector of "persecuted" Igbo minorities. This happened amidst a rising undercurrent of deep-seated competition between the two groups dating back to the political rivalry between Obafemi Awolowo and Nnamdi Azikiwe in the 1950s for control of Lagos. A chain of separate but interrelated incidents resurrected this dormant Igbo-Yoruba acrimony. In his 2012 memoirs, Chinua Achebe, the acclaimed writer of Igbo descent, accused Obafemi Awolowo, the revered leader of Yorubas, of devising the blockade which led to starvation of over 1 million Igbos during the Nigerian civil war of 1967–1970.[99] Yoruba intellectuals disputed this revisionist account. At around the same time, the Fashola administration in an urban renewal drive had forcibly "resettled" destitute individuals. This so-called resettlement incensed some Igbo political leaders, resulting in heated debates between Igbo and Yoruba intelligentsia on who "owns" Lagos.[100] If this sectarian rhetoric persists, stoked and weaponized in partisan politics, it could unravel the consensus which has erstwhile rallied diverse communities towards a shared vision for Lagos.

With increased scrutiny and demands for accountability around PFM, there is rising popular discontent over the perceived hegemony of Tinubu in governance in Lagos. In public procurement, there is widespread inflation of contracts, cronyism, and lack of competitive bidding. In 2015 for instance, a controversy erupted over the upgrades to Fashola's personal website at an inflated cost of N78 million.[101] Yet it is these selective privileges to the private firms like Alpha-Beta Consulting (ABC), rumored to be owned by Tinubu, that were instrumental to initial successes in raising tax revenues when the government's bureaucratic apparatus was weak. As de Gramont explains, policy coherence and institution-building were helped by Tinubu's realization in his second term in office that he could extend his political influence in Lagos and expect to benefit from future improvements in tax collection.[102] Although a procurement law supported by the World Bank was enacted in 2011 and a procurement agency set up, the influence of crony firms like ABC persists and remains a sore point for civil society activists. In the End SARs mass protests against police brutality in October 2020, hotels, shopping malls, and other assets rumored to be linked to Bola Tinubu were deliberately vandalized.

****

In conclusion, Lagos has become Nigeria's largest and most diversified subnational economy that would rank as one of Africa's top ten economies if it were a separate country. Public policies implemented within a specific political settlement in Lagos greatly contribute to these economic outcomes. Specifically, a reform-oriented political coalition is coordinating the state's factor endowments, skillfully harnessing the institutional provisions of Nigerian federalism, and strengthening the state's

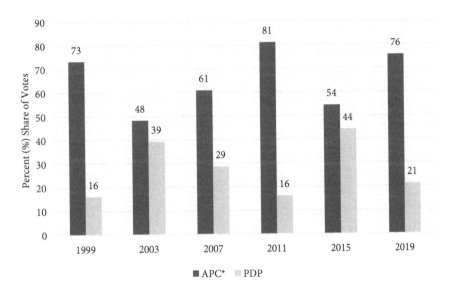

Figure 7.10 Political Parties' Share of Votes (%) in Lagos Governorship Elections, 1999–2019.

*The APC in Lagos was previously AD until 2007, then it became ACN, then AC, and then APC from 2013
Source: African elections database/INEC Figures.

administrative capacity for tax reforms. And this policy effectiveness in Lagos was neither coincidental nor a matter of luck, but a response to the severe constraints that threatened the very survival of Lagos ruling elites. The constraints of horizontal–elite factionalization within the APC ruling party compelled successive governors to secure external validation from ordinary Lagosians through service delivery. Vertical–societal pressures from severe urban decay necessitated infrastructure rehabilitation. External pressures of fiscal insolvency incentivized meaningful tax and PFM reforms. As these policy reforms result in fiscal diversification, urban renewal, and an emerging if fragile social compact, the true test for Lagos is whether it can sustain the momentum of effective leadership through greater accountability to its residents. In the absence of stronger accountability, its fragile state-society compact could be consumed by cronyism and the sectarian rhetoric of partisan politics. In the next chapter, we look at the failed industrial transition in Kano, a major agro-industrial hub in Nigeria, due in part to the absence of a pro-business political coalition to mitigate the global forces of deindustrialization.

8

Kano: The Political Foundations of Nigeria's Failed Agro-industrial Transition

The evening of July 14, 2016 was the culmination of months of efforts by Abdulmumin Jibrin. Standing in the packed conference hall of the upscale Tahir Guest Palace Hotel, Jibrin, a lawmaker in Nigeria's House of Representatives, presented his vision for establishing a world-class film village in his hometown in Kano State. Modeled on Chinese and Indian film centers, the twenty-hectare Kano film village would be equipped with state-of-the-art facilities and equipment for film making. It would have a "… cinematography center, 400-capacity auditorium, hostel, sound stage, eatery block, three-star hotel, shopping mall, stadium, clinic, among others…," he explained.[1] Through months of persistent advocacy, Honorable Jibrin had secured a $1 million commitment from the federal government to invest in the film village project that would standardize film production in *Kanywood*, the Hausa language film industry in Nigeria. The initiative would also create up to 10,000 jobs, attract private investment in the region and generate tax income for the government. Jibrin's message was delivered to an audience that included the governor and other high-level officials of Kano State, top actors, producers, and other professionals in the industry and government regulators. Unfortunately, it all went downhill from there.

The backlash against the proposed Kano film village project was swift and ferocious. Led by a handful of conservative Muslim clerics, a tiny but vocal minority in Kano condemned the project in its entirety. One of the leading critics, Sheikh Abdallah Usman Gadan Kaya, denounced the project as one that would encourage outsiders to "to come and practice immorality and destroy our values."[2] Those who heeded Sheikh Kanya's call to campaign against the film village took to Facebook, WhatsApp, and other social media as the cleric had instructed, the very tools of the modernity they seemed to despise. In their fierce opposition to the initiative, the critics argued that the government should instead focus on reviving dams for agricultural development in the region. Still, many more residents of Kano including the then Emir Muhammad Sanusi II, who is a hereditary Muslim ruler, mounted a spirited defense of the film village initiative for all its socio-economic benefits. Strangely, the federal government caved-in to the demands of the conservative critics and swiftly backed away from the project.[3]

Within days, an ambitious million-dollar plan to elevate Nigeria's Hausa movie industry was savagely derailed by a vocal minority. Kannywood had already been disadvantaged by an alleged "southern bias" in 2013 in the distribution of a N3 billion fund established by then President Goodluck Jonathan to empower Nigeria's creative industries.[4] The Kano film village project was, thus, a way to "redress" the grievances of film makers and other creatives who did not benefit from the first presidential fund.[5]

This derailment of the Kano film village was a gut punch in a series of crippling actions that undermined Kannywood's attempts to realize its full potential as a modern movie industry. Even in its present confined form, Kannywood caters to a market of nearly 100 million Hausa speakers across Nigeria, Republic of Niger, Chad, Ghana, Cameroon, and other parts of West Africa. It accounts for at least 30% of the Nigerian film industry called Nollywood, which produces more than 1,500 movies a year, second in number only to India's Bollywood and more than Hollywood.[6] The Hausa language film industry in Kano has survived despite hostility by successive Kano State governments pushed to police the industry by some fundamentalist gatekeepers of social norms. The government swiftly clamps down on cinema's attempts at creativity and innovation to tackle socially sensitive subjects on the prodding of some conservative Muslim clerics. A former Kano State governor, Ibrahim Shekarau, went to extra lengths to crack down on the industry for not conforming to strict religious norms. During his administration between 2007 and 2011, over 1,000 people employed in Kannywood were arrested, fined, or imprisoned including singers, editors, and video viewing center owners, for violating strict regulations around dancing, singing, or wearing attire that did not conform to local customs as defined by the Kano State Censorship Board.[7] A small minority, thus, incinerated the opportunities in the Kano film village project to create thousands of jobs, attract private investment, and generate non-oil tax income for the state.

At first glance, the Kano film village controversy seemed to demonstrate the incompatibility of northern Nigeria's cultural norms with economic modernization. To some, the incident illustrated yet again, Kano and northern Nigeria's obstinate unwillingness to march into the twenty-first century with the rest of the country. For instance, in a blow to Kano's creative industries in 2007, then Governor Ibrahim Shekarau publicly burnt thousands of Hausa language romance novels at an all-girls boarding school.[8] Even more cynical is that Shekarau, an experienced educationist who before becoming governor rose to the rank of Director at the Kano Ministry of Education, embarked on this book-burning exercise using the bogus claim that the books were "pornographic" and leading to the "moral decadence" of northern Nigeria society.[9]

Yet, this controversy does not reflect Kano's thriving entrepreneurial culture, large and dynamic population, and centuries-long history of transnational commerce. Indeed, Kano was a southern hub of the trans-Saharan trade routes that extended from Africa to Western and Central Asia peaking between the 1500 and 1800s even before Nigeria's incorporation into the European system of global commerce. It is described as "The Manchester of West Africa" by the historian A. G. Hopkins because, by the nineteenth century, Kano was one of Africa's great commercial centers producing and trading textiles.[10] Kano is currently one of the country's major economic hubs. It is the hometown of Africa's richest man, Aliko Dangote, industrialists such as Abdulsamad Rabiu, and some of Nigeria's wealthiest dynasties. Kano has several modern shopping malls including the Ado Bayero Mall, which, until 2015, was Nigeria's largest. Against this backdrop, the religious restrictions imposed by a vocal minority of conservative Muslim clerics on creative industries and economic modernization are a recent phenomenon unleashed by the forces of globalization, political liberalization, and Islamist revivalism in post-military Nigeria in the 2000s.

What is the relationship between these socio-political currents in Kano and economic diversification in Nigeria? In post-military Nigeria, Kano's ruling elites were engulfed in the tide of Islamist revivalism to prioritize public policies that shepherd society towards stricter religious norms. In this endeavor, successive Kano ruling elites have not envisioned a strong economic strategy to mitigate the deindustrialization that has swept across Nigeria, Africa, and the developing countries since the 1980s. As such, Kano's political elites have been unable to reimagine a growth agenda that harnesses the region's comparative advantage of agro-industrial activities and supports new industries such as creative arts, entertainment, and the digital economy.

Kano is a microcosm of Nigeria and, indeed, Africa's failed industrialization in the last four decades in the agro-allied sectors decimated by the forces of globalization. Kano's agriculture and manufacturing sectors, especially the CTG industry, have been rendered uncompetitive by Nigeria's chaotic economic policies and a hostile business environment. There may be an element of determinism here—that Kano, with its agro-industrial endowment structure, has a comparative advantage in sectors doomed to deindustrialization and is therefore locked on a path of inevitable economic decline. However, geography, history, culture, and resources are not destiny. The worst impacts of Kano's deindustrialization could be mitigated by a consistent pro-business leadership that boldly envisions an economic strategy in mapping out and enabling new industries. However, as argued in the theoretical discussion in Chapters 2 and 3, the quality of leadership depends on the distribution of power in society. In Kano, for their political survival, the ruling elite have succumbed to the tiny but influential minority of ultra-conservative Muslim clerics to implement a puritanical vision of Islamic public morality without a strong economic strategy. By contrast, political elites have ignored or antagonized the established but fragmented Kano business community. Therefore, one of Nigeria's most strategic hubs holding the reins of the country's post-oil economy is stunted, engulfed in strong headwinds of globalization, Islamist revivalism, and political liberalization, and incapable of realizing its vast economic potential due to the nature of its political settlement.

In this chapter therefore, we argue that Kano state-ruling elites have not built a pro-growth coalition to address deindustrialization and its socio-economic impacts due to the political constraints they faced. Kano's ruling elites were swept away by the tide of the Islamist revivalism of the early 2000s to extend strict shari'ah law as the vehicle to address rising poverty, inequality, and socio-economic concerns. Although some governance reforms were effectively implemented in 2011, these were not tied to a defined economic strategy. For their political survival, Kano's ruling elites succumbed to the vociferous demands for Shariah implementation from an influential minority of advocates. Against the backdrop of the Shariah movement of the 2000s in northern Nigeria, Kano's policymakers pursued a sectarian policy orientation excluding the business community and lacking an economic strategy to mitigate deindustrialization. Thus, in a time of economic globalization, democratization, and Islamist revivalism, Kano has struggled to carve out a viable path to modern economic development.

The chapter is structured as follows. I first present the Kano economy: as Nigeria's fourth-largest non-oil subnational economy, characterized by low productivity and fiscal dependence. I then explain how Kano's structural attributes position the state towards the agro-industrial activities ravaged by the global forces of deindustrialization of the past four decades. Then the chapter examines in more detail how the balance of power in Kano has created the conditions for the absence of a proactive reform-orientation in Kano to mitigate the worst impacts of deindustrialization and carve out an alternative path for economic modernization for the state.

The Agrarian and Trading Economy of Kano

Let us now look at the size and composition of Kano's economy. Like our analysis of Lagos in Chapter 7, three important characteristics are relevant here. First, Kano is Nigeria's fourth-largest non-oil subnational economy. Second, it is comprising mostly agriculture, services, and trading activities with a large number of microenterprises in the informal sector. Third, Kano's fiscal revenue base is heavily dependent on federal oil revenue transfers rather than internal non-oil sources. These three characteristics provide a snapshot of an important regional hub and an anchor of Nigeria's post-oil future.

To begin with, Kano is Nigeria's fourth-largest non-oil economy, after Lagos, the FCT, and Anambra. With a GDP of N2.9 trillion in 2017, it contributes 2.6% to the national economy (Figure 8.1). It is the largest economy in Nigeria's north, and an important commercial hub for agriculture produce, manufacturing, and the trading of imported goods. Over the period 2013–2017 for which data are available, total output increased slightly, from N1.8 trillion in 2013 to N2.9 trillion in 2017 not accounting for inflation.

A second characteristic of the Kano economy is its agrarian, services, and trading composition. The five largest sector groups that account for at least 10% of Kano GDP are services (56%), information and communications (19%), agriculture (18%), trade (14%) and manufacturing (11%) (Figure 8.2.). Services is Kano's largest economic sector category and produces 56% of GDP. The largest activity within the services category is information and communications at 19%. Trade is the third-largest sector category. As one of Nigeria's largest commercial centers, Kano has over sixteen markets for textiles, commodities, and livestock, such as the Dawanau market—the largest grains market in West Africa—and the Kwari textile market.[11] On agriculture, Kano's aggregate output of N533 billion places it as the thirteenth-largest producer among the twenty-two states surveyed by the Nigerian Bureau of Statistics (Figure 8.3). The sector employs over 75% of the state's population, is the source of food and incomes for households and supplier of raw materials to industries.[12]

However, relative to several other states, Kano's agriculture output is low. Of the 22 states surveyed by the NBS, Kano has a landmass of 20,280 square kilometers placing it as the ninth-largest of the group and the smallest of the northern states, yet

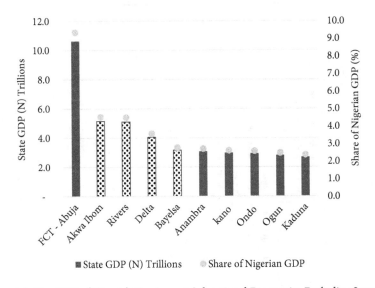

Figure 8.1 The GDP of Nigeria's Ten Largest Subnational Economies Excluding Lagos.

Source: Author's calculations from NBS dataNote: Lagos is excluded because it was not included in the twenty-two-state GDP survey by the NBS. Bars shaded with dots represent oil-producing states in the Niger Delta.

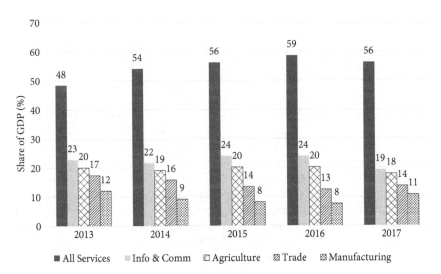

Figure 8.2 The Five Largest Sectors Comprising at Least 10% of the Kano Economy, 2013–2017.

Source: Author's calculations from NBS Data.

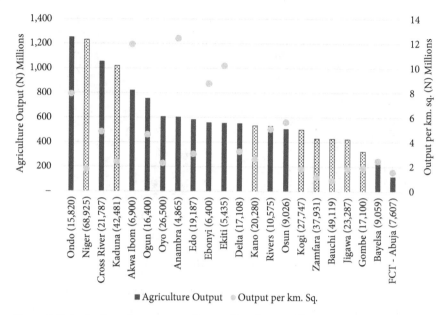

Figure 8.3 Agriculture Output across Twenty-Two States in Nigeria in 2017.

Source: Author's calculations from NBS data on agriculture output and annual abstract of statistics 2017 on landmass.
Note: Figures in brackets represent the landmass of the state in question; bars shaded with dots represent northern
states, those shaded in solid color represent southern states, the FCT—Abuja is the federal capital.

its agriculture output ranks thirteenth. However, even southern states with a smaller
landmass and with a climate less conducive to agriculture record more agriculture
output than Kano (Figure 8.3). Using a rough measure of output in (N) millions per
square kilometer, Kano has an agriculture output of N3 million per square kilometers.
It does not even feature in the top ten of these twenty-two states for which we have
data. The top-ranking states in terms of agriculture output per square kilometers are
Anambra (N12m), Akwa Ibom (N12m), Ekiti (N10m), Ebonyi (N9m) and Ondo (8m),
and all except Ondo have a landmass that is less than half of Kano's. Kano however has
higher agriculture output per square kilometers than the other northern states in the
survey all of which are geographically larger, including Kaduna and Niger which are
more than double its size. Of course, certain caveats apply here, including the kind of
agriculture activity—it is possible that the southern states produce cash crops, like oil
palm, that are traded for a higher value than food crops produced in the north.

Overall, these figures point to a sobering and deeper problem of low agriculture
productivity in Kano as with most of northern Nigeria. Indeed, the issue of declining
agriculture productivity is confirmed by more detailed figures on output in Kano
State government documents. Across various types of food and cash crops, output
has declined (Figures 8.4). Between 2011 and 2014 alone, crops such as cowpea,
soybeans, cotton, wheat, rice, millet, etc., have declined by more than 50%.
However, livestock and poultry production increased or remained stable during this

(a) Crops with Export Potential

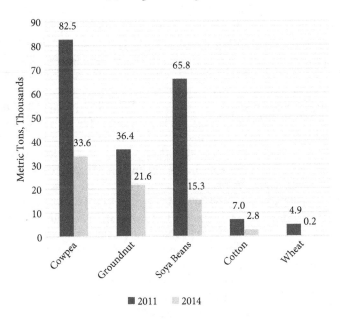

(b) Food Crops

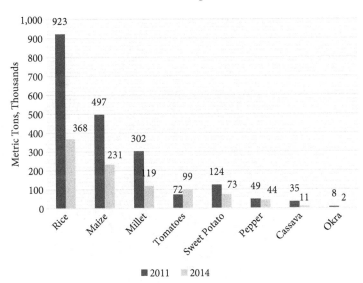

Figure 8.4 Production of Key Crops in Kano, 2011 and 2014.

Source: Author's calculations from Kano State Development Plan (2015, pp. 35–36).

period. Overall, there appears to be distorted and poor resource optimization, low productivity in other words. The cultivation and production of commodities in Kano is generally at subsistence levels. Yield is low from farmland, ponds, trees, livestock, and other agricultural units, with limited private investments overall. Most of Kano's twenty freshwater dams are non-operational, impeding irrigation agriculture, and only about 30% of total cultivable land is currently being used.[13] Production remains labor intensive and largely at subsistence level.

These problems of low productivity in agriculture affect the manufacturing sub-sectors.[14] The CTG sub-sector has been hit hardest. According to the trade association the Manufacturers Association of Nigeria (MAN), just about two of the over thirty textile factories in Kano are functioning: Tofa Textiles and African Textiles.[15] The food and beverages sub-sector fares better, although producing at suboptimal levels according to industrialist, Ali Madugu, who is the chief executive of a major food-processing company in Kano, Dala Foods and vice president of MAN.[16] In the leather industry, only eighteen out of over 40 tanneries are in operation; an industry that engages about 40,000 people in the value chain and produces for export.

Within these major economic sectors, as with national trends, there is a prevalence of micro enterprises and informal activity. Kano State has 1.9 million MSMEs, employing around 3.5 million individuals and contributing over nearly 70% of the state's GDP.[17] Of these MSMEs, 1.8 million, or 99.5%, are micro enterprises which employ fewer than ten people (Figure 8.5a/b). In a survey of 1,829 small and

(a) SMEs in Kano compared to the Rest of Gigeria

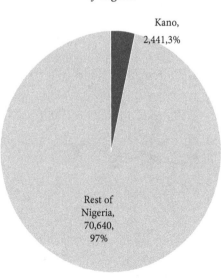

Kano, 2,441,3%

Rest of Nigeria, 70,640, 97%

■ Kano   ▨ Rest of Nigeria

*(b) Micro Enterprises in Kano Compared
to the Rest of Nigeria*

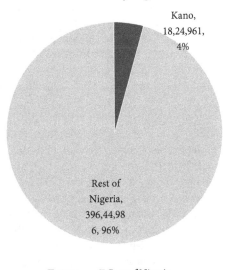

(c) Distribution of Kano SMEs

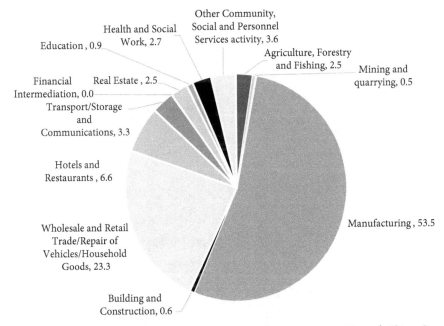

Figure 8.5 Kano Has One of the Largest Numbers of MSMEs among Nigeria's Thirty-Six States (2017 figures).

Source: Author's calculations from SMEDAN & NBS (2017).
Source: Authors' calculation from NBS/SMEDAN 2012 in Kano State Development Plan (2015, p. 14).

medium-scale enterprises (SMEs) in Kano which employ between ten and 200 people, 54% were found to be in manufacturing, 23% in trade, and 7% in hotels and restaurants (Figure 8.5c). Most SMEs are in the manufacturing sector, indicating that it is a solid but underperforming pillar of the economy. The informal MSME sector in Kano, as in other parts of Nigeria, is a safety net for millions who lack the skills to venture into the formal labor market or the resources to thrive in the formal economy. The agriculture and manufacturing sectors along with Kano's rich history commerce hold the key to growth, wealth creation, and employment generation for millions in a post-oil Nigeria.

The third characteristic of the Kano economy is that its fiscal revenue base is highly dependent on federal oil revenue transfers. In 2008, Kano's IGR constituted 18% of total revenue, meaning that federal receipts, mainly oil revenue and VAT, constituted over 82% (Figure 8.6a). In 2009, IGR rose to 25%, and then to a high of 39% in 2010. Across an eleven-year period for which data are available, from 2008 to 2019, Kano's IGR has increased somewhat staying at an average of 30% of all fiscal revenues. Taxes and fines and fees have expanded the most since 2008. In 2008, taxes, fines and fees collectively accounted for 40% of IGR or around N5 billion. By 2014, they accounted for 81% or around N27 billion of all internal revenue (Figure 8.6b). This rising tax and other earnings point to an improvement in PFM and is corroborated by my discussions with state government officials and independent analysts. The growth in IGR was mainly driven by fiscal prudence, increased transparency, and improved tax collection by the Kano State Government with the explicit aim of generating

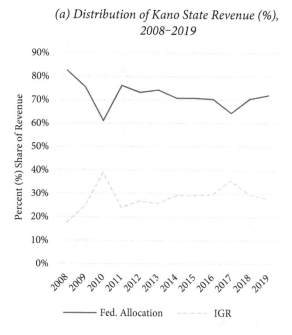

(a) Distribution of Kano State Revenue (%), 2008–2019

(b) Distribution of Kano IGR, 2008–2016

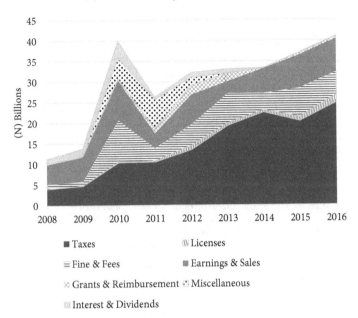

Figure 8.6 Composition of Kano State Revenue, 2008–2019.

Source: Author's calculations from Kano State Government (2009–2019) Report of the Accountant-General of Kano State together with the audited financial statements for the year.

internal non-oil revenue. Despite the steady increase in non-oil IGR, Kano State overwhelmingly depends on federal oil receipts, for 72% of total revenues in 2019 (Figure 8.6a).

Kano State has broadened its revenue base since 2011 by focusing on domestic sources. There is improved tax administration and fiscal prudence without tapping external sources such as domestic capital markets or multilateral agencies such as the African Development Bank and the World Bank, as peer states such as Lagos have done. In the Kano State Development Plan, the government says that "does not anticipate any borrowing within the three-year financial projections, several options do exist for possible future consideration."[18]

This discussion on the current state of the Kano economy provides some insight into Nigeria's fourth-largest non-oil subnational economy, which is comprising agriculture, trade, and services. Agriculture output is on a declining trend. Kano also has a fiscal revenue base dependent on federal oil revenue transfers despite recent improvements in non-oil revenue generation. What structural and political factors explain Kano's economic status, its low productivity, and fiscal dependence of federal revenue transfers?

Kano's Endowment Structure is Oriented towards an Agro-industrial Economy

There are structural reasons for Kano's status as one of Nigeria's largest non-oil subnational economies characterized by low productivity and fiscal dependence. Its factor endowments orient the state towards the agro-industrial activities that have undergone deindustrialization during the past four decades. This endowment structure in terms of natural resources and geography, labor and human capital, infrastructure and finance capital, and entrepreneurial skills provides vast opportunities but also imposes significant limitations on Kano's prospects for economic transformation.

Natural Resources and the Limitations of Kano's Geography

With considerable renewable and non-renewable natural resources, Kano is positioned to thrive as an agro-industrial economy. It is a historic gateway to a vast transnational market, but its location in the Nigerian hinterland with poor transport infrastructure connectivity limits this agro-industrial potential.

Due to natural endowments in arable land, crops, and livestock, Kano is well suited to a strong agro-industrial economy. It has a landmass of 20,280 square kilometers, the twentieth-largest among Nigeria's thirty-six states. Of this landmass, there is a cultivable land area of 1.7 million hectares.[19] Its semi-arid Sudan savannah climate is suitable for crop production, livestock rearing, and the movement of manufactured goods. Kano has food crops (millet, cowpeas, sorghum, maize, and rice), export crops (sesame, soybeans, cotton, garlic, ginger, sugar cane, etc.), and fruit (oranges, banana, and mango) as well as a sizeable land mass for commercial agriculture and food processing for domestic and international markets.[20] With a headcount of 22 million livestock in 2014, the state houses over 80% of Nigeria's tanneries which produce high-quality leather for supply to high-end European designers such as Louis Vuitton.[21] Kano also has about forty mineral and metal resources, with more than a dozen in commercial quantities.[22] These include kaolin, gold, feldspar, and precious stones including aquamarine, amethyst, emerald, and quartz. Thus, there is enormous potential to produce and distribute edible oils, animal feed, soap, food and beverages, meat and dairy, horticulture, leather products, textiles, metals industries, and gemstones.

Policymakers and trade associations acknowledge the imperative to add value to Kano's vast resources through manufacturing for domestic consumption and exports. One of the state's main development objectives is to build: "A fast growing and diversified economy whose development is firmly rooted in local resources. Its agricultural sector shall be modernized… Its manufacturing sector shall be competitive… and shall hold the key to wealth creation, employment generation and poverty eradication."[23] Both policy makers and business leaders have sought to achieve backward integration of domestic manufacturing with local agriculture, and forward integration with the trade, hospitality, and service industries. Kano is central to a textile belt in northern Nigeria, including Zaria, southern Katsina and Zamfara, and a wider region of cotton and grain production.[24] Kano is also identified as one of Nigeria's eight industrial economic zones by the Ministry of Industry Trade and Investment, for agro-industry. However, as discussed in the previous section, there is low productivity in agriculture.

In terms of its geography, Kano's location on the fringes of the Sahara is a gateway to a vast transnational market in West, North, and Central Africa. As an historic trading hub, Kano was an important entry port in the trans-Saharan trades from the eighth century, peaking between the 1500 and 1800s. It was the richest province of the Sokoto Caliphate, one of Africa's most powerful precolonial empires.[25] Even after the British conquest of the Sokoto Caliphate in 1903, Kano remained the economic hub of northern Nigeria. Its commercial reach was transnational with significant relations with the Republic of Niger, Chad, Mali, Sudan, Mauritania, Libya, and Morocco for trade in textiles, leather, commodities, and crafts all reinforced by linguistic and cultural ties.[26] Kano's status as an historic gateway to this vast transnational market orients it to trading commodities and domestic manufactures.

Kano's location in the interior of Nigeria also imposes severe but surmountable limitations to its full industrial potential. It is 1,080 kilometers away from Nigeria's main seaport in the south in Lagos. This distance from the ports poses major problems for industry mainly due to inadequate transport infrastructure. According to a Chatham House report, the expansion of Nigeria's transport infrastructure has not kept up with the needs of farmers and agro-businesses inland, the growth of urban centers, and has not improved rural-urban connectivity.[27] It can take up to a month to deliver a container by road from shipside in Lagos to its destination in Kano, whereas rail transport can halve this time. From 2014, the Lagos–Kano rail line was partially restored to offer a weekly freight service of twenty containers. This weekly service represents only 1% of the daily freight volume bound for northern destinations.[28] Thus, road transport is the primary means by which most goods are carried across Nigeria.

This poor infrastructure to transport shipments from the southern coast adds significant cost to doing business in Kano. The deplorable situation was vividly explained to me by a leading businessman, former chairman of the Kano Chamber of Commerce, Industry, Mines and Agriculture (KACCIMA) and then vice president of the National Chamber NACCIMA.[29] Instead of cargo arriving in Kano from Lagos within 18–30 hours, it takes more than a week to arrive, and the empty container takes the same time to return to Lagos. "Those in the south-west or south-east receive their cargo within a day, while those in the hinterland receive theirs about 10 days later or more… there is a loss of man-hours as raw materials that do not arrive on time delay production…" he explained.

The inadequate transport infrastructure creates several challenges for Kano's manufacturing industry. First, as the CEO of Dala Foods Ali Madugu explained to me, it increases the production costs of local manufacturers who rely on these imported inputs, such as the food and beverages sub-sector.[30] Since the roads are in such a poor state, there are delays, breakage, spoilage, or theft of manufacturing input which amount to an additional cost of about 4% of total sales.[31] The poor state of transport infrastructure also enables smuggling to thrive, thereby aggravating the deindustrialization of Kano and other parts of northern Nigeria. Apparently, it is far easier to unload a shipping container at the port in Cotonou in the Republic of Benin, truck it up north through to Maradi in south-central Republic of Niger, and then drive it southward to Kano in Nigeria, than to move this same shipment through the congested ports in Lagos and through the bad roads up north (see map 8.1).[32] Due to poor transport infrastructure therefore, Kano's geography imposes costs on doing business especially for the manufacturing sector.

Solutions exist to the challenge of efficient transport connectivity to Kano and other parts of northern Nigeria. There are ongoing federal road and rail projects along the Kano-Lagos route (Map 8.1). The use of Nigeria's inland waterways is another alternative for transporting merchandise. This would allow large boats to carry goods bound for the north from the Lagos coast of the Atlantic up the River Niger. For this river to be navigable by large vessels, however, it needs to be dredged or have silt removed across 572 kilometers from Baro in Niger State in central Nigeria to Warri in the Niger Delta (Map 8.1) This dredging has been going on and off since 2009. As the Kano businessman and VP of NACCIMA explained thus:[33]

> ... If [the government is] able to make the river ports functional... and certain tonnage of ships could come all the way, it is going to reduce the journey to the

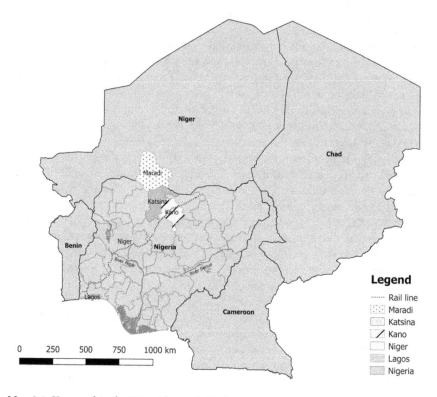

Map 8.1 Kano within the West Africa sub-Region.

Source: Author's construction.

hinterland by half. Once you get to the River Niger, you have gone halfway. Therefore you will do the rest on both railway and by road. You… reduce the cost of doing business… therefore you can have goods from anywhere in the world… to… any of these ports in Nigeria, and then the smaller vessels would have the goods transferred to them and within hours, you have the goods delivered to the destination

If the River Niger is successfully dredged, it would ease these transportation challenges which have made it difficult to haul consumer and capital goods from the southern seaports to the northern hinterland and contributed to undermining Kano's industrial competitiveness.

Kano's Unskilled Human Capital Potential

As one of Nigeria's most populous states, Kano should be able to meet the demands of labor-intensive industries in agriculture, manufacturing, and services. It has over 13 million people, accounting for roughly 7% of the country's population. Over 50% of the population is in the 15–64 age group, 47% is below the age of 15 and 3% is above 65.[34] However, Kano's human capital potential to man the formal economy in general and these labor-intensive industries specifically is hampered by low skills, low productivity, and high rates of poverty.

Across various indicators for skills acquisition, Kano underperforms the national average. These indicators include youth literacy, educational attainment, and computer skills. Just over half or 57% of Kano youth between 15 and 35 years is literate (Figure 8.7a), lower than a national average of 74%. These aggregate figures mask the extremely low attainment across different educational levels. Consider this: there are more young people with only a primary education (29%), than with a secondary (24%) or post-secondary (5%) education (Figure 8.7b). There are fewer literate young people in Kano compared to the national average.

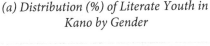

(a) Distribution (%) of Literate Youth in Kano by Gender

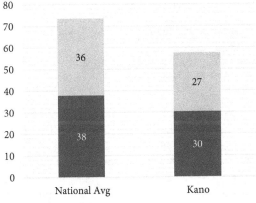

(b) Distribution (%) of Youth by Level of Education in Kano, 2012

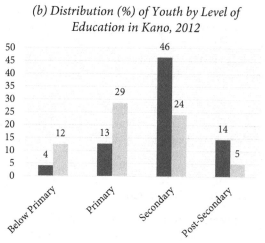

■ National Avg   ▪ Kano

(c) Distribution (%) of Kano Youth with Computer Literacy

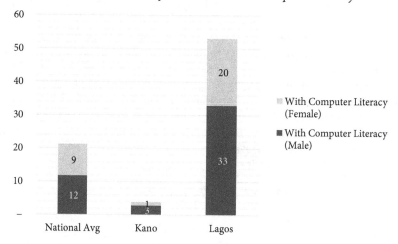

▪ With Computer Literacy (Female)

■ With Computer Literacy (Male)

Figure 8.7 Educational Attainment among the Youth Population (15–35 years) in Kano is below the National Average (2012 figures).

*Literate youth is defined here as those with a minimum of primary education.
Source: Author's calculations from *NBS* (2012, pp. 72–73; 106).

The problem of Kano's low educational attainment is two-pronged: low enrollments and high dropout rates. According to the Kano State Government, many young people do not get enrolled in school, and of those enrolled, only four in ten finish basic education, and less than 10% of those who finish secondary school are enrolled in university.[35] Crucially, the capacity of Kano's young people to thrive in a modern service economy is also low. Across the third indicator, computer skills, Kano youth perform far below the national average. Only 4% have computer skills compared to a national average of 21%, and 53% in Lagos, the heart of the country's service economy (Figure 8.7c). There are also severe disparities based on gender and geography with worse outcomes for females and rural dwellers. Male youth literacy (31%) is much higher than for females (27%) (Figure 8.7a).

Due in part to low skills acquisition, Kano suffers from low labor productivity in terms of value-added per worker. In a survey of eleven states by the World Bank, average value added per worker is highest in Lagos ($6,740), followed by Ogun ($5,170) and Nigeria's capital city FCT-Abuja ($5,038) while Kano as well as the northern states of Kaduna and Sokoto registered labor productivity of about $3,000.[36] Unit labor costs in Kano (18%) are low, however, which suggests low wages in the north, compared to the national average (31%) and Lagos (57%) according to the World Bank.[37] Still, there are too few cognitive skills in northern states like Kano, compared to southern states.[38] Firms find it difficult to hire workers as the skills content of the job role increases.

The problem of skills shortage was illustrated further in a discussion with a business executive in Kano. The manager one of Nigeria's largest shopping malls, the Ado Bayero Mall in Kano, explained to me that for highly technical jobs roles "the local population lacks skills. Contractors, laborers are outsourced from Lagos and even South Africa… [There are] unnecessary delays due to the need to outsource facility and service providers."[39] The skills shortage therefore increases the costs of labor—through larger expatriate salaries for instance—further adding to the costs of doing business.

A third factor undermining the potential of Kano's human capital is poverty. Despite having the fourth-largest non-oil economy, Kano State's high rate of poverty outstrips the national average. In 2019, over half (55%) of the Kano population was in absolute poverty, compared to the national average of 40% (Figure 8.8). These poverty numbers are an improvement from the year 2010 when more than seven out of ten people in the state lived in absolute poverty.

Insufficient Physical, Finance, and Social Capital in Kano

Kano's capital stock affects its agro-industrial potential. Capital, as defined here, includes physical capital in infrastructure, financial capital, and social capital in terms of access to global networks.

Given Kano's size and economic potential, there is insufficient physical capital especially transport and electricity infrastructure. As one of Nigeria's major economic hubs, Kano has received abundant federal investments in transport infrastructure in the past. The country's first airport, the Malam Aminu Kano International Airport, was established in Kano in 1936. Data from the Federal Ministry of Works shows that Kano had 973 kilometers of federal roads in 2011 commensurate to its landmass and relative to other Nigerian states.[40] With Kano's large rural-agricultural economy comprising several towns and village beyond the state capital, feeder roads are necessary to connect to regional markets and processing facilities. While systematic data on Kano's road networks is scarce, analysts explained to me that public investment

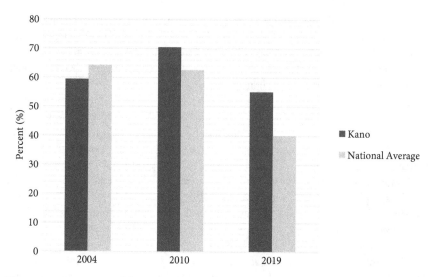

Figure 8.8 Percentage of the Population in Absolute Poverty, 2004–2019.

Source: Author's calculations from NBS (Nigeria poverty profile 2010, 2012; 2019 Poverty and inequality in Nigeria: Executive summary, 2020).

in road infrastructure has an urban bias. There is also underinvestment in transport infrastructure linking Kano to the ports in the south of Nigeria.

Electricity access in Kano is also far below the national average. As discussed in Chapter 5, erratic power supply is debilitating to Nigeria's productivity. The situation is much worse in Kano where, according to a 2009 survey, the total outage duration averages 393 hours per month or 16 days and is twice the national average of 196 hours per month or eight days.[41] The Secretary to the Kano State Government further contextualized the situation, that Kano requires "close to 500MW, unfortunately we get 200MW, sometimes 30MW or even just 10MW from the national grid... We have so many factories that have closed... because of this."[42] There is a power supply gap of over 400MW daily. These power outages and the supply gap increase production costs because costly self-generation adds about 40% to firms' operational costs.[43] For the Ado Bayero shopping mall, 80% of its electricity in 2014 was from backup generators while only 20% came from the national grid.[44] The haphazard deregulation of AGO-diesel fuel, as discussed in Chapter 6, used in self-generation has hurt manufacturers. As the managing director of Flour Mills in Kano explained to me:[45]

> ... They said by deregulation, private investors could supply fuel [diesel] from outside the country... Something we were buying for less than N50 shot up to... N100... The consequence was that... [those] operating three shifts... went down to... one shift and not working Saturdays and Sundays, and some... had to close down. Now, not more than... two textile industries are operating in Kano, while [in] those days, we had more than 15 textile industries...

Like Lagos, Kano has also been delayed by approvals from the federal government in pursuing its IPP because their two large dams, Tiga and Challawa, fall under the authority of the federal government.[46] Few attempts have been made to explore alternatives such as solar energy. Therefore, inadequate power supply is further undermining the state's economic productivity.

In terms of financial capital, the challenges in accessing business finance are not unlike those experienced across the rest of Nigeria. Various enterprise surveys show that large firms in Kano are not short of finance as they run with capital from diversified commercial business interests especially the indigenous trading families such as the Dantatas and the Rabius. It is rather, MSMEs that find it difficult to access business finance limiting their ability to expand operations and adopt new technology. Thus, like the rest of Nigeria, only 1% of investment finance in Kano comes from financial institutions, start-up investment is self-financed, while continuing operations are funded through retained earnings.[47] Consequently, local enterprises are disadvantaged relative to foreign firms, which have better access to cheaper finance from abroad.

What may be unique to Kano is that the collapse of banks with northern shareholders may have worsened the prospects for business finance to MSMEs. In an economy with a high rate of informality, the evisceration of mid-tier financial institutions in between the extremes of the big banks and microfinance undermined financial inclusion in northern states. Specifically, the banking recapitalization of 2004, discussed in Chapter 5, resulted in the collapse of regional, northern banks which could not meet the statutory requirements of a minimum capital base of N25 billion. This severely affected MSME lending in the north as banks often allocate loans in ways that are not based upon economic criteria.[48] Nigerian banks rarely engage in the high-risk MSME lending preferring well-capitalized clients like governments, large corporations, and oil and forex traders. Where they do venture into MSME lending, commercial banks over-collateralize in excess of 100% of the loan in the shape of guarantee by land, they have high interest rates, impose short repayment periods and offer a limited range of credit instruments.[49]

Finally, Kano is endowed with social capital and soft infrastructure as a commercial, industrial, and metropolitan center. As discussed already, Kano's economic status is in part built on its history as a gateway to the centuries-old trans-Saharan trade. At its peak in the sixteenth century, Emir Muhammad Rumfa established the Kurmi market which contributed to the city's emergence as a leading commercial center in West Africa.[50] Kano's businessmen had long-established contacts with strategic markets in West, Central, and North Africa, the Middle East, and parts of Asia. By the 1980s, Kano was Nigeria's second-largest industrial and commercial center with five industrial estates (in Sharada, Challawa, Bompai, Tokarawa, and Zaria Road). At their peak in the early 1990s, these industrial parks had over 400 large-scale and 600 medium-sized manufacturing firms.[51] There are also shopping malls, hotels, and restaurants; the Kanywood movie industry, schools, hospitals, and other urban facilities. This soft infrastructure comprises of business networks, learning opportunities, and a large consumer market beyond Nigeria.

However, compared to Lagos, Kano's soft infrastructure has deteriorated. For instance, by June 2012, all European airlines had discontinued their flights to Kano, the last being KLM Airlines, due in part to low passenger numbers.[52] In the 2000s the U.S. and other Western countries closed their consulates in Kano, especially since 2011 when Boko Haram's terrorist attacks intensified. Many NGOs, multinationals and their expatriate staff closed or moved down south either for fear of insecurity or due to low consumer demand as business executives said to me.[53] Consequently, Kano has declining access to global networks because diplomatic missions, MNCs, international media and NGOs largely operate from Abuja or Lagos, hundreds of kilometers away. This deprives local firms and individuals of learning opportunities, creates higher information asymmetry and other associated costs on economic activity.

Entrepreneurial Capacity and the Challenge of Industrial Upgrading in Kano

Kano's large and established entrepreneurial class has struggled to transition from trading to industrial production. The reasons can be found in Nigeria's challenging business environment in a time of hyper globalization. We also consider the hypothesis that aspects of Islamic inheritance laws may not be allowing capital accumulation on a scale big enough to support industrial upgrading. Therefore, Kano's manufacturing sector is now the realm of foreign enterprises while most indigenous firms are MSMEs enterprises engaged in commerce due to difficulties in climbing up the value chain.

As the economic nerve center of northern Nigeria, Kano has some of Nigeria's most established entrepreneurs. Kano's centuries-old status as a commercial hub was built on artisan industry including leather works and traditional dyeing pits, and its attraction to commodities merchants from West, Central, East, and North Africa. Many of Kano's leading businessmen descend from the long-distance traders of the precolonial past.[54] For instance, Alhassan Dantata, West Africa's richest man in the early 1900s, and Ibrahim Gashash who were appointed as Nigeria's first Licensed Buying Agents (LBA) in commodities, were ancestors of more recent industrial investors including Aminu Dantata, the Gashash brothers, and Aliko Dangote. Other industrial investors who were initially in transport, haulage, and trade include Muhammadu Nagoda, Haruna Kassim, Sani Marshal, Garba Bichi and Sons, Nababa Badamasi of Gaskiya Textiles, Baba Nabegu of Nabegu tannery, etc.[55] In the 1950s and 1960s, the aristocracy, whose sources of income had been eroded under colonial rule, became involved in business through board memberships of foreign firms and public–private partnerships. The indigenization policies of the 1970s, as discussed in Chapter 4, opened up further opportunities for industrial investment. There was activity in manufacturing industries including CTG, plastic and rubber, paper products, leather, food and beverages, chemicals, metals, and basic industrial products.

This robust history of entrepreneurship notwithstanding, Kano's entrepreneurial class has struggled to transition to industrial production. Most of Kano's 1.9 million MSMEs are in the trade sector. Even the well-capitalized business dynasties such as Dantata and Isiyaka Rabiu engaged in industrial production have barely moved up the value chain, although their other business holdings in construction and services are profitable. As the Kano-based vice president of NACCIMA explained:[56]

> this issue of capacity underscores the reason why most existing industries in Kano that are operating... are owned largely by foreigners... when you are talking of industrial production, you don't talk of those producing bottled water... not even the one which produces food... grains... and package[s] them... Not much value is added. By now, we would have thought that it could have graduated to producing goods for export in a very large scale... and... for sale to other parts of the country. That is not happening...

Even the medium and large-scale firms engaged in manufacturing have struggled to stay afloat. By 2013, of the 181 industrial establishments in Bompai industrial estate, 128 or 71% were non-operational (Figure 8.9). At the Sharada Industrial Estate, 106 or 69% of the 152 establishments were closed. Those firms still operating work at less than 40% capacity. The hardest hit sub-sectors are the textiles, leather, chemicals, plastics, food & beverages and pharmaceuticals. Overall, according to the Kano State Government nearly 40% of Nigeria's moribund textile firms are in Kano.[57]

The difficulty of industrial upgrading in Kano and indeed the rest of Nigeria is linked to structural factors in the business environment that affect productivity, as discussed in Chapter 5. Yet, the role of national trade policy in Kano's deindustrialization looms large. As Murtala Muhammad and others argue convincingly, Kano's challenges

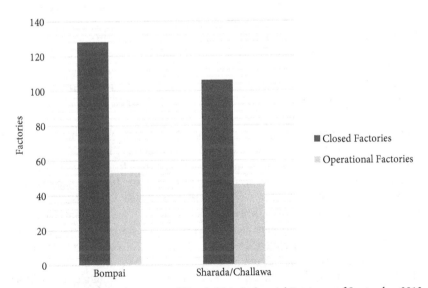

Figure 8.9 List of Factories in Two of Kano's Main Industrial Estates as of September 2013.

Source: Author's calculations from MAN Kano Branch Data.

in industrial upgrading marks the latest phase in a long history of assault by global forces to its industrial potential.[58] In their 2019 analysis of the decimation of Kano's CTG industry, they identify three such phases of deindustrialization. Phase one began during the British colonial conquest of Kano in 1903 which redirected the thriving trans-Saharan trade in local textiles to the coastal transatlantic trade in commodities and European manufactures. Thus, the local merchants in Kano were forced to alter their centuries-old commercial systems in local commodities, cloths, textiles, leather, etc., with West and North Africa to the demands of buying and distributing European manufactures. Phase two was induced by the free market policies of structural adjustment from the 1980s which removed trade controls and reduced government support to industry. As discussed in Chapter 4, structural adjustment did not stimulate the expected supply-side response and, as such, manufacturing capacity utilization fell, eroding the sector's competitiveness. Phase three was marked by trade liberalization amidst the rise of China as an industrial behemoth in the twenty-first century. Muhammad et al. show how the dumping and smuggling of Chinese textile products since the year 2000 flooded Kano, forcing its textile industries to reduce production, retrench workers, and eventually close.

There may be another dynamic to consider. Specifically, the application of Islamic inheritance law in northern Nigeria may be at odds with capital accumulation to support industrial upgrading. The economist, Timur Kuran argues that "certain elements of Islamic law dampened individual incentives to build larger and longer-lasting commercial organizations, thus limiting entrepreneurial possibilities."[59] Kuran notes that:[60]

> ... the Islamic inheritance system made it difficult to preserve a successful enterprise. By premodern standards the Islamic inheritance system is highly egalitarian. It mandates individual shares for all members of the nuclear family, male and female, and... also for the decedent's more distant relatives. Thus, for all its distributional advantages, it led to the fragmentation of successful enterprises... The problem was particularly acute for highly successful businessmen, because they tended to have more children, often from multiple wives.

Some of my anecdotal findings in Kano appear to support Kuran's thesis about the impact of Islamic inheritance law on capital accumulation. I learnt from the MAN Kano branch that several notable indigenous manufacturing firms collapsed after their founders' death.[61] Companies such as Gaskiya Textiles, Kaura Biscuits, Nabegu and Ila tanneries to name but a few, established in the 1970s by indigenous industrial investors, were dealt fatal blows by inheritance squabbles among the founders' surviving wives and children. Only in cases where heirs stayed strongly committed to the enterprise's continuity did it survive. Dala Foods is one such example. Established in 1979, Dala Foods is one of Kano's leading indigenous food and beverages companies run by Ali Madugu. From adolescence, the younger Madugu was committed to his father's enterprise. Upon the latter's death, the son strived to preserve his father's legacy despite acrimonious inheritance disputes within the family. Thus, it may seem that applications of Islamic inheritance could undermine capitalization on a scale that supports industrial upgrading in Kano. Yet, this theory raises more questions than it provides answers. For instance, several instruments exist such as the establishment of trusts and public listings on a stock market, to prevent the disintegration of these family enterprises. Besides, entrepreneurs the Muslim-majority countries of Indonesia and Malaysia have built globally competitive industrial conglomerates. Further empirical work will be needed to test this theory about Islamic inheritance law and enterprise longevity.

With the weak capacity of indigenous entrepreneurs, foreign enterprises prevail in Kano's manufacturing industry. The manufacturing landscape is comprising Levantine (Lebanese, Syrian and Israeli) and Asian (Indian and increasingly Chinese) firms with some indigenous entrepreneurs interspersed.[62] This foreign participation dates to 1917, when Lebanese and Tripolitanian Arabs started participating in the commodities trade.[63] As discussed in Chapter 4, after the Second World War, there was a strategic withdrawal of European firms such as UAC, Leventis, and G.B. Oliver and they were replaced by Eastern firms.[64] Lebanese entrepreneurs such as K. Maorun, George Calil, and the Moukarim brothers thus diversified from the groundnut trade to oil milling, confectionery, plastics, iron and wood processing, and textiles. The Lebanese in particular, were instrumental to early efforts to promote industry in Nigeria in the 1950s.[65]

After independence, there was a re-entry of foreign capital into industrial production in Nigeria when the technical deficiencies of indigenous enterprises became apparent. As discussed in Chapter 4, the indigenization policies of the 1970s aimed to nurture industrialization by nationalizing and restricting the oil industry, light manufacturing, services, and retail trade to Nigerians. Research by Ankie Hoogvelt shows that, in Kano, entrepreneurs received business assistance and SOEs were established by the Kano State Investment Corporation, although foreign partners retained technological control.[66] Indigenous trading families such as the Dantatas acquired shares in Flour Mills, while the state government established the Kano State Oil and Allied Products (KASOP), Kano Textile Printers, and other SOEs. On the realization that local firms lacked the capacity to drive this industrial take-off, there was a re-entry of foreign capital into light manufacturing, food processing, and CTG. This was further enabled by the NIPC Act of 1995 which allowed for 100% foreign ownership.

Since the turn of the century, the dominance of foreign ownership in Kano's manufacturing industry illustrates challenges for indigenous enterprises in climbing up the industrial value chain. Of Kano's two main operating textile manufacturers, African Textiles has Lebanese shareholders while Tofa Textiles is fully Kano-owned. Tanneries are also operated by southern entrepreneurs or foreign firms such as the Lebanese in Mamuda Ltd. Even the major trading supply chains are largely southern-Nigerian-based multinationals, a few Lebanese (pharmaceutical products), Chinese (textiles and apparels), and Kano indigenes (household goods, building materials, and agricultural produce) although some large indigenous supermarkets such as Sahad Stores, Jifatu, and Country Mall have emerged recently. Most of the enterprises established with the equity participation of the Kano State Government in the 1970s are now moribund. These include the National Truck Manufacturers Limited, Giwarite Nig. Limited, Northern Nigeria Flour Mills, Nigerian Medical Pharmaceutical Products Limited, Ceramic Manufacturers Limited, and Garment

Manufacturers Limited.[67] Instead, the informal sector is a safety net for more than a million micro and small enterprises lacking the skills and capital to operate in the formal economy.

The analysis of Kano's factor endowments helps explain its status as status as one of Nigeria's largest non-oil subnational economies ravaged by deindustrialization, characterized by low productivity and fiscal dependence on federal transfers. Despite the limitations posed by these structural attributes to Kano's agro-industrial potential, proactive public policies can and should be able to mitigate the worst impacts of deindustrialization and economic decline. However, Kano's ruling elites have not pursued reform-oriented public policies due to the nature of politics in the state. The next section examines the reasons behind the absence of a consistent reform-orientation in Kano and the underlying politics of it all.

Subnational Policy Reforms do not Mitigate Kano's Deindustrialization

Kano's economic performance as one of Nigeria's largest non-oil subnational economies and fiscal dependence on federal oil revenues appears to be predetermined by its structural attributes. After all, the whole of Nigeria and indeed most African countries have struggled against the headwinds of globalization to maintain the competitiveness of their manufacturing industries. Yet, Kano's economy is not permanently locked on a certain path of decline without any alternative trajectory. Politics rather than history, culture or structural attributes plays a decisive role here. Since democratization in 1999, Kano's public policies have not been consistently pro-growth as those in Lagos, for example. This applies across the administrations of Governors Rabiu Musa Kwankwaso (1999–2003), Ibrahim Shekarau (2003–2011), Kwankwaso's second administration (2011–2015)[68] and Abdullahi Ganduje (2015–present). Kano's ruling elites have not outlined a clear economic strategy to mitigate the global forces of deindustrialization, overcome the limitations imposed by geography, upskill their state's abundant human capital stock and generally improve the business environment to strengthen the entrepreneurial base. Kano's ruling elites have not aligned their economic policies with the needs of their large business community nor mapped out and supported new industries such as the large Hausa language film industry. Although some governance reforms were effectively implemented from 2011, these were not tied to a broader economic strategy.

In this section, we discuss why and how Kano's ruling elites have built a pro-Shariah but not a pro-business political coalition to address their socio-economic challenges. Using the political settlements framework outlined in earlier chapters, I argue that the external fiscal constraints from insufficient federal oil revenues and vertical–societal pressures of poor human development played out differently in Kano. Kano's ruling elites were pressured by relentless advocacy to implement Islamic Shariah law as the vehicle to address economic redistribution concerns of rising poverty and governance challenges of political accountability. In this endeavor, Kano's ruling elites did not form strong coalitions with the business community to drive growth, generate alternative revenue streams and implement economic redistribution policies. The horizontal constraints of elite competition made elites concerned about their political survival to succumb to vociferous demands for Shariah implementation from an influential minority of conservative Muslim clerics, the failure of which came at great political costs. A social compact emerged between some political elites and the organized pro-Shariah advocates excluding the established but fragmented business class. Therefore, swept up in the tide of Islamic revivalism of the 2000s in northern Nigeria and across the Muslim world, Kano's policymakers pursued a sectarian policy orientation without a defined economic strategy.

The Kano Ruling Elite is Constrained towards a pro-Shariah Policy Orientation

After the transition to electoral rule in 1999 Kano, like much of Nigeria, was at a critical juncture experiencing significant socio-economic challenges. The way these problems affected key constituencies and their framing by political actors did not immediately catalyze a pro-growth reform-orientation, as was the case at the federal level under Obasanjo's administration (2001–2007), and in Lagos State (1999–2015). Fiscal pressures from insufficient federal oil revenue allocations, rising poverty and low human development of a rapidly growing population did create severe pressures for Kano's ruling elites but in vastly different ways. What threatened their political survival was the bottom-up advocacy for the implementation of strict Islamic law across northern Nigeria led by some Muslim clerics and their political collaborators. Although there was a brief spell of reform-orientation around PFM and social development in the second administration of Governor Rabiu Kwankwaso (2011–2015), the Shariah movement remained strong. Why was the pro-Shariah movement more effective in shaping the policy orientation of Kano's ruling elites than other constituencies such as the business community?

At the turn of the century, Kano experienced its own share of external fiscal pressures. By virtue of its size and population Kano is one of the lowest recipients of federal oil revenues per capita. In the early 2000s, low global oil prices and the resulting smaller federal oil receipts for the states was compounded by federal legislation in 2004 to cede revenues from offshore oil production to the littoral states of the Niger Delta. Prominent northern policy elites from Kaduna, Kano, Gombe, and Borno were at the forefront of resisting the On-Shore Off-Shore Dichotomy Abrogation Act in the national debates that ensued between 2002 and 2003.[69] The legislation passed in 2004, and drastically reduced federal oil receipts for non-oil-producing states. Interestingly, within Kano itself, this national debate and fiscal pressures from low oil receipts were overshadowed by other matters that posed far severe threats to the political survival of ruling elites.

It was vertical–societal pressures conveyed in the vehicle of Islamist revivalism that profoundly shaped public policy orientation in Kano. Throughout the first decade of the 2000s, Kano along with several states in northern Nigeria were engulfed in the Shariah movement. As discussed earlier, the pressures from population growth, deindustrialization, rising poverty, poor human development in terms of low educational attainment and limited job opportunities across Nigeria were especially acute in Kano and the rest of northern Nigeria. Across economic and human development indicators, northern states lagged their southern counterparts. In fact, the shari'ah movement was ignited by Sani Yarima the Governor of Zamfara, a state with the highest incidence of poverty in Nigeria.

In northern Nigeria, people advocated for Shariah as a solution to the persistent governance and human development challenges they experienced daily. Advocates saw Shariah law as the solution to problems brought on by years of misrule by secular military rulers and the administrative distortions of British colonial rule. In surveys, people associated positive things with Shariah law because it was practiced in the powerful Sokoto Caliphate and Kanem-Bornu empires in northern Nigeria prior to British colonial rule in the twentieth century.[70] As these empires were prosperous and powerful entities, many wanted to "return to the glory of former times" and had expressed this aspiration through calls since to reintroduce Shariah law.[71] They believed the application of full Islamic law would correct the decades of venal rule of secular leaders, by enthroning a "just" system of governance and creating economic opportunity. As the political scientist Brandon Kendhammer notes, Shariah implementation movements in Muslim-majority societies gained popular support by framing problems common to new democracies around economic redistribution and political accountability (corruption, inequality, poor governance) as moral concerns to be addressed by the state's enforcement of ethical conduct.[72]

Crucially, the advocacy for Shariah implementation succeeded because democratization allowed advocates use electoral politics to mobilize popular support. In other words, in northern Nigeria, the Shariah project overlapped with the democracy project of the 2000s. In Kano, the first post-military governor Rabiu Kwankwaso was pressured by clerics and other advocates to extend strict Islamic law in 2000—what Alex Thurston refers to as "politics from below." Thurston documents the sequence of events thus:[73] in October 1999, a group of Kano ulama or clerics in public lectures began pressuring Kwankwaso to introduce a Shariah bill. In December 1999, thousands of women marched on the governor's residence to call for Shariah implementation. Kwankwaso eventually caved into this pressure in February 2000 by signing the Shariah and Islamic Administration of Justice Reform Law but stopped short of signing a Shariah Penal Code. Although Kwankwaso eventually signed the Shariah Penal Code in November 2000, this delay came at a political cost because the advocates interpreted it as reluctance on his part. On several occasions, Kwankwaso's convoy was pelted with stones. He eventually lost his re-election bid in 2003. As Kendhammer astutely observes, there were dozens of newspaper editorials, pamphlets, and thousands of hours of radio and television discussions to legally mobilize support on the Shariah project by journalists, Islamic educators, jurists, and intellectuals.[74]

The pro-Shariah advocacy also played out in the horizontal–elite competition in Kano (Figure 8.10). A perception among pro-Shariah advocates that Kwankwaso was out of step with their demands contributed to his defeat in the 2003 governorship election. His challenger, Ibrahim Shekarau (2003–2011) of the ANPP campaigned as an enthusiastic promoter of Shariah. Across several northern states as well, including

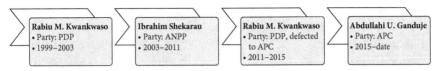

Figure 8.10 Timeline of Kano State Governors and their Political Parties since 1999.

Source: Author's construction.

Borno and Gombe, governors lost their re-election to pro-Shariah challengers.[75] Shekarau successfully mounted his challenge in 2003, as a grassroots champion of Shariah persecuted by Kwankwaso when the latter demoted him in the Kano State civil service for attending a pro-Shariah meeting.

From 2011 to 2015 however, Kano experienced a brief spell of reform-orientation that stemmed from Kwankwaso's personal circumstances. His government made visible efforts to increase IGR, adopt fiscal prudence in PFM, rehabilitate urban infrastructure, invest in rural infrastructure especially roads linking farming communities to urban markets, and invest in education, all of which made national headlines. The catalyst for this reform-orientation was Kwankwaso's reawakening after he lost his re-election in 2003 and descended into political oblivion, as his cabinet members and aides explained to me.[76] Even though he got a strategic national assignment, as Defense Minister from 2003–2007, it seemed to him a ministerial position did not command the same executive power as being the governor of one of Nigeria's most populous states.

In this so-called political obscurity, Kwankwaso vowed to, if given a second chance as governor, immortalize his legacy by tackling the socio-economic problems in Kano.[77] He wanted to join the list of Kano's revered leaders such as military governor Audu Bako and Abubakar Rimi, and position himself for a potential presidential run, which he attempted in 2015.[78] He became an influential figure in national opposition politics to then President Jonathan's PDP government and played an instrumental role in the creation of the national APC which unseated the PDP in the presidential election of 2015. Kwankwaso was personally motivated to do things differently by building legacy infrastructure and improving the lives of people in Kano to pave the way for a bigger national role.

A Pro-Shariah and Idiosyncratic Agenda Characterizes the Policy Orientation of Kano's Ruling Elites

The policy orientation of Kano's ruling elites since the turn of the century has been characterized by a pro-Shariah agenda lacking a growth-oriented economic strategy. Well-credentialed and worldly policymakers in Kano expended resources to build the machinery of government devoted to implementing Shariah law, from enacting legislation to empowering courts to creating administrative agencies. When a brief pivot toward a programmatic reform-orientation occurred around 2011, it was idiosyncratic in ways that did not create strong coalitions to sustain the momentum of change and strengthen institutions.

Despite their high levels of educational attainment, Kano's post-military ruling elites have not articulated a clear vision for economic modernization in the twenty-first century. An engineer by training, Rabiu Kwankwaso studied in the UK from 1982 to 1985, first at the Middlesex Polytechnic and then at Loughborough University of Technology, where he received a Master's degree in water engineering. He was Nigeria's Defense Minister from 2003 to 2007. Ibrahim Shekarau is an experienced educationalist, who rose through the ranks of the civil service to reach the position of Director in the Kano State Ministry of Education, before joining partisan politics. The current governor, Abdullahi Ganduje, has a doctorate in Public Administration. Therefore, using any benchmark of educational attainment, experience, or worldliness, Kano's governors cannot be found wanting. Similarly, many of the state's government agencies and departments are staffed/headed by professionals educated in Nigerian and, in some cases, Western universities with backgrounds in journalism, engineering, law, and education.[79]

In fact, one would expect an engineer, an educationist, and a public administrator to outline a strategy for overcoming Kano's structural limitations imposed by geography, investing in human capital, and mitigating the impacts of globalization on the state's agro-allied industries. Yet, they did not espouse a discernible pro-business policy orientation not for lack of ability, but because being devout Muslims, it would have been political suicide not to yield to the powerful Shariah movement of the early 2000s. As Kwankwaso experienced in his first term in office, the perception that he was reluctant to enact legislation and set up Shariah implementation agencies resulted in the loss of his re-election bid in 2003. Although Kano's political elites also express a desire to "reposition the state back to its leading role..."[80] as a center of commerce, these aspirations are platitudes that have not translated into a practical economic strategy.

Rather, Kano's post-military leaders have devoted public resources to building administrative structures to implement Shariah law. After Kwankwaso's administration caved into the unrelenting demands for Shariah in 2000, Kano became one of twelve states to enact legislation to extend Islamic law "in the conduct of governance but as a way of life to all Muslims in the State."[81] In addition to enacting legislation, Kwankwaso created new shari'ah courts and the *Hisbah*, a Shariah police with partial responsibility for enforcing public morality. Ibrahim Shekarau's administration from 2003 enthusiastically advanced Shariah implementation by creating government bureaucracies towards this end. These include a *Shura* (Consultative) Council, the Shari'ah Commission, the *Zakat* and *Hubusi* (Obligatory Alms and Endowments) Commission, and *A Daidaita Sahu*, a directorate for the reorientation of Kano society—headed by a former World Bank staff—which organized the burning of romance novels in 2007.[82] Thus, of the four proclaimed achievements of Shekarau's first term in office, two relate to shari'ah and none relates to the economy. These are "(a) protecting the sanctity of Islam; (b) providing security to the populace; (c) Upholding and preserving our religious and cultural values; and (d) promotion of education... to build a disciplined society."[83] To date, Kano is the only state in Nigeria with an entire machinery of government, from legislation to courts to administrative agencies devoted to implementing the "visions of Islamic public morality."[84]

When a paradigm shift towards programmatic policies happened from 2011, the reforms were idiosyncratic and not part of a broader economic strategy. Across all of Kano's post-military governments, one could find some useful reforms if one looked hard enough. However, it was from 2011 in Kwankwaso's second tenure that a discernible policy shift occurred. Indeed, one of his first tasks after inauguration was to undertake a study tour in Lagos to "learn their ways." Although Kwankwaso had an evident pro-reform mindset, he personalized policymaking. As the chief executive of a state government agency explained to me,[85] "[Kwankwaso] ha[d] the intention and the will, but he lack[ed] a competent and credible team." The three high-level reform committees in the Ministry of Commerce, including the Investment Climate Committee and the Technical Advisory Committee that the government "copied" from Lagos, only met about twice a year, they were "committees on paper."[86] Contracts were awarded without a defined economic objective, there was a weak record-keeping culture and 70–80% of government policy was issued verbally.[87] Furthermore, revenues for MDAs and local councils were centralized in the governor's office, every line of expenditure had to be approved personally by the governor. As one of the cabinet commissioners explained to me, Kwankwaso's hawkish vigilance brought down the ministry's overhead from N5 million per month to just N300,000 per month.[88] Bureaucrats were made to explain their budgets in detail thereby reducing waste and blocking leaks.

Kwankwaso's micro-management helped achieve fiscal prudence but deprived cabinet commissioners of financial autonomy and did not strengthen administrative structures. Yet, this personalistic approach to governance can be attributed to Kwankwaso's personal ambition to join the ranks of "great" Kano leaders and position him to pursue his presidential ambition. Indeed, within this time, Kwankwaso emerged as an influential figure in the national opposition against the then ruling party the PDP. However, within Kano, his commissioners did not feel like members of a bigger economic team working to actualize a singular vision. Many of the government's core agencies, including the Ministries of Finance, Budget and Planning, Land, Women Affairs and Social Development, etc., were staffed with well-educated professionals.

These idiosyncrasies notwithstanding, the Kwankwaso administration implemented important governance reforms in PFM, urban renewal, and social development that drew national attention. Without attempting to be exhaustive, let us examine in more detail some of these reforms that affect the economy and the business environment.

The first pillar of the Kwankwaso reforms is PFM for fiscal prudence and revenue generation. A notable PFM reform is the digitization of land administration, with the establishment of the Kano Geographic Information System (KANGIS) in January 2014.[89] Seven months after inception, KANGIS raised N700 million just from issuing formal land titles to landowners, as the agency's director-general explained to me.[90] Relatedly, initial reforms at the Board of Internal Revenue (BIR) resulted in an IGR increase from N500 million per month in June 2011 to N1.2 billion in early 2012.[91] To block leaks, the expenditure of all MDAs and local councils was centralized to the office of the governor, and by 2014, the government had saved over N6 billion per annum on overheads. To institute transparency in public contracting, Kano became the first state to publish its Executive Council (cabinet) proceedings in national newspapers and on social media.[92] The overall aim of these PFM reforms was to block leaks and free up resources to finance infrastructure projects, as the Kano

Commissioner of Budget and Planning explained to me.[93] But the state stopped short of sourcing external finance, from multilateral agencies or through the bond market, as Lagos has done.

The second pillar of reforms was improving the business environment through urban renewal, infrastructure rehabilitation, and tax harmonization. Notable urban renewal initiatives include the establishment of the Kano Road Transport Agency (KAROTA) modeled on the LASTMA in Lagos. There were also efforts at consistent garbage collection, waste disposal, and construction of streetlights. The infrastructure completed or that was underway during my field work in Kano in 2014 includes roads and overhead bridges within Kano metropolis, the construction of 5-kilometer length of roads in each of the state's forty-four local governments to connect rural areas to urban centers;[94] the construction of a 42-kilometer Kano metro project connecting Dawanau grains market financed by Chinese partners[95] and independent hydro power projects at Tiga and Challawa to power industrial areas. There were also reforms to unclog bureaucratic bottlenecks for business in Kano. Stemming from consultations with business leaders, the Kano State legislature passed a law in 2013 to harmonize over 220 taxes and levies to 18, according to the managing director of the Kano Flour Mills.[96] Overall, there were efforts to oprove the state's business climate.

The third pillar of Kwankwaso's reforms was social development initiatives aimed at job creation and poverty reduction with a strong gender component. For instance, 47% of the 1,000 pioneer students in a newly established North West University are female. More than twenty-six entrepreneurial institutes and business assistance programs in the film industry, and journalism also targeted women. The government also invested more funds in education. The education budget increased from N1.6 billion or 2.2% of total expenditure in 2010 to N6.2 billion or 5.3% in 2012. As the Secretary to the Kano State Government explained to me, the higher expenditure aimed to increase enrollment and completion rates for girls through the provision of school uniforms, teacher recruitment and training, a school feeding program and the construction of schools and facilities.[97] In fact, the Shariah police the Hisbah Board, was a strategic partner in public sensitization to encourage women's participation in these social programs. In higher education, they established two state universities—University College Wudil and North-West University—to complement the one federal university, the Bayero University of Kano, that hitherto had served the 12 million plus population. There was also an overseas scholarship scheme for more than 2,000 postgraduate students in medical sciences, engineering, and aviation.

Unfortunately, many of these projects have been abandoned or discontinued due to elite factionalization, weak implementation mechanisms, and questions around their sustainability. The relationship between Kwankwaso and his protégé, the present Governor Abdullahi Ganduje, progressively deteriorated into full-blown animosity by early 2016. A casualty of this fallout has been Kwankwaso's numerous flagship projects. Most of the twenty-six entrepreneurial institutes have been abandoned.[98] Scholarship schemes and other empowerment programs have been discontinued. The modest efforts of the Kwankwaso administration have been undermined by the absence of a strong coalition to weather elite factionalization and electoral politics.

Kano's Business Class is Alienated from the Post-military and Pro-Shariah Social Compact

Since the turn of the century, Kano's ruling elites have not aligned their policy orientation with the needs of the state's large business community. While political leaders are subject to the dictates of conservative Muslim clerics, their relations with the business community are often ambiguous and downright conflictual. The business community itself is fragmented and lacks the capacity for collective action to advocate pro-productivity policies. Consequently, challenges in the business environment that require strong state–business coordination are not prioritized by the Kano ruling elites in their negotiations with the federal government.

There are deep fissures within the large business community in Kano that undermine their collective bargaining power with the political elite on economic policies. As discussed already, Kano became Nigeria's second-largest industrial center by the 1970s building on a centuries-long history of commerce and industry. With various large-scale entrepreneurs, wealthy dynasties, and 1.9 million MSMEs, the Kano business community has strong representation in national trade associations. These include MAN, NACCIMA, the Supermarkets Associations, among scores of others. At the time of writing in January 2021, the president of MAN is of Kano heritage. Yet, Kano's business community has deep fissures that undermine their collective action and bargaining power in state–business relations.

A fissure between industrialists who favor protectionism and the merchants who support liberal trade, inhibits collective action.[99] With Nigeria's haphazard trade policies characterized by arbitrary import bans, some prominent merchants are susceptible to smuggling of contraband items, according to several analysts and merchants I spoke to.[100] Consumer goods, textiles, and some light manufactures which are officially under varying degrees of protection are routinely smuggled or dumped from China into the Kano market, as the manager of a manufacturing enterprise explained,[101] to the detriment of locally produced equivalents. The menace of smuggling and its decimation of the CTG industry in Kano through the old trans-Saharan trade routes across West Africa is well-documented in the analysis by Murtala and colleagues.[102] For instance, they calculate the value of contraband textiles smuggled into Kano from less than $500 million in 2001 to $1.5 billion by 2006, and $3.4 billion by 2014. More striking, the percentage of textile imports from China destined for Kano via the Sahara increased from about 20% of the total textile imports in 2001 to nearly 60% in 2006 and over 92% by 2014.[103] The smuggling kingpins are politically connected, according to Kano industrialists.[104] These manufacturers bear the brunt of smuggling that undercuts their locally produced goods.

Even among manufacturers, the fissure between the large-scale industrialists and the smaller and medium-sized players undermines cohesion to collectively influence economic policies. As discussed in previous chapters, large enterprises in Nigeria crowd out business finance from the banking sector. Large firms are also accused of policy capture to the detriment of smaller players. For instance, Aliko Dangote, Nigeria's most prominent industrialist who is of Kano heritage, is accused of leveraging his political connections to secure personal rather than industry-wide benefits. Smaller manufacturing firms find it difficult to obtain low-pour black oil to generate electric power because Dangote's factories often crowd out demand.[105] As we saw in Chapter 6, Dangote brushes off these accusations on the grounds that he receives incentives from government in return for the investments he makes in infrastructure which become public goods, to be freely used by communities and other firms.

These fissures within the Kano business community undermine collective action in state–business relations on pro-productivity policies. Economic policy is thus largely detached from the realities of the business community. And even under Kwankwaso's brief pivot to a reform-orientation, governance reforms were not guided by an overarching economic strategy, but by the governor's idiosyncrasies. His administration's larger education budget, the overseas scholarship scheme, road projects, and business support programs for micro enterprises ostensibly aimed to rejuvenate Kano's economy. In reality, these initiatives did not align with the needs of industry. For instance, the economic benefit of the $6.7 million spent by the government to train over 100 commercial pilots is hard to fathom since Kano is no longer a large aviation hub, has no state airline, and there is a national supply glut of commercial pilots. Most of these pilots returned home to Kano in 2016 and had to switch careers to teaching or civil service jobs.[106] Several of such well-intentioned initiatives did not align with industry needs around addressing burdensome regulation, providing reliable electricity, investing in transport infrastructure and combating the menace of smuggling and dumping of cheap imports.

The weak state–business relations in turn affect the capacity of the Kano government to harness federal institutional arrangements to the benefit of the state's economy. On matters outlined in the Exclusive List of the constitution such as trade policy, infrastructure, and security, the Kano government has not strongly advocated for the business community in its jurisdiction. On trade policy, Nigeria's inconsistency in its "gradual liberalization" strategy has decimated industrial clusters across the country, including those in Kano. When China joined the World Trade Organization (WTO) in 2001 and became the "factory of the world," it outcompeted Nigeria's industrial clusters including those in Kano. The China influence served to aggravate challenges induced by trade liberalization during the structural adjustment of the 1980s and 1990s as we discussed in Chapter 4 and the earlier diversion of Kano's trades by British colonialism as documented by Muhammad and others.[107] As local manufacturing became uncompetitive, the federal government was unable to address business constraints that affect productivity, including irregular power supply, insufficient transport infrastructure, the high cost of credit, multiple taxation, and the pervasiveness of smuggling. Even well-capitalized, foreign-owned firms in Kano struggle to stay afloat. Executives at Lebanese-owned African Textiles and Chinese-owned Lee Plastics explained that they are only able to stay open by rationing their operations.[108] In the absence of adjustment support, many MSMEs either closed or moved into the informal economy to survive. Thus, Kano has the highest number of closed factories and millions of micro enterprises.

The weak intergovernmental coordination between the federal and Kano State governments on industry is reflected in the exclusion of smaller business groups from economic policy. MSMEs are marginalized in economic policy formulation and are often unaware of incentives such as pioneer status, manufacturing-in-bond scheme, the export expansion grant, the agriculture development fund, and the textiles development fund, which inadvertently benefit large-scale firms over small ones. According to some manufacturers in Kano, federal business assistance programs are haphazardly designed, their implementation vehicles are not well established, they are often not well publicized among target recipients who are not based in places like Lagos and are often suspended arbitrarily.[109] There are also frequent and arbitrary import restrictions to "promote local industry," for instance when Nigeria abruptly closed its land borders in 2019 to tackle smuggling from neighboring West African countries.[110]

Thus, smaller-scale enterprises entrepreneurs in Kano and indeed the rest of Nigeria are frequently excluded from federal programs for MSME such as the Nollywood grant discussed at the beginning of this chapter. The Kano government's inability to advocate for Kano business community in its interactions with the federal government on infrastructure, trade policy, security, and finance all contribute to a hostile business environment. A fragmented Kano business community is unable to overcome its collective action problems to advocate for pro-productivity policies.

*****

As Nigeria's fourth-largest non-oil subnational economy, Kano is an important regional anchor for various agriculture, trade, and services activities. Yet it is characterized by low and declining agriculture output and its fiscal revenue base is dependent on federal oil revenue transfers. To a large extent, Kano's structural attributes, such as its hinterland location, a large unskilled labor force and comparative advantage in the agro-industrial activities that have undergone deindustrialization, impose significant but not insurmountable limitations to its economic transformation. In many ways, Kano is a microcosm of a broader experience of deindustrialization across Nigeria, Africa, and much of the developing world since the 1980s. However, these limitations are offset by the opportunities presented by its factor endowments including arable land, mineral resources, a large population, and its centuries-old history of commerce and transnational trading linkages. More importantly, proactive public policies can mitigate some of the impacts of deindustrialization and the limitations imposed by its structural attributes. The question is: why have Kano's ruling elites not espoused a proactive strategy to reimagine the possibilities for structural economic transformation?

The answer to this question lies in Kano's underlying power configuration. Since the transition to democracy in 1999, the state's ruling elites have built a pro-Shariah, but not pro-business, political coalition to address their socio-economic challenges. Using the lens of political settlements, we have shown in this chapter that Kano's leaders were engulfed by a wave of Islamist revivalism to implement Shariah law, from enacting legislation to empowering courts to creating administrative agencies as the vehicle to address economic redistribution concerns of rising poverty and governance deficits of political accountability. Although Kano had external fiscal pressures and vertical–societal pressures of poor human development, these did not push ruling elites towards outlining an economic strategy to address these challenges. Thus, the ruling elites have not defined a clear vision to mitigate the global forces of deindustrialization, overcome the limitations imposed by geography, upskill their state's human capital stock, and strengthen the business environment. Neither have they aligned their economic policies with the needs of their large business community to tackle declining agriculture productivity and the smuggling that costs the CTG industry $3.4 billion annually, nor have they mapped out and supported new industries such as the large Hausa language film industry. A brief pivot toward a programatic reform-orientation from 2011 was idiosyncratic and not tied to a broader economic strategy. Thus, PFM reforms increased IGR from 18% of total revenue in 2008 to nearly 30% by 2019, but Kano State overwhelmingly depends on federal oil receipts for more than 70% of its revenues.

Conclusion

Nigeria is not a powerless victim of an "oil curse." It achieved strong economic growth for over a decade in the twenty-first century and became Africa's largest economy. It is also a large and complicated country with profound economic development challenges, chief of which is diversifying its economy. Nigeria is not alone in this. Countries like Chile and Malaysia have been able to achieve significant economic diversification from copper and oil respectively, while others like Botswana, Saudi Arabia and the UAE that are still dependent on their resource wealth have strong economies and high per capita incomes. Nigeria is also not uniquely characterized by an African political culture of neopatrimonialism which undermines bureaucratic capabilities, rational decision-making, and service delivery. Nigeria's challenge of economic diversification is situated within a political setting of an unstable distribution of power among individual, group, and institutional actors. In this volatile balance of power, ruling elites have lurched from one political crisis to another throughout the country's history and even after the transition to democratic rule at the turn of the century. A perpetual state of crisis management orients economic policy to be episodic focused on stabilization rather than a systematic focus to drive the structural economic transformation Nigeria aspires for.

To come up with effective solutions, a more accurate diagnosis of the economic development challenge that afflicts countries like Nigeria is an important step. That is the endeavor this book has attempted. What have we learnt so far?

Nigeria's Challenge of Economic Diversification

Throughout the book, I have explained how Nigeria's main economic development challenge is not a resource curse. Rather, it is a challenge of diversifying the economy mainly from the oil sector, but also subsistence agriculture and informal activities across its subnational entities. Economic diversification is an expansion of the sources of production, employment, trade, revenues, and expenditures and it is associated with the process of structural economic transformation. There are at least three pathways to achieving this economic transformation: through manufacturing and resource-based industrialization, leapfrogging through digital technologies and industries without smokestacks. Drawing on the comparative historical experience of countries in Europe, North America, and Asia, there is no doubt that governments play a critical role in guiding this economic transition by coordinating a country's factor endowments, creating markets, and correcting market failures. However, this effective guiding role depends on the state's institutional capacity which is, in turn, determined by its political character. By political character, I am specifically referring to the distribution of power in society and how it shapes the government's economic policy orientation.

Nigeria's challenge of economic diversification predates its first oil boom of the 1970s but was exacerbated by oil wealth and has persisted since then. As presented in Chapter 4, both the pathologies of oil wealth and the sources of resilience of the Nigerian economy predate the oil boom. Contrary to the narratives of resource curse theories, the challenge of economic diversification was already evident before the first shipment of oil was exported in 1958. Even before Nigeria transitioned to become Africa's largest oil exporter in 1973, policymakers were already expressing a desire to diversify the economy beyond the production and export of unprocessed agriculture and solid mineral resources. After military rule ended in 1999, the challenge of economic diversification persisted but in a somewhat different manner. By 2014, Nigeria became Africa's largest economy due to the growth of non-oil sectors and a rebasing of its GDP. Presently, more than 90% of the economy of Lagos, Nigeria's commercial capital, is comprising non-oil activities especially in trade and real estate. Indeed, if Lagos were a separate country, it would rank as Africa's seventh-largest economy as its GDP of $107 billion in 2014 was larger than Kenya, Ethiopia, Ghana, and Tanzania. Similarly, the largest subnational economy in Nigeria's north, Kano, is wholly comprising non-oil activities.

In the twenty-first century, the challenge of exports and fiscal diversification persists even as the economy's composition has changed. As discussed in Chapter 5, the oil sector today contributes only around 10% of GDP even though it accounts for more than 90% of exports and 50% of government revenues. It is illustrative that most Nigerians, over 76% of the labor force, are engaged in small-scale activities in agriculture and trade in the informal economy. Nigeria's thirty-six states, except for Lagos and more recently Ogun, depend on federal oil revenue transfers for more than 50% of their budgets. This situation in which a more diversified economic activity on one hand does not translate into more diversified exports and revenue sources on the other, has to do with low levels of productivity growth since the 1980s. Although labor productivity began to pick up in the decade of the 2000s and is now higher than the Africa average, output per worker is still below the 1970s levels.

We have also learnt that the orientation of economic policies in Nigeria towards stabilization rather than transformation has contributed to this challenge of economic diversification. These policies have not had the consistently systematic focus of coordinating resource endowments and addressing market failures necessary to enable economic transformation. In Chapter 4, I explained how economic policy priorities shifted from the laissez-faire approach of the colonial period to the state-led capitalism in global fashion post-independence, and a brief pivot towards creating conditions for a market economy in the late 1980s. At the end of the century, Nigeria's structural economic problems and dependence on the oil sector were severe, productivity was low, growth was a sluggish 2% per annum outstripped by population growth of over 3%. From the 2000s after democratization, policymaking was geared towards macroeconomic and political stabilization, rather than sustained economic transformation. As discussed in Chapters 5 and 6, the economic policy agenda focused on macroeconomic stabilization to address the fiscal pressures resulting from oil price volatility; economic liberalization to generate and sustain growth, and selective public sector reforms to improve transparency, fight corruption, and enhance government coordination.

Even though all post-military governments identified economic diversification as a national aspiration, their policy direction did not consistently and proactively tackle market failures. There have been no consistent efforts to address the supply-side constraints of productivity. Until the recent rail and power projects from the 2010s, there have been no serious efforts to improve the business environment through investment in infrastructure. There has not been a comprehensive overhaul of Nigeria's civil service. It is the same story on the demand-side. For a long time, there was no formal social safety net system for the poor in Nigeria until the NSIP was launched in 2016. Even though it has over 12 million beneficiaries and for the first time Nigeria now has a social registry for the poor, social spending is only 2.6% of GDP and lags low-income countries in Africa and around the world.

At the subnational level, differences in policy orientation among Nigeria's states also shape economic outcomes. In Lagos State, the governors articulated a clear vision to transform the megalopolis to a world-class city by adopting a pro-business orientation, upgrading urban infrastructure, and implementing tax reforms for non-oil revenue generation. To implement this vision, they expediently harnessed the fiscal and political authority provided by the constitution to strengthen their administrative capacity. Thus, Lagos has attained atypical fiscal diversification among Nigeria's thirty-six states. Their IGR increased steadily to 84% of total revenues in 2017, of which taxes contributes 86%. By contrast, in Kano State, the ruling elites have not outlined a clear vision to mitigate the global forces of deindustrialization, overcome the limitations imposed by geography, upskill their state's human capital stock and strengthen the business environment. They have neither aligned their economic policies with the needs of their large business community to tackle declining agriculture productivity and the smuggling that causes $3.4 billion worth of losses in the CTG industry, nor mapped out and supported new industries such as the large Hausa language film industry. Swept up in the tide of Islamist revivalism, Kano's well-credentialed policymakers instead pursued the implementation of Shariah law, from enacting legislation to empowering courts to creating administrative agencies. A brief pivot toward a programmatic reform-orientation from 2011 was idiosyncratic and not tied to a broader economic strategy. Thus, PFM reforms increased IGR from 18% of total revenue in 2008 to nearly 30% by 2019 but Kano State depends on federal oil receipts for more than 70% of its revenues.

These policies, that have not helped to achieve Nigeria's economic diversification, were pursued in a political setting of an unstable distribution of power. The four dimensions of the distribution of power are: elite bargains, wider coalitions with non-elite societal groups, an economic agenda or policy regime, and institutionalization or enforcement. As discussed in Chapter 3, this balance of power shapes the composition of ruling coalitions and what their economic policy priorities are. In Nigeria, the distribution of power results in unstable coalitions that do not allow for smooth transitions across governments. In this volatile power configuration, policy making is oriented towards stabilization to pacify competing political actors and respond to external shocks rather than a long-term focus on structural economic transformation. With such a power configuration, Nigeria is an "intermediate" state which intermittently implements reforms that produce growth spurts rather than sustained policy reforms that diversify the economy. But this institutional environment is not static. It can change suddenly at critical junctures when powerful actors are constrained by horizontal, vertical, and external pressures to act in specific ways. In Nigeria, even when changes in the distribution of power have engendered pro-growth policies, this policy pivot has been insufficient to sustain economic transformation as in the upper middle-income countries across Asia and Latin America. As an oil exporter, these disruptions to the power configuration tend to happen during oil boom-and-bust cycles which swiftly reinforce or reconfigure the status quo. Oil price volatility is politically disruptive in Nigeria because a consensus on the allocation of externally derived oil rents which account for the bulk of foreign exchange and fiscal revenue is central to the country's distribution of power. Thus, policy choices of ruling elites with allocative powers at this critical juncture is especially decisive in shaping institutions.

Throughout the twentieth century, Nigeria's unstable balance of power engendered a policy approach of stabilization rather than structural transformation to diversify the economy. Intense ethno-regional and religious competition shaped policy design and implementation towards institutional centralization to stabilize the polity and economy in ways that compounded the challenge of economic diversification. As discussed in Chapter 4, Nigeria's military rulers centralized institutions to better capture the oil windfall of the 1970s and to stabilize a polity torn apart by a civil war in the 1960s. This explanation contradicts resource curse theories because policy choices were not driven by oil wealth but were executed with oil windfall revenues in ways that amplified the challenge of economic diversification. Thus, the concentration of fiscal powers in a federal government engaged in post-war state building of a fragmented society came at the expense of effective subnational autonomy. The Nigerian state also took on new responsibilities for economic management through public investment, import substitution, nationalization, and the establishment of SOEs in major industries to rebuild the economy. Thus, Nigeria's post-war reconstruction by unaccountable military regimes financed by the oil windfall corroded institutions that were battered to begin with. During this time, Nigeria diverged from its peers in Asia which were transitioning to middle- and high-income countries: from those led by military dictatorships such as South Korea's General Park Chung Hee and Indonesia's General Suharto, described as the most corrupt leader in modern history by Transparency International,[1] to the one-party democracies like Lee Kuan Yew's Singapore and Malaysia under Mahathir Mohamed.

After military rule ended in 1999, Nigeria's balance of power again engendered a policy orientation of stabilization with proclaimed aspirations for economic diversification. In Chapter 5, we discussed how an elite consensus on power-sharing called "zoning" was the basis on which Nigeria exited decades of military rule. Zoning aimed to stabilize Nigeria's volatile political competition by rotating presidential power and other principal elective positions between the north and the south, Christians and Muslims. The economic aspect of this stabilization responded to the severe fiscal crisis caused by external constraints of low global oil prices on which Nigeria depended for over 90% of exports and 80% of government revenues. Debt relief and a series of economic reforms were therefore pursued to simultaneously relieve the fiscal pressures, enable growth, and improve transparency in PFM.

These stabilization reforms, continued in varying degrees by successor administrations, fell short of the structural transformation needed to achieve economic diversification. Nevertheless, these reforms enabled Nigeria to break the cycle of economic stagnation and become Africa's largest economy by 2014. As discussed in Chapter 6, it was the fiscal pressures from the external constraints of volatile oil prices that pushed Nigeria's policymakers to successfully liberalize the telecoms sector in 2001 as part of the drive to generate non-oil growth. Yet, at this critical juncture, several efforts to reform the downstream oil sector stalled. These fiscal pressures were insufficient to drive the successful deregulation of the downstream sector by boosting domestic refining and cleaning up the wasteful fossil fuel subsidy regime. Instead, wider redistribution concerns for cheap fuel used in private generators due to insufficient grid electricity, for passenger vehicles in the absence of sufficient mass transit and to compensate for the absence of social protection services disincentivized downstream oil sector reforms.

The interaction between the power configuration and policy orientation can also be found among Nigeria's states. In Lagos in the early 2000s, severe crises that threatened the very survival of ruling elites compelled a reform-orientation, as discussed in Chapter 7. The horizontal constraints of elite factionalization within the APC ruling party forced successive governors to secure external validation from ordinary Lagosians through service delivery. Vertical–societal pressures from urban decay necessitated investment in infrastructure rehabilitation. External pressures from fiscal insolvency incentivized meaningful tax and PFM reforms. Overall, a ruling coalition that was administratively capable of policy reforms espoused a grand vision for the city's rehabilitation and leveraged Nigeria's federal institutions. Consequently, Lagos is achieving fiscal diversification, implementing urban renewal, and developing a fragile social contract.

By contrast, as we saw in Chapter 8, the power configuration in Kano has not enabled ruling elites to build a pro-growth coalition to address the decades-old challenge of deindustrialization and its implications. In the early 2000s, Kano's ruling elites were engulfed by the tide of the Islamist revivalism to extend strict Shariah law as the vehicle to address rising poverty, inequality, and socio-economic concerns. Although some governance reforms were effectively implemented from 2011, these were not tied to a defined economic strategy. For their political survival, Kano's ruling elites succumbed to the vociferous demands for Shariah implementation from an influential minority of advocates. Kano's policymakers pursued a religious policy orientation excluding the large business community and lacking an economic strategy to mitigate deindustrialization.

Thus, in a time of economic globalization, democratization, and Islamist revivalism, Kano has struggled to carve a viable path to modern economic development.

*****

With this diagnosis, how do we address the challenge of economic diversification in resource-rich countries like Nigeria? These five building blocks can pave the path to addressing the challenge of economic diversification in resource-rich countries especially those in Africa. Economic diversification must be seen for what it truly is: a political project of development. This project would entail an arrangement that stabilizes Nigeria's volatile distribution of power and develops a shared vision for achieving structural economic transformation. This political project should also outline the urgent policy priorities for a post-oil Nigerian future. Finally, scholars and analysts would need to update mental models for analyzing the challenges of economic development.

Economic Diversification is a Political Project of Development

The challenge of economic diversification must be seen for what it is: a political project for economic development. The aim of this political project would be to stabilize Nigeria's political economy and generate shared prosperity rather than just aiming to "build a strong economy" or achieve "industrialization" as an end in itself. As the experience of late industrializers in Europe and East Asia show, the drive for successful economic transformation was a political objective of attaining self-sufficiency against external aggression. The threat of military aggression from neighbors—North Korea, China, and Malaysia—compelled the ruling elites in South Korea, Taiwan, and Singapore respectively to drive industrial transformation for their security.[2] As we discussed in Chapter 3, this impetus is often lacking in oil-rich countries, where billions of dollars in oil earnings allow the state to acquire military capabilities without the need to build an industrial economy. Viewed thus through this prism, Saudi Arabia has a strong military without being an industrial powerhouse because it uses its petrodollars to import weapons from countries like the USA, the UK, and Ukraine.

Since Nigeria is a regional power in West Africa without a peer competitor, it has not really faced existential threats from external aggressors. Like China in the early twentieth century, the more immediate existential threats to Nigeria are largely internal—including the volatile competition for power among elites which erupted into civil war in 1967. As scholars frequently note, the opening up of China under Deng Xiaoping from 1979 was a political project of economic transformation to unify and rebuild the country after the destructive Mao years and decades of intense chaos and turmoil.[3] More recently, violent armed groups in the Niger Delta, the neo-Biafra extremists in the South East, the Boko Haram terrorists in the North East, the herdsmen–farmer clashes, and an upsurge in violent crime across the country are tearing apart the very fabric of Nigerian society. The threat to Nigeria's survival comes from within. Economic diversification should thus be a political project aimed at building a strong Nigeria that delivers shared prosperity and is inclusive of rival elites and the potential foot soldiers from armed groups threatening the country's very survival. Without such a political project of economic diversification, it is not a stretch to say that Nigeria could violently implode.

Stabilizing Nigeria's Volatile Balance of Power

One of the core objectives of the political project of economic diversification is to stabilize Nigeria's volatile balance of power. This is crucial to resolving the collective action problems that plague long-term development efforts and institution-building. Due to the relatively equal power of the "big three" ethnic groups—Hausas and Fulanis in the North, Igbos in the South-East, and Yorubas in the South-West—as well as the coalitions of minority groups in the oil-producing Niger Delta and the Middle Belt, no one group can singularly establish an enduring hegemony without destabilizing the political settlement to the point of violent collapse. As discussed in Chapters 4 and 5, attempts at various unilateral hegemonic agendas led to the collapse of the First Republic in 1966, the civil war in 1967, the succession of military coups between the 1970s and 1990s, Obasanjo's failed presidential third term bid in the mid-2000s, and the electoral defeat of the PDP in 2015 after Jonathan's breach of the "zoning" power-sharing agreement in 2011.

I believe a systematic adoption of the zoning power-sharing arrangement can help to resolve collective action problems and stabilize Nigeria's volatile balance of power. As we discussed in Chapter 5, zoning was incubated in the PDP, formed the basis of the military's departure from politics in 1999, and has undergone a reset in 2015. Despite its elitist origins, the idea of a power swing between the north and the south, Christians and Muslims, every eight years is a norm most Nigerians loosely recognize. Given the intense instability that characterizes political transitions due to historic distrust, zoning can be fully adopted in the country's party system until the polity reaches a certain level of maturity before discarding it. What I am proposing is nothing new. An elaborate system of power-sharing to give all Nigerians a sense of belonging, gradually erase the layers of ethno-regional and religious distrust, and reduce the volatility of political competition was proposed in the 1994–1995 constitutional conference, as discussed in Chapter 4. I believe these recommendations on power-sharing which came out of a robust deliberative process managed by Nigerians should be revisited and repurposed for the modern era.

For zoning to work, it should be institutionalized in a constitutional amendment and consistently enforced. The reason why zoning has not previously succeeded in dousing this volatility is the frequent noncompliance which then breaches trust and destabilizes the polity during every election cycle. This was the case when Obasanjo attempted a third term in 2007, when Yar'Adua passed away in his third year in office, and when Jonathan breached the agreement to run for office in 2011. Zoning is an institutional innovation that emerged from Nigeria's unique socio-political context to provide political stability. Such a power-sharing agreement, however, is not without precedence. Switzerland, one of the wealthiest and most stable countries in the world, has a form of power-sharing built around "consensus" among its twenty-six cantons, political parties, interest groups, and other constituencies. Other varieties of power-sharing arrangements can be found in Belgium and the Netherlands.[4] Therefore, maintaining a stable balance of power such that various individual, group, and organizational actors are not mortally terrified of the implications of losing elections can help resolve the collective action problems needed to pursue the political project of economic diversification. A systematic and enforceable power-sharing mechanism will go a long way towards stabilizing Nigeria's volatile distribution of power, the absence of which will be perilous for the country's continued existence.

A Shared Vision for Transforming the Nigerian Economy

Another core objective of the political project of economic diversification is to generate shared prosperity. There needs to be a shared vision for how the Nigerian economy can be best positioned to work for all Nigerians. Developing this shared vision is absolutely critical to addressing the deep structural challenges of the economy. As we have discussed in this book, even the rare reform episodes in Nigeria have been ad hoc reactionary responses to external constraints of oil shocks rather than proactive attempts at sustained economic transformation. Thus, once global oil prices revert to historic highs, as was the case between 2008 and 2015 when oil prices were over $100 per barrel, and again from 2021 as prices climb up the reform momentum decelerates as the status quo prevails. Long-term reform plans are also frequently thwarted by the short-term political calculations of Nigeria's chaotic electoral transitions. To be clear, this ebb and flow of a reform-orientation is not a uniquely Nigerian phenomenon. Saudi Arabia also struggles to sustain the pace of implementing its ambitious plans for economic diversification when oil prices are high. Similarly, analysts point to the fickleness of politicians in Western Europe and the United States in executing the lofty initiatives promised during electioneering campaigns. The universal difficulty of maintaining a long-term planning horizon should by no means induce complacency among Nigerians.

How can Nigeria build this shared vision for transforming the economy? This is no easy task. Nigeria is a large country with a turbulent past. Various constituencies have deep-seated distrust for promises that have never materialized. Yet, I believe a shared vision for economic transformation can be built on at least three core pillars.

First, what should be the balance of state–market relations in Nigeria? This question has not been recently posed, tackled, and settled by the country's intelligentsia. For this reason, the ideas shaping public policies are all over the place without harmonization among various actors. For instance, among public officials of a certain generation is an often rigidly statist mindset of government intervention in everything. Then among some of the Lagos finance types is an emerging libertarian (as distinct from "liberal") streak imported from a misapplication of right-wing-leaning scholars like Milton Friedman, Ayn Rand, and Thomas Sowell. These American thinkers developed their extreme ideas of limited government, massive deregulation, hyper individualism, and disdain for social policies to address inequality, from the United States' unique history. To an extent though, this emerging libertarianism in these Lagos circles is also borne of a perception of an overbearing, inept, and predatory government that appears eager to extract from—by imposing arbitrary taxes and onerous regulations—rather than supporting the private sector. While these Lagos perceptions have some truth to them, they are not representative of the rest of Nigeria. Many of Nigeria's backwater states like Cross River, Benue, Jigawa, Ebonyi, Gombe, Ekiti, and Zamfara need first and foremost market-creation public policies that actually build a private sector. Indeed, it was the absence of effective government services that allowed extremist armed groups make headway in the Niger Delta and the North-East by providing social assistance as well as terrorizing destitute communities. Of course, even in the United States, extreme libertarianism is a privileged indulgence of some intellectual and business elites who are able to ignore the role of public roads, schools, libraries, and law enforcement in society.

Thus, an internal debate is desperately needed among the Nigerian intelligentsia to settle on the appropriate role of the state and the market in organizing the Nigerian economy. This debate should be attuned to the realities of the twenty-firat century, considering the fourth industrial revolution, decarbonization, climate change, trade integration, and protectionism, etc. What roles should governments play: in supporting business; in providing public goods such as infrastructure, education, security; in effective regulation for consumer and environmental protection; in helping the poor and the vulnerable; and in preventing capture by monopolists?

A second pillar of this shared vision should be an appreciation of regional differentiations within Nigeria and their unique but complimentary policy needs. As we discussed in Chapters 7 and 8, there are strong differentiations in factor endowments across Nigeria which necessitate different policy tools for effective coordination. One could say that Nigeria has four distinct regional economies. There is an oil economy in the south–south or the Niger Delta, a manufacturing and service economy in the south-west and the south-east, an agricultural and solid minerals economy in the north-central, and an agro-industrial economy in the north-west and north-east. As the analyses of the two subnational cases of agro-industrial and services-oriented regional economies of Kano and Lagos respectively show, these regions require distinct approaches to economic management. Here is the punchline though. These different economies are also highly complementary. Unfortunately, this important nuance sometimes eludes many Nigerians who entertain dark ideas of balkanizing Nigeria to address a vexatious policy challenge that other countries also grapple with. Take the United States for example: New York, on the east coast, is the financial capital where Wall Street is located; the southern and the mid-western states are agro-industrial; Silicon Valley in California is the tech capital and so on. The effective management of socio-economic diversity cannot be simply to espouse dark visions of chaos when coexistence can be achieved through policy complementarity.

Let me illustrate the idea of regional policy complementarity a bit more. From the discussion in Chapter 7, there is no doubt that Lagos and the broader south-west region, are well suited to a market economy driven by an already existing private sector and foreign investors. The higher relative literacy rates and stronger civil society presence can both constrain ruling elites to be more accountable. Kano and much of northern Nigeria, where the private sector is weak among several other market failures, requires a more statist economic model in the interim to eventually midwife a market economy in the long term. The purpose of a stronger state intervention in this case would be to coordinate a balanced allocation of labor, capital, and technology within its endowment structure. As we discussed in Chapter 8, due in part to Kano's unskilled human capital stock, large but weak private sector and weak civil society presence, these secular forces have limited influence in the policy process compared to the well-organized and vocal minority of conservative Islamists. Thus, a strong, capable, and dynamic government can push through necessary economic and governance reforms to enable the industrial economic transformation that empowers other secular actors in the long term in society. Unfortunately, some Nigerian analysts engrossed in a virulent bigotry of low expectations wrongfully assume that regional differentiations should translate into division, conquest, and chaos, rather than mutual understanding, coexistence, and complementarity.

The final pillar for a shared vision is a mechanism for the management of oil revenues in equitable and pragmatic ways. This is crucial since the sector provides the bulk of foreign exchange and government revenues. Where Nigeria has failed, Botswana and Norway are successfully managing their diamond and oil wealth respectively. Today, the average Nigerian is poorer and less secure than when the first oil boom happened in 1970. Managing oil revenues should be guided by an overarching principle of gradually achieving resource decentralization for both equity and efficiency. A mindset of equity is needed to address the environmental and underdevelopment challenges in the oil-producing region, the Niger Delta. There are initiatives to build on, including derivation, the Niger-Delta Development Commission, and the environmental clean-up plan developed in collaboration with the United Nations Environment Program. The efficiency aspect of revenue management should build time-bound conditions for revenue diversification. Incentives and sanctions should be imposed on federal oil revenue disbursements to the states. State governments should account for these federal allocations and be sanctioned for wasteful expenditures. Overall, the time-bound aspect of this revenue management should be carried out with the realization that the impending global transition to a low-carbon future will eventually result in the decline of global demand for fossil fuels. Such a systematic approach to oil revenue management with a timeline, incentives, and sanctions could spur states to be innovative in achieving fiscal diversification and support their private sector. This systematic approach will also depart from the prevailing toxic discourse on "resource control" often driven by an impulse to exact retribution that disincentivizes meaningful action.

Addressing Market Failures: The Policy Priority for a Post-Oil Nigeria

The political project of economic diversification should also outline the urgent policy priorities for a post-oil Nigerian future. A more stable distribution of power with a shared vision for the Nigerian economy should allow for a shift in policy orientation from stabilization to supporting economic transformation. What should a policy orientation of supporting structural economic transformation entail? In addition to coordinating Nigeria's resource endowments, it should proactively tackle the market failures of economic transformation. These market failures include the supply-side constraints on the productivity of firms and workers and the demand-side constraints on people's incomes and their capacity to consume goods and services.

To address market failures on the supply side, policies are needed that increase productivity of workers and firms. These include the provision of physical infrastructure (electricity, transportation, and digital infrastructure), access to business finance, closing the knowledge and technological gap among firms and workers, and institutional reform all of which help to increase the output of workers and firms. At a bare minimum Nigeria must do all it can to address the vexatious lack of affordable and reliable electric power to have a real shot at diversifying its economy. As we discussed in Chapter 5, unreliable electricity is not only an inconvenience but it also undermines productivity, especially of its MSMEs and the informal sector. Indeed, Nigeria cannot realistically hope to be a serious participant in the fourth industrial revolution, to build a nationwide digital economy and to navigate the global energy transition without affordable and reliable electricity.[5] Thus, a national emergency ought to be declared with a time-bound action plan, to overhaul Nigeria's power sector and address the debilitating problems around generation, transmission, and distribution.

Policies that are pro-poor can also help address market failures on the demand side. As we discussed in Chapter 5, social protection instruments help individuals and households to increase both their income and consumption, strengthen their resilience to shocks, and prevent destitution. Nigeria must prioritize sustained investments in social protection to increase the resilience of informal enterprizes to shocks that disrupt their incomes and wipe out their assets. The Bolsa Familia in Brazil gained global acclaim for helping to pull millions out of poverty by providing cash transfers to poor households. To help weather the shocks of the COVID-19 pandemic, over eighty-eight countries across Africa, Asia, Europe, and North America have provided wage subsidies, cash transfers, and other support to households, small businesses, and workers since March 2020.[6] Nigeria has only recently started to build a comprehensive social safety net system through the NSIP. More needs to be done to support vulnerable individuals and households so that they can move out of destitution and strengthen their resilience to shocks. This will include increasing social spending; expanding coverage of social protection programs across Nigeria's 200 million people; harmonizing the parallel initiatives across various ministries; and investing in collecting and maintaining demographic data including an updated census and national identity management. These social investments will also help to ensure that when an economic shock occurs, Nigerian incomes do not slip precipitously pushing individuals and households back into hardship.

To successfully tackle these market failures in the Nigerian economy requires a capable government. Such a capable government supports and facilitates economic activity without being overbearing, designs and implements effective regulation, is responsive and dynamic. These are the tasks to be undertaken by the civil service or the bureaucracy. In other words, Nigeria can no longer afford to postpone the necessary but difficult endeavor of comprehensive civil service reform. A hollowed-out, aging, and incompetent bureaucracy cannot take on the daunting tasks of addressing market failures in a large and complicated economy like Nigeria in the era of a fourth industrial revolution and climate change. Comprehensive civil service reform must therefore be on the policy agenda.

Updating our Mental Models on the Challenges of Economic Development

Finally, we need to update our mental models for analyzing the challenges of economic development in resource-rich, African countries like Nigeria. Economic development is a political process: it occurs within a society's power configuration and is undertaken by various individual, group, and organizational actors in society all aiming to exercise power and influence in pursuit of their interests. Economic development is not just undertaken by the private sector in a vacuum and the market does not just will itself into existence. Policy choices made overtly or covertly shape the existence of a market economy. Thus, the act of deregulating an industry, establishing or privatizing SOEs, reducing or increasing taxes, investing in infrastructure and other public goods are all political decisions made by powerful individuals, groups, or organizations. In pursuing any market-creating policy, decision-makers must prioritize from among a plethora of choices. Choosing which policy to prioritize entails negotiations among various stakeholders advocating for a specific course of action—entrepreneurs large and small may want tax breaks, trade associations may favor less-stringent regulations, labor unions may want legislation to protect minimum wages, and grassroots activists may want stronger environmental protections. The technocratic government agencies that efficiently facilitate economic activity do not just come to be on their own. Political leaders must understand the need for a capable bureaucracy, appoint competent managers to oversee these entities, and provide these technocrats with both political backing and sufficient autonomy to act in the public interest.

Using a framework for analysis that is centered on power relations allows us a better appreciation of the political nature of economic development. In this interplay of power, policy, and economic outcomes, certain policies are more likely to materialize than others. When we map out the distribution of power in a society, how this configuration persists or changes and identify what constrains decision-makers to lean towards certain actions from a range of policy choices available to them, we are better able to understand whether the policies we advocate for and prescribe are actually feasible within that institutional context or whether we are better off doing something else. Using the lens of power relations, we can see the mechanisms through which "bad" policies like fuel subsidies are preferred or "good" ones like social protection for the poor are ignored by seemingly rational, well-educated, and well-credentialed ruling elite.

It is crucial, however, not to confuse this framework with a discussion on regime type to assess a country's "democratic or authoritarian" credentials, whether it conducts good or bad elections, whether it has robust or weak civil societies, etc. Enquiries on the quality of a country's democracy are, of course, important but they are entirely different from an analysis of the negotiations in the policy process, the winners and losers of such policies and the administrative competence to implement them. In Nigeria, large infrastructure projects were completed by the undemocratic post-war military governments which also hollowed out the civil service. Billions of dollars of oil revenues were mismanaged by democratic civilian administrations under whom Nigeria's media and civil society have also flourished. Applying a framework focused on the dynamic interplay of power, policymaking, and economic outcomes gives us important insights into the political process of economic development that pure focus on the democratic or authoritarian nature of regimes does not.

Finally, using the lens of power relations confirms what we have always known—that no country is "cursed" by its hydrocarbons and other such resources or culturally averse to development. Oil and mineral resources can indeed shape the calculus of decision-makers, but so do new technologies, development and trade partners, industrial tycoons, neighboring countries, armed groups, and others various factors that could disrupt revenue streams, tilt the balance of power in a society and constrain ruling elites to pursue specific courses of action. Oil and other mineral resources can magnify challenges and opportunities of economic transformation especially during the boom-and-bust cycle, but these resources hardly have the power to curse any country to tread the path of economic stagnation ad infinitum. Our frameworks for analysis should be dynamic enough to account for the ebbs and flows and recognize new opportunities to address old challenges. In a world of accelerated technological change, global warming, and the necessity of finding clean energy solutions, the pathways available to countries aspiring to economic development will continuously change thereby necessitating openness on the part of scholars and policymakers to ensure that existing mental models are fit for purpose.

Notes

Chapter 1

1 PricewaterhouseCoopers (X-Raying the Nigerian Palm Oil Sector, 2019).
2 The other two companies in the top five list are Singaporean Wilmar International Ltd and Golden Agri-Resources, see: Statista (Leading Palm Oil Companies Worldwide in 2018, based on Market Capitalization, 2019).
3 Tony Elumelu Foundation (We are an African Private-Sector-Led Philanthropy Empowering African Entrepreneurs, 2020).
4 Nsehe Mfonobong (Meet Tony Elumelu, Africa's Frontline Business Leader, 2012).
5 African Business Magazine (Special Report: Africa's Top 100 Banks 2019, 2019).
6 Other inherent attributes invoked as reasons for economic underperformance include geography, such as the seventeen landlocked countries in Africa, and having a hot tropical climate. A large literature disputes these claims because modern infrastructure can help overcome these geographic limitations, as in the case of Luxembourg and Switzerland, some of the world's wealthiest countries per capita, which are also both landlocked.
7 The phrase "Dutch Disease" was coined by *The Economist* in 1977 with respect to the macroeconomic challenges in the Netherlands resulting from the extraction of hydrocarbons in the North Sea. Since then, economists have examined ways in which commodity booms cause economic problems. Landmark publications include: Max Corden and Peter Neary ('Booming Sector and De-Industrialization in a Small Open Economy', 1982), Richard Auty (*Sustaining Development in Mineral Economies: the Resource Curse Thesis*, 1993), Jeffrey Sachs and Andrew Warner ('Natural Resources and Economic Development: the Curse of Natural Resources', 2001) and Macartan Humphreys, Jeffrey Sachs and Joseph Stiglitz (*Escaping the Resource Curse*, 2007).
8 Tradeable sectors are industries whose goods and services can be sold internationally. They can be resource sectors (oil and minerals) or non-resource sectors (agriculture and manufacturing). By contrast, the output of non-tradable sectors, such as services like haircuts or a massage, can only be consumed within the domestic economy (Auty, 1993; Sachs and Warner, Natural Resource Abundance and Economic Growth, 1995). More recently however, new technologies are blurring these boundaries because they allow services, especially in finance and health, to be traded across borders.
9 Hazem Beblawi defines a "rentier economy" with respect to Arab and Middle Eastern oil producers as one in which hydrocarbons contribute 60–80% of GDP (The Rentier State in the Arab World, 1987, p. 53).
10 Notable proponents of the socio-political dimension of the resource curse include Alan Gelb and Henry Bienen (Nigeria: From Windfall Gains to Welfare Losses, 1988) and Michael Ross (The Political Economy of the Resource Curse, 1999; Does Oil Hinder Democracy?, 2001; The Oil Curse: How Petroleum Wealth Shapes the Development of Nations, 2012).

11 Beblawi (1987, pp. 51–52).

12 On Botswana's defiance of the Dutch Disease, see Amy Poteete (Is Development Path Dependent or Political? A Reinterpretation of Mineral-Dependent Development in Botswana, 2009).

13 Jean-Philippe Stijns (Natural Resource Abundance and Economic Growth Revisited, 2005).

14 Others making this argument include David de Ferranti, Guillermo Perry et al. (From Natural Resources to the Knowledge Economy: Trade and Job Quality, 2002), Gavin Wright (The Origins of American Industrial Success, 1879–1940, 1990; Resource Based Growth, Then and Now, 2001) and Amir Lebdioui, Keun Lee, and Carlo Pietrobelli (Local-Foreign Technology Interface, Resource-Based Development, and Industrial Policy: How Chile and Malaysia are Escaping the Middle-Income Trap, 2020).

15 A commodities super cycle is a ten to forty-year period of rapidly rising commodity prices resulting from the demand for input from industrial production and the urban development of an emerging economy. Four super cyles have occurred since the 1800s. See Bilge Erten and Jose A. Ocampo (Super Cycles of Commodity Prices Since the Mid-Nineteenth Century, 2013).

16 He lists these unusual properties of oil revenues as their Scale (volume of oil rents), Source (not from taxes), Stability (volatile and unpredictable) and Secrecy (easily hidden) (2012, p. 1). See other publications (Ross, 1999; 2001).

17 Ross (2012, p. 13).

18 Ibid, p. 196; 213.

19 James Cust reviews these international initiatives including the EITI, the Kimberley Process and the Natural Resource Charter (The Role of Governance and International Norms in Managing Natural Resources, 2017).

20 Clare Short (The Development of the Extractive Industries Transparency Initiative, 2014).

21 Siri A. Rustad, Philippe Le Billon and Paivi Lujala (Has the Extractive Industries Transparency Initiative been a Success? Identifying and Evaluating EITI Goals, 2017).

22 Collier's commentary begins thirty-nine minutes into the video of the opening plenary session of the 2015 Natural Resource Governance Institute's (NRGI) conference. Available at: www.youtube.com/watch?time_continue=2467&v=k8BDT9 hzqwk&feature=emb_logo

23 Ha-Joon Chang and Amir Lebdioui (From Fiscal Stabilization to Economic Diversification: a Developmental Approach to Managing Resource Revenues, 2020). See also Rustad, Le Billon and Lujala (2017).

24 Notable proponents include Jean-Francois Médard (The Underdeveloped State in Tropical Africa: Political Clientelism or Neo-Patrimonialism?, 1982), Christopher Clapham (Third World Politics: an Introduction, 1986), Patrick Chabal and Jean-Pascal Daloz (Africa Works: Disorder as Political Instrument, 1999).

25 Peter Evans (Embedded Autonomy: States and Industrial Transformation, 1995, pp. 12, 60).

26 For instance, Peter Lewis compares Nigeria's neopatrimonial state with Indonesia's quasi-developmental state in the 1980s and 1990s (Growing Apart: Oil, Politics and Economic Change in Indonesia and Nigeria, 2007) and Atul Kohli describes Nigeria as "neopatrimonial" in comparison to Brazil, India and South Korea (State-Directed Development: Political Power and Industrialization in the Global Periphery, 2004).

27   For instance, Weeda Mehran writes on Afghanistan (Neopatrimonialism in Afghanistan: Former Warlords, New Democratic Bureaucrats?, 2018), David Lewis writes on Central Asia (Understanding the Authoritarian State: Neopatrimonialism in Central Asia, 2012) and Francis Fukuyama summarizes the application of the concept to Southern Europe (Political Order and Political Decay: from the Industrial Revolution to the Globalization of Democracy, 2014).

28   Thandika Mkandawire (Neopatrimonialism and the Political Economy of Economic Performance in Africa: Critical Reflections, 2015).

29   Daloz devotes an entire article describing the pathologies of the African "Big Man" ("Big Men" in Sub-Saharan Africa: How Elites Accumulate Positions and Resources, 2003).

30   Hazel Gray and Lindsay Whitfield (Reframing African Political Economy: Clientelism, Rents and Accumulation as Drivers of Capitalist Transformation, 2014, p. 3).

31   Ha-Joon Chang (23 Things They Don't Tell You about Capitalism, 2011, pp. 123–124).

32   Jason Mitchell (IMF: African Economies are the World's Fastest Growing, 2019).

33   Meagan Dooley and Homi Khara (How Inclusive is Growth?, 2019).

34   Fukuyama (2014, pp. 96–100).

35   Thomas Philippon (The Great Reversal: How America Gave Up on Free Markets, 2019).

36   Mushtaq Khan, Antonio Andreoni, and Pallavi Roy (Anti-Corruption in Adverse Contexts: Strategies for Improving Implementation, 2019).

Chapter 2

1   Nigeria Planning Commission (National Economic Empowerment and Development Strategy, 2004; Nigeria Vision 20:2020: Economic Transformation Blueprint, 2009; The Transformation Agenda 2011–2015: Summary of Federal Government's Key Priority Policies, Programmes and Projects, 2013).

2   National Planning Commission (2009, p. 10).

3   Federation of Nigeria (First National Development Plan, 1962–68, 1961) and Federal Republic of Nigeria (Second National Development Plan, 1970–74: Programme of Post-War Reconstruction and Development, 1970; Guideposts for the Second National Development Plan, 1966) Federal Republic of Nigeria (Third National Development Plan, 1975–1980, 1975).

4   Federal Republic of Nigeria (1975); Guidelines for the Fourth National Development Plan, 1981–1985, 1980, pp. 11–19).

5   See, for instance, the summary of this webinar published in one of Nigeria's largest newspapers, The Punch (Stakeholders Urge Govt to Diversify Economy, Spend Wisely, 2020).

6   See: Celestin Monga and Justin Yifu Lin (Introduction: Overcoming the Curse of Destiny, 2019, p. 1) and John Black, Nigar Hashimzade and Gareth Myles (Oxford Dictionary of Economics, 2017).

7   Although there have been debates as to whether variation in productivity is the outcome of differences in factor accumulation or total factor productivity, the consensus seems to settle on the latter. Summarized in Cesar Calderon (Boosting

Productivity in Sub-Saharan Africa: Policies and Institutions to Promote Efficiency, 2021) and Young Eun Kim and Norman Loayza (Productivity Growth: Patterns and Determinants across the World, 2019). See also, Robert E. Hall and Charles I. Jones (Why Do Some Countries Produce So Much More Output Per Worker than Others?, 1999), Francesco Caselli (Accounting for Cross-Country Income Differences, 2005) and Chang-Tai Hsieh and Peter J. Klenow (Development Accounting, 2010).

8   Kim and Loayza (2019).

9   Other drivers of productivity growth include factor reallocations across the rate of firm turnover in an industry, i.e., the barriers for entry and exit for high- vs. low-productivity firms, summarized in Calderon (2021).

10 See: Chad Syverson (What Determines Productivity?, 2011) and Kim and Loayza (2019). On managerial capabilities, see: Xavier Cirera and William F. Maloney (The Innovation Paradox: Developing-Country Capabilities and the Unrealized Promise of Technological Catch-Up, 2017).

11 Calderon (2021).

12 Zainab Usman and David Landry (Economic Diversification in Africa: How and Why it Matters, 2021).

13 See: Margaret McMillan and Dani Rodrik (Globalization, Structural Change, and Productivity Growth, with an Update on Africa, 2014), Chris Papageorgiou and Nikola Spatafora (Economic Diversification in LICs: Stylized Facts and Macroeconomic Implications, 2012).

14 See also: Atish R. Ghosh and Jonathan D. Ostry (Export Instability and the External Balance in Developing Countries, 1994), Marc J. Melitz (The Impact of Trade on Intra-Industry Reallocations and Aggregate Industry Productivity, 2003); Robert Feenstra and Hiau Looi Kee (Export Variety and Country Productivity: Estimating the Monopolistic Competition Model with Endogenous Productivity, 2008), Vera Songwe and Deborah Winkler (Exports and Export Diversification in Sub-Saharan Africa: A Strategy for Post-Crisis Growth, 2012), Felicity J. Proctor (Rural Economic Diversification in Sub-Saharan Africa, 2014), and UNCTAD (Export Diversification and Employment, 2018).

15 Francisco Buera et al. (Finance and Development: A Tale of Two Sectors, 2011). See also Raghuram Rajan and Luigi Zingales (Financial Dependence and Growth, 1998) and Thorsten Beck et al. (Finance, Firm Size, and Growth, 2008).

16 See among others: Michael Michaely (Concentration of Exports and Imports: an International Comparison, 1958), Ricardo Hausmann, Jason Hwang and Dani Rodrik (What You Export Matters, 2007), Olivier Cadot Céline Carrère and Vanessa Strauss-Kahn (Trade Diversification, Income and Growth: What do We Know?, 2012), Daniel Lederman and William Maloney (Does What You Export Matter? In Search of Empirical Guidance for Industrial Policy, 2012) and Luc Désiré Omgba (Institutional Foundations of Export Diversification Patterns in Oil-Producing Countries, 2014).

17 Charlotte J. Lundgren, Alun H. Thomas and Robert C. York (Boom, Bust or Prosperity? Managing Sub-Saharan Africa's Natural Resource Wealth, 2013).

18 See among others: Alberto Amurgo-Pacheco and Martha D. Pierola (Patterns of Export Diversification in Developing Countries: Intensive and Extensive Margins, 2008), and Marion Jansen, Carolina Lennon and Roberta Piermartini (Income Volatility: Whom You Trade with Matters, 2016).

19 See: Auty (1993) and Thomas Baunsgaard et al. (Fiscal Frameworks for Resource-Rich Developing Countries, 2012).

20   Robin Burgess and Nicholas Stern (Taxation and Development, 1993).
21   Timothy Besley and Torsten Persson (The Origins of State Capacity: Property Rights, Taxation and Politics, 2009).
22   See, for example, Vito Tanzi (Structural Factors and Tax Revenue in Developing Countries: A Decade of Evidence, 1992), Roger Gordon and Wei Li (Tax Structures in Developing Countries: Many Puzzles and a Possible Explanation, 2009), and Henrik J. Kleven, Claus T. Kreiner, and Emmanuel Saez (Why Can Modern Governments Tax So Much? An Agency Model of Firms as Fiscal Intermediaries, 2016).
23   By easing financial frictions and credit constraints, see Rajan and Zingales (1998), Beck et al. (2008) and Buera, Kaboski, and Shin (2011) or by targeting public spending to motivate tax compliance, see Timmons (The Fiscal Contract: States, Taxes and Public Services, 2005).
24   Hazem Beblawi (1987).
25   Mick Moore et al. (Taxing Africa: Coercion, Reform and Development, 2018).
26   World Bank's World Development Indicators.
27   See: BBC News (Africa Debate: Will Africa Ever Benefit from its Natural Resources?, 2012), EY calculations of data from US Department of Energy/EIA database (26 October 2015).
28   EIA, *U.S. Imports of Nigeria Crude Oil.* (EIA Database, 30 September).
29   Carbon Tracker Initiative (Beyond Petrostates: The Burning Need to Cut Oil Dependence in the Energy Transition, 2021).
30   Of these sixteen, four are the "Asian miracles" that industrialized, while the others are either the Gulf Arab monarchies that discovered large quantities of oil or countries that joined the European Union. (Cherif and Hasanov, 2019, p. 12).
31   UNCTAD and UNIDO (Economic Development in Africa Report 2011: Fostering Industrial Development in Africa in the New Global Environment, 2011, p. 5) and Mary Hallward-Driemeier and Gaurav Nayyar (Trouble in the Making? The Future of Manufacturing-Led Development, 2018, p. 3).
32   On the centrality of manufacturing for industrialization and sustained economic transformation, see: Nicholas Kaldor (Strategic Factors in Economic Development, 1967), and Nobuya Haraguchi, Charles Fang Chin Cheng and Eveline Smeets (The Importance of Manufacturing in Economic Development: Has this Changed?, 2017). On linkages, see: Albert Hirschman (The Strategy of Economic Development, 1958; A Generalised Linkage Approach to Development, with Special Reference to Staples, 1977). On social transformation, see: Michael L. Ross (Oil, Islam and Women, 2008).
33   For an iteration of this argument with respect to Morocco, see Ross (2008).
34   Szirmai (Industrialisation as an Engine of Growth in Developing Countries, 1950-2005, 2012; Manufacturing and Economic Development, 2013), Haraguchi et al (2017).
35   Ha-Joon Chang (2011, pp. 88–101).
36   On natural resources, see: UNECA (Making the Most of Africa's Commodities: Industrializing for Growth, Jobs and Economic Transformation, 2013) On exploiting low labor costs, see: AfDB, OECD and UNDP (African Economic Outlook 2014: Global Value Chains and Africa's Industrialisation, 2014).
37   Justin Yifu Lin (From Flying Geese to Leading Dragons: New Opportunities and Strategies for Structural Transformation in Developing Countries, 2013; China's Light Manufacturing and Africa's Industrialization, 2019).

38 See, Arkebe Oqubay and Deborah M. Kefale (A Strategic Approach to Industrial Hubs: Learnings in Ethiopia, 2020) and Sonia Hoque (Ethiopia's Economic Transformation and Job Creation: the Role of Hawassa Industrial Park, 2017).

39 Amir Lebdioui, Keun Lee and Carlo Pietrobelli (Local-Foreign Technology Interface, Resource-Based Development, and Industrial Policy: How Chile and Malaysia are Escaping the Middle-Income Trap, 2020).

40 UNCTAD (World Investment Report 2019: Special Economic Zones, 2019).

41 UNCTAD (2019, p. 149).

42 On mixed performance of China-Africa SEZs, see: Tang Xiaoyang (Chinese Economic and Trade Cooperation Zones in Africa, 2020) and Douglas Zhihua Zeng (Special Economic Zones in sub-Saharan Africa: What Drives their Mixed Performance, 2020).

43 Kevin Acker and Deborah Brautigam (Twenty Years of Data on China's Africa Lending, 2021).

44 UNECA (Electronic Trade Rekindling Sales for African Businesses during COVID-19, 2020).

45 Author calculations from official Chinese and U.S. government, and European Commission data.

46 Yomi Kazeem (Samsung is Making a Comeback but China's Transsion is still Africa's Top Phone Maker, 2019)

47 Gyude Moore (A New Cold War is Coming. Africa Should not Pick Sides, 2020).

48 For more on disruptive technologies and the implications of the digital transformation, see: World Economic Forum (Digital Transformation Initiative: Unlocking $100 Trillion for Business and Society from Digital Transformation, 2018) and World Bank Group (World Development Report 2019: the Changing Nature of Work, 2019).

49 See for instance, Andrew Fish and Honora Spillane (Reshoring Advanced Manufacturing Supply Chains to Generate Good Jobs, 2020).

50 Keith Belton (COVID-19 Makes the Case for Resilient Manufacturing: Six Policy Proposals that Merit Newfound Attention, 2020).

51 Yuka Hayashi (Biden Signs Buy American Order for Government Procurement, 2021).

52 Dani Rodrik (Premature Deindustrialization, 2016).

53 See: World Bank Group (2019) and Van Waijenburg and Frankema (2019).

54 Chris Blattman, Simon Franklin, and Stefan Dercon (Impacts of Industrial and Entrepreneurial Jobs on Youth: 5-Year Experimental Evidence on Factor Job Offers and Cash Grants in Ethiopia, 2019).

55 A counterargument can be found in: Haraguchi et al. (2017). See also the works of Ha-Joon Chang, Justin Yifu Lin, Celestin Monga, Arkebe Oqubay and others for the pushback on premature deindustrialization.

56 See the edited volume by Richard Newfarmer, John Paige, and Finn Tarp (Industries without Smokestacks and Structural Transformation in Africa, 2018).

57 Saurabh Mishra, Susanna Lundstrom, and Rahul Anand (Service Export Sophistication and Economic Growth, 2011), Ejaz Ghani and Stephen O'Connell (Can Service Be a Growth Escalator in Low Income Countries?, 2014) and Ejaz Ghani and Homi Kharas (The Service Revolution in South Asia: An Overview, 2010).

58 See edited volume by Ghani for instance (The Service Revolution in South Asia, 2010).

59 On a distinct "African model" that caters to domestic and regional markets, see Ewout Frankema and Marlous van Waijenburg (Africa Rising? A Historical Perspective, 2018).

60 On services in Kenya, see: Anupam Khanna, Phyllis Papadavid, Judith Tyson, and Dirk Willem te Velde (The Role of Services in Economic Transformation—with an Application to Kenya, 2016) and Dianah Ngui Muchai and Peter Kimuyu (Prospects for Information and Communications Technology-Enabled Services in Kenya: The Case of the Mobile Money Transfer Industry, 2017). On healthcare in South Africa, see: John Connell (Medical Tourism: Sea, Sun, Sand and... Surgery, 2006). See also the edited volume by Newfarmer, Page and Tarp (2018) for examples on Rwanda, Senegal, and Tanzania.

61 Definition of "Market" adapted from Black, Hashimzade, and Myles (Oxford Dictionary of Economics, 2017).

62 These include the following publications: Justin Yifu Lin and Ha-Joon Chang (Should Industrial Policy in Developing Countries Conform to Comparative Advantage or Defy it? A Debate Between Justin Lin and Ha-Joon Chang, 2009), Joseph Stiglitz, Justin Lin, and Celestin Monga (The Rejuvenation of Industrial Policy, 2013), Joseph Stiglitz and Justin Lin (The Industrial Policy Revolution I: The Role of Government beyond Ideology, 2013), Joseph Stiglitz, Justin Lin, and Ebrahim Patel (The Industrial Policy Revolution II: Africa in the 21st Century, 2013), Akbar Noman et al. (Good Growth and Governance in Africa: Rethinking Development Strategies, 2011) and ECA (Transformative Industrial Policy for Africa, 2016). Other more general works on industrial policy include Cherif and Hasanov (2019) and Mariana Mazzucato (The Entrepreneurial State: Debunking Public vs. Private Sector Myths, 2013).

63 Chang (2002).

64 The theory of comparative advantage was initially proposed by David Ricardo in 1817 (On the Principles of Political Economy and Taxation (introd by Michael P. Fogarty), 1817 [1955]). Eli Heckscher and Bertil Ohlin expanded this to the factor endowment- based comparative advantage theory (Heckscher-Ohlin Trade Theory, 1991). See also Ricardo Hausmann and Dani Rodrik (Economic Development as Self-Discovery, 2003, p. 605).

65 Lin in Lin and Chang (2009, pp. 485–486).

66 This was packaged as "Washington Consensus" policies, a term coined by John Williamson with respect to Latin America, and later applied to other developing countries. See: John Williamson (What Washington Means by Policy Reform, 1990; The Washington Consensus as a Policy Prescription for Development, 2004).

67 Robert Bates (Markets and States in Tropical Africa: the Political Basis of Agricultural Policies, 1981).

68 See these landmark IMF publications: the edited volume by Olivier Blanchard et al. (In the Wake of the Crisis: Leading Economists Reassess Economic Policy, 2012) and Jonathan D. Ostry, Prakash Loungani. and David Furceri (Neoliberalism: Oversold?, 2016).

69 Lin in Lin and Chang (2009, pp. 484–485),

70 World Bank (The East Asian Miracle: Economic Growth and Public Policy, 1993), Kohli (2004), Akbar Noman and Joseph Stiglitz (Strategies for African Development, 2012), Stiglitz, Lin, and Monga (2013b, p. 7) and Economic Commission for Africa (2016).

71   Albert Hirschman (The Strategy of Economic Development, 1958) and Alexander Gerschenkron (Economic Backwardness in Historical Perspective: A Book of Essays, 1962).

72   See: April Dembosky (Silicon Valley Rooted in Backing from US Military, 2013).

73   Stiglitz, Lin, and Monga (2013, pp. 7–9).

74   On steel tariffs, see: IHS Markit (Trump Steel and Aluminium Tariffs Analysis, n.d.). On reshoring supply chains, see: Andrea Shalal, Alexandra Alper, and Patricia Zengerle (U.S. Mulls Paying Companies, Tax Breaks to Pull Supply Chains from China, 2020).

75   On EU agriculture subsidies, see: Selam Gebrekidan, Matt Apuzzo, and Benjamin Novak (The Money Farmers: How Oligarchs and Populists Milk the E.U. for Millions, 2019). On EU renewable energy subsidies, see: Marcella Nicolini and Massimo Tavoni (Are Renewable Energy Subsidies Effective? Evidence from Europe, 2017) and Irina Slav (The Sky is the Limit for Clean Energy Subsidies in Europe, 2020).

76   Lin in Lin and Chang (2009, pp. 492 and 500).

77   Joe Studwell (How Asia Works: Success and Failure in the World's Most Dynamic Region, 2014).

78   Reda Cherif and Fuad Hasanov The Return of the Policy that Shall not be Named: Principles of Industrial Policy.Working Paper No. 19/74, 2019)

79   Ibid.

80   A country's comparative advantage is "dynamic" when growth is sustained because its endowment structure is also transforming. Unless this is factored into an economic strategy, policymakers would be working with a "static" comparative advantage which would condemn the economy to primary activity with minimal prospects of upgrading to higher-productivity activities. See: Noman and Stiglitz (2012), Justin Yifu Lin and Celestin Monga (Comparative Advantage: the Silver Bullet of Industrial Policy, 2013, p. 20 and 29) and Hausmann and Rodrik (2003, p. 605).

81   Lebdioui, Lee and Pietrobelli (2020).

82   Lin in Lin and Chang (2009, pp. 489 and 500) and Stiglitz et al. (2013, p. 12).

83   Alice Amsden (Asia's Next Giant: South Korea and Late Industrialization, 1989) and Studwell (2014).

84   Cherif and Hasanov (2019, p. 60).

85   Arkebe Oqubay (Made in Africa: Industrial Policy in Ethiopia, 2015).

86   Noman and Stiglitz (2012, p. 4) and Joel S. Migdal (Strong Societies and Weak States: State-Society Relations and State Capabilities in the Third World, 1988, p. 4).

87   These include Chalmers Johnson (MITI and the Japanese Miracle, 1982), Amsden (1989), Robert Wade (Governing the Market: Economic Theory and the Role of Government in East Asian Industrialization, 1990), Evans (1995 and1998), Adrian Leftwich (Bringing Politics Back In: Towards a Model of the Developmental State, 1995), Doner, Ritchie and Slater (2005) and Kohli (2004) among many others.

88   See Kohli (2004), Khan (2010; 2012a), Thandika Mkandawire (Institutional Monocropping and Monotasking in Africa, 2012), Noman and Stiglitz (2012, p. 4), Gray and Whitfield (2014).

89   Thandika Mkandawire (2012) and Mushtaq Khan (Khan, Governance and Growth: History, Ideology and Methods of Proof, 2012a).

90   Mushtaq Khan (Governance and Growth Challenges for Africa, 2011b). See also Kunal Sen and Dirk Willem te Velde (State-Business Relations, Investment Climate Reform, and Economic Growth in Sub-Saharan Africa, 2011).

91   See Richard Doner (Limits of State Strength: Toward an Institutionalist View of
      Economic Development, 1992), Adrian Leftwich (1995) and David Kang (Crony
      Capitalism: Corruption and Development in South Korea and the Philippines, 2004,
      p. 9).

Chapter 3

1   The Economist (Hopeless Africa, 2000).
2   David Sebudubudu and Mokganedi Zara Botlhomilwe (The Critical Role of
      Leadership in Botswana's Development: What Lessons?, 2011).
3   Amy Poteete (Is Development Path Dependent or Political? A Reinterpretation of
      Mineral-Dependent Development in Botswana, 2009, p. 555) and Sebudubudu and
      Botlhomilwe (2011).
4   Mo Ibrahim Foundation (News Release: President Moghae Receives 2008 Ibrahim
      Prize for Achievement in African Leadership, 2008).
5   Africa Natural Resources Centre (Botswana's Mineral Revenues, Expenditure and
      Savings Policy: A Case Study, 2016).
6   Poteete (2009, p. 555) and Sebudubudu and Botlhomilwe (2011).
7   Zsuzsánna Biedermann in Ha-Joon Chang and Amir Lebdioui (From Fiscal
      Stabilization to Economic Diversification: a Developmental Approach to Managing
      Resource Revenues, 2020, p. 7).
8   Daily Trust (Nigeria: Yar'Adua Admits Election Flaws, 2007).
9   World Bank's World Development Indicators.
10   NBC (No Winner for African Leadership Prize, 2009).
11   The challenge of providing a cohesive definition of the "elite" persists in elite
      theory according to Mike Woods (Re-thinking Elites: Network, Space and Local
      Politics, 1998, p. 2101) and Suzanne Keller (Beyond the Ruling Class: Strategic
      Elites in Modern Society, 1979, p. 201). John Scott (Modes of Power and the Re-
      Conceptualization of Elites, 2008, p. 33) conceptualizes elites within the context
      of their access to power. He classifies such elite into four categories based on the
      structures of domination: coercive elite (control over the means of violence);
      inducing elite (economic power); a commanding elite (institutional hierarchies);
      and an expert elite (professional expertise). C. Wright Mills (The Power Elite: New
      Edition, 1956 [2000], p. 9) also identifies three pillars of power in America: the
      military, corporate, and political elite.
12   On the state as theater of "economic accumulation," see Michael Watts (Peasantry,
      Merchant Capital and the Colonial State: Class in Northern Nigeria, 1900–1945,
      1987) and as the prize of "domestic political struggle," see Ricardo Soares de Oliveira
      (Oil and Politics in the Gulf of Guinea, 2007, p. 20).
13   On the generation and appropriation of economic surplus from agriculture
      producers during colonial rule in Nigeria, see: James S. Coleman (Nigeria:
      Background to Nationalism, 1958), Robert Shenton (The Development of Capitalism
      in Northern Nigeria, 1986), and Okello Oculi (Green Capitalism in Nigeria, 1987).
      On the persistence of subsistence agriculture in Nigeria, see: Watts (1987) and Gavin
      Williams (Why is there no Agrarian Capitalism in Nigeria?, 1988).
14   On marketing boards in Nigeria, see: E. K. Hawkins (Marketing Boards and
      Economic Development in Nigeria and Ghana, 1958), Oculi (1987), Toyin Falola

and Matthew Heaton (A History of Nigeria, 2008) and Murray Last (Governance and the Public at the Local Level: from Revenue-Raising to Benign Neglect, 1960–2010, 2011).

15 On this overlap between the political and economic spheres, see Tom Forrest (The Advance of African Capital: the Growth of Nigerian Private Enterprise, 1994, p. 27; 246). Jean-Pascal Daloz defines straddling strategies as situations where elites use a first position, mostly political to either obtain another one or to strengthen the original one which is economic or traditional (2003, p. 276). On the "fusion of elites," see Richard Sklar (The Nature of Class Domination in Africa, 1979, p. 537).

16 (1979, p. 534).

17 Dozie Okoye and Roland Pongou analyze the regional differentiations in the spread of Western education in colonial Nigeria (Historical Missionary Activity, Schooling, and the Reversal of Fortunes: Evidence from Nigeria, 2014). Peter Kazenga Tibenderana, however, documents at length how the British administrators, who had the final decision-making power even under indirect rule, were chiefly responsible for delaying and limiting the spread of Western education in northern Nigeria due to fears about empowering future intellectual resistance to colonial rule in the North (The Emirs and the Spread of Western Education in Northern Nigeria, 1910–1946, 1983). Although the emirs retained their leadership positions in the North, in reality, they were deprived of decision-making power on fiscal and other crucial matters.

18 On economic, political, and social inequalities, see Frances Stewart (Horizontal Inequalities: A Neglected Dimension of Development, 2005) and Abdul Raufu Mustapha (Institutionalising Ethnic Representation: How Effective is the Federal Character Commission in Nigeria?, 2009, p. 562).

19 The idea that social classes emerge from the process of production and their ownership of the means of production (i.e., whether they are entrepreneurs or workers) originates from Karl Marx. Max Weber includes "status" groups and parties, along with social classes as the major elements of social structure and the distribution of power in society (Economy and Society: an Outline of Interpretive Sociology, 1922 [1978], pp. 302–307). However, there is no consensus on any of the core concepts of Marxist class analysis according to Erik Wright (Foundations of a Neo-Marxist Class Analysis, 2005), and Richard Breen notes that Weber's comments on class are also fragmentary (Foundations of a Neo-Marxist Class Analysis, 2005). Although the concept of class is a useful analytical tool, I do not share Marx's conclusions about the organization of society.

20 For an elaboration of this point, see Richard Sklar (1979, p. 537) and Soares de Oliveira (2007, p. 125).

21 Soares de Oliveira (2007, p. 125). The term "ruling elite" goes back to the concept of "ruling class" in classical elite theories of Vilfredo Pareto and Gaetano Mosca which saw the dialectic conflict in society as that between the elite who hold power and those who seek power (Keller, 1979, p. 11). Subsequent studies identified a "power elite" (Mills, 1956 [2000]), a "governing elite" according to Siegfried Nadel (The Concept of Social Elites, 1956) or a "strategic elite" (Keller, 1979) as different from other privileged groups.

22 See: Edward Laws (Political Settlements, Elite Pacts and Governments of National Unity, 2012) and Jonathan Di John and James Putzel (Political Settlements: Issue Paper, 2009, p. 14).

23 Di John and Putzel (2009, p. 14).

24 On powerful actors beyond the capital city, see Mariz Tadros and Jeremy Allouche (Political Settlements as a Violent Process: Deconstructing the Relationship between Political Settlements and Intrinsic, Instrumental and Resultant Forms of Violence, 2017, p. 198). On transnational actors, see Anthony Bebbington et al. (Resource Extraction and Inclusive Development: Extending the Bases of the Political Settlements Approach, 2018), and Samuel Hickey and Angelo Izama (The Politics of Governing Oil in Uganda: Going against the Grain?, 2017).

25 Mushtaq Khan (Rents, Efficiency and Growth, 2000), Khan (2010) and Laws (2012, pp. 20, 36).

26 Tadros and Allouche (Political Settlements as a Violent Process: Deconstructing the Relationship between Political Settlements and Intrinsic, Instrumental and Resultant Forms of Violence, 2017).

27 On rent management, see: Khan (2000).

28 The literature on business–state relations and their growth implications is large. It includes: Sylvia Maxfield and Ben Ross Schneider (Business and the State in Developing Countries, 1997), Richard Doner and Ben Ross Schneider (Business Associations and Economic Development, 2000), Deborah Brautigam, Lise Rakner, and Taylor Scott (Business Associations and Growth Coalitions in Sub-Saharan Africa, 2002).

29 Khan (2010, pp. 20–21).

30 For more on growth coalitions, see for instance: Richard Doner (Limits of State Strength: Toward an Institutionalist View of Economic Development, 1992), Peter Evans (1992) and Brautigam, Rakner and Scott (2002).

31 Khan (2010, p. 16; 2018, p. 26) and Lindsay Whitfield et al. (The Politics of African Industrial Policy: a Comparative Perspective, 2015).

32 Adam Przeworski (Institutions Matter?, 2004, p. 529).

33 Khan (2018).

34 On contingent conditions, see: James Mahoney and Celso M. Villegas (Historical Enquiry and Comparative Politics, 2009).

35 Giovanni Capoccia and R. Daniel Kelemen (The Study of Critical Junctures: Theory, Narrative and Counterfactuals in Historical Institutionalism, 2007, p. 343).

36 Daron Acemoglu and James Robinson (Paths of Economic and Political Development, 2008).

37 On persistence, see also James Robinson (Elites and Institutional Persistence, 2010).

38 Capoccia and Kelemen (2007, p. 352).

39 On historical breaking points, see: Wolfgang Streeck and Kathleen Thelen (Introduction: Institutional Change in Advanced Political Economies, 2005). On new equilibria, see Peter Hall and Rosemary Taylor (Political Science and the Three New Institutionalisms, 1996).

40 James Mahoney (Path Dependence in Historical Sociology, 2000).

41 Capoccia and Kelemen (2007).

42 Similarly, Lindsay Whitfield and Ole Therkildsen examine how policies are influenced by the characteristics of ruling coalitions. They define these characteristics in terms of the vulnerability, fragmentatio, and financing of ruling coalitions (What Drives States to Support the Development of Productive Sectors? Strategies Ruling Elites Pursue for Political Survival and their Policy Implications, 2011, pp. 17–26).

43 Richard Doner, Bryan Ritchie, and Dan Slater (Systemic Vulnerability and the Origins of Developmental States: Northeast and Southeast Asia in Comparative Perspective, 2005, pp. 328–330).

44   His typology of state–business relations has combinations of a coherent/fractured state and a concentrated/dispersed business sector resulting in four scenarios (2004, pp. 7, 11–18).
45   Khan (2000).
46   See: Dani Rodrik (Sense and Nonsense in the Globalization Debate, 1997).
47   See: Doner, Ritchie and Slater (2005). This also echoes the argument by Charles Tilly that strong states in Europe emerged in response to security threats (cited in Doner, Ritchie, and Slater).
48   Anjli Raval and Andrew Ward (Saudi Aramco Plans for a Life after Oil, 2017).

Chapter 4

1   Terry-Lynn Karl (The Paradox of Plenty: Oil Booms and Petro States, 1997).
2   NNPC (History of the Nigerian Petroleum Industry, 2020).
3   On colonial export agriculture, see: Gavin Williams (Colonialism and Capitalism, the Nigeria Case. A Review, 1974), Gerald K. Helleiner (Peasant Agriculture, Government and Economic Growth in Nigeria, 1966), R. Olufemi Ekundare (An Economic History of Nigeria 1860–1960, 1973, p. 112) and Toyin Falola (Development Planning and Decolonization in Nigeria, 1996, p. 4).
4   Federation of Nigeria (1961, p. 38).
5   Federal Republic of Nigeria, FRN (Federal Republic of Nigeria, 1970, pp. 17 and 137).
6   FRN (1970).
7   See Sayre Schatz (Nigerian Capitalism, 1977, p. 26).
8   FRN (1975, pp. 8 and 28–29).
9   See, FRN (1975, p. 10) and Schatz (1977, p. 45).
10   FRN (1975, p. 47).
11   Tom Forrest (The Advance of African Capital: the Growth of Nigerian Private Enterprise, 1994, pp. 41, 159).
12   I. William Zartman and Sayre Schatz (Introduction, 1983, p. 15).
13   Adebayo Olukoshi (1993, p. 3) and Shehu Yahaya (State versus Market: the Privatization Programme of the Nigerian State, 1993, p. 17).
14   On class formation in Nigeria, see: James S. Coleman (Nigeria: Background to Nationalism, 1958), Kalu Ezera (Constitutional Developments in Nigeria: an Analytical Study of Nigeria's Constitution-Making Developments, and the Historical and Political Factors that Affected Constitutional Change, 1964, p. 94). Billy J. Dudley (An Introduction to Nigerian Government and Politics, 1982), Gavin Williams (1974) and Robert Shenton (1986).
15   See: Billy J. Dudley (1982, pp. 57, 61–73) and Falola and Heaton (1996, p. 165).
16   Frederick J. D. Lugard (The Dual Mandate in British Tropical Africa, 1922, p. 210).
17   John Mackintosh (Nigerian Government and Politics, 1966, p. 44).
18   Remi Adekoya (Awolowo, Azikiwe and the Igbo-Yoruba "Lagos Press War," 2019).
19   Dudley (1982, p. 62).
20   Dudley (1982, p. 80).
21   See: John de St. Jorre (The Brothers' War: Biafra and Nigeria, 1972, p. 116) and Karl Maier (This House Has Fallen: Nigeria in Crisis, 2000, pp. 84–85).
22   See Max Siollun (Oil, Politics and Violence: Nigeria's Military Coup Culture, 2009, pp. 167–168).

23 Ajani (2009).
24 Interview with Babangida in: Maier (2000, p. 59).
25 Tom Forrest (Politics and Economic Development in Nigeria, 1995).
26 See Dudley (1982) and Siollun (2013) for the religious tensions which preceded and succeeded the decision on joining the OIC.
27 See: Siollun (2013, p. 247). On alliances in the civil war, see de St. Jorre (1972).
28 Abdul Raufu Mustapha (Ethnic Structure, Inequality and Governance of the Public Sector in Nigeria, 2006, pp. 18–19).
29 Interview, Abuja, Nigeria, April 14, 2014.
30 Barbara Geddes (1999, p. 136).
31 See: Coleman (1958, p. 59), Forrest (1994, p. 19) and Williams (1988).
32 Dudley (1982, p. 45).
33 A second generation of universities was established between 1970 and 1985, to meet the manpower needs of the post-civil war reconstruction and industrialization drive. A shift in orientation from broad-based university education to specialized education motivated the birth of the third-generation universities in the 1990s, focused on technology and agriculture. See: Williams E. Nwagwu and Omoverere Agarin (Nigerian University Websites: a Webometric Analysis, 2008).
34 See: Segun Osoba (The Nigerian Power Elite, 1952-65, 1977, pp. 370–371) and Forrest (1994, p. 27).
35 See: Alan Gelb and Henry Bienen (Nigeria: from Windfall Gains to Welfare Losses?, 1988, pp. 234–235) and Valerie P. Bennett and A. H. Kirk-Greene (Back to the Barracks: a Decade of Marking Time, 1978).
36 On the salience of class issues, see: Richard Sklar (Political Science and National Integration: a Radical Approach, 1967, p. 6) and Larry Diamond (Social Change and Political Conflict in Nigeria's Second Republic, 1983, p. 74).
37 Henry Bienen (Income Distribution and Politics in Nigeria, 1983, p. 102) and Okwudiba Nnoli (Ethnic Politics in Nigeria, 1978, p. 289).
38 Lewis (1994, p. 445).
39 Ibid., p. 441.
40 Maier (2000, p. 65).
41 See: Forrest (1995, p. 110) and Siollun (2013, pp. 247–248).
42 See: Enemaku Idachaba (Chronology of Major Political Events in the Abacha Era (1993–1998), 2001).
43 Interview, Abuja, Nigeria, April 30, 2014.
44 Lugard (1922, p. 617).
45 Falola (1996, p. 3).
46 Ibid.
47 Ibid.
48 FoN (1961, p. 6).
49 Legislative Council Nigeria (A Ten Year Plan of Development and Welfare for Nigeria, 1946, 1946, pp. 3–5).
50 Williams (1974, p. 9).
51 See: Ankie Hoogvelt (Indiginisation and Foreign Capital: Industrialisation in Nigeria, 1979) and Thomas J. Biersteker (Indigenisation and the Nigerian Bourgeoisie: Dependent Development in African Context, 1987, p. 258).
52 Sayre Schatz (1977, p. 3) and Tom Forrest (1994).
53 FoN (1961, pp. 23–24; 60).
54 Federation of Nigeria (1961).

55 Yakubu Gowon (Second National Development Plan 1970–74: Broadcast, 1970, p. 2).
56 Federation of Nigeria (1961) and FRN (1970, p. 75).
57 On the attempt at a green revolution, see: Okello Oculi (Green Capitalism in Nigeria, 1987, p. 178).
58 FRN (1970, pp. 145–146) and (Broadcasts by His Excellency, Major General Yakubu Gowon, Head of the Federal Military Government, Commander in Chief of the Armed Forces, 1970, p. 3).
59 FRN (1975, p. 17), Schatz (1977, p. 59).
60 FRN (1975).
61 Gowon (1970, p. 2) and FRN (1975, pp. 27–31).
62 Lewis (1994, p. 443).
63 FRN (1980, p. 52).
64 Olukoshi (1993, p. 3) and Yahaya (1993, p. 17).
65 Ibid., p. 72.
66 World Bank (Nigeria Structural Adjustment Program: Policies, Implementation, and Impact, 1994).
67 Emmanuel Uche (Development Plans and Policies in Nigeria: Observed Impediments and Practical Best Alternatives, 2019).
68 Discussion in this paragraph draws on World Bank (1994, p. ix).
69 Paul Lubeck and Michael Watts (An Alliance of Oil and Maize? The Response of Indigenous and State Capital to Structural Adjustment in Nigeria, 1994, p. 223).
70 Lewis (1994, pp. 437–438).
71 Lubeck and Watts (1994, p. 206).
72 World Bank (1994, p. ix).
73 Thandika Mkandawire and Charles Soludo (African Voices on Structural Adjustment, 2003).
74 Forrest (1994, p. 38).
75 Ibid., p. 250.
76 On the regional disparities resulting from indigenization, see: Peter Lewis (Economic Statism, Private Capital and the Dilemmas of Accumulation in Nigeria, 1994, p. 443) and Biersteker (1987).
77 On this point, see Siollun (2013, pp. 176–177).
78 Nigeria Vision 2010 Committee (Report of the Vision 2010 Committee, 1997).
79 Mustapha (2006, p. iv).
80 On the divide and rule tactics of British colonial rule in India, see Shashi Tharoor (Inglorious Empire: What the British Did to India, 2016, pp. 101–148), and in Nigeria, see: Coleman (1958, p. 53), Ezera (1964) and Nnoli (1978).
81 Falola and Heaton (2008, p. 155).
82 Richard Sklar (Democracy for the Second Republic, 1981).
83 Dudley (1982, p. 58).
84 Ibid.
85 Ibid., pp. 67–73.
86 Mustapha (2006).
87 For an extensive analysis of the history of intergovernmental revenue-sharing arrangements in Nigeria, see the research paper by Ehtisham Ahmad and Raju Singh (Political Economy of Oil-Revenue Sharing in a Developing Country: Illustrations from Nigeria, 2003, pp. 9–11).

88 On federal character, see research papers by Ladipo Adamolekun, John Erero and Basil Oshionebo ("Federal Character" and Management of the Federal Civil Service and the Military, 1991) and Mustapha (2009).

89 Richard Joseph assesses the crisis of governance and clientelistic politics in the elections of 1979 and 1983, through the prism of "prebendalism," the intense struggle between opposing ethno-clientelist groups, to control and exploit the offices of the state (1987). See also interview with Second Republic politician, Tanko Yakassai, in The Nigerian Voice (Why the North Abandoned Ekwueme for Obasanjo in 1999—Tanko Yakassai, 2013).

90 See: Siollun (2013, p. 225).

91 Alex Ekwueme (What Nigeria Lost by Abacha's Untimely Death: Well-thought out Provisions of the 1995 Constitution, 2005).

92 Terry-Lynn Karl (The Paradox of Plenty: Oil Booms and Petro States, 1997, p. 7).

93 Ibid., p. 41.

94 Lubeck and Watts (1994, p. 41).

95 Forrest (1994, p. 243).

Chapter 5

1 See also, Sherelle Jacobs (How Big Really is Africa's Middle Class?, 2015) and the report in question by the AfDB (The Middle of the Pyramid: Dynamics of the Middle Class 48 in Africa, 2011).

2 Aljazeera America (Nigeria Emerges as Africa's Largest Economy, 2014).

3 World Bank (Gross Domestic Product 2020). Available at: https://databank. worldbank.org/data/download/GDP.pdf.

4 IMF (Staff Report for the 2016 Article IV Consultation, 2016).

5 NBS (Nigeria Manufacturing Sector: Summary Report 2010–2012, 2014b, p. 9).

6 NBS (2014a).

7 IMF (Nigeria: Request for Purchase under the Rapid Financing Instrument—Press Release; Staff Report; and Statement by the Executive Director for Nigeria, 2020).

8 Hazem Beblawi (The Rentier State in the Arab World, 1987, pp. 51–53).

9 IMF (2020, p. 4).

10 Author interview, Kano, August 23, 2014.

11 Author interview, Abuja, May 14, 2014.

12 See: Jide Ajani (G-34 / PDP: The risks we took under Abacha, by Alex Ekwueme, 2009).

13 Author interview, Abuja, May 14, 2014.

14 Inge Amundsen (Who Rules Nigeria?, 2012, p. 3).

15 Abubakar Siddique Mohammed (The Masquerade Unmasked: Obasanjo and the Third-term Debacle, 2010, p. 179).

16 See: BBC News (Nigeria's Military Purges Gather Pace, 1999)(1999).

17 John Campbell (Nigeria: Dancing on the Brink, 2011, p. 18) and Amundsen (2012, p. 6).

18 Author interviews at the NGF secretariat. Abuja, 10 March 2014. This is not an unconstitutional body. There are several other groupings of governors along regional or partisan lines, such as the Northern Governors' Forum, the South–South Governors' Forum and the APC's Progressive Governors' Forum (PGF).

19 Rory Carroll (Nigerian State Governor Dresses up to Escape £1.8m Charges in UK, 2005).

20 Thisday (Nigeria: Obasanjo Promises Private Sector Good Governance, 2003) and Olalekan Adetayo (Governors, Businessmen, Others Donate N21.27bn to Jonathan, 2014).

21 Author interview, Abuja, March 24, 2014

22 U.S. Embassy Abuja (Goodluck Jonathan Remains Acting President of Nigeria #251113, 2010).

23 Letter published in Sahara Reporters (Don't Field Goodluck Jonathan In Northern Slot, Adamu Ciroma Group Writes PDP, 2010).

24 Author interview, Abuja, May 14, 2014.

25 Olly Owen and Zainab Usman (Why Goodluck Jonathan Lost the Nigerian Presidential Election of 2015, 2015).

26 Author interview with managing editor of a national newspaper in Lagos, July 8, 2014.

27 Pew Research Centre (Nigeria—The Future of World Religions: Population Growth Projections, 2010–2050, 2020).

28 Monica Toft, Daniel Philpott, and Timothy S. Shah (God's Century: Resurgent Religion and Global Politics, 2011).

29 When northern Nigeria was colonized by the British in the late nineteenth century, colonial laws modified or restricted certain aspects of shari'ah. Shari'ah courts–then known as area courts–had jurisdiction only over matters of personal status law. Criminal matters were dealt with under the Penal Code for Northern Nigeria (See: HRW, 2004:13).

30 Brandon Kendhammer (Muslims Talking Politics: Framing Islam, Democracy and Law in Northern Nigeria, 2016, p. 3).

31 Author interview with leadership of Christian Association of Nigeria (CAN), Abuja, May 16, 2014.

32 Section 10 of the 1999 Constitution states that "the Government of the Federation or of a State shall not adopt any religion as State Religion."

33 Sabina Alkire, Usha Kanagaratnam and Nicolai Suppa (The Global Multidimensional Poverty Index (MPI) 2019, 2019).

34 HRW ("Political Shari'a"? Human Rights and Islamic Law in Northern Nigeria, 2004, pp. 90–92).

35 Fatima Adamu (Gender, Hisba and the Enforcement of Morality in Northern Nigeria, 2008, p. 136).

36 Excerpt of keynote speech by CAN president obtained from the non-participant observation of Christian conference on ecumenism organized by the Association of Catholic Bishops in Nigeria, Abuja, April 23, 2014

37 Mfonobong Nsehe (The Five Richest Pastors in Nigeria, 2011).

38 See: Premium Times (CAN President, Oritsejafor, Admits Ownership of Cash-stacked Jet Seized in South Africa, 2014) (2014).

39 Ebenezer Obadare (The Muslim Response to the Pentecostal Surge in Nigeria: Prayer and the Rise of Charismatic Islam, 2016).

40 Said Adejumobi (Introduction: State, Economy and Society in a Neo-Liberal Regime, 2011, pp. 12–13).

41 Council on Foreign Relations (Boko Haram in Nigeria, 2020). For more on Boko Haram's origins and impacts, see edited volume by Abdul Raufu Mustapha and Kate Meagher (Overcoming Boko Haram: Faith, Society and Islamic Radicalization in Northern Nigeria, 2020).

42 While oil theft was started in the 1970s by military officers, democratization enabled participation by politicians and through an Amnesty programme from 2008 for "repentant militants," many moved to crude oil theft, piracy, and organized crime. See: Christina Katsouris and Aaron Sayne (Nigeria's Criminal Crude: International Options to Combat the Export of Stolen Oil, 2013).

43 Author interviews in Abuja between April and May 2014.

44 According to internet subscriber data from the Nigerian Communications Commission.

45 Stephanie Busari (What is Behind Nigeria's Fuel Protests?, 2012).

46 See: Jamie Hitchen, Jonathan Fisher, Idayat Hassan and Nic Cheeseman (WhatsApp and Nigeria's 2019 Elections: Mobilising the People, Protecting the Vote, 2019).

47 See el-Rufai (2013, p. 197).

48 DMO (Annual Report and Statement of Accounts 2005, 2005, pp. 40–44).

49 In 2003, British Prime Minister Tony Blair, promised to champion Nigeria's cause for debt relief if it were to develop and implement an economic reform program (el-Rufai, 2013, p. 189; Okonjo-Iweala N., 2012, p. 27).

50 Okonjo-Iweala (2012, p. 151).

51 OSSAP-MDGs (Monitoring and Evaluation for Accountability: The Case of Nigeria's Virtual Poverty Fund, 2006, p. 3).

52 Summarized in Ngozi Okonjo-Iweala (Point of View: Nigeria's Shot at Redemption, 2008).

53 Okonjo-Iweala (2012, p. 120).

54 For analyses of the Amnesty Programme, see: Mark Davidheiser and Kialee Nyiayaana (Demobilization or Remobilization? The Amnesty Program and the Search for Peace in the Niger Delta, 2011) and Iro Aghedo (Winning the War, Losing the Peace: Amnesty and the Challenges of Post-Conflict Peace-Building in the Niger Delta, Nigeria, 2012, p. 273).

55 Ibid.

56 Author interview, March 8, 2015.

57 Peter Lewis and Howard Stein (Shifting Fortunes: The Political Economy of Financial Liberalization in Nigeria, 1997, p. 6).

58 Charles Soludo (Beyond Banking Sector Consolidation in Nigeria, 2006).

59 Keynote speech by Lamido Sanusi (The Nigerian Banking Industry: What Went Wrong and the Way Forward, 2010).

60 Central Bank of Nigeria (Central Bank of Nigeria Advertorial [List of Debtors], 2009).

61 Sanusi (2010).

62 Author interview with senior official at Central Bank of Nigeria. Abuja, March 16, 2014.

63 Mutsa Chironga, Hilary De Grandis, and Yassir Zouaoui (Mobile Financial Services in Africa: Winning the Battle for the Customer, 2017).

64 Bright Okogu and Philip Osafo-Kwaako (Issues in Fiscal Policy Management Under the Economic Reforms (2003–2007), 2008, p. 197).

65 Joe Abah (Strong Organisations in Weak States: Atypical Public Sector Performance in Dysfunctional Environments, 2012).

66 The analysis in this paragraph is largely drawn from Abah (2012, pp. 2–5) and Nasir el-Rufai who was head of Obasanjo's Public Service Reform Team from 2005 to 2007 (2013, pp. 313–327).

67 The Guardian (Oronsaye Panel Report and Sundry Consequences, 2020).

68 Derived from summary fact-sheet provided to the author by a Special Assistant to President Buhari.

69 Definition adapted from World Bank Group (The State of Social Safety Nets 2018, 2018).

70 See report by the Overseas Development Institute (ODI) (Social Protection in Nigeria: Mapping Programmes and their Effectiveness, 2012, p. 50).

71 Figures derived from summary provided to the author by a Special Assistant to President Buhari.

72 See ODI (2012) and the World Bank (Advancing Social Protection in a Dynamic Nigeria, 2020)for further elaboration.

73 IRIN (Nigeria: House Gives Reason for Obasanjo Impeachment Threat, 2002).

74 Craig Timberg (Nigerian Senate Blocks Bid for Third Presidential Term, 2006).

75 Success Nwogu, Mudiaga Affe, Alexander Okere and Friday Amobi (Are State Houses of Assembly Executive Rubber Stamps?, 2017).

76 Nicolas Van de Walle and Kimberly S. Butler (Political Parties and Party Systems in Africa's Illiberal Democracies, 1999, p. 15).

77 Author interviews at the NGF secretariat, and with the manager of a bilateral donor initiative, Abuja, March 10–11 2014.

Chapter 6

1 Author interview, Lagos, 20 March 2014.

2 U.S. Embassy Abuja (Nigeria: Tariff and Ban Information, 2003).

3 Sahara Reporters (CBN's List of Bank Debtors, 2009).

4 Dangote Group (About Us, 2020).

5 Forbes (#191 Aliko Dangote, 2021).

6 Akinyinka Akinyoade and Chibuike Uche argue that Dangote's entrepreneurial skills explain his success in cement manufacturing (Dangote Cement: An African Success Story?, 2016).

7 U.S. Embassy Lagos (Aliko Dangote and Why You Should Know about Him, 2005).

8 Taiwo A. Gbenga et al. (Privatization and Commercialization of Nigerian National Petroleum Corporation Oil Refineries in Nigeria, 2014).

9 William Wallis (The Telecoms Numbers that Didn't Add Up, 2013).

10 BBC News (Nigeria Awards Telecoms Licenses, 2001).

11 Interview with an advisor for Obasanjo's government, Abuja, 13 May 2014.

12 Strive Masiyiwa (It's Time to Play by a Different (Ethical) Set of Rules (Part 7) Nigeria I, 2015).

13 Chukwudiebube Opata (Transplantation and Evolution of Legal Regulation of Interconnection Arrangements in the Nigerian Telecommunications Sector, 2011).

14 BBC (2001).

15 On share ownership for the pioneering telecoms firms, see: Masiyiwa (2015) and Fola Akanbi (Forbes: Nigerian New Entrants to Rich List Grew Wealth through Investments in Oil and Gas, 2012).

16 Ibid.

17 See: Masiyiwa (2015).

18 Nigeria Communications Commission NCC (Subscriber Statistics, 2021).

19 MTN Group Limited (Quarterly Update for the Period Ended 30 September 2020, 2020).

20 Crusoe Osagie (Nigeria: As Dangote Transforms Nigeria into an Export Nation, 2015).

21 CBN (Annual Economic Report for 2013, 2013).

22 U.S. Energy Information Administration—EIA (Nigeria, 2013).

23 AU and ECA (Report of the High Level Panel on Illicit Financial Flows from Africa, 2014) and Sanusi L. Sanusi (Memorandum Submitted to the Senate Committee on Finance on the Non-Remittance of Oil Revenue to the Federation Account, 2014).

24 Alex Gboyega et al. (Political Economy of the Petroleum Sector in Nigeria, 2011, p. 15).

25 The key unions in the sector are the Petroleum and Natural Gas Senior Staff Association (PENGASSAN) and the Nigerian Union of Petroleum and Natural Gas Workers (NUPENG). They represent the white-collar and blue-collar workers respectively.

26 Busari (What is Behind Nigeria's Fuel Protests?, 2012).

27 These are mostly econometric analyses on economic impacts, see: Michael Plante (The Long-Run Macroeconomic Impacts of Fuel Subsidies, 2014); on social and distributional impacts, see: Francisco Javier Arze del Granado, David Coady and Robert Gillingham (The Unequal Benefits of Fuel Subsidies: A Review of Evidence for Developing Countries, 2012) and Ismail Soile and Xiaoyi Mu (Who Benefit Most from Fuel Subsidies? Evidence from Nigeria, 2015); on environmental impact, see: David Coady, Ian Parry, Louis Sears, and Baoping Shang (How Large are Global Energy Subsidies?, 2015).

28 See for instance: David Victor (The Politics of Fossil-Fuel Subsidies, 2009); Masami Kojima (Fossil Fuel Subsidy and Pricing Policies: Recent Developing Country Experience, 2016), Gabriela Inchauste and David Victor (The Political Economy of Energy Subsidy Reform, 2017) and Harro van Asselt and Jakob Skovgaard (The Politics of Fossil Fuel Subsidies and their Reform, 2018).

29 See for instance, background papers and report published as part of the Rethinking Power Sector Reforms in the Developing World Project: www.worldbank.org/en/topic/energy/publication/rethinking-power-sector-reform.

30 International Energy Agency—IEA (Nigeria Energy Outlook, 2019).

31 Ibid.

32 Anthony Black, Brian Makundi and Thomas McLennan (Africa's Automotive Industry: Potential and Challenges, 2017, pp. 12–16).

33 IEA (2019).

34 Author interviews.

35 Olumide Adeosun and Ayodele Oluleye (Nigeria's Refining Revolution, 2017, p. 4).

36 Felix Jaro and Noma Garrick (Privatisation of Refineries: the Panacea to Nigeria's Refining Problems?, n.d.).

37 Modular refineries are available in capacities of 1,000–30,000 bpd, have low capital requirements of around $100–$200 million, can be constructed within a short time span of under twenty months, and provide for flexibility to be built and upgraded in a phased manner. Conventional refineries by contrast are usually larger with capacities higher than 100,000 bpd, require larger capital investments and specialized labor to run, maintain and upgrade, and also allow for economies of scale and thus higher margins on products (Adeosun and Oluleye, 2017, p. 12).

38 Olumide Adeosun and Ayodele Oluleye (Nigeria's Refining Revolution, 2017).

39 Tume Ahemba (Obasanjo Ally Buys Second Nigerian Oil Refinery, 2007).

40 Hydrocarbons Technology (Dangote Refinery, Lagos, 2020).

41   Aaron Sayne, Alexandra Gillies and Christina Katsouris (Inside NNPC Oil Sales: A Case for Reform in Nigeria, 2015, pp. 42–43).

42   Ibid.

43   Sanusi (2014, p. 3).

44   Elisha Bala-Gbogbo and Anthony Osae-Brown (Nigeria to Keep Oil-for-Fuel Swap for at Least Three More Years, 2019).

45   House of Representatives (Report of the Ad-hoc Committee "To Verify and Determine the Actual Subsidy Requirements and Monitor the Implementation of the Subsidy Regime in Nigeria").

46   HoR (2012, p. 7).

47   Ike Abonyi and Akinwale Akintunde (Subsidy Fraud: EFCC to Prosecute 23 Oil Marketers, 2012).

48   Michael Eboh (FG Spent N1.5trn to Subsidise Petrol in 2019— Enang, 2020).

49   Eklavya Gupte (Nigeria's President Confirms Removal of Gasoline Subsidies, 2020).

50   On public support for fuel subsidies, see: Neil McCulloch, Tom Moerenhout, and Joonseok Yang (Fuel Subsidy Reform and the Social Contract in Nigeria: A Micro-economic Analysis, 2020), on impacts on firm productivity, see: Morgan Bazilian and Ijeoma Onyeji (Fossil Fuel Subsidy Removal and Inadequate Public Power Supply: Implications for Businesses, 2012).

51   World Bank (Advancing Social Protection in a Dynamic Nigeria, 2020, p. 26).

52   Priscilla Atansah, Masoomeh Khandan, Todd Moss, Anit Mukherjee, and Jennifer Richmond (When do Subsidy Reforms Stick? Lessons from Iran, Nigeria and India, 2017).

Chapter 7

1   Xan Rice (Africa: Lessons from Lagos, 2012).

2   UN Habitat (The State of African Cities 2018: the Geography of African Investment, 2018, p. 157).

3   Adrienne LeBas and Nic Cheeseman (The Lagos Experiment: Services Delivery, Tax Collection, and Popular Attitudes, 2013).

4   Existing Lagos State Government estimates are widely divergent from NBS data. For instance, NBS data estimates manufacturing at 8.75% while Lagos State puts the figure at almost 29.6%. For consistency, I use state GDP data from the NBS and fiscal data from state government sources.

5   African Markets (Nigeria Starts Crude Oil Production in Lagos, 2016).

6   Zwile Nkosi (Lagos, Nigeria Listed by Mercer as the fourth costliest city in Africa, 2019).

7   Lagos State Government (Lagos State Development Plan 2012-2025, 2013).

8   John Black, Nigar Hashimzade, and Gareth Myles (Oxford Dictionary of Economics, 2017).

9   Sue Ann Batley Blackman and William J. Baumol (Natural Resources, n.d.).

10   Laurent Fourchard (Lagos, Koolhas and Partisan Politics in Nigeria, 2011, p. 67).

11   Nigeria has six ports in total. The others are Calabar, Rivers, Delta and Onne Ports mostly in the Niger Delta where the oil export terminals are.

12   Lagos State Government (2013, p. 105) and UN Habitat (The State of African Cities 2014: Re-Imagining Sustainable Urban Transitions, 2014, p. 135).

13 On the flooding challenge in Lagos, see: Ibudun O. Adelekan 'Vulnerability of Poor Urban Coastal Communities to Flooding in Lagos, Nigeria', 2010.

14 Lagos State Government (2013, p. 57).

15 Ibid.

16 UN Habitat (2014, p. 270).

17 Ibid., p. 103; 2020, p. 331).

18 According to the ILO, the labor force includes those 15 years old and over who are either employed, unemployed, or seeking employment (Black, Hashimzade, and Myles, 2017).

19 Kaye Whiteman (Lagos: a Cultural and Historical Companion, 2012, pp. 30–31), Laurent Fourchard (Lagos, 2012, p. 67).

20 Akin L. Mabogunje (Urbanization in Nigeria, 1968, p. 264) and Ayodeji Olukoju (Population Pressure, Housing and Sanitation in West Africa's Premier Port-City: Lagos, 1900–1939, 1993).

21 Whiteman (2012, pp. 30–31) and Fourchard (2012, pp. 70–71).

22 Nicholas A. Nwagwu (The Politics of Universal Primary Education in Nigeria, 1955–1977, 1978).

23 Giuseppe Larossi, Peter Mousley and Ismail Radwan (An Assessment of the Investment Climate in Nigeria, 2009, pp. 2, 13).

24 Gary S. Becker (Human Capital, 2008).

25 Eko Atlantic (About Eko Atlantic, 2020, p. 151).

26 Matthew Gandy (Planning, Anti-Planning and the Infrastructure Crisis Facing Metropolitan Lagos, 2006) and Laurent Fourchard (Lagos, 2012).

27 Whiteman (2012, pp. 34 and 73).

28 Ibid., p. 84.

29 Ibid., p.86.

30 Lagos State Government (2013, p. 45).

31 Ibid., p. 53.

32 UN Habitat (2018, p. 118).

33 Central Bank of Nigeria (Commercial Banks, 2020).

34 Larossi, Mousley, and Radwan (2009, p. 60).

35 Author interview, October 27, 2015, London, United Kingdom.

36 Author interview, July 8, 2014, Lagos, Nigeria.

37 Author interview, October 27, 2015, London, United Kingdom.

38 Stuart R. Lynn (Economic Development: Theory and Practice for a Divided World, 2003, p. 92).

39 Russell S. Sobel (Entrepreneurship, 2008).

40 See rich list reports by Damilare Opeyemi (Meet the Five Nigerians who Made the Forbes 2016 World Billionaires List, 2016).

41 Whiteman (2012, p. 78).

42 Author interview, 20 March 2014, Lagos, Nigeria.

43 Dario Giuliani and Sam Ajadi (618 Active Tech Hubs: The Backbone of Africa's Tech Ecosystem, 2019).

44 Marc Jean Yves Lixi et al. (Nigeria Digital Economy Diagnostic Report, 2019, p. 30).

45 Gbenga Onalaja (TechCabal Explains: Yaba i-HQ, 2015).

46 Author interview with Founder of BudgIT, one of the start-up operating from the Co-Creation Hub spaces, July 21, 2014, Lagos, Nigeria.

47 Co-Creation Hub (Startups, 2020).

48 Giuliani and Ajadi (2019).

49 Lixi et al. (2019, p. 2).
50 See, e.g., reports by Colin Freeman (Meet the Man Who Tamed Africa's Most Lawless City, 2014) and *The Economist* (Learning from Lagos, 2015).
51 These include, among others, Laurent Fourchard (2011), Diane de Gramont (Governing Lagos: Unlocking the Politics of Reform, 2015), Nic Cheeseman and Diane de Gramont (Managing a Mega-City: Learning the Lessons from Lagos, 2017) and Daniel Agbiboa (Informal Urban Governance and Predatory Politics in Africa: the Role of Motor-Park Touts in Lagos, 2018).
52 Robert Kaplan (The Coming Anarchy: How Scarcity, Crime, Overpopulation, Tribalism, and Disease are Rapidly Destroying the Social Fabric of Our Planet, 1994).
53 de Gramont (2015, p. 6).
54 Abubakar Momoh (The Elections in Lagos State as a Political Monologue, 2011, p. 205).
55 Tonye Bakare (Why I Dumped Ambode—Tinubu, 2018).
56 Gandy (2006, p. 372).
57 Author interview, 17 July 2014, Lagos, Nigeria.
58 Cited in Gandy (2006, p. 390).
59 Berg, Julie et al. (Contested Social Orders: Negotiating Urban Security in Nigeria and South Africa, 2013, pp. 171–172).
60 Author interview, July 16, 2014, Lagos, Nigeria.
61 Author interview, July 13, 2014, Lagos, Nigeria.
62 de Gramont (2015, p. 7).
63 Chief Obafemi Awolowo as premier of the western region in the 1950s established universal primary education and extended health and agricultural services. Lateef Jakande, the first elected governor of Lagos State (1979–1983) developed a strategic plan for Lagos and undertook large municipal investments (Nwagwu, 1978; Gandy, 2006).
64 de Gramont (2015, p. 10).
65 See Fourchard (2011, p. 47) for an assessment of the resulting tensions between Lagos State and the federal government on this extra-constitutional creation of local councils.
66 Author interview, July 13, 2014, Lagos, Nigeria.
67 Ibid.
68 Author interview, July 17, 2014, Lagos, Nigeria.
69 Babatunde Fashola's inauguration speech on May 29, 2007, reproduced in Nigeria Governors' Forum (Inaugural Speeches of Presidents (1999–2011) and Governors (2007–2013) of the Federal Republic of Nigeria, 2013, p. 254).
70 Author interview with a senior analyst at a bilateral development agency, July 16, 2014, Lagos, Nigeria.
71 de Gramont (2015, p. 11).
72 Author interview, July 17, 2014, Lagos, Nigeria.
73 There are sixty-nine items in the Exclusive List and thirty items in the Concurrent List. See: Parts I and II, Second Schedule of the 1999 Constitution of the Federal Republic of Nigeria.
74 For full list of powers of a state governor, see: Chapter VI, Part II, of the 1999 Constitution of the Federal Republic of Nigeria.
75 Author interview with Ministry of Finance official, July 3, 2014, Lagos, Nigeria.
76 Author interview, July 17, 2014, Lagos, Nigeria.
77 Ibid.

78 Author interview with Ministry of Finance official, July 3, 2014, Lagos, Nigeria. See also report by Chukwuemeka Eze (VAT: Why Lagos Lost at Supreme Court, 2014).

79 Author interview, July 17, 2014, Lagos, Nigeria.

80 Fourchard (2011, p. 52).

81 Author interview, July 17, 2014, Lagos, Nigeria.

82 Author interview, LCCI, July 8, 2014, Lagos, Nigeria.

83 See: "Lagos Economic Summit Group" website. Available at: http:// lagoseconomicsummit.org/.

84 Author interview with Commissioner for Economic Planning and Budget, July 17, 2014, Lagos, Nigeria.

85 Ibid.

86 de Gramont (2015, p. 16).

87 Ibid.

88 Ibid.

89 Author interview, Ministry of Finance, July 3, 2014, Lagos, Nigeria.

90 Alemika and Omotosho, 2009 and Alemika, Cheeseman and LeBas, 2010 in de Gramont (2015, pp. 15–16).

91 de Gramont (2015, p. 10).

92 Ibid., pp. 19, 24

93 For a detailed analysis of the compact between the politicians and informal sector associations, see: Pauline Baker (1974), Fourchard (2011, pp. 50–52; 2012), Whiteman (2012, pp. 206–207) and Agbiboa (2018).

94 Fourchard (2012, p. 52).

95 de Gramont (2015, p. 16).

96 Author interview, Ministry of Finance, July 3, 2014, Lagos, Nigeria.

97 Whiteman (2012, p. 207).

98 On intra-party fragmentation, see: Momoh (2011, p. 211).

99 This spat is documented in a news report by Ini Ekott (Igbo, Yoruba at War Over Chinua Achebe's Criticism of Awolowo in New Book, 2012). See the book itself by Chinua Achebe (There was a Country: a Personal History of Biafra, 2012).

100 See. for instance: Idowu Akinlotan (The Lagos Deportation Saga and 2015 Politics, 2013).

101 Nicholas Ibekwe (How I Spent N78 Million on Website, Mobile Applications, Others—Fashola, 2015).

102 de Gramont (2015, p. 12).

Chapter 8

1 Mohammed Lere (Kannywood: Nigeria to Establish World-Class Film Village in Kano, 2016).

2 Christopher Vourlias (Nigeria Scraps Plans for $10 Million Film Village After Muslim Clerics Protest, 2016).

3 BBC News (Nigeria Shelves Plans for "Kannywood" Film Village, 2016).

4 The Punch (Jonathan Splashes N3 Billion New Grant on Nollywood, 2013).

5 Shaibu Husseini (A Film Village for Kannywood to Compensate for a "Lopsided" Project Act Nollywood, 2016).

6   Carmen McCain (The "Second Coming" of Kannywood, 2011) and Elizabeth Flock (Inside Nollywood, the Booming Film Industry that Makes 1,500 Movies a Year, 2017).

7   Carmen McCain (Nollywood, Kannywood, and a Decade of Hausa Film Censorship in Nigeria, 2013, p. 232).

8   Kate Bubacz and Monica Mark (These Muslim Women are Fluent in the Language of Love, 2016).

9   Premium Times (VIDEO: Why I Set Books Ablaze as Kano Governor—Shekarau, Education Minister, 2014).

10   A. G. Hopkins cited in Murtala Muhammad et al. (China's Involvement in the Trans-Saharan Textile Trade and Industry in Nigeria: The Case of Kano, 2019, p. 3).

11   Kano State Government (2015, p. 39).

12   Ibid., p. 35.

13   Kano State Government (2015, p. 36).

14   By order of output, these manufacturing sub-sectors are: food, beverage, and tobacco; textile, apparel, and footwear; wood and wood products; pulp and paper products; chemicals and pharmaceuticals; non-metallic products; plastic and rubber products; electrical and electronics; basic metal, iron, and steel; motor vehicles and assembly and other manufacturing. See: NBS (2014).

15   Author interviews at MAN Kano branch, August 20–21, 2014

16   Author interview, August 20, 2014, Kano, Nigeria.

17   Kano State Government (2015, p. 40).

18   Kano State Government (Kano State Development Plan 2013–2015, 2012).

19   Kano State Government (Kano State Development Plan 2016–2018, 2015).

20   Kano State Government (2015, p. 35).

21   See news report by Barbara Jones and Sanchez Manning (Your aid helps fashion giants: Just when you thought you'd read all about foreign aid waste... the astonishing story of how UK money funded factory clothing catwalk queens, 2016).

22   KACCIMA (35th Kano International Trade Fair: Promoting Agricultural and Other Non-Oil Business Sector for Sustainable Development, 2014).

23   Kano State Development Plan (2012, p. 9).

24   Forrest (1994, p. 197).

25   On precolonial Nigeria, see: Anthony G. Hopkins (An Economic History of West Africa, 1973), Shenton (1986, p. 57), and Forrest (1994, p. 197).

26   Murtala Muhammad et al. (China's Involvement in the Trans-Saharan Textile Trade and Industry in Nigeria: the Case of Kano, 2019).

27   Leena K. Hoffman and Paul Melly (Nigeria's Booming Borders: the Drivers and Consequences of Unrecorded Trade, 2015, p. 28).

28   Ibid.

29   Author interview, August 12, 2014, Kano, Nigeria.

30   Author interview, August 20, 2014, Kano, Nigeria.

31   Giuseppe Iarossi, Peter Mousley, and Ismail Radwan (An Assessment of the Investment Climate in Nigeria, 2009, p. 24).

32   Hoffman and Melly (2015, p. 15).

33   Author interview, August 12, 2014, Kano, Nigeria.

34   Kano State Government (2015, p. 27).

35   Kano State Government (2012).

36   Iarossi, Mousley, and Radwan (2009, p. 13).

37 World Bank (An Assessment of the Investment Climate in Nigeria: The Challenges of Nigeria's Private Sector, 2016, pp. 77–78).
38 World Bank (2016, p. 91).
39 Author interview, August 22, 2014, Kano, Nigeria.
40 Federal Ministry of Works (Digest of Statistics, 2011, p. 85).
41 Iarossi, Mousley and Radwan (2009, p. 24).
42 Author interview, August 26, 2014, Kano, Nigeria.
43 Khan (2012, p. 34).
44 Author interview, August 22, 2014, Kano, Nigeria.
45 Author interview, August 15, 2014, Kano, Nigeria.
46 Author interview with Commissioner for Budget and Planning, August 18, 2014, Kano, Nigeria.
47 Giuseppe Iarossi and George Clarke (Nigeria 2011: An Assessment of the Investment Climate in 26 States, 2011, pp. 14–15).
48 Iarossi and Clarke (2011, p. 25).
49 Ibid., p. 27.
50 Usman Khan (GEMS3 Supporting an Improved Business Environment: Assess Level of Need for Support to KSG, 2012, p. 16).
51 Khan (2012, p. 17).
52 See news report by International Flyerz (KLM to Discontinue Flights to Kano, 2012).
53 Author interviews with Manager of Ado Bayero Mall, the MAN Kano branch, and with the chief executive of Country Mall, August 2014, Kano, Nigeria.
54 Forrest (1994, p. 197).
55 Ibid., pp. 199–200.
56 Author interview, August 12, 2014, Kano, Nigeria.
57 Kano State Government (2015, p. 27).
58 Murtala Muhammad, Ramatu Buba, Muhammad Danial Azman and Abubakar Ahmed (Muhammad, Buba, Azman, and Ahmed, 2019).
59 Timur Kuran (The Scale of Entrepreneurship in Middle Eastern History: Inhibitive Roles of Islamic Institutions, 2010, p. 81).
60 Ibid., p. 69.
61 Author interviews, August 20–21, 2014, Kano, Nigeria.
62 Ibid.
63 Forrest (1994, p. 18).
64 Author interviews with industrialists in Kano, August 2014.
65 Adebayo Olukoshi cited in Forrest (1994, p. 201).
66 Ankie Hoogvelt (Indiginisation and Foreign Capital: Industrialisation in Nigeria, 1979, pp. 61–67).
67 Kano State Government (2012).
68 Rabiu Kwankwaso was elected governor of Kano State in 1999 on the platform of the PDP. In 2003, he lost his re-election bid to ANPP's Ibrahim Shekarau. He ran for the same position again eight years later, in 2011, and won. In 2013, Kwankwaso defected to the newly formed APC while Shekarau moved to the PDP.
69 See opinion analysis by federal legislator Ahmed M. Salik (Onshore-Offshore Dichotomy and the Abrogation Act, 2016).
70 See for instance, media report by Katrin Gansler (Nigeria Looks Back on 20 Years of Sharia Law in the North, 2019).
71 Ibid.

72 Brandon Kendhammer (Muslims Talking Politics: Framing Islam, Democracy and Law in Northern Nigeria, 2016, p. 17).

73 Alex Thurston (Muslim Politics and Shari'a in Kano State, Northern Nigeria, 2014, pp. 36–37).

74 Kendhammer (2016, p. 17).

75 Franz Kogelmann in Thurston (2014, p. 37).

76 Author interviews, August 2014, Kano, Nigeria.

77 Ibid.

78 Author interview with political analyst, August 20, 2014, Kano, Nigeria.

79 Thurston (2014, p. 40).

80 Author interview with former commissioner for budget and planning, August 18, 2014, Kano Nigeria.

81 Rabiu Kwankwaso's inauguration speech on May 29, 2011, reproduced in NGF (2013, p. 477).

82 Thurston (2014, pp. 40–41).

83 Ibrahim Shekarau's May 29, 2007 inauguration speech, reproduced in NGF (2013, p. 213).

84 Fatima Adamu (Gender, Hisba and the Enforcement of Morality in Northern Nigeria, 2008)and Thurston (2014).

85 Author interview in Kano, Nigeria, August 2014.

86 Ibid.

87 Ibid.

88 Author interview, August 2014, Kano, Nigeria.

89 KANGIS is modeled along the federal government's competently managed Abuja Geographic Information Systems (AGIS). It is run by a former AGIS director.

90 Author interview, August 11, 2014, Kano, Nigeria.

91 Muhammad Sagagi (Budget Analysis: Kano State Government Budget 2012) and Kano State Government (2012).

92 Author interview with Secretary to the State Government, August 26, 2014, Kano, Nigeria.

93 Author interview August 18, 2014, Kano, Nigeria.

94 Author interview with the Secretary to the State Government, August 26, 2014, Kano, Nigeria.

95 Author interviews with analyst, August 20, 2014, Kano, Nigeria.

96 Author interview, August 15, 2014. Kano, Nigeria.

97 Author interview, August 26, 2014, Kano, Nigeria.

98 See news report by Y. A. Ibrahim (Inside Kwankwaso's Abandoned Billion Naira Institutes, 2016).

99 Author interview with Kano-based economist, August 10, 2014, Kano, Nigeria.

100 Author interviews, August 2014, Kano, Nigeria.

101 Author interview with senior manager at Lee Group, August 20, 2014, Kano, Nigeria.

102 Murtala et al. (2019).

103 Ibid., pp. 5–7.

104 Author interviews, August 2014, Kano, Nigeria.

105 Author interview with industrialists, August 2014, Kano, Nigeria.

106 See news report by Nuruddeen M. Abdallah et al. (80 Kano Gov't-Trained Pilots Now Teachers, Civil Servants, 2016).

107 Muhammad et al. (2019).

108 Author interviews with industrialists, August 2014, Kano, Nigeria.

109 Author interviews, August 2014, Kano, Nigeria.
110 Aljazeera English (Nigeria's Land Borders Closed to all Goods, Official Confirms, 2019).

Conclusion

1 BBC News (Suharto Tops Corruption Ranings, 2004).
2 Richard Doner, Bryan Ritchie, and Dan Slater (Systemic Vulnerability and the Origins of Developmental States: Northeast and Southeast Asia in Comparative Perspective(2005).
3 See edited volume by Ross Garnaut, Ligang Song, and Cai Fang (China's 40 Years of Reform and Development: 1978–2018, 2018).
4 On the Swiss consensus democracy, see: Wolf Linder and Sean Mueller (Swiss Democracy: Possible Solutions to Conflict in Multicultural Societies, 2021).
5 Rose Mutiso and Katie Hill (Why Hasn't Africa Gone Digital? One Major Reason is a Lack of Reliable, Affordable Electricity, 2020).
6 Ugo Gentilini, Mohamed Almenfi, Ian Orton, and Pamela Dale (Social Protection and Jobs Responses to COVID-19: A Real-Time Review of Country Measures, 2020).

References

Abah, J. (2012). *Strong Organisations in Weak States: Atypical Public Sector Performance in Dysfunctional Environments*. Unpublished PhD Thesis: Maastricht University.

Abdallah, N. M., Sule, I. K., Ibrahim, Y. A., & Aliyu, A. (2016, February 20). *80 Kano Gov't-Trained Pilots Now Teachers, Civil Servants*. Retrieved July 8, 2016, from Daily Trust: https://dailytrust.com/80-kano-govt-trained-pilots-now-teachers-civil-servants

Abonyi, I., & Akintunde, A. (2012, July 25). *Subsidy Fraud: EFCC to Prosecute 23 Oil Marketers*. Retrieved October 25, 2015, from Thisday: www.thisdaylive.com/articles/subsidy-fraud-efcc-to-prosecute-23-oil-marketers/120779/

Acemoglu, D., & Robinson, J. A. (2008). Paths of Economic and Political Development. In B. R. Weingast, & D. A. Wittman, *The Oxford Handbook of Political Economy* (pp. 673–693). Oxford: Oxford University Press.

Achebe, C. (2012). *There was a Country: a Personal History of Biafra*. London: Penguin Books.

Acker, K., & Brautigam, D. (2021). *Twenty Years of Data on China's Africa Lending*. No. 4. Boston University Global Development Centre; Johns Hopkins School of Advanced and International Studies.

Adamolekun, L., Erero, J., & Oshionebo, B. (1991). "Federal Character" and Management of the Federal Civil Service and the Military. *Publius: the Journal of Federalism, 21*(4), 75–88.

Adamu, F. (2008). Gender, Hisba and the Enforcement of Morality in Northern Nigeria. *Africa, 78*(01), 136–152.

Adejumobi, S. (2011). Introduction: State, Economy and Society in a Neo-Liberal Regime. In S. Adejumobi, *State, Economy and Society in Post-Military Nigeria* (pp. 1–23). New York: Palgrave Macmillan.

Adekoya, R. (2019, August 22). *Awolowo, Azikiwe and the Igbo-Yoruba "Lagos Press War."* Retrieved May 1, 2020, from Business Day: https://businessday.ng/columnist/article/awolowo-azikiwe-and-the-igbo-yoruba-lagos-press-war/

Adelekan, I. O. (2010). Vulnerability of Poor Urban Coastal Communities to Flooding in Lagos, Nigeria. *Environment and Urbanization, 22*(2), 433–450.

Adeosun, O., & Oluleye, A. (2017). *Nigeria's Refining Revolution*. www.pwc.com/ng/en/assets/pdf/nigerias-refining-revolution.pdf: PwC.

Adetayo, O. (2014, December 21). *Governors, Businessmen, Others Donate N21.27bn to Jonathan*. Retrieved May 15, 2015, from Sahara Reporters: http://saharareporters.com/2014/12/21/govs-businessmen-others-donate-n2127bn-jonathan.

AfDB. (2011). *The Middle of the Pyramid: Dynamics of the Middle Class in Africa*. Abidjan: African Development Bank.

AfDB; OECD; UNDP. (2014). *African Economic Outlook 2014: Global Value Chains and Africa's Industrialisation*. Paris: African Development Bank; Organisation for Economic Cooperation and Development; United Nations Development Programme.

Africa Natural Resources Centre. (2016). *Botswana's Mineral Revenues, Expenditure and Savings Policy: A Case Study*. Abidjan: African Development Bank Group.

African Business Magazine. (2019, November 4). Special Report: Africa's Top 100 Banks 2019. *African Business Magazine*. Retrieved from http://africanbusinessmagazine.com/africas-top-100-banks/special-report-africas-top-100-banks-2019/

African Markets. (2016, May 5). *Nigeria Starts Crude Oil Production in Lagos*. Retrieved December 1, 2020, from African Markets: www.african-markets.com/en/news/west-africa/nigeria/nigeria-starts-crude-oil-production-in-lagos

Agbiboa, D. E. (2018). Informal Urban Governance and Predatory Politics in Africa: The Role of Motor-Park Touts in Lagos. *African Affairs, 117*(466), 62–82.

Aghedo, I. (2012). Winning the War, Losing the Peace: Amnesty and the Challenges of Post-Conflict Peace-Building in the Niger Delta, Nigeria. *Journal of Asian and African Studies, 48*(3), 267–280.

Ahemba, T. (2007, May 28). *Obasanjo Ally Buys Second Nigerian Oil Refinery*. Retrieved August 11, 2020, from Reuters: https://uk.reuters.com/article/nigeria-refinery/obasanjo-ally-buys-second-nigerian-oil-refinery-idUKL2854224220070528

Ahmad, E., & Singh, R. (2003). *Political Economy of Oil-Revenue Sharing in a Developing Country: Illustrations from Nigeria*. International Monetary Fund, Fiscal Affairs Department WP/03/16. Washington D.C.: International Monetary Fund.

Ajani, J. (2009, August 22). *G-34 / PDP: The Risks We Took under Abacha, by Alex Ekwueme*. Retrieved from Vanguard: www.vanguardngr.com/2009/08/g-34-pdp-the-risks-we-took-under-abacha-by-alex-ekwueme/

Akanbi, F. (2012, November 25). *Forbes: Nigerian New Entrants to Rich List Grew Wealth through Investments in Oil and Gas*. Retrieved October 20, 2015, from Thisday: www.thisdaylive.com/articles/forbes-nigerian-new-entrants-to-rich-list-grew-wealththrough-investments-in-oil-and-gas/131583/

Akinlotan, I. (2013, August 18). *The Lagos Deportation Saga and 2015 Politics*. Retrieved from The Nation: https://thenationonlineng.net/the-lagos-deportation-saga-and-2015-politics/

Akinyoade, A., & Uche, C. (2016). *Dangote Cement: an African Success Story?* ASC Working Paper 131/2016. Leiden: African Studies Centre.

Aljazeera America. (2014, April 6). *Nigeria Emerges as Africa's Largest Economy*. Retrieved from Aljazeera America: http://america.aljazeera.com/articles/2014/4/6/nigeria-biggest-economy.html

Alkire, S., Kanagaratnam, U., & Suppa, N. (2019). *The Global Multidimensional Poverty Index (MPI) 2019*. OPHI MPI Methodological Notes 47. Oxford: Oxford Poverty and Human Development Initiative, University of Oxford.

Amsden, A. (1989). *Asia's Next Giant: South Korea and Late Industrialization*. New York; Oxford: Oxford University Press.

Amundsen, I. (2012). *Who Rules Nigeria?* Oslo: NOREF - Norwegian Peacebuilding Resource Centre. Retrieved from www.cmi.no/publications/4623-who-rules-nigeria

Arze Del Granado, F. J., Coady, D., & Gillingham, R. (2012). The Unequal Benefits of Fuel Subsidies: A Review of Evidence for Developing Countries. *World Development, 40*(11), 2234–2248.

AU and ECA. (2014). *Report of the High Level Panel on Illicit Financial Flows from Africa*. Conference of Ministers of Finance, Planning and Economic Development.

Auty, R. (1993). *Sustaining Development in Mineral Economies: The Resource Curse Thesis*. London: Routledge.

Bakare, T. (2018, September 30). *Why I Dumped Ambode - Tinubu*. Retrieved December 3, 2020, from The Guardian: https://guardian.ng/news/why-i-dumped-ambode-tinubu/

Baker, P. (1974). *Urbanization and Political Change: The Politics of Lagos, 1917–1967.* Berkeley: University of California Press.

Bala-Gbogbo, E., & Osae-Brown, A. (2019, September 2). *Nigeria to Keep Oil-for-Fuel Swap for at Least Three More Years.* Retrieved August 10, 2020, from BNN Bloomberg: www.bnnbloomberg.ca/nigeria-to-keep-oil-for-fuel-swap-for-at-least-three-more-years-1.1309963

Bates, R. (1981). *Markets and States in Tropical Africa: the Political Basis of Agricultural Policies.* Berkeley: University of California Press.

Bazilian, M., & Onyeji, I. (2012). Fossil Fuel Subsidy Removal and Inadequate Public Power Supply: Implications for Businesses. *Energy Policy, 45*, 1–5.

BBC News. (1999, June 11). *Nigeria's Military Purges Gather Pace.* Retrieved May 18, 2015, from BBC Nes: http://news.bbc.co.uk/2/hi/africa/366259.stm

BBC News. (2001, January 19). *Nigeria Awards Telecoms Licenses.* Retrieved June 07, 2015, from BBC News: http://news.bbc.co.uk/1/hi/business/1126538.stm

BBC News. (2004, March 25). *Suharto Tops Corruption Ranings.* Retrieved from BBC News: http://news.bbc.co.uk/2/hi/business/3567745.stm

BBC News. (2012, October 15). *Africa Debate: Will Africa Ever Benefit from its Natural Resources?* Retrieved October 26, 2015, from BBC News: www.bbc.com/news/world-africa–19926886

BBC News. (2016, July 25). *Nigeria Shelves Plans for "Kannywood" Film Village.* Retrieved December 14, 2020, from www.bbc.com/news/world-africa–36883949

Bebbington, A., Abdulai, A.-G., Bebbington, D. H., Marja, H., & Sanborn, C. A. (2018). Resource Extraction and Inclusive Development: Extending the Bases of the Political Settlements Approach. In A. Bebbington, A.-G. Abdulai, D. H. Bebbington, H. Marja, & C. A. Sanborn, *Governing Extractive Industries: Politics, Histories and Ideas* (pp. 11–21). Oxford: Oxford University Press.

Beblawi, H. (1987). The Rentier State in the Arab World. In H. Beblawi, & G. Luciani, *The Rentier State* (pp. 49–63). London: Primo.

Beck, T., Demirgüç-Kunt, A., Laeven, L., & Levine, R. (2008). Finance, Firm Size, and Growth. *Journal of Money, Credit, and Banking, 40*(7), 1379–1405.

Becker, G. S. (2008). *Human Capital.* Retrieved from *The Concise Encyclopaedia of Economics*: www.econlib.org/library/Enc/HumanCapital.html

Belton, K. B. (2020, April 20). *COVID-19 Makes the Case for Resilient Manufacturing: Six Policy Proposals that Merit Newfound Attention.* Retrieved September 7, 2020, from Industry Week: www.industryweek.com/the-economy/public-policy/article/21129255/covid19-makes-the-case-for-resilient-manufacturing

Bennett, V. P., & Kirk-Greene, A. H. (1978). Back to the Barracks: A Decade of Marking Time. In S. K. Panter-Brick, *Soldiers and Oil: the Political Transformation of Nigeria* (pp. 1–26). London: Cass.

Berg, J., Akinyele, R., Fourchard, L., Van Der Waal, K., & Williams, M. (2013). Contested Social Orders: Negotiating Urban Security in Nigeria and South Africa. In S. Bekker, & L. Fourchard, *Governing Cities in Africa: Politics and Policies* (pp. 169–188). Cape Town: HSRC Press.

Besley, T., & Persson, T. (2009). The Origins of State Capacity: Property Rights, Taxation and Politics. *American Economic Review, 99*(4), 1218–1244.

Bienen, H. (1983). Income Distribution and Politics in Nigeria. In W. I. Zartman, *The Political Economy of Nigeria* (pp. 85–104). New York: Praeger.

Biersteker, T. J. (1987). Indigenisation and the Nigerian Bourgeoisie: Dependent Development in African Context. In P. M. Lubeck, *The African Bourgeoisie: Capitalist*

Development in Nigeria, Kenya and the Ivory Coast (pp. 249–279). Boulder: Lynne Rienner.

Black, A., Makundi, B., & McLennan, T. (2017). *Africa's Automotive Industry: Potential and Challenges.* Working Paper Series No. 282. Abidjan: African Development Bank.

Black, J., Hashimzade, N., & Myles, G. (2017). *Oxford Dictionary of Economics.* Oxford: Oxford University Press.

Blackman, S. A., & Baumol, W. J. (n.d.). *Natural Resources.* Retrieved from The Library of Economics and Liberty: www.econlib.org/library/Enc/NaturalResources.html

Blanchard, O., Romer, D., Spence, M., & Stiglitz, J. E. (2012). *In the Wake of the Crisis: Leading Economists Reassess Economic Policy.* Cambridge, MA: MIT Press.

Blattman, C., Franklin, S., & Dercon, S. (2019). *Impacts of Industrial and Entrepreneurial Jobs on Youth: 5-Year Experimental Evidence on Factor Job Offers and Cash Grants in Ethiopia.* SocArXiv. doi:10.31235/osf.io/zrqe4

Brautigam, D., Rakner, L., & Scott, T. (2002). Business Associations and Growth Coalitions in Sub-Saharan Africa. *Journal of Modern African Studies, 40*(4), 519–547.

Breen, R. (2005). Foundations of a Neo-Marxist Class Analysis. In E. O. Wright, *Approaches to Class Analysis* (pp. 31–50). Cambridge: Cambridge University Press.

Bubacz, K., & Mark, M. (2016, February 17). *These Muslim Women are Fluent in the Language of Love.* Retrieved December 31, 2020, from BuzzFeed News: www.buzzfeednews.com/article/katebubacz/meet-the-women-behind-nigerias-most-subversive-novellas

BudgIT. (2019). *Nigeria's Petrol Subsidy Regime: Dilemma of the World's Most Populous Black Nation.* Lagos: BudgIT.

Buera, F. J., Kaboski, J. P., & Shin, Y. (2011). Finance and Development: A Tale of Two Sectors. *American Economic Review, 101*(5), 1964–2002.

Burgess, R., & Stern, N. (1993). Taxation and Development. *Journal of Economic Literature, 31*(2), 762–830.

Busari, S. (2012, January 13). *What is Behind Nigeria's Fuel Protests?* Retrieved April 5, 2019, from CNN: www.cnn.com/2012/01/06/world/africa/nigeria-fuel-protest-explained/index.htm

Calderon, C. (2021). *Boosting Productivity in Sub-Saharan Africa*: Policies and Institutions to Promote Efficiency. Washington D.C.: World Bank.

Campbell, J. (2011). *Nigeria: Dancing on the Brink.* Lanham: Rowman & Littlefield Publishers Inc.

Capoccia, G., & Kelemen, D. R. (2007). The Study of Critical Junctures: Theory, Narrative and Counterfactuals in Historical Institutionalism. *World Politics, 49*(3), 341–369.

Carbon Tracker Initiative. (2021). *Beyond Petrostates: The Burning Need to Cut Oil Dependence in the Energy Transition.* Carbon Tracker Initiative. Retrieved from https://carbontracker.org/reports/petrostates-energy-transition-report/

Carroll, R. (2005, November 22). *Nigerian State Governor Dresses up to Escape £1.8m Charges in UK.* Retrieved from *The Guardian*: www.theguardian.com/world/2005/nov/23/hearafrica05.development

Caselli, F. (2005). Accounting for Cross-Country Income Differences. In P. Aghion, & S. Durlauf, *Handbook of Economic Growth* (Vol. 1, Part A, pp. 679–741). Amsterdam: Elsevier.

CBN. (2009). *Central Bank of Nigeria Advertorial [List of Debtors].* Abuja: Central Bank of Nigeria (CBN).

CBN. (2013). *Annual Economic Report for 2013.* Abuja: Central Bank of Nigeria.

Central Bank of Nigeria. (2020). *Commercial Banks*. Retrieved from Central Bank of Nigeria: www.cbn.gov.ng/Supervision/Inst-DM.asp

Chabal, P., & Daloz, J.-P. (1999). *Africa Works: Disorder as Political Instrument*. London: James Currey.

Chalmers, J. (1982). *MITI and the Japanese Miracle*. Stanford: Stanford University Press.

Chang, H.-J. (2002). *Kicking Away the Ladder: Development Strategy in Historical Perspective*. London: Anthem Press.

Chang, H.-J. (2011). *23 Things They Dont Tell You about Capitalism*. London: Penguin.

Chang, H.-J., & Lebdioui, A. (2020). *From Fiscal Stabilization to Economic Diversification: a Developmental Approach to Managing Resource Revenues*. WIDER Working Paper 2020/108. Helsinki: UNU-WIDER.

Cheeseman, N., & de Gramont, D. (2017). Managing a Mega-City: Learning the Lessons from Lagos. *Oxford Review of Economic Policy, 33*(3), 457–477.

Cherif, R., & Hasanov, F. (2019). *The Return of the Policy that Shall not be Named: Principles of Industrial Policy*. Working Paper No. 19/74. Washington D.C.: International Monetary Fund.

Chironga, M., De Grandis, H., & Zouaoui, Y. (2017, September 1). *Mobile Financial Services in Africa: Winning the Battle for the Customer*. Retrieved from McKinsey & Company: www.mckinsey.com/industries/financial-services/our-insights/mobile-financial-services-in-africa-winning-the-battle-for-the-customer

Cirera, X., & Maloney, W. F. (2017). *The Innovation Paradox: Developing-Country Capabilities and the Unrealized Promise of Technological Catch-Up*. Washington D.C.: World Bank.

Clapham, C. (1986). *Third World Politics: an Introduction*. Madison: The University of Wisconsin Press.

Coady, D., Parry, I., Sears, L., & Shang, B. (2015). *How Large are Global Energy Subsidies?* IMF Working Paper WP/15/105. Washington D.C.: International Monetary Fund. Retrieved from www.imf.org/external/pubs/ft/wp/2015/wp15105.pdf

Co-Creation Hub. (2020). *Startups*. Retrieved December 9, 2020, from Co-Creation Hub: https://cchubnigeria.com/startups/

Coleman, J. S. (1958). *Nigeria: Background to Nationalism*. Berkeley: University of California Press.

Connell, J. (2006). Medical Tourism: Sea, Sun, Sand and… Surgery. *Tourism Management, 27*(6), 1093–1100.

Corden, W. M., & Neary, J. P. (1982). Booming Sector and De-Industrialization in a Small Open Economy. *The Economic Journal, 92*(368), 825–848.

Council on Foreign Relations. (2020, June 25). *Boko Haram in Nigeria*. Retrieved from Global Conflict Tracker: www.cfr.org/global-conflict-tracker/conflict/boko-haram-nigeria

Cust, J. (2017). *The Role of Governance and International Norms in Managing Natural Resources*. Working Paper 2017/203. Helsinki: UNU-WIDER.

Daily Trust. (2007, May 30). *Nigeria: Yar'Adua Admits Election Flaws*. Retrieved from Daily Trust: https://allafrica.com/stories/200705300320.html

Daloz, J.-P. (2003). "Big Men" in Sub-Saharan Africa: How Elites Accumulate Positions and Resources. *Comparative Sociology, 2*(1), 271–285.

Dangote Group. (2020). *About Us*. Retrieved July 15, 2020, from Dangote Group: www.dangote.com/about-us

Davidheiser, M., & Nyiayaana, K. (2011). Demobilization or Remobilization? The Amnesty Program and the Search for Peace in the Niger Delta. *African Security, 4*(1), 44–64.

de Ferranti, D., Perry, G. E., Lederman, D., & Maloney, W. E. (2002). *From Natural Resources to the Knowledge Economy: Trade and Job Quality*. Washington D.C.: World Bank. Retrieved from https://openknowledge.worldbank.org/handle/10986/14040

de Gramont, D. (2015). *Governing Lagos: Unlocking the Politics of Reform*. Washington D.C.: Carnegie Endowment for International Peace.

de St. Jorre, J. (1972). *The Brothers' War: Biafra and Nigeria*. Boston: Houghton Mifflin.

Dembosky, A. (2013, June 9). *Silicon Valley Rooted in Backing from US Military*. Retrieved September 19, 2020, from *The Financial Times*: www.ft.com/content/8c0152d2-d0f2-11e2-be7b-00144feab7de

Di John, J., & Putzel, J. (2009). *Political Settlements: Issue Paper*. Governance and Social Development Resource Centre. Birmingham: International Development Department, University of Birmingham. Retrieved January 13, 2013

Diamond, L. (1983). *Social Change and Political Conflict in Nigeria's Second Republic*. New York: Praeger.

DMO. (2005). *Annual Report and Statement of Accounts 2005*. Abuja: DMO- Debt Management Office.

Doner, R. F. (1992). Limits of State Strength: Toward an Institutionalist View of Economic Development. *World Politics, 44*(03), 398–431.

Doner, R., & Schneider, B. R. (2000). Business Associations and Economic Development. *Business and Politics, 2*(3), 261–288.

Doner, R. F., Ritchie, B. K., & Slater, D. (2005). Systemic Vulnerability and the Origins of Developmental States: Northeast and Southeast Asia in Comparative Perspective. *International Organization, 59*(2), 327–361.

Dooley, M., & Khara, H. (2019, November 22). *How Inclusive is Growth?* Retrieved from Brookings: www.brookings.edu/blog/future-development/2019/11/22/how-inclusive-is-growth/

Dudley, B. J. (1982). *An Introduction to Nigerian Government and Politics*. London: Macmillan.

Eboh, M. (2020, April 9). *FG Spent N1.5trn to Subsidise Petrol in 2019— Enang*. Retrieved August 10, 2020, from Vanguard: www.vanguardngr.com/2020/04/fg-spent-n1-5trn-to-subsidise-petrol-in-2019-enang/

Economic Commission for Africa. (2013). *Making the Most of Africa's Commodities: Industrializing for Growth, Jobs and Economic Transformation*. Addis Ababa: United Nations Economic Commission for Africa.

Economic Commission for Africa. (2016). *Transformatiive Industrial Policy for Africa*. Addis Ababa: UN Economic Commission for Africa.

EIA. (2013). *Nigeria*. United States Energy Information Administration.

Eko Atlantic. (2020). *About Eko Atlantic*. Retrieved from Eko Atlantic: www.ekoatlantic.com/about-us/

Ekott, I. (2012, October 8). *Igbo, Yoruba at War Over Chinua Achebe's Criticism of Awolowo in New Book*. Retrieved July 15, 2016, from *Premium Times*: www.premiumtimesng.com/news/102820-igbo-yoruba-at-war-over-chinua-achebes-criticism-of-awolowo-in-new-book.html

Ekundare, R. O. (1973). *An Economic History of Nigeria 1860-1960*. London: Methuen.

Ekundayo, K. (2017, November 2). *Nigeria Spent N9tr on Fuel Subsidy in 10 Years— PPPRA*. Retrieved from Daily Trust: https://dailytrust.com/nigeria-spent-n9tr-on-fuel-subsidy-in-10-years-pppra

Ekwueme, A. (2005, May 29). *What Nigeria Lost by Abacha's Untimely Death: Well-thought out Provisions of the 1995 Constitution*. Retrieved April 14, 2015, from Dawodu.com: https://dawodu.com/ekwueme1.htm

el-Rufai, N. A. (2013). *The Accidental Public Servant*. Ibadan: Safari Books.

Erten, B., & Ocampo, J. A. (2013). Super Cycles of Commodity Prices since the Mid-Nineteenth Century. *World Development, 44*, 14–30.

Evans, P. (1992). The State as Problem and Solution: Predation, Embedded Autonomy and Structural Change. In S. Haggard, & R. Kaufman, *The Politics of Economic Adjustment* (pp. 139–181). Princeton: Princeton University Press.

Evans, P. (1995). *Embedded Autonomy: States and Industrial Transformation*. Princeton: Princeton University Press.

Eze, C. (2014, May 20). *VAT: Why Lagos Lost at Supreme Court*. Retrieved July 12, 2016, from The Nation: https://thenationonlineng.net/vat-lagos-lost-supreme-court/

Ezera, K. (1964). *Constitutional Developments in Nigeria: an Analytical Study of Nigeria's Constitution-Making Developments, and the Historical and Political Factors that Affected Constitutional Change*. Cambridge: Cambridge University Press.

Falola, T. (1996). *Development Planning and Decolonization in Nigeria*. Gainesville: University Press of Florida.

Falola, T., & Heaton, M. (2008). *A History of Nigeria*. New York: Cambridge University Press.

Federal Ministry of Works. (2011). *Digest of Statistics*. Abuja: Federal Ministry of Works, Nigeria.

Federal Republic of Nigeria. (1966). *Guideposts for the Second National Development Plan*. Lagos: Federal Republic of Nigeria (FRN) Ministry of Economic Development.

Federal Republic of Nigeria. (1970). *Broadcasts by His Excellency, Major-General Yakubu Gowon, Head of the Federal Military Government, Commander in Chief of the Armed Forces*. Lagos: Federal Republic of Nigeria.

Federal Republic of Nigeria. (1970). *Second National Development Plan, 1970–1974: Programme of Post-War Reconstruction and Development*. Lagos: Federal Ministry of Information.

Federal Republic of Nigeria. (1975). *Third National Development Plan, 1975–1980*. Lagos: Federal Republic of Nigeria (FRN), Federal Ministry of Economic Development.

Federal Republic of Nigeria. (1980). *Guidelines for the Fourth National Development Plan, 1981–1985*. Lagos: Federal Ministry of National Planning.

Federation of Nigeria. (1961). *First National Development Plan, 1962–1968*. Lagos: Federal Ministry of Economic Development.

Fish, A., & Spillane, H. (2020, July 23). *Reshoring Advanced Manufacturing Supply Chains to Generate Good Jobs*. Retrieved September 7, 2020, from Brookings Institution: www.brookings.edu/research/reshoring-advanced-manufacturing-supply-chains-to-generate-good-jobs/

Flock, E. (2017, October 24). *Inside Nollywood, the Booming Film Industry that Makes 1,500 Movies a Year*. Retrieved December 31, 2020, from PNS News Hour: www.pbs.org/newshour/arts/inside-nollywood-the-booming-film-industry-that-makes-1500-movies-a-year

Forbes. (2021, September 2). *#191 Aliko Dangote*. Retrieved September 2, 2021, from *Forbes*: www.forbes.com/profile/aliko-dangote/?sh=3c6f29dd22fc

Forrest, T. (1994). *The Advance of African Capital: the Growth of Nigerian Private Enterprise*. Edinburgh: Edinburgh University Press for the International African Institute.

Forrest, T. (1995). *Politics and Economic Development in Nigeria*. Boulder; Oxford: Westview.

Fourchard, L. (2011). Lagos, Koolhas and Partisan Politics in Nigeria. *International Journal of Urban and Regional Research, 35*(1), 40–56.

Fourchard, L. (2012). Lagos. In S. Bekker, & G. Therborn, *Power and Powerlessness: Capital Cities in Africa* (pp. 65–82). Cape Town: HSRC Press.

Frankema, E., & Van Waijenburg, M. (2018). Africa Rising? A Historical Perspective. *African Affairs, 117*(469), 543–568.

Freeman, C. (2014, October 24). *Meet the Man Who Tamed Africa's Most Lawless City.* Retrieved July 12, 2016, from *The Telegraph*: www.telegraph.co.uk/news/worldnews/africaandindianocean/nigeria/11184759/Meet-the-man-who-tamed-Nigerias-most-lawless-city.html

Fukuyama, F. (2014). *Political Order and Political Decay: From the Industrial Revolution to the Globalization of Democracy.* New York: Farrar, Straus and Giroux.

Gandy, M. (2006). Planning, Anti-Planning and the Infrastructure Crisis Facing Metropolitan Lagos. *Urban Studies, 43*(2), 371–396.

Gansler, K. (2019, October 27). *Nigeria Looks Back on 20 Years of Sharia Law in the North.* Retrieved December 29, 2020, from Deutsche Welle: www.dw.com/en/nigeria-looks-back-on-20-years-of-sharia-law-in-the-north/a–51010292

Garnaut, R., Song, L., & Fang, C. (2018). *China's 40 Years of Reform and Development: 1978–2018.* Acton: Australian National University Press.

Gbenga, T. A., Mukaila, A. A., Micheal, A. O., & Olayiwola, S. A. (2014). Privatization and Commercialization of Nigerian National Petroleum Corporation Oil Refineries in Nigeria. *International Journal of Science and Research, 3*(8), 643–648.

Gboyega, A., Soreide, T., Minh Le, T., & Shukla, G. P. (2011). *Political Economy of the Petroleum Sector in Nigeria.* Washington D.C.: World Bank.

Gebrekidan, S., Apuzzo, M., & Novak, B. (2019, November 3). *The Money Farmers: How Oligarchs and Populists Milk the E.U. for Millions.* Retrieved September 9, 2020, from The New York Times: www.nytimes.com/2019/11/03/world/europe/eu-farm-subsidy-hungary.html?auth=login-google

Geddes, B. (1999). What Do We Know about Democratization after 20 Years? *Annual Review of Political Science*, 115–144.

Gelb, A., & Bienen, H. (1988). Nigeria: From Windfall Gains to Welfare Losses. In A. Gelb, *Oil Windfalls: Blessing for Curse?* (pp. 227–261). New York: Oxford University Press.

Gentilini, U., Almenfi, M., Orton, I., & Dale, P. (2020). *Social Protection and Jobs Responses to COVID-19: A Real-Time Review of Country Measures.* Washington D.C.: World Bank. Retrieved July 22, 2020, from https://openknowledge.worldbank.org/handle/10986/33635

Gerschenkron, A. (1962). *Economic Backwardness in Historical Perspective: A Book of Essays.* Cambridge, MA: Harvard University Press.

Ghani, E. (2010). *The Service Revolution in South Asia.* Oxford: Oxford University Press.

Ghani, E., & Kharas, H. (2010). The Service Revolution in South Asia: An Overview. In E. Ghani, *The Service Revolution in South Asia.* Oxford: Oxford University Press.

Ghani, E., & O'Connell, S. D. (2014). *Can Service Be a Growth Escalator in Low Income Countries?* Policy Research Working Paper No. 6971. Washington D.C.: World Bank.

Giuliani, D., & Ajadi, S. (2019, July 10). *618 Active Tech Hubs: The Backbone of Africa's Tech Ecosystem.* Retrieved December 2, 2020, from GSMA: www.gsma.com/mobilefordevelopment/blog/618-active-tech-hubs-the-backbone-of-africas-tech-ecosystem/

Gordon, R., & Li, W. (2009). Tax Structures in Developing Countries: Many Puzzles and a Possible Explanation. *Journal of Public Economics, 93*(7–8), 855–866.

Gowon, Y. (1970). *Second National Development Plan 1970–1974: Broadcast.* Lagos: Federal Republic of Nigeria.

Gray, H., & Whitfield, L. (2014). *Reframing African Political Economy: Clientelism, Rents and Accumulation as Drivers of Capitalist Transformation.* Working Paper Series (159). London: International Development, LSE.

Gupte, E. (2020, June 5). *Nigeria's President Confirms Removal of Gasoline Subsidies.* Retrieved June 06, 2020, from S&P Global Platts: www.spglobal.com/platts/en/market-insights/latest-news/oil/060520-nigerias-president-confirms-removal-of-gasoline-subsidies

Hall, P. A., & Taylor, R. C. (1996). Political Science and the Three New Institutionalisms. *Political Studies, 44*(5), 936–957.

Hall, R. E., & Jones, C. I. (1999). Why Do Some Countries Produce So Much More Output Per Worker than Others? *The Quarterly Journal of Economics, 114*(1), 83–116.

Hallward-Driemeier, M., & Nayyar, G. (2018). *Trouble in the Making? The Future of Manufacturing-Led Development.* Washington D.C.: World Bank.

Haraguchi, N., Cheng, C. F., & Smeets, E. (2017). The Importance of Manufacturing in Economic Development: Has this Changed? *World Development, 93*, 293–315.

Hausmann, R., & Rodrik, D. (2003). Economic Development as Self-Discovery. *Journal of Development Economics*, 603–633.

Hawkins, E. K. (1958). Marketing Boards and Economic Development in Nigeria and Ghana. *The Review of Economic Studies, 26*(1), 51–62.

Hayashi, Y. (2021, January 25). *Biden Signs Buy American Order for Government Procurement.* Retrieved January 26, 2021, from *The Wall Street Journal*: www.wsj.com/articles/biden-to-sign-buy-american-order-for-government-procurement-11611568806

Heckscher, E., & Ohlin, B. (1991). *Heckscher-Ohlin Trade Theory.* Cambridge, MA: MIT Press.

Helleiner, G. K. (1966). *Peasant Agriculture, Government and Economic Growth in Nigeria.* Homewood: Richard D. Irwin.

Hickey, S., & Izama, A. (2017). The Politics of Governing Oil in Uganda: Going against the Grain? *African Affairs, 116*(463), 163–185.

Hirschman, A. (1958). *The Strategy of Economic Development.* New Haven, CT: Yale University Press.

Hirschman, A. (1977). A Generalised Linkage Approach to Development, with Special Reference to Staples. *Economic Development and Cultural Change, 25*(Supplement), 67–98.

Hitchen, J., Hassan, I., Fisher, J., & Cheeseman, N. (2019). *Whatsapp and Nigeria's 2019 Elections: Mobilising the People, Protecting the Vote.* Abuja; Birmingham: Centre for Democracy and Development; University of Birmingham.

Hoffman, L. K., & Melly, P. (2015). *Nigeria's Booming Borders: The Drivers and Consequences of Unrecorded Trade.* London: Chatham House.

Holmes, R., Akinrimisi, B., Morgan, J., & Buck, R. (2012). *Social Protection in Nigeria: Mapping Programmes and their Effectiveness.* London: Overseas Development Institute.

Hoogvelt, A. (1979). Indiginisation and Foreign Capital: Industrialisation in Nigeria. *Review of African Political Economy, 6*(14), 56–58.

Hopkins, A. G. (1973). *An Economic History of West Africa.* London: Longman.

Hoque, S. (2017, August 24). *Ethiopia's Economic Transformation and Job Creation: the Role of Hawassa Industrial Park.* Retrieved September 7, 2020, from Supporting Economic Transformation: https://set.odi.org/sonia-hoque-odi-ethiopias-economic-transformation-job-creation-role-hawassa-industrial-park/

House of Representatives. (2012). *Report of the Ad-hoc Committee "To Verify and Determine the Actual Subsidy Requirements and Monitor the Implementation of the Subsidy Regime in Nigeria."* Resolution No. (HR.1/2012).

HRW. (2004, September 21). *"Political Sharia"? Human Rights and Islamic Law in Northern Nigeria.* Retrieved from Human Rights Watch: www.hrw.org/report/2004/09/21/political-sharia/human-rights-and-islamic-law-northern-nigeria

Hsieh, C.-T., & Klenow, P. J. (2010). Development Accounting. *American Economic Journal: Macroeconomics, 2*(1), 207–223.

Humphreys, M., Sachs, J. D., & Stiglitz, J. E. (2007). *Escaping the Resource Curse.* New York: Columbia University Press.

Husseini, S. (2016, July 24). *A Film Village for Kannywood to Compensate for a "Lopsided" Project Act Nollywood.* Retrieved December 14, 2020, from https://guardian.ng/life/film/a-film-village-for-kannywood-to-compensate-for-a-lopsided-project-act-nollywood/

Hydrocarbons Technology. (2020). *Dangote Refinery, Lagos.* Retrieved July 27, 2020, from Hydrocarbons Technology: www.hydrocarbons-technology.com/projects/dangote-refinery-lagos/

Iarossi, G., & Clarke, G. R. (2011). *Nigeria 2011: An Assessment of the Investment Climate in 26 States.* Washington D.C.: World Bank.

Iarossi, G., Mousley, P., & Radwan, I. (2009). *An Assessment of the Investment Climate in Nigeria.* Washington D.C.: World Bank.

Ibekwe, N. (2015, August 13). *How I Spent N78 Million on Website, Mobile Applications, Others - Fashola.* Retrieved July 16, 2016, from *Premium Times:* www.premiumtimesng.com/news/top-news/188365-how-i-spent-n78-million-on-website-mobile-applications-others-fashola.html

Ibrahim, Y. A. (2016). *Inside Kwankwaso's Abandoned Billion Naira Institutes.* Retrieved July 8, 2016, from Daily Trust: www.dailytrust.com.ng/news/general/inside-kwankwaso-s-abandoned-billion-naira-institutes/145723.html

Idachaba, E. (2001). Chronology of Major Political Events in the Abacha Era (1993–1998). In K. Amuwo, D. C. Bach, & Y. Lebeau, *Nigeria During the Abacha Years (1993–1998): The Domestic and International Politics of Democratization* (pp. 341–363). Ibadan: IFRA-Nigeria.

IEA. (2019). *Nigeria Energy Outlook.* Retrieved from IEA: www.iea.org/articles/nigeria-energy-outlook

IHS Markit. (n.d.). *Trump Steel and Aluminium Tariffs Analysis.* Retrieved September 9, 2020, from IHS Markit: https://ihsmarkit.com/solutions/trump-steel-aluminum-tariffs.html

ILO. (2018). *Women and Men in the Informal Economy: A Statistical Picture (Third Edition).* Geneva: International Labour Office.

IMF. (2016). *Staff Report for the 2016 Article IV Consultation.* Washington D.C.: International Monetary Fund.

IMF. (2020). *Nigeria: Request for Purchase under the Rapid Financing Instrument – Press Release; Staff Report; and Statement by the Executive Director for Nigeria.* Country Report No. 20/142. Washington D.C.: International Monetary Fund African Department.

Inchauste, G., & Victor, D. (2017). *The Political Economy of Energy Subsidy Reform.* Washington D.C.: World Bank.

International Flyerz. (2012). *KLM to Discontinue Flights to Kano.* Retrieved July 1, 2016, from International Flyerz: www.internationalflyerz.co.za/viewtopic.php?t=1524

IRIN. (2002, September 5). *Nigeria: House Gives Reason for Obasanjo Impeachment Threat.* Retrieved May 20, 2015, from IRIN: www.thenewhumanitarian.org/report/34153/nigeria-house-gives-reasons-obasanjo-impeachment-threat

Jacobs, S. (2015, September 8). *How Big Really is Africa's Middle Class?* Retrieved from African Business: https://africanbusinessmagazine.com/uncategorised/continental/how-big-really-is-africas-middle-class/

Jaro, F., & Garrick, N. (n.d.). *Privatisation of Refineries: the Panacea to Nigeria's Refining Problems?* Retrieved August 11, 2020, from Energy Mix Report: www.energymixreport.com/privatisation-of-refineries-the-panacea-to-nigerias-refining-problems/

Jones, B., & Manning, S. (2016, April 30). *Your Aid Helps Fashion Giants: Just when You Thought You'd Read All about Foreign Aid Waste . . . the Astonishing Story of How UK Money Funded Factory Clothing Catwalk Queens.* Retrieved June 30, 2016, from *Daily Mail*: www.dailymail.co.uk/news/article-3567648/Your-aid-helps-fashion-giants-Just-thought-d-read-foreign-aid-waste-astonishing-story-UK-money-funded-factory-clothing-catwalk-queens.html

Joseph, R. A. (1987). *Democracy and Prebendal Politics in Nigeria: The Rise and Fall of the Second Republic.* Cambridge: Cambridge University Press.

KACCIMA. (2014). *35th Kano International Trade Fair: Promoting Agricultural and Other Non-Oil Business Sector for Sustainable Development.* Kano: Kano Chamber of Commerce, Industry, Mines and Agriculture - KACCIMA.

Kaldor, N. (1967). *Strategic Factors in Economic Development.* New York: New York State of School of Industrial and Labor Relations.

Kang, D. (2004). *Crony Capitalism: Corruption and Development in South Korea and the Philippines.* Cambridge: Cambridge University Press.

Kano State Government. (2012). *Kano State Development Plan 2013–2015.* Kano: Ministry of Planning and Budget.

Kano State Government. (2015). *Kano State Development Plan 2016–2018.* Kano: Kano State Ministry of Planning and Budget.

Kaplan, R. (1994, February). *The Coming Anarchy: How Scarcity, Crime, Overpopulation, Tribalism, and Disease are Rapidly Destroying the Social Fabric of Our Planet.* Retrieved December 3, 2020, from *The Atlantic*: www.theatlantic.com/magazine/archive/1994/02/the-coming-anarchy/304670/

Karl, T.-L. (1997). *The Paradox of Plenty: Oil Booms and Petro States.* Berkeley; London: University of California Press.

Katsouris, C., & Sayne, A. (2013). *Nigeria's Criminal Crude: International Options to Combat the Export of Stolen Oil.* London: Chatham House.

Kazeem, Y. (2019, December 10). *Samsung is Making a Comeback but China's Transsion is Still Africa's Top Phone Maker.* Retrieved from Quartz Africa: https://qz.com/africa/1765210/transsion-is-africas-top-phone-maker-but-samsung-is-back/

Keller, S. (1979). *Beyond the Ruling Class: Strategic Elites in Modern Society.* New York: Arno Press.

Kendhammer, B. (2016). *Muslims Talking Politics: Framing Islam, Democracy and Law in Northern Nigeria.* Chicago: University of Chicago Press.

Khan, M. (2000). Rents, Efficiency and Growth. In M. Khan, & J. K. Sundaram, *Rents, Rent-Seeking and Economic Development: Theory and Evidence in Asia* (pp. 21–60). Cambridge: Cambridge University Press.

Khan, M. (2010). *Political Settlements and the Governance of Growth-Enhancing Institutions.* (Unpublished).

Khan, M. (2011). Governance and Growth Challenges for Africa. In A. Noman, K. Botchwey, H. Stein, & J. E. Stiglitz, *Good Growth and Governance in Africa: Rethinking Development Strategies* (pp. 114–139). Oxford: Oxford University Press.

Khan, M. (2012). Governance and Growth: History, Ideology and Methods of Proof. In A. Noman, K. Botchwey, H. Stein, & J. E. Stiglitz, *Good Growth and Governance in Africa: Rethinking Development Strategies* (pp. 51–79). Oxford: Oxford University Press.

Khan, M. (2018). Political Settlements and the Analysis of Institutions. *African Affairs, 117*(469), 636–655.

Khan, U. (2012). *GEMS3 Supporting an Improved Business Environment: Assess Level of Need for Support to KSG.* (Unpublished).

Khanna, A., Papadavid, P., Tyson, J., & Te Velde, D. W. (2016). *The Role of Services in Economic Transformation—with an Application to Kenya.* London: ODI - Supporting Economic Transformation.

Kim, Y. E., & Loayza, N. V. (2019). *Productivity Growth: Patterns and Determinants across the World.* Policy Research working paper; no. WPS 8852. Washington D.C.: World Bank.

Kleven, H. J., Kreiner, C. T., & Saez, E. (2016). Why Can Modern Governments Tax So Much? An Agency Model of Firms as Fiscal Intermediaries. *Economica, 83*(330), 219–246.

Kohli, A. (2004). *State-Directed Development: Political Power and Industrialization in the Global Periphery.* Cambridge: Cambridge University Press.

Kojima, M. (2016). *Fossil Fuel Subsidy and Pricing Policies: Recent Developing Country Experience.* Washington D.C.: World Bank.

Kuran, T. (2010). The Scale of Entrepreneurship in Middle Eastern History: Inhibitive Roles of Islamic Institutions. In D. S. Landes, J. Mokyr, & W. J. Baumol, *The Invention of Enterprise: Entrepreneurship from Ancient Mesopotamia to Modern Times* (pp. 62–87). Princeton: Princeton University Press.

Lagos State Government. (2013). *Digest of Statistics: 2013.* Ikeja: Lagos Bureau of Statistics.

Lagos State Government. (2013). *Lagos State Development Plan 2012–2025.* Lagos: Ministry of Economic Planning and Budget.

Lagos State Government. (2015). *Digest of Statistics: 2015.* Ikeja: Lagos Bureau of Statistics.

Lagos State Government. (2018). *Digest of Statistics: 2018.* Ikeja: Lagos Bureau of Statistics.

Larossi, G., Mousley, P., & Radwan, I. (2009). *An Assessment of the Investment Climate in Nigeria.* Directions in Development. Washington D.C.: World Bank.

Last, M. (2011). *Governance and the Public at the Local Level: From Revenue-Raising to Benign Neglect, 1960–2010.* Unpublished Paper.

Laws, E. (2012). *Political Settlements, Elite Pacts and Governments of National Unity.* Background Paper No.10. Development Leadership Program.

LeBas, A., & Cheeseman, N. (2013). *The Lagos Experiment: Services Delivery, Tax Collection, and Popular Attitudes.* SSRN.

Lebdioui, A., Lee, K., & Pietrobelli, C. (2020). Local-Foreign Technology Interface, Resource-Based Development, and Industrial Policy: How Chile and Malaysia are Escaping the Middle-Income Trap. *The Journal of Technology Transfer.* doi:https://doi.org/10.1007/s10961-020-09808-3

Leftwich, A. (1995). Bringing Politics Back In: Towards a Model of the Developmental State. *The Journal of Development Studies, 31*(3), 400–427.

Legislative Council Nigeria. (1946). *A Ten Year Plan of Development and Welfare for Nigeria, 1946.* Lagos: Nigeria.

Lere, M. (2016, July 15). *Kannywood: Nigeria to Establish World-Class Film Village in Kano*. Retrieved December 14, 2020, from www.premiumtimesng.com/entertainment/206947-kannywood-nigeria-establish-world-class-film-village-kano.html

Lewis, D. (2012). Understanding the Authoritarian State: Neopatrimonialism in Central Asia. *The Brown Journal of World Affairs, 19*(1), 115–126.

Lewis, P. (1994). Economic Statism, Private Capital and the Dilemmas of Accumulation in Nigeria. *World Development, 22*(3), 437–451.

Lewis, P. (2007). *Growing Apart: Oil, Politics and Economic Change in Indonesia and Nigeria*. University of Michigan Press: Ann Arbor.

Lewis, P., & Stein, H. (1997). Shifting Fortunes: The Political Economy of Financial Liberalization in Nigeria. *World Development, 25*(1), 5–22.

Lin, J. Y. (2013). From Flying Geese to Leading Dragons: New Opportunities and Strategies for Structural Transformation in Developing Countries. In J. E. Stiglitz, J. Y. Lin, & E. Patel, *The Industrial Policy Revolution II: Africa in the 21st Century* (pp. 50–70). London: Palgrave Macmillan.

Lin, J. Y. (2019). China's Light Manufacturing and Africa's Industrialization. In A. Oqubay, & J. Y. Lin, *China-Africa and an Economic Transformation* (pp. 265–282). Oxford: Oxford University Press.

Lin, J. Y., & Monga, C. (2013). Comparative Advantage: The Silver Bullet of Industrial Policy. In J. E. Stiglitz, & J. Y. Lin, *The Industrial Policy Revolution I: The Role of Government Beyond Ideology* (pp. 19–38). London: Palgrave Macmillan.

Lin, J. Y., & Chang, H.-J. (2009). Should Industrial Policy in Developing Countries Conform to Comparative Advantage or Defy it? a Debate Between Justin Lin and Ha-Joon Chang. *Development Policy Review, 27*(5), 483–502.

Linder, W., & Mueller, S. (2021). *Swiss Democracy: Possible Solutions to Conflict in Multicultural Societies* (4th Edition). Cham: Palgrave Macmillan.

Lixi, M. J., Zottel, S., Neto, M. I., Boroffice, F. A., Karpinski, K., Lim, L. T.,... Bra, P. (2019). *Nigeria Digital Economy Diagnostic Report*. Washington D.C.: World Bank Group.

Lubeck, P. M., & Watts, M. J. (1994). An Alliance of Oil and Maize? The Response of Indigenous and State Capital to Structural Adjustment in Nigeria. In B. J. Berman, & L. Colin, *African Capitalists in African Development* (pp. 205–234). Boulder: Lynne Rienner.

Lugard, F. J. (1922). *The Dual Mandate in British Tropical Africa*. Edinburgh; London: William Blackwood and Sons.

Lundgren, C. J., Thomas, A. H., & York, R. C. (2013). *Boom, Bust or Prosperity? Managing Sub-Saharan Africa's Natural Resource Wealth*. African Department. Washington D.C.: International Monetary Fund. Retrieved from www.imf.org/en/Publications/Departmental-Papers-Policy-Papers/Issues/2016/12/31/Boom-Bust-or-Prosperity-Managing-Sub-Saharan-Africas-Natural-Resource-Wealth-40476

Lynn, S. R. (2003). *Economic Development: Theory and Practice for a Divided World*. New Jersey: Prentice Hall.

Mabogunje, A. L. (1968). *Urbanization in Nigeria*. New York: University of London Press.

Mackintosh, J. P. (1966). *Nigerian Government and Politics*. London: Allen & Unwin.

Mahoney, J., & Villegas, C. M. (2009). Historical Enquiry and Comparative Politics. In C. Boix, & S. C. Stokes, *The Oxford Handbook of Comparative Politics* (pp. 507–548). Oxford: Oxford University Press.

Maier, K. (2000). *This House Has Fallen: Nigeria in Crisis*. London: Penguin Press.

Masiyiwa, S. (2015, October 4). *It's Time to Play by a Different (Ethical) Set of Rules (Part 7) Nigeria I*. Retrieved October 20, 2015, from Econet: www.econetafrica.com/strive-masiyiwa-blog/index.php/its-time-to-play-by-a-different-ethical-set-of-rules-part-7-nigeria-1-of-5/

Maxfield, S., & Schneider, B. R. (1997). *Business and the State in Developing Countries*. Ithaca: Cornell University Press.

Mazzucato, M. (2013). *The Entrepreneurial State: Debunking Public vs. Private Sector Myths*. New York: Public Affairs.

McCain, C. (2011, May 21). *The "Second Coming" of Kannywood*. Retrieved December 31, 2020, from Daily Trust: https://dailytrust.com/the-second-coming-of-kannywood

McCain, C. (2013). Nollywood, Kannywood, and a Decade of Hausa Film Censorship in Nigeria. In D. Biltereyst, & R. V. Winkel, *Silencing Cinema: Film Censorship around the World* (pp. 223–240). New York: Palgrave Macmillan.

McCulloch, N., Moerenhout, T., & Yang, J. (2020). *Fuel Subsidy Reform and the Social Contract in Nigeria: A Micro-economic Analysis*. ICTD Working Paper 104. Brighton: Institute for Development Studies.

Médard, J.-F. (1982). The Underdeveloped State in Tropical Africa: Political Clientelism or Neo-Patrimonialism? In C. S. Clapham, *Private Patronage and Public Power: Political Clientelism in the Modern State* (pp. 162–192). London: Pinter.

Mehran, W. (2018). Neopatrimonialism in Afghanistan: Former Warlords, New Democratic Bureaucrats? *Journal of Peacebuilding & Development, 13*(2), 91–105.

Mfonobong, N. (2012, January 9). *Meet Tony Elumelu, Africa's Frontline Business Leader*. Retrieved January 5, 2020, from Forbes: www.forbes.com/sites/mfonobongnsehe/2012/01/09/meet-tony-elumelu-africas-frontline-business-leader/#6f9e896639b8

Migdal, J. S. (1988). *Strong Societies and Weak States: State-Society Relations and State Capabilities in the Third World*. Princeton: Princeton University Press.

Mills, C. W. (1956 [2000]). *The Power Elite: New Edition*. Oxford: Oxford University Press.

Mishra, S., Lundstrom, S., & Anand, R. (2011). *Service Export Sophistication and Economic Growth*. World Bank Policy Research Working Paper No. 5606. Washington D.C.: World Bank.

Mkandawire, T. (2012). Institutional Monocropping and Monotasking in Africa. In A. Noman, K. Botchwey, H. Stein, & J. E. Stiglitz, *Good Growth and Governance in Africa: Rethinking Development Strategies* (pp. 80–113). Oxford: Oxford University Press.

Mkandawire, T. (2015). Neopatrimonialism and the Political Economy of Economic Performance in Africa: Critical Reflections. *World Politics, 67*(03), 563–612.

Mkandawire, T., & Soludo, C. C. (2003). *African Voices on Structural Adjustment*. Trenton, NJ; Dakar, Senegal; Ottawa: Africa World Press.

Mo Ibrahim Foundation. (2008, November 15). *News Release: President Moghae Receives 2008 Ibrahim Prize for Achievement in African Leadership*. Retrieved from Mo Ibrahim Foundation: https://mo.ibrahim.foundation/sites/default/files/2017-10/president-mogae-receives-2008-ibrahim-prize-for-achievement-in-african-leadership.pdf

Mohammed, A. S. (2010). The Masquerade Unmasked: Obasanjo and the Third-Term Debacle. In S. Adejumobi, *Governance and Politics in Post-Military Nigeria* (pp. 173–207). New York: Palgrave Macmillan.

Momoh, A. (2011). The Elections in Lagos State as a Political Monologue. In J. A. Ayoade, & A. A. Akinsanya, *Nigeria's Critical Election* (pp. 203–228). Plymouth: Lexington Books.

Monga, C., & Lin, J. Y. (2019). Introduction: Overcoming the Curse of Destiny. In C. Monga, & J. Y. Lin, *The Oxford Handbook of Structural Transformation* (pp. 1–34). Oxford: Oxford University Press.

Moore, G. (2020, August 21). *A New Cold War is Coming: Africa Should not Pick Sides.* Retrieved September 12, 2020, from Mail & Guardian: https://mg.co.za/africa/2020-08-21-a-new-cold-war-is-coming-africa-should-not-pick-sides/

Moore, M., Prichard, W., & Fjeldstad, O.-H. (2018). *Taxing Africa: Coercion, Reform and Development.* London: Zed Books.

Muchai, D. N., & Kimuyu, P. (2017). *Prospects for Information and Communications Technology-Enabled Services in Kenya: The Case of the Mobile Money Transfer Industry.* WIDER Working Paper 2017/86. Helsinki: UNU-WIDER.

Muhammad, M., Buba, R., Azman, M. D., & Ahmed, A. (2019). China's Involvement in the Trans-Saharan Textile Trade and Industry in Nigeria: The Case of Kano. *Review of African Political Economy.* doi:10.1080/03056244.2019.1680356

Mustapha, A. R. (2006). *Ethnic Structure, Inequality and Governance of the Public Sector in Nigeria.* Democracy, Governance and Human Rights. Geneva: United Nations Research Institute for Social Development. Retrieved from www.unrisd.org/unrisd/website/document.nsf/(httpPublications)/C6A23857BA3934CCC12572CE0024BB9E?OpenDocument

Mustapha, A. R. (2009). Institutionalising Ethnic Representation: How Effective is the Federal Character Commission in Nigeria? *Journal of International Development, 21*(4), 561–576.

Mustapha, A. R., & Meagher, K. (2020). *Overcoming Boko Haram: Faith, Society & Islamic Radicalization in Northern Nigeria.* London: James Currey.

Mutiso, R., & Hill, K. (2020, August 11). *Why Hasn't Africa Gone Digital? One Major Reason is a Lack of Reliable, Affordable Electricity.* Retrieved February 5, 2021, from Scientific American: www.scientificamerican.com/article/why-hasnt-africa-gone-digital/

Nadel, S. (1956). The Concept of Social Elites. *International Social Science Bulletin, 8,* 413–424.

NBC. (2009, October 19). *No Winner for African Leadership Prize.* Retrieved from NBC: www.nbcnews.com/id/33378461/ns/world_news-africa/t/no-winner-african-leadership-prize/#.XnZ79KhKiUk

NBS. (2012). *National Baseline Youth Survey.* Abuja: National Bureau of Statistics.

NBS. (2012). *Nigeria Poverty Profile 2010.* Abuja: National Bureau of Statistics.

NBS. (2014a). *Measuring Better: Frequently Asked Questions on the Rebasing/Re-Benchmarking of Nigeria's Gross Domestic Product (GDP).* Abuja: Nigerian Bureau of Statistics.

NBS. (2014b). *Nigeria Manufacturing Sector: Summary Report 2010–2012.* Abuja: Nigeria National Bureau of Statistics.

NBS. (2016). *Banks Credit and Deposit by States in Nigeria: 2010–2015.* Abuja: National Bureau of Statistics.

NBS. (2016). *Formal and Informal Sector Split of Gross Domestic Product 2015.* Abuja: National Bureau of Statistics.

NBS. (2020). *2019 Poverty and Inequality in Nigeria: Executive Summary.* Abuja: National Bureau of Statistics.

NCC. (2020, August 10). *Subscriber Statistics.* Retrieved 2020, from Nigeria Communications Commission: www.ncc.gov.ng/stakeholder/statistics-reports/subscriber-data#annual-subscriber-technology-data

Newfarmer, R., Page, J., & Tarp, F. (2018). *Industries without Smokestacks and Structural Transformation in Africa*. Oxford: Oxford University Press.

Nicolini, M., & Tavoni, M. (2017). Are Renewable Energy Subsidies Effective? Evidence from Europe. *Renewable and Sustainable Energy Reviews, 74*, 412–423.

Nigeria Governors' Forum. (2013). *Inaugural Speeches of Presidents (1999–2011) and Governors (2007–2013) of the Federal Republic of Nigeria*. Lagos: Kachifo.

Nigeria Vision 2010 Committee. (1997). *Report of the Vision 2010 Committee*.

Nkosi, Z. (2019, June 26). *Lagos, Nigeria Listed by Mercer as the 4th Costliest City in Africa*. Retrieved December 1, 2020, from Mercer: https://africa.mercer.com/newsroom/lagos-nigeria-listed-by-mercer-as-the-4th-costliest-city-in-africa.html

Nnoli, O. (1978). *Ethnic Politics in Nigeria*. Enugu: Fourth Dimension.

NNPC. (2019). *Annual Statistics Bulletin 2019*. Abuja: Nigeria National Petroleum Corporation.

NNPC. (2020, May 1). *History of the Nigerian Petroleum Industry*. Retrieved from Nigerian National Petroleum Corporation: https://nnpcgroup.com/NNPC-Business/Business-Information/Pages/Industry-History.aspx

Noman, A., & Stiglitz, J. E. (2012). Strategies for African Development. In A. Noman, B. Kwesi, H. Stein, & J. Stiglitz, *Good Growth and Governance in Africa: Rethinking Development Strategies* (pp. 3–47). New York: Oxford University Press.

Noman, A., Botchwey, K., Stein, H., & Stiglitz, J. (2011). *Good Growth and Governance in Africa: Rethinking Development Strategies*. Oxford: Oxford University Press.

NPC. (2004). *National Economic Empowerment and Development Strategy*. Abuja: National Planning Commission.

NPC. (2009). *Nigeria Vision 20:2020: Economic Transformation Blueprint*. Abuja: National Planning Commission.

NPC. (2013). *The Transformation Agenda 2011–2015: Summary of Federal Government's Key Priority Policies, Programmes and Projects*. Abuja: National Planning Commission.

Nsehe, M. (2011, June 7). *The Five Richest Pastors in Nigeria*. Retrieved from *Forbes*: www.forbes.com/sites/mfonobongnsehe/2011/06/07/the-five-richest-pastors-in-nigeria/#3773e2b56031

Nwagwu, N. A. (1978). The Politics of Universal Primary Education in Nigeria, 1955–1977. *Compare: A Journal of Comparative and International Education, 8*(2), 149–157.

Nwagwu, W. E., & Agarin, O. (2008). Nigerian University Websites: A Webometric Analysis. *Webology, 5*(4).

Nwogu, S., Affe, M., Okere, A., & Amobi, F. (2017, July 4). *Are State Houses of Assembly Executive Rubber Stamps?* Retrieved July 9, 2020, from *The Punch*: https://punchng.com/are-state-houses-of-assembly-executive-rubber-stamps/

Obadare, E. (2016). The Muslim Response to the Pentecostal Surge in Nigeria: Prayer and the Rise of Charismatic Islam. *Journal of Religious and Political Practice*, 75–91.

Oculi, O. (1987). Green Capitalism in Nigeria. In P. M. Lubeck, *The African Bourgeoisie: Capitalist Development in Nigeria, Kenya and the Ivory Coast* (pp. 167–184). Boulder: Lynne Rienner.

Okogu, B., & Osafo-Kwaako, P. (2008). Issues in Fiscal Policy Management under the Economic Reforms (2003–2007). In P. Collier, C. P. Soludo, & C. Pattilo, *Economic Policy Options for a Prosperous Nigeria* (pp. 187–219). London: Palgrave Macmillan.

Okonjo-Iweala, N. (2008). Point of View: Nigeria's Shot at Redemption. *Finance and Development, 45*(4), 42–44.

Okonjo-Iweala, N. (2012). *Reforming the Unreformable: Lessons from Nigeria*. Cambridge, MA; London: MIT Press.

Okoye, D., & Pongou, R. (2014, August 20). *Historical Missionary Activity, Schooling, and the Reversal of Fortunes: Evidence from Nigeria*. Retrieved from SSRN: http://dx.doi.org/10.2139/ssrn.2484020

Olukoju, A. (1993). Population Pressure, Housing and Sanitation in West Africa's Premier Port-City: Lagos, 1900–1939. *The Great Circle, 15*(2), 91–106.

Olukoshi, A. O. (1993). General Introduction: from Crisis to Adjustment in Nigeria. In A. O. Olukoshi, *The Politics of Structural Adjustment in Nigeria* (pp. 1–16). London; Ibadan: James Currey.

Onalaja, G. (2015, November 11). *TechCabal Explains: Yaba i-HQ*. Retrieved December 9, 2020, from TechCabal: https://techcabal.com/2015/11/11/techcabal-explains-yaba-i-hq/

Opata, C. (2011). Transplantation and Evolution of Legal Regulation of Interconnection Arrangements in the Nigerian Telecommunications Sector. *International Journal of Communications Law and Policy, 14*(1), 1–14.

Opeyemi, D. (2016, March 2). *Meet the Five Nigerians who Made the Forbes 2016 World Billionaires List*. Retrieved July 10, 2016, from Ventures Africa: http://venturesafrica.com/meet-the-five-nigerians-on-forbes-world-billionaires-ranking–2016/

Oqubay, A. (2015). *Made in Africa: Industrial Policy in Ethiopia*. Oxford: Oxford University Press.

Oqubay, A., & Kefale, D. (2020). A Strategic Approach to Industrial Hubs: Learnings in Ethiopia. In A. Oqubay, & J. Y. Lin, *The Oxford Handbook of Industrial Hubs and Economic Development*. Oxford: Oxford University Press.

Osagie, C. (2015, April 14). *Nigeria: As Dangote Transforms Nigeria into an Export Nation*. Retrieved July 04, 2016, from Thisday: http://allafrica.com/stories/201504140084.html

Osoba, S. (1977). The Nigerian Power Elite, 1952–65. In P. C. Gutkind, & P. Waterman, *African Social Studies: a Radical Reader* (pp. 368–382). London: Heinemann.

OSSAP-MDGs. (2006). *Monitoring and Evaluation for Accountability: The Case of Nigeria's Virtual Poverty Fund*. Office of the Senior Special Assistant to the President on MDGs (OSSAP-MDGs).

Ostry, J. D., Loungani, P., & Furceri, D. (2016). Neoliberalism: Oversold? *Finance and Development, 53*(2), 38–51.

Owen, O., & Usman, Z. (2015). Why Goodluck Jonathan Lost the Nigerian Presidential Election of 2015. *African Affairs, 114*(456), 1–17.

Pew Research Centre. (2020). *Nigeria - The Future of World Religions: Population Growth Projections, 2010–2050*. Retrieved from Global Religious Futures: http://globalreligiousfutures.org/countries/nigeria/religious_demography#/?affiliations_religion_id=0&affiliations_year=2020

Philippon, T. (2019). *The Great Reversal: How America Gave Up on Free Markets*. Cambridge, MA: The Belknap Press of Harvard University Press.

Plante, M. (2014). The Long-Run Macroeconomic Impacts of Fuel Subsidies. *Journal of Development Economics, 107*, 129–143.

Poteete, A. (2009). Is Development Path Dependent or Political? A Reinterpretation of Mineral-Dependent Development in Botswana. *Journal of Development Studies, 45*(4), 544–571.

Premium Times. (2014, August 24). *VIDEO: Why I Set Books Ablaze as Kano Governor – Shekarau, Education Minister*. Retrieved December 15, 2020, from www.premiumtimesng.com/news/top-news/167208-video-why-i-set-books-ablaze-as-kano-governor-shekarau-education-minister%E2%80%8E.html

Premium Times. (2014, September 16). *CAN President, Oritsejafor, Admits Ownership of Cash-Stacked Jet Seized in South Africa*. Retrieved from Premium Times: www.premiumtimesng.com/news/headlines/168224-can-president-oritsejafor-admits-ownership-of-cash-stacked-jet-seized-in-south-africa.html

Przeworski, A. (2004). Institutions Matter? *Government and Opposition, 39*(4), 527–540.

PwC. (2019). *X-Raying the Nigerian Palm Oil Sector*. PricewaterhouseCoopers.

Rajan, R. G., & Zingales, L. (1998). Financial Dependence and Growth. *American Economic Review, 88*(3), 559–586.

Raval, A., & Ward, A. (2017, December 10). *Saudi Aramco Plans for a Life after Oil*. Retrieved March 30, 2018, from The Financial Times: www.ft.com/content/e46162ca-d9a6-11e7-a039-c64b1c09b482

Ricardo, D. (1817 [1955]). *On the Principles of Political Economy and Taxation (introd by Michael P. Fogarty)*. London: John Murray Dent.

Rice, X. (2012, June 28). *Africa: Lessons from Lagos*. Retrieved July 12, 2016, from *The Financial Times*: www.ft.com/content/8b24d40a-c064-11e1-982d-00144feabdc0

Robinson, J. (2010). *Elites and Institutional Persistence*. WIDER Working Paper 2010/85. Helsinki: UN World Institute of Development Economics Research. Retrieved from http://www.wider.unu.edu/publications/working-papers/2010/en_GB/wp2010-85/

Rodrik, D. (1997, Summer). Sense and Nonsense in the Globalization Debate. *Foreign Policy, 107*, pp. 19–37.

Rodrik, D. (2016). Premature Deindustrialization. *Journal of Economic Growth, 21*, 1–33.

Ross, M. (1999). The Political Economy of the Resource Curse. *World Politics, 51*(2), 297–322.

Ross, M. (2001). Does Oil Hinder Democracy? *World Politics, 53*(03), 325–361.

Ross, M. (2012). *The Oil Curse: How Petroleum Wealth Shapes the Development of Nations*. Princeton; Oxford: Princeton University Press.

Ross, M. L. (2008). Oil, Islam and Women. *American Political Science Review, 102*(1), 102–123.

Rustad, S. A., Le Billon, P., & Lujala, P. (2017). Has the Extractive Industries Transparency Initiative been a Success? Identifying and Evaluating EITI Goals. *Resources Policy, 17*, 151–162.

Sachs, J., & Warner, A. M. (1995). Natural Resource Abundance and Economic Growth. *NBER Working Paper, Working Paper No. 5398*.

Sachs, J., & Warner, A. M. (2001). Natural Resources and Economic Development: The Curse of Natural Resources. *European Economic Review, 45*(4-6), 827–838.

Sagagi, M. (2012). *Budget Analysis: Kano State Government Budget 2012*. (Unpublished).

Sahara Reporters. (2009, August 18). *CBN's List of Bank Debtors*. Retrieved August 12, 2020, from Sahara Reporters: http://saharareporters.com/2009/08/18/cbns-list-bank-debtors

Sahara Reporters. (2010, September 17). *Don't Field Goodluck Jonathan in Northern Slot, Adamu Ciroma Group Writes PDP*. Retrieved from Sahara Reporters: http://saharareporters.com/2010/09/17/don%E2%80%99t-field-goodluck-jonathan-northern-slot-adamu-ciroma-group-writes-pdp

Salik, A. M. (2016, May 15). *Onshore-Offshore Dichotomy and the Abrogation Act*. Retrieved December 29, 2020, from Daily Trust: https://dailytrust.com/onshore-offshore-dichotomy-and-the-abrogation-act

Sanusi, L. S. (2010). The Nigerian Banking Industry: What Went Wrong and the Way Forward. *Convocation Lecture Delivered at the Convocation Square, Bayero University Kano*. Kano: Central Bank of Nigeria.

Sanusi, L. S. (2014, February 3). Memorandum Submitted to the Senate Committee on Finance on the Non-Remittance of Oil Revenue to the Federation Account.

Sayne, A., Gillies, A., & Katsouris, C. (2015). *Inside NNPC Oil Sales: A Case for Reform in Nigeria*. Natrual Resource Governance Institute. Retrieved from https://resourcegovernance.org/sites/default/files/documents/nrgi_insidennpcoilsales_mainreport.pdf

Schatz, S. (1977). *Nigerian Capitalism*. Berkeley; London: University of California Press.

Scott, J. (2008). Modes of Power and the Re-Conceptualization of Elites. *Sociological Review, 56*(Issue Supplement s1), 28–43.

Sebudubudu, D., & Botlhomilwe, M. Z. (2011). The Critical Role of Leadership in Botswana's Development: What Lessons? *Leadership, 8*(1), 29–45.

Sen, K., & Te Velde, D. W. (2011). State-Business Relations, Investment Climate Reform, and Economic Growth in Sub-Saharan Africa. In A. Noman, K. Botchwey, H. Stein, & J. E. Stiglitz, *Good Growth and Governance in Africa: Rethinking Development Strategies* (pp. 303–321). Oxford: Oxford University Press.

Shalal, A., Alper, A., & Zengerle, P. (2020, May 18). *U.S. Mulls Paying Companies, Tax Breaks to Pull Supply Chains from China*. Retrieved September 9, 2020, from Reuters: www.reuters.com/article/us-usa-china-supply-chains/u-s-mulls-paying-companies-tax-breaks-to-pull-supply-chains-from-china-idUSKBN22U0FH

Shenton, R. (1986). *The Development of Capitalism in Northern Nigeria*. London: James Currey.

Short, C. (2014). The Development of the Extractive Industries Transparency Initiative. *The Journal of World Energy Law and Business, 7*(1), 8–15.

Siollun, M. (2009). *Oil, Politics and Violence: Nigeria's Military Coup Culture*. New York: Algora Publishing.

Siollun, M. (2013). *Soldiers of Fortune: Nigerian Politics under Buhari and Babangida (1983-1993)*. Abuja: Cassava Republic.

Sklar, R. (1967). Political Science and National Integration: A Radical Approach. *The Journal of Modern African Studies, 5*(1), 1–11.

Sklar, R. (1979). The Nature of Class Domination in Africa. *Journal of Modern African Studies, 17*(4), 531–552.

Sklar, R. L. (1981). Democracy for the Second Republic. *Issue: A Journal of Opinion, 11*(1/2), 14–16.

Slav, I. (2020, August 3). *The Sky is the Limit for Clean Energy Subsidies in Europe*. Retrieved September 9, 2020, from *Energy World Magazine*: www.energyworldmag.com/the-sky-is-the-limit-for-clean-energy-subsidies-in-europe/

SMEDAN & NBS. (2017). *National Survey of Micro, Small and Medium Scale Enterprises (MSMEs) 2017*. Abuja: National Bureau of Statistics.

Soares De Oliveira, R. (2007). *Oil and Politics in the Gulf of Guinea*. London: Hurst & Co.

Sobel, R. (2008). *Entrepreneurship*. Retrieved July 11, 2016, from *The Concise Encyclopaedia of Economics*: http://www.econlib.org/library/Enc/Entrepreneurship.html

Soile, I., & Mu, X. (2015). Who Benefit Most from Fuel Subsidies? Evidence from Nigeria. *Energy Policy, 87*, 314–324.

Soludo, C. C. (2006). *Beyond Banking Sector Consolidation in Nigeria*. London: Presentation at the Global Banking Conference on Nigerian Banking Reforms.

Statista. (2019, September 23). *Leading Palm Oil Companies Worldwide in 2018, based on Market Capitalization*. Retrieved January 5, 2020, from Statista: www.statista.com/statistics/477252/leading-global-plam-oil-companies-based-on-market-capitalization/

Stewart, F. (2005). Horizontal Inequalities: A Neglected Dimension of Development. In W. P. Development, *UNU-WIDER* (pp. 101–135). London: Palgrave Macmillan UK.

Stiglitz, J., & Lin, J. (2013). *The Industrial Policy Revolution I: The Role of Government beyond Ideology*. London: Palgrave Macmillan.

Stiglitz, J., Lin, J., & Monga, C. (2013a). *The Rejuvenation of Industrial Policy*. Washington D.C.: World Bank.

Stiglitz, J., Lin, J., & Monga, C. (2013b). Introduction: The Rejuvenation of Industrial Policy. In J. Stiglitz, & J. Lin, *The Industrial Policy Revolution I: The Role of Government Beyond Ideology* (pp. 1–15). London: Palgrave Macmillan.

Stiglitz, J., Lin, J., & Patel, E. (2013). *The Industrial Policy Revolution II: Africa in the 21st Century*. London: Palgrave Macmillan.

Stijns, J.-P. (2005). Natural Resource Abundance and Economic Growth Revisited. *Resources Policy, 30*(2), 107–130.

Studwell, J. (2014). *How Asia Works: Success and Failure in the World's Most Dynamic Region*. London: Grove Press.

Syverson, C. (2011, June). What Determines Productivity? *Journal of Economic Literature, 49*(2), 326–365.

Szirmai, A. (2012). Industrialisation as an Engine of Growth in Developing Countries, 1950–2005. *Structural Change and Economic Dynamics, 23*(4), 406–420.

Szirmai, A. (2013). Manufacturing and Economic Development. In A. Szirmai, W. Naude, & L. Alcorta, *Pathways to Industrialzation in the Twenty-First Century: New Challenges and Emerging Paradigms* (pp. 54–75). Oxford: Oxford University Press.

Tadros, M., & Allouche, J. (2017). Political Settlements as a Violent Process: Deconstructing the Relationship between Political Settlements and Intrinsic, Instrumental and Resultant Forms of Violence. *Conflict, Security and Development, 17*(3), 187–204.

Tanzi, V. (1992). Structural Factors and Tax Revenue in Developing Countries: A Decade of Evidence. In I. Goldin, & L. A. Winters, *Open Economies: Structural Adjustment and Agriculture* (pp. 267–285). Cambridge, MA: Cambridge University Press.

Tharoor, S. (2016). *Inglorious Empire: What the British Did to India*. Victoria: Scribe.

The Economist. (2000, May 11). *Hopeless Africa*. Retrieved from The Economist: www.economist.com/leaders/2000/05/11/hopeless-africa

The Economist. (2015, July 2). *Learning from Lagos*. Retrieved July 12, 2016, from The Economist: www.economist.com/middle-east-and-africa/2015/07/02/learning-from-lagos

The Guardian. (2020, May 15). *Oronsaye Panel Report and Sundry Consequences*. Retrieved July 6, 2020, from The Guardian Nigeria: https://guardian.ng/opinion/oronsaye-panel-report-and-sundry-consequences/

The Nigerian Voice. (2013, November 23). *Why the North Abandoned Ekwueme for Obasanjo in 1999 - Tanko Yakassai*. Retrieved April 14, 2015, from The Nigerian Voice: www.thenigerianvoice.com/news/129699/why-north-abandoned-ekwueme-for-obasanjo-in-1999-tanko-yak.html

The Punch. (2013, March 4). *Jonathan Splashes N3 Billion New Grant on Nollywood*. Retrieved December 15, 2020, from www.vanguardngr.com/2013/03/jonathan-splashes-n3-billion-new-grant-on-nollywood/

The Punch. (2020, June 19). *Stakeholders Urge Govt to Diversify Economy, Spend Wisely*. Retrieved September 7, 2020, from *The Punch*: https://punchng.com/stakeholders-urge-govt-to-diversify-economy-spend-wisely/

Thisday. (2003, March 27). *Nigeria: Obasanjo Promises Private Sector Good Governance*. Retrieved May 19, 2015, from allAfrica: http://allafrica.com/stories/200303270705.html

Thurston, A. (2014). Muslim Politics and Shari'a in Kano State, Northern Nigeria. *African Affairs, 114*(454), 28–51.

Tibenderana, P. K. (1983). The Emirs and the Spread of Western Education in Northern Nigeria, 1910-1946. *The Journal of African History, 24*(4), 517–534.

Timberg, C. (2006, May 17). *Nigerian Senate Blocks Bid for Third Presidential Term*. Retrieved May 18, 2015, from The Washington Post: www.washingtonpost.com/wp-dyn/content/article/2006/05/16/AR2006051600705.html

Timmons, J. (2005). The Fiscal Contract: States, Taxes and Public Services. *World Politics, 57*(4), 530–567.

Toft, M. D., Philpott, D., & Shah, T. S. (2011). *God's Century: Resurgent Religion and Global Politics*. New York and London: W.W. Norton & Company Inc.

Tony Elumelu Foundation. (2020). *We are an African Private-Sector-Led Philanthropy Empowering African Entrepreneurs*. Retrieved January 5, 2020, from The Tony Elumelu Foundation: www.tonyelumelufoundation.org/about-us

U.S. Embassy Abuja. (2010, February 26). *Goodluck Jonathan Remains Acting President of Nigeria*. Retrieved January 24, 2015, from Wikileaks: http://wikileaks.org/cable/2010/02/10ABUJA215.html

U.S. Embassy Lagos. (2005, March 7). *Aliko Dangote and Why You Should Know about Him*. Retrieved from Wikileaks: https://wikileaks.org/plusd/cables/05LAGOS362_a.html

UN Habitat. (2014). *The State of African Cities 2014: Re-Imagining Sustainable Urban Transitions*. Nairobi: United Nations Human Settlements Programme.

UN Habitat. (2020). *World Cities Report 2020: The Value of Sustainable Urbanization*. Nairobi: United Nations Human Settlements Programme.

UN Habitat; IHS-Erasmus University Rotterdam. (2018). *The State of African Cities 2018: the Geography of African Investment*. United Nations Human Settlements Programme (UN-Habitat).

UNCTAD. (2019). *World Investment Report 2019: Special Economic Zones*. New York: United Nations Publications.

UNCTAD and UNIDO. (2011). *Economic Development in Africa Report 2011: Fostering Industrial Development in Africa in the New Global Environment*. New York and Geneva: United Nations.

UNECA. (2020, May 15). *Electronic Trade Rekindling Sales for African Businesses during COVID-19*. Retrieved September 12, 2020, from UNECA: www.uneca.org/stories/electronic-trade-rekindling-sales-african-businesses-during-covid–19

Usman, Z., & Landry, D. G. (2021). *Economic Diversification in Africa: How and Why it Matters*. Washington D.C.: Carnegie Endowment for International Peace.

Van Asselt, H., & Skovgaard, J. (2018). *The Politics of Fossil Fuel Subsidies and their Reform*. Cambridge: Cambridge University Press.

Van De Walle, N., & Butler, K. S. (1999). Political Parties and Party Systems in Africa's Illiberal Democracies. *Cambridge Review of International Studies, 13*(1), 14–28.

Van Waijenburg, M., & Frankema, E. (2019, January 31). *The African Model: Asia's Path May not Work, but there is an Alternative*. Retrieved from African Arguments: https://

africanarguments.org/2019/01/31/the-african-model-asias-path-may-not-work-but-there-is-an-alternative/

Victor, D. (2009). *The Politics of Fossil-Fuel Subsidies*. Geneva: International Institute for Sustainable Development.

Vourlias, C. (2016, August 2). *Nigeria Scraps Plans for $10 Million Film Village after Muslim Clerics Protest*. Retrieved December 14, 2020, from https://variety.com/2016/film/global/nigeria-scraps-plans-for-10-million-film-village-after-muslim-clerics-protest-1201827887/

Wade, R. (1990). *Governing the Market: Economic Theory and the Role of Government in East Asian Industrialization*. Princeton: Princeton University Press.

Wallis, W. (2013, March 10). *The Telecoms Numbers that Didn't Add Up*. Retrieved June 08, 2015, from Financial Times: www.ft.com/cms/s/0/155b347c-87e6-11e2-b011-00144feabdc0.html#axzz3cPtrPXQd

Watts, M. J. (1987). Peasantry, Merchant Capital and the Colonial State: Class in Northern Nigeria, 1900–1945. In P. M. Lubeck, *The African Bourgeoisie: Capitalist Development in Nigeria, Kenya and the Ivory Coast* (pp. 59–96). Boulder: Lynne Rienner.

Weber, M. (1922 [1978]). *Economy and Society: an Outline of Interpretive Sociology*. Berkeley: University of California.

Whiteman, K. (2012). *Lagos: A Cultural and Historical Companion*. Oxford: Signal.

Whitfield, L., & Therkildsen, O. (2011). *What Drives States to Support the Development of Productive Sectors? Strategies Ruling Elites Pursue for Political Survival and their Policy Implications*. DIIS Working Paper 2011:*15*. Copenhagen: Danish Institute for International Studies. Retrieved from www.jstor.org/stable/resrep13341

Whitfield, L., Buur, L., Therkildsen, O., & Kjaer, A. M. (2015). *The Politics of African Industrial Policy: A Comparative Perspective*. New York: Cambridge University Press.

Williams, G. (1974). Colonialism and Capitalism, the Nigeria Case. A Review. *ASAUK Conference*. Liverpool.

Williams, G. (1988). *Why is There no Agrarian Capitalism in Nigeria?* Queen Elizabeth House, University of Oxford. (Unpublished Manuscript).

Williamson, J. (1990). What Washington Means by Policy Reform. In J. Williamson, *Latin American Adjustment: How Much Has Happened?* Washington D.C.: Institute for International Economics.

Williamson, J. (2004). The Washington Consensus as a Policy Prescription for Development. *Practitioners of Development*. Washington D.C.: Institute for International Economics.

Wolfgang, S., & Kathleen, T. (2005). Introduction: Institutional Change in Advanced Political Economies. In S. Wolfgang, & T. Kathleen, *Beyond Continuity: Institutional Change in Advanced Political Economies* (pp. 1–39). Oxford: Oxford University Press.

Woods, M. (1998). Re-thinking Elites: Network, Space and Local Politics. *Environment and Planning A: Economy and Space, 30*(12), 2101–2119.

World Bank. (1993). *The East Asian Miracle: Economic Growth and Public Policy*. New York: Oxford University Press.

World Bank. (1994). *Nigeria Structural Adjustment Program: Policies, Implementation, and Impact*. Washington D.C.: World Bank.

World Bank. (2007). *Nigeria – Lagos State: States Finances Review and Agenda for Action*. Washington D.C.: World Bank.

World Bank. (2016). *An Assessment of the Investment Climate in Nigeria: The Challenges of Nigeria's Private Sector*. Washington D.C.: World Bank.

World Bank. (2018). *The State of Social Safety Nets 2018*. Washington D.C.: World Bank.

World Bank. (2020). *Advancing Social Protection in a Dynamic Nigeria*. Washington D.C.: World Bank Group.

World Bank Group. (2019). *World Development Report 2019: The Changing Nature of Work*. Washington D.C.: World Bank.

World Economic Forum; Accenture. (2018). *Digital Transformation Initiative: Unlocking $100 Trillion for Business and Society from Digital Transformation*. Geneva: World Economic Forum.

Wright, E. O. (2005). Foundations of a Neo-Marxist Class Analysis. In E. O. Wright, *Approaches to Class Analysis* (pp. 4–30). Cambridge: Cambridge University Press.

Wright, G. (1990). The Origins of American Industrial Success, 1879-1940. *American Economic Review, 80*(4), 651–668.

Wright, G. (2001). *Resource Based Growth, Then and Now*. Washington D.C.: Stanford University and World Bank.

Xiaoyang, T. (2020). Chinese Economic and Trade Cooperation Zones in Africa. In A. Oqubay, & J. Y. Lin, *The Oxford Handbook of Industrial Hubs and Economic Development* (pp. 950–966). Oxford: Oxford University Press.

Yahaya, S. (1993). State versus Market: The Privatization Programme of the Nigerian State. In A. Olukoshi, *The Politics of Structural Adjustment in Nigeria* (pp. 16–32). London; Ibadan: James Currey.

Zartman, I. W., & Schatz, S. (1983). Introduction. In I. W. Zartman, *The Political Economy of Nigeria* (pp. 1–24). New York: Praeger.

Zeng, D. Z. (2020). Special Economic Zones in sub-Saharan Africa: What Drives their Mixed Performance. In A. Oqubay, & J. Y. Lin, *The Oxford Handbook of Industrial Hubs and Economic Development* (pp. 1008–1025). Oxford: Oxford University Press.

Annex 1: Nigeria's Thirty-Six States and Six Geopolitical Zones

North Central	South East
Benue	Abia
Kogi	Anambra
Kwara	Ebonyi
Nasarawa	Enugu
Niger	Imo
Plateau	
North East	**South South**
Adamawa	Akwa Ibom
Bauchi	Cross River
Borno	Bayelsa
Gombe	Rivers
Taraba	Delta
Yobe	Edo
North West	**South West**
Jigawa	Ekiti
Kaduna	Lagos
Kano	Ogun
Katsina	Ondo
Kebbi	Osun
Sokoto	Oyo
Zamfara	
Other	
Federal Capital Territory, Abuja	

Annex 2: Nigeria's Heads of States since Independence

Queen Elizabeth II was head of state from October 1, 1960 until October 1, 1963 and ruled with a governor general and prime minister until a republic was declared in 1963.

First Republic (1963–1966)

Nnamdi AZIKIWE (president, ceremonial): Oct 1, 1963 to Jan 16, 1966 (overthrown).
Abubakar Tafawa BALEWA (Prime Minister): Oct 1, 1963 to Jan 16, 1966 (assassinated).

Military rule (1966–1979)

General Johnson Thomas AGUIYI-IRONSI: Jan 16, 1966 to Jul 29, 1966 (overthrown).
General Yakubu GOWON: Jul 29, 1966 to Jul 29, 1975 (overthrown).
General Murtala MOHAMMED: Jul 29, 1975 to Feb 13, 1976 (assassinated).
General Olusegun OBASANJO: Feb 13, 1976 to Oct 1, 1979 (handover to elected successor).

Second Republic (1979–1983)

Shehu SHAGARI: Oct 1, 1979 to Dec 31, 1983 (overthrown).

Military rule (1983-1993)

General Muhammadu BUHARI: Dec 31, 1983 to Aug 27, 1985 (overthrown).
General Ibrahim BABANGIDA: Aug 27, 1985 to Aug 26, 1993 (resigned).

Third Republic (1993)

Ernest SHONEKAN: Aug 26, 1993 to Nov 17, 1993 (overthrown).

Military rule (1993–1999)

General Sani ABACHA: Nov 17, 1993 to Jun 8, 1998 (died in office).
General Abdulsalam ABUBAKAR: Jun 8, 1998 to May 29, 1999 (handover to elected successor).

Fourth Republic (1999–present)

Olusegun OBASANJO: May 29, 1999 to May 29, 2007 (completed two constitutional terms).
Umaru Musa YAR'ADUA: May 29, 2007 to May 5, 2010 (died in office).
Goodluck JONATHAN: May 5, 2010 to May 29, 2015 (lost re-election).
Muhammadu BUHARI: May 29, 2015 to present.

Annex 3: Nigeria's Development Plans and Economic Strategies

	Plan	Head of State
The Fixed-Term Planning Era		
1	First National Development Plan (1962–1968)	Dr. Nnamdi Azikiwe and Sir Abubakar Tafawa Balewa
2	Second National Development Plan (1970–1974)	General Yakubu Gowon
3	Third National Development Plan (1975–1980)	General Yakubu Gowon
4	Fourth National Development Plan (1981–1985)	Alhaji Shehu Shagari
The Rolling Plan Era		
5	The First National Rolling Plan (1990–1992)	General Ibrahim B. Babangida
6	The Second National Rolling Plan (1993–1995)	General Ibrahim B. Babangida
7	The Third National Rolling Plan (1994–1996)	General Sani Abacha
8	The Fourth National Rolling Plan (1997–1999)	General Sani Abacha
The Medium Term Planning Era		
9	National Economic Direction (1999–2003)	Olusegun Obasanjo
10	National Economic Empowerment and Development Strategy (2003–2007)	Olusegun Obasanjo
11	Seven-Point Agenda (2007–2010)	Umaru Musa Yar'Adua
12	Transformation Agenda (2011–2015)	Dr. Goodluck Jonathan
13	Economic Recovery and Growth Plan (2017–2021)	Muhammadu Buhari

Index

Economic Diversification in Nigeria (Usman)
An 'f' following a page number indicates information in a figure. Information in notes is indicated by 'n' following the page number.

CPSIA information can be obtained
at www.ICGtesting.com
Printed in the USA
LVHW081330070722
722971LV00001B/2